A History of the World
in the Twentieth Century

PART ONE: 1899–1918

D. C. Watt

'The political history of the period is treated with great
professional skill and in considerable detail by the three
collaborators . . .

Mr Watt shows how the gradual breakdown of the whole
diplomatic system of Europe, declining from its zenith of
power, led to the most terrible and destructive war in all
European history; he sees the divisive and destructive
powers which tore European civilization in pieces as the
reflection of the deep discontent of social groupings which
had been denied any share in the political processes which
governed their destinies . . .

The outstanding feature of this history with its good
bibliographies, maps and statistical tables, is the way in
which the three authors have set themselves to see and
explain the pattern of inter-connecting world forces
during the whole of this troubled period.

They accept Wendell Wilkie's phrase, that it is now one
world, as the keynote of their history, and they succeed
in weaving together the infinitely varied and complex
strands of international politics, emphasizing not so much
those events which have been peculiar to particular
nations as those which have been common to them all.

The book must be rated as a quite outstanding achievement.'
                                                    Church Times

Also available

A History of the World in the Twentieth Century
PART TWO: 1918–1945
by Frank Spencer

A History of the World in the Twentieth Century
PART THREE: 1945–1968
by Neville Brown

A History of the World in the Twentieth Century

PART ONE: 1899–1918

D. C. WATT

PAN BOOKS LTD · LONDON

First published as *A History of the World in the Twentieth Century* (one volume complete) 1967 by Hodder and Stoughton Ltd.
This edition published 1970 by Pan Books Ltd., 33 Tothill Street, London, S.W.1.

330 02466 3

Printed in Great Britain by
Cox & Wyman Ltd., London, Reading and Fakenham

Contents

Section Two

The Breakdown of the European System

Section Three

The War of 1914–1918

List of Maps

Preface

(This preface appeared in the complete one-volume edition)

IN writing this book, we have attempted to compose a history of the world seen as a whole. That is to say, we have started with the assumption that in this century most of the barriers and divisions which made different areas of the world into selfcontained compartments, whose histories could be studied in isolation since the events which they recorded were not influenced by any causes from outside each individual area, most of these barriers, we say, have disappeared. In this century the chain of causation in each area can as well originate outside as within it. The divisions are down, the old compartments unreal. In Wendell Wilkie's phrase, it is one world.

For the historian this assumption, if defensible, is at first an unwelcome one. The study of history has become more specialized because of the increasing range of source materials and the growing variety of languages needed to study them, not to speak of their sheer volume. For example the records of the German Foreign Ministry for the years 1880–1936 which were captured by the Allies in 1945 comprised some 400 tons of documents. And this is only one source for today's diplomatic historians. To command the source materials of a single major area of the world even within the last sixty-seven years takes a considerable part of a historian's career. And it is only through such specialization, or so it is believed, that the historian learns his craft.

For this reason much of what has come to pass as world history is not written as such. Rather it appears as a series of short histories of its major component areas, a chapter on France, a chapter on Russia, a chapter on India, a chapter on China.

In contrast, what we have attempted to do is to weave together the histories of the separate states and areas so as to make one history of them. Inevitably this has imposed certain limitations on the scope of our study. Our history concentrates on the political events of the world since 1900. That is, it concerns itself mainly with the political and power relationships between the recognized component political units of the twentieth-century world. Events in the sphere of economics, technology, ideas, demography are of importance to this study only in so far as they affect or have affected the course of political developments.

Secondly, our history inevitably focuses more on the international aspects of world history, since it is in the relations between states that the stuff of a world history must soon be found. This restriction has proved less hampering than might have been thought, since in this century no state, no political unit, is an island to itself. Inevitably, however, some things will have been omitted. Thus out of necessity some details of purely parochial interest must fail to appear on so broad a canvas, even though we have preferred the attention to detail of a Peter Breughel rather than the broad impressions of a Turner or a Cézanne.

Lastly, this book is written in the belief, which is not purely confined to its authors, that nationalism has too long made slaves of the historical profession. The historian now has to try to single out not those events which are peculiar to each political unit, but those common to them: to concentrate not on the unique but the common characteristics. Other more senior historians have pointed the way. It is our hope that this book will encourage others to follow. Although economics, war and technology have made us one world, men still believe that history has made them uniquely different from others. Such beliefs will continue to keep the world divided. If men wish to believe in their uniqueness, that is their affair and their blindness but it is no business of the historian to organize his work so as to lend them support. True history cannot serve the partisans of a creed, a nation, an ideology or a race.

The authors would like to express their thanks to Dr Frank O. Marzari, now of the University of British Columbia for his help in the preparation of the statistical tables, to Mr R. Urwin, who compiled the index, and to Mr A. Spark, who drew the maps.

D. C. Watt
Frank Spencer
Neville Brown

A History of the World in the Twentieth Century

PART ONE: 1899–1918

D. C. WATT

D. C. WATT, MA Oxon, is a Reader in International
History at the London School of Economics and Political
Science and editor of *Survey of International Affairs* in
the Royal Institute of International Affairs. Author of
many books and articles, he was formerly a member of
the international team of historians responsible for the
publication of *Documents in German Foreign Policy,
1918–1945*.

Section One

The World on the
Eve of the Twentieth Century:
Europe at its Zenith

Chapter 1

Europe and the External World

INTRODUCTION

A MARTIAN visiting our world in 1900 could have been forgiven for regarding it as completely dominated by Europe. Six European powers, Britain, France, Germany, Austria-Hungary, Italy, and Russia bestrode the globe. Their fleets policed the oceans. Their soldiers, explorers, traders and missionaries were busy bringing under Europe's sway the last areas of Asia and Africa. The last great non-European empires, Ottoman Turkey and Manchu China, were falling apart under the impact of those Europeans they had so long regarded as infidels and barbarians. Japan in the Far East and the United States in the western hemisphere counted as powers in their own parts of the world. But elsewhere only a few isolated statelets, like Abyssinia in Africa or Siam in South-East Asia, retained their independence; and they owed their survival only to the agreement of the great powers of Europe that to recognize their independence was a better course than to fight over their possession.

Our Martian visitor might, it is true, have balked a little at counting Russia as truly European. And, traversing the Pacific, he might well have been equally hesitant at counting Japan and the United States as parts of the European system. But a closer look would have shown him that all three were firmly tied into the European system by the web of capital investment and trade which financed and furthered the massive economic expansion through which they were passing. In Japan he would have recognized a state which had embraced European political models as firmly as it had adopted European weapons and money. And both in America and Russia he would have found the ruling *élites* thoroughly Europeanized, often educated at European universities, such as Oxford, the Sorbonne, Heidelberg or

Uppsala, and regular visitors to Paris, London, and the spas of Central Europe. In the salons of St Petersburg he would have been addressed in the language of Paris. In New York he would have been more conscious of the influence of London. But in both countries he would have easily recognized opposed wings of the great central spread of European culture and power. Moreover, when he returned to London and Paris he would have discovered that each of the two countries, Russia and America, were in turn beginning to contribute their share towards the enrichment of Europe's culture. Within ten years of his visit, in fact, Dostoevsky, Pushkin and Tolstoy, Chekhov, Borodin and Moussorgsky, Diaghilev, Pavlova, and Chaliapin were to be the toast of Europe. And from the United States, American painters and writers, Whistler, Henry James, Ezra Pound, and T. S. Eliot, would be adding their contributions to the great panoply of English art and literature.

On his return sixty-six years later, he would find a very different scene. The heartland of the culture and power of 1900, the continent of Europe, he would find divided between two great and hostile coalitions. America and Russia, in 1900 only wings of the great central spread of European power and culture, have each developed their own culture and ideologies and have grown into super-powers dominating the Europe they have divided between them. In Europe itself he would find the inhabitants torn between the pulls of a movement for European unity and those of the two super-powers in much the same way as his Russian and American contacts in 1900 had been torn between their own emergent cultures and those of Europe. Of the great powers of 1900, the Habsburg Empire has disappeared entirely. Germany is divided by concrete, cement and barbed-wire and part of its oldest territories in the east have been recolonized by Russians and Poles. Only Britain and France preserve any claims to great power status and any role beyond the confines of Europe. But how much that role has changed since 1900.

The most far-reaching changes in the sixty-six years since his last visit would only strike the visitor from Mars when he left Europe for Asia and Africa. From the Mediterranean to the Zambesi, he would find in Africa independent African states where he had previously seen European colonies. Even southwards of the Zambesi, always supposing he passed the racial standards of the Rhodesian and South African governments, he would find that the ruling groups, though of European extraction, were largely or entirely composed of persons born in Africa. As he moved from Africa to Asia, he would find still greater changes. The Indian sub-continent no longer lies subject to British rule. Instead it lies divided between Pakistan and India, both recognized as being among the powers. Farther east the former Chinese empire has recovered its strength and fallen subject to a new crusading expansionist creed – while losing none of its old contempt for, and isolation from, the rest of the world. China's rate of expansion into her borderlands, so our Martian will learn, has already led to armed clashes with India and caused the United States to commit a large section of its armed forces to intervention in South-East Asia. Japan is tied, albeit reluctantly, the American security system, and all the central and northern cific lies under the shadow of American power. And wherever e goes in Asia or Africa, the Martian will find the attitudes of those with whom he speaks dominated by the values and vocabulary of anti-colonialism as the non-European world slowly recovers its balance and the tide of European dominion, at its full in 1900, ebbs finally away.

If he should inquire as to the causes of these changes, the visitor from Mars will hear of two intensely destructive wars which devastated Europe's heart and spread death and destruction across much of the rest of the world. He will discover that the demonic forces which led the European powers so rapidly to dominate the rest of the world drove them also into near-suicidal conflict with one another. And he will perhaps marvel that no one could be found, within so creative and dynamic a culture, capable of controlling its destructive impulses and diverting them to more fruitful purposes.

THE WORLD AND EUROPEAN EXPANSION
TO 1900

European expansion overseas had begun slowly enough in the fifteenth century, with Henry the Navigator's caravels inching their way in successive expeditions down the coast of Africa; until finally, within two years of one another, Vasco da Gama had burst into the Indian Ocean, and Columbus, taking ship westwards for Cathay, instead had re-discovered America. The next fifty years had seen a spasmodic outburst of Spanish and Portuguese power which divided the Americas, settled colonies on the coasts of India, Africa and the East Indies, and captured for their coffers the specie of the Peruvian empire and the riches of the Indian spice trade. They had been followed at a slower pace by the Dutch, the British, and the French. Meanwhile new powers had arisen in Central Europe with the disintegration of the Holy Roman Empire, the rise of Prussia, the withdrawal of the Ottoman Empire under Austrian pressure from the plains of Hungary and Croatia, the decay and partition of the Polish state, and the rise of Russia. And with this ferment in Europe, Britain had become residual legatee to the bulk of the overseas empires of France and the Netherlands. In 1776 she had seen her own earliest overseas colonies seek the road to independen and in the first decades of the nineteenth century she had aid. and abetted the Latin American revolt against Spain.

But all of this was in slow motion compared with the speed with which the new powers of Europe had moved in the three decades before 1900. In 1870 a map of Africa would have shown a continent sprinkled only with the coastal stations of Spain, Portugal, France and Britain. In the north, only Algeria acknowledged European rule, that of France. In the south, the British colonies of the Cape and Natal were expanding slowly in the wake of the retreating republics of the Boers, quondam Dutch settlers, trekking northwards to get away from the alien rule of Britain. The northern Mediterranean coast was lined with states nominally in tributary relationship with the Sultan of the Ottoman Empire, but in fact virtually independent, Morocco, Tunis, Tripoli, Egypt. Inland from the Red Sea lay the Amharic kingdom of Abyssinia, chastised by a British expedition in the 1860s but otherwise independent. Further south lay the Arab sultanate of Zanzibar, founded by the Arabs of Muscat and Oman in the early years of the nineteenth century, now independent, its ruler passing under the magnetic influence of the great British consul, Sir John Kirk. Otherwise the continent was *terra incognita*, the only European presence that of missionaries (the first mission stations were established in the Nyasa highlands in the 1850s) and of explorers.

By 1900 the picture had completely changed. Britain occupied Egypt and the whole Nile valley of the Sudan. Italian colonies lay at Eritrea and on the Somali coast, dividing the horn of

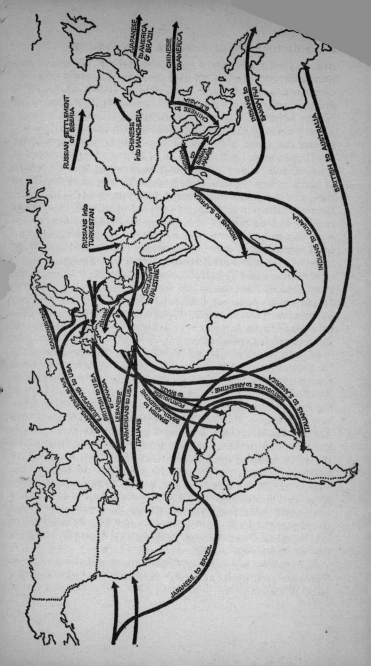

Africa with Britain and France. Zanzibar and the mainland up to and beyond the Great Lakes were British. Below this the German colony of Tanganyika bordered on to the expanded Portuguese colony of Mozambique. Below this again, Natal and British South Africa swung around the embattled Boer states. To the west lay the long tongue of British Bechuanaland, and beyond this to the north lay the two Rhodesias and Nyasaland. West again lay German South-West Africa, to its north Portuguese Angola, and then a chain of French and British colonies alternating with the occasional Spanish station, and the German colony of the Cameroons. Central Africa north of the Rhodesias lay under the personal rule of Leopold of the Belgians, whose ruthless and, on the whole, inefficient exploitation of the Congo was soon to lead to a European outcry. North of that lay the great hinterland of West Africa, which the French were in the midst of bringing under their sway. On the Mediterranean coast only Morocco and Tripoli still remained outside European rule. Elsewhere in Africa only Abyssinia was to survive, after the Italian armies had been defeated at Adowa in 1896. The only other independent state in all Africa was that of Liberia, founded by philanthropic Americans as a home for American Negroes some sixty-plus years before.

As with Africa so with the Far East and the vast expanses of the Pacific. In 1900 Russian troops occupied Manchuria. A mixed force of western troops had marched under German command (the German contingent did not arrive there in time) to relieve the foreign legations at Peking besieged by the Populist rebels against the west, the Boxers. Germany occupied Kiaou-Chou, Britain Wei-Hei-Wei and Hong Kong. The Germans claimed the Shantung peninsula as their sphere of interest, Britain took the great valley of the Yangtse-Kiang, the French that of the Si-Kiang towards the Indo-Chinese border. Indo-China was French, the Philippines American, the Malay archipelago largely Dutch, all but the large island of Singapore, which with Malaya itself was British. India, Burma, Ceylon came under the British government of India. In Asia only Japan remained free. Within two years she was to become Britain's ally. Two years later she was to perform the inconceivable and attack and defeat Russia (as in 1896 she had defeated China), the first major defeat of a European great power at the hands of an Asiatic state since the siege of Vienna.

In the Pacific the picture was the same. Japan's fleet was modern and efficient and soon to win a great naval victory. Elsewhere everything was for the Europeans or the Americans. The isles of the Hawaiian cluster had passed finally under American rule in 1898. International crisis had flared briefly over Samoa before its partition in 1900 between Germany and the United States. The islands of the central and southern Pacific, for years the prey of the guano trader and the 'black-birder', the slave-raider of the Pacific, had passed with few exceptions under German, French, or British rule. In the south, Australia and New Zealand were on the last stages of the road to self-government. In the Far South, Antarctica remained an imminent lure to explorers, the South Pole as yet undiscovered.

One section of the world remained for the powers of Europe to partition, the Near and Middle East, the Islamic world from the Golden Horn to Kabul, from the Red Sea to the Black. Egypt was occupied by the British. Morocco and Tripoli were nominally tributary to the Ottoman Sultan. Palestine, Syria, the Lebanon, Mesopotamia were provinces of the Ottoman Empire, which also claimed sovereignty over the Islamic holy land of the Hejaz, and the adjoining Yemen; claimed, too, sway over the rest of the Arabian peninsula including Nejd, home of the Saud family, and the waterless but strategically important sheikhdom of Kuwait. The sheikhdoms of the Gulf lived in enforced peace with one another under the benign and protecting eye of the government of British India. On the northern side of the Gulf the ancient kingdom of Persia lay between the naval pressure of Britain and the land pressure of Russia in the north, seething with discontent and seeking German aid as a balance. Oil was suspected but had not yet been struck in commercial quantities. Britain's interest was everywhere. France entered as the traditional protector of the Catholic Arabs, her claims vindicated by the Crimean War. American missionaries were active working through colleges in Beirut and Istanbul. Otherwise the area was given to Islam. By 1920 it would be all under European dominion, virtual or actual, save only Persia, the Nejd and the Anatolian heartland of Turkey. One other state remained, an agreed buffer between British India and Russia, the state of Afghanistan which British India had three times tried to subjugate but each time in vain, an area of feudal near-anarchy, its Amir a pensionary of India.

THE BASES OF WESTERN STRENGTH

The superiority which the great powers of Europe displayed over the states and political systems of the rest of the world rested essentially on two items. First, in population resources they were superior to any non-European power except China with its three hundred odd millions. The rough population tables of 1900 show that apart from British India and the Tsarist Empire, the population statistics of the great powers lie in a solid lump at the top of the table ranging from Italy's 31 million at the bottom, Britain and France at 37·9 and 38·9 million each, Austria-Hungary at 45·2 million, Germany at 56 million, to the United States at 62 million at the top. Second, and more important, the European powers commanded a series of techniques for the mobilization of their natural resources different, both in degree and kind from those employed by their victims.

The first of these techniques was the use of mechanical power, generated mostly by coal (though oil was coming to supersede it in places where motive power was important), to extract and process the raw materials of iron and steel. The second was a command of technological innovation, which in the period between 1880 and 1913 was running at one of the highest rates of development in history. The third was the evolution of systems of administration, management and public finance capable of mobilizing the wealth of individual states for the purposes of state in a manner inconceivable to the older empires of Rome or China. Hand in hand with this went a system of financial institutions like the joint-stock companies, the banks and the investment houses which produced both private and collective wealth by allowing investors to take far greater risks than was ever possible during the days of the mercantile powers of medieval Arabia, India, or China.

The technological superiority enjoyed by the European powers expressed itself most markedly in the control they exercised over international transport and communications. The growth of cables, news agencies and, in the decade after 1900, long-distance wireless stations, meant that their owners came naturally to control the flow and dissemination of information and intelligence, and to enjoy an immediacy of command denied to their opponents and bitterly contested among themselves. Their mobility enabled them to magnify their strength and to mobilize its potential in a way impossible to conceive in the earlier empires, so making the concept of the *levée en masse*, the nation in arms, realizable in a way undreamt of by the Jacobin originators of the idea. For, ultimately, the superiority of the European great powers lay on the battlefield. The revolution through which they had passed had as one of its essential elements a revolution in the technology of war.

This last great outburst of European expansionism was accompanied by a series of economic and social developments which are easy to describe, but whose causal interconnexions are still controversial and difficult to explain. To begin with there was a very considerable increase in population, usually accounted for by a rapid fall in the overall death rate in the 1880s in various countries (the birth rate remaining more or less standard). Thus the total population of Europe, excluding Russia, rose by some 80 millions between 1880 and 1913, the most rapid expansion being in Britain (12 million) and in Germany (22 million), Italy (7 million) and Austria-Hungary (12 million). Between 1900 and 1913 the population of Germany was actually increasing by a million a year.

This growth in population was accompanied by an even more striking increase in industrial production. In a civilization founded on coal as the source of energy for mechanical power European production rose from 238 million tons in 1880 to 563 million tons in 1913; between 1900 and 1913 the rise in production was 163 million tons alone. Steel production rose with equal speed from a mere $9\frac{1}{2}$ million tons in 1880 to 42 million in 1913. Similar figures can be adduced in all the other major heavy industries. Only in agriculture did Europe remain depressed.

Almost all of this growth in manufacturing capacity and power took place in three countries, Britain, France and the new German Empire. Together they accounted for about 70 per cent of Europe's total manufacturing capacity. In the key fields of coal, steel and machinery production, the figures were 93, 78 and 80 per cent respectively. Their domestic markets were large enough to provide an adequate framework for their own industries. Together they dominated the world market for manufactured products, commanding about 60 per cent of world exports. In fact, France's share alone was larger than that of

America, while Britain's and Germany's were each two to three times as large.

Of the three European powers, the fastest growing was Germany, which between 1895 and 1905 overtook Britain in most fields except textiles. In 1900 Germany was in fact entering on a period of growth which was to lead to a virtual doubling of her steel, iron and coal manufacturing capacity over the next ten years.

To these fantastic rates of growth in population and economic and industrial power one must add Europe's superiority in the technology of war. The long-range rifle, the Maxim machine-gun, quick-firing artillery with high explosive and shrapnel, gave European troops an immense superiority of fire over their non-European opponents. As Hilaire Belloc wrote of such engagements

> *Whatever happens, we have got*
> *The Maxim gun, and they have not.*

The defence was being greatly strengthened with the advent of landmines and barbed wire, first invented in the 1850s to enclose the great American desert.

But there was more to modern European warfare than superiority in weapons technology. Discipline was something that Europe had evolved with the professional armies of the eighteenth century, as they had the rudiments of army staff organization. In the mid-nineteenth century the Prussian army had adapted the railways to its purposes, making out of them an instrument of speed in the mobilization and concentration of military strength which had brought Prussia two immensely rapid victories in 1866 and 1870 and made Germany the premier power in Europe. They had also evolved the concept of war economics, the harnessing of modern industrial methods and productivity for war. But the idea of mobilizing the economy of a country for war demanded more than military staff work and the ability to organize railway timetables. It called for effective central administrative systems in government and for the mobilization of the nation's financial strength.

The administrative apparatus of two of the three greatest European powers, France and Germany, had in fact been directly evolved out of the need to make the state a more efficient machine for waging war. The French administrative system had its origin

in the aggressive absolutism of Louis XIV, as modernized and
harnessed to the idea of the national will by Napoleon. Its
equivalent in Germany developed first under the militant
absolutism of the first four Hohenzollern monarchs of Prussia,
to be profoundly modernized under the impact of defeat at
Napoleon's hands at Jena in 1806. Common elements to both
were a national system of state finance and public accounting,
national conscription in which every citizen served two to three
years with the active forces and a further twenty-five to twenty-
eight years with the reserves. Common, too, was the idea of
universal compulsory public education to produce an educated
citizenry, and a bureaucracy selected and recruited by competitive examination from the best products of the national educational system.

The effect was to produce in each country a military strength
that could be immediately mobilized for national purposes and
which proved much greater than that controlled by any non-
western political unit. The only major weakness in each country
lay in its financial machinery, which rested mainly on indirect
taxation of the customs, tariff, and excise type. Easy to administer, these forms of taxation provided a regular income adequate
to the normal purposes of the state. However, they lacked devices
by which reserves of financial strength could be quickly tapped
in times of national emergency other than those provided by
public loans.

In contrast to the continental bureaucracies which were
designed to cope with the problems of war, the British administrative machinery was largely concerned with economic growth,
industrialization and the social services. Like France and
Germany, Britain had a professional civil service recruited by
open competition from the educated *élites* of the nation. Britain's
educational system was a curious *mélange* of state, religious and
independent schools with a much smaller university system at
its head than that of Germany, even though a system of free
scholarships and the like ensured that reserves of talent among
the lower levels of society did not go totally untapped. Its private
sector of education, far more highly developed than that of the
continental powers, was geared to the task of producing a
governing class not only for Britain but also for the colonial and
Indian empires, one in which the virtues of character and
initiative were as highly valued as those of intellect alone.

By contrast with the continental powers Britain relied on professional military and naval forces designed mainly for overseas operations. For home defence a militia, formerly conscript, but voluntary since the mid-nineteenth century, and other volunteer forces sufficed. Not until 1907 was the militia incorporated into the Army Reserve and the other volunteer forces reorganized into the Territorial Army. In matters of military organization the South African War of 1899–1901 was to show that Britain lacked any kind of military staff capable of dealing with the problems of large-scale warfare. Her first line of defence remained the Royal Navy, in 1900 more than twice as strong as that of any potential rival, and still dominant over every part of the seven seas.

Britain's great strength *vis-à-vis* her continental rivals lay in her financial machinery which had evolved in part in response to the needs of financing coalition warfare against the dominant powers of the continent during the eighteenth century. The problems of administering a standing public debt had long been solved in Britain, and British systems of public accounting and political regulation of government expenditure were equal to those of France on which they had originally been modelled. British resistance to indirect taxation as an impediment to trade had led in 1842 to the revival of the idea of a direct tax on incomes, originally introduced during the Napoleonic wars. The British government drew its other revenues from excise and customs duties on luxury goods, and from a tax on inherited wealth introduced in 1894. The inheritance duties and the graduated income tax together gave Britain an immense reservoir of taxable wealth, hardly tapped at all in 1900, but available for times of national emergency.

If this ability to mobilize for the purposes of state their full material and human resources had given the powers of Europe the necessary margin of strength against the much more numerous populations of the older non-European empires, the most important advantage enjoyed by them had come much earlier. This was the control of the oceans which gave them access to every part of the world except the centre of the Eurasian landmass. The last major challenges to European naval power had been defeated in the sixteenth century with the Portuguese victories in the Indian Ocean over the sea powers of the Indian littoral, and the Spanish-Venetian defeat of Ottoman sea power at Lepanto in 1571. From that date the only threats to the ships of the west had come from the Barbary pirates, whose strongholds had finally been cleaned up in the early nineteenth century with the French occupation of the Algerian coast. Similar piracy, though on a smaller scale, had led the British to intervene in the Persian Gulf in the mid-nineteenth century. Thereafter the general adoption of steam propulsion and coal-fired boilers had made piracy virtually impossible, except under the guise of state action, since the steamship needed elaborate bases and frequent coaling. The armoured warship of the 1900s could only be produced by the steel and engineering techniques of the major industrial powers, by the yards of Britain, France, Germany, Italy, the United States, Russia or Japan. The steamship made western commerce normally independent of wind and tide; though the disaster which struck the SS *Titanic* in 1912 was to show that nature could still set limits on men's pride.

From the conquest of the oceans, western man stood in 1900 on the edge of controlled flight in heavier-than-air vehicles. Men had been ballooning since the eighteenth century. The first successful airship, driven by steam, had been demonstrated in Paris in 1812. In 1884, also in Paris, an airship had flown with electric motors. The first rigid airship was demonstrated in Germany in 1897, and the first of the famous Zeppelins made its maiden flight in July 1900 over Lake Constance. In ten years they were to be running passenger services. Moreover, the initial steps necessary for the development of the aeroplane were also being taken. Otto Lilienthal made the first successful glider flight in 1891. The box-kite followed in 1893, the kite balloon in 1896. The glider and the box-kite had solved the aerodynamic problems and the advance of technology in the nineteenth century had given men the ability to power the aeroplane. On December 17th, 1903, at Kitty Hawk, North Carolina, the Wright brothers of the United States flew their first heavier-than-air vehicle. In the next five years, monoplanes and biplanes multiplied in England, France, Germany, and Italy. In 1909 M. Blériot flew across the English Channel, and Britain's isolation from attack was about to end.

Mobility by air followed mobility on land. The steam engine and the railway locomotive had already carried western power and ideas everywhere. But from the 1880s onwards, with German engineers taking the lead, the internal combustion engine had been developed, first burning coal-gas (N. A. Otto, 1878), then oil (Priestman, 1886), and petrol (Daimler, 1885), with the carburettor (Daimler, 1885), and electric ignition (Karl Benz, 1885). The application of these devices to driving vehicles was almost immediate. Karl Benz built his first petrol-driven three-wheeler car in 1885 and his first four-wheeler in 1893. By 1900 Daimler cars were in full production in Germany (1894) and Britain (1896). Peugeot (1889), Panhard and Lavassor (1891), and Renault (1899) had built cars in France, Wolseley (1895), Lanchester (1895–96) and Austin were at work in Britain, and Henry Ford had built his first car (1896) in the United States. The first Model-T was to be produced eight years later, and the motor-car became the vehicle of the new middle class.

To mobility (and the car was to conquer deserts hitherto only accessible to the camel caravan), the west added ease in verbal communication. Submarine cables were laid in the 1850s after the invention of telegraphy and the Morse code. The electric telephone followed in the 1870s (Bell, 1876), and in 1900 the world stood on the edge of long-distance wireless communication. Hertz had taken out his patents in 1887 and Lodge in 1897. The first successful trans-Atlantic transmission came in 1901 between St John's, Newfoundland, and Poldhu in Cornwall in the British Isles. The man responsible was the Italian Marconi, who, thereafter, settled in Britain.

Other major technological advances came in the widespread use of electricity for lighting purposes with the development of the electric dynamo in the 1880s, of street lighting, high-voltage transmission, and the filament lamp. Other changes included the development of photography on celluloid film, the beginnings of the cinema in Britain and France, the invention of the rotary press and of rotogravure and the introduction of steel and new types of cement and concrete for construction. The cities grew towards the sun as the Americans developed the skyscraper, and burrowed into the earth when the British pioneered the underground railway.

A significant development in this rapid advance of technology in all fields was the general shortening of time between the original innovation and its general application to the needs of society. In part this was due to the great effort put into research, in that the same innovation would emerge from widely separated laboratories and workshops more or less simultaneously. But it was much more the product of the industrial enterprise of the west, and the ease with which the device of the joint stock company made available the stored savings of the multitude rather than the inherited wealth of the individual few. Moreover, the technological initiative had begun to pass from Britain to Germany in the last decades of the nineteenth century, the only major British inventions being Parson's steam turbine and Dunlop's pneumatic tyre to compare with the great German lead in electric engineering, in the motor-car and in dye stuffs and chemicals. Germany, however, was handicapped by Britain's and America's capture of the great new source of power, oil. Indeed, British capital was engaged in oil exploration throughout the world, including such diverse places as Rumania, Russia, Burma, the East Indies, Mexico, and, above all, the Middle East.

Despite the fact that Germany led Britain in many industrial fields, and also in the race for technological innovation, Britain remained the paramount source of capital for a developing world industrialization. In the first decade of the twentieth century, Britain was investing 10 per cent of her national income overseas (one-half of her current savings), as compared with a mere 2 per cent for Germany, and her total overseas investments stood at £3,763 million sterling, one quarter of her national wealth. The London market offered the largest range of investment agencies, from the great commercial banks, with their overseas branches, and the old-established merchant banking houses, to the small specialized investment agencies. The Stock Exchange was a self-governing institution with rigid rules for the enforcement of financial probity. The three hundred thousand odd substantial investors included many who were inclined to take serious risks and finance long-term private investment abroad, the largest share going to investments in the Empire, in the United States, and in Latin America.

The Paris market stood in direct contrast to that of London, except that there were even fewer opportunities for profitable investment in France than in Britain. French investment first stemmed from the *rentier* tradition, which had bred a class of small investors looking for income investment rather than capital appreciation as did their opposite members in London. The ten million would-be *rentiers* placed their money first of all with a small group of banks, the *Banques des Depots* and the *Banques des Affaires*, and preferred above all to invest in the security of governmental loans, especially those made to foreign governments like that of Tsarist Russia, which accounted for one quarter of all French investment abroad. The Paris market was, above all, the market for foreign governmental loans. Unlike Britain, France lacked an industrial organization able to carry out great industrial enterprise overseas, and the French investor had therefore an added inducement to entrust his money to those who would absolve him of all risks.

To these two international centres of overseas investment funds, Berlin stood a poor third, mainly because of the great demands on German capital made by the domestic economy. Germany lacked both the *rentier* class of France or the large investors of Britain, and control of her investment funds was much more institutionalized than among either of her two rivals. Capital funds were concentrated in the hands of the great banks, who acted in combination to take up large demands for investment loans rather than in competition with one another. This concentration of power made German investment leadership overseas much more dominant than that of Britain or France, though lack of funds circumscribed Germany's freedom of action.

A characteristic feature of German overseas investment was the expansion of German banks especially in the Balkans and in South America, a form of financial imperialism much more resented by its recipients than either the political direction of French funds by the French government or the *de haut en bas* inquisitiveness of British investors. The bulk of German funds invested abroad went to South-Eastern Europe, the United States and Latin America.

THE CHARACTERISTIC PHENOMENA OF IMPERIALISM

Behind this last great spasm of European expansion and the immense technological advances which gave the European powers their strength lay a deeper drive, the will to Empire. As a mass movement imperialism affected the major powers at different times, coming mainly in two great waves, in the late 1880s and again in the following decade. Contemporary writers such as J. A. Hobson in Britain and Charles Sumner in America were to find economic causes for its strength and persistence, failing to recognize it for what it was, a peculiar and viciously atavistic form of nationalism. It dominated British politics first in the mid-1880s, and swept back in the 1890s to rule unchallenged until 1903–4, when the Liberal party began to regain its balance. In France it held sway in the 1890s until the entire country became absorbed in the Dreyfus case. Imperialism maintained its grip over Germany for a longer period until checked in 1908–9. United States imperialism lasted from 1898 to 1912 when Wilson's victory in the Presidential election marked the end of 'dollar diplomacy'.

In all countries the main strength of imperialism lay among a determined, oligarchically-minded minority who formed a number of middle-class pressure groups. In Britain the Primrose League, the Imperial Federation League, in France the Committee for French Africa, in Germany the German Colonial League organized demonstrations, lobbied MPs, influenced or dominated the press and raged generally at the pusillanimity of their governments and the lack of interest in imperial matters of the average citizen. In such a mood, Rudyard Kipling wrote his famous *Recessional*. But the reluctance of the governments to act was often circumvented by the drive and opposition of the imperialists in the field. Frequently, these were consuls, such as Nachtigall who secured the German Cameroons, Roustan who played a major part in the French annexation of Tunis, Kirk at Zanzibar, Willard Straight, the American vice-consul, who played so large a part in involving America in her first clash with Japan over Manchurian railroads. Often they were explorers like Karl Peters who secured Tanganyika for Germany, Marchand who led his men halfway across Africa to the head waters of the Nile at Fashoda to provoke an international crisis with Britain, or Stanley who marked out the Congo for Leopold. Sometimes they were visionaries like Cecil Rhodes, sometimes concession hunters. Often they formed chartered companies which operated ahead of their own governments. Typical examples were Rhodes' British South Africa Company, which settled the Rhodesias and attempted unsuccessfully to annex the Boer Republic in the Jameson Raid of 1897, Sir George Taubman Goldie's Royal Nigerian Company, and the Imperial British East Africa Company that deliberately intervened in East Africa to keep the Germans out. Most believed they were serving the national interest, even when their countries disowned them. For most of them nationalism was their religion.

It is this ideological element in imperialism which at bottom casts doubt on the economic theories of the origin of imperialism so popular around the turn of the century and taken over lock, stock and barrel by Lenin. These theories sought to explain imperialism in terms of the marginal return to capital invested. When this return became too small in relation to opportunities at home, so it was claimed, capital was exported, and where capital went the government which represented the interests of those capitalists had to follow. There were, of course, instances of such economic and financial imperialism. The French action against Tunis, the British occupation of Egypt, the Anglo-German action against Venezuela in 1903, the American actions in Central America are examples of this debt-collecting, financial imperialism. But there are so many cases of imperialism which fail to fit this thesis; including that of Germany, where there was an actual shortage of capital on the home market and the returns on capital invested abroad were less than the profits earned at home, or those of Italy and Japan which were net importers of capital during the whole of their most imperialist periods. Moreover, there are even cases, such as those of the American banks in China under President Taft, or the French financial interests in Morocco which behaved in an imperialist manner only after their governments forced them to do so to provide them with an excuse for an intervention on which they had already decided.

The truth is that imperialism was an emotion which often clothed itself in economic arguments, often in pseudo-Darwinian racialist arguments, often in a historicist appeal to the 'world-historical' process, whatever that might mean. It represented an exaggerated form of nationalism from which it developed with awful inevitability. Where this emotion did not classify itself as imperialism, it took other forms, of irredentist nationalism like pan-Germanism or pan-Slavism. Its explanation had to be sought in the processes which were at work in Europe. For it was a social not an economic phenomenon, a product of the strains and stresses of Europe itself.

Chapter 2

Europe at Home

THE NEWNESS OF EUROPE

As a collection of political units defined by geography, Europe is old. But the precise collection of these units which made up Europe in 1900 were all newly created, or had at least passed in the nineteenth century through social and political upheavals on such a scale as to make them comparatively young in appearance. In general the socio-political set-up within the individual states and the international system which held them together were barely thirty years old.

In Britain the electoral reform of 1867, taken with the beginning of universal primary education in the 1870s, had completely transformed the nature of British politics, ushering in an era of mass political parties. Party organization and discipline became of the first importance, and control of the party organization at the grass-roots the key to political power. To lead these parties, at first the charisma of a great personality was necessary. Such a charisma was won at this date only by personal appearance over as wide an area as possible and by the oratorical powers displayed, for example, by the British statesman, William Ewart Gladstone, whose great Midlothian campaign of 1879 marked the first tentative essay of the mid-nineteenth century parliamentary leader in the techniques of mass persuasion to be so widely used in the twentieth century. Under the organizatory talents of Mr Joseph Chamberlain for the Liberals, and his opposite numbers on the Tory side, Lord Randolph Churchill and Sir John Gorst, the two loose coalitions of the mid-nineteenth century grew into disciplined and unified parties, though the strain of maintaining a doctrinal unity was to prove too much for the Liberals who suffered their first, though not their last, great schism with the resignation of Mr Chamberlain in 1886. The Tory party had already been organizing support among the new industrial working class and the divisions in the ranks of its rival did much to consolidate their influence among them.

In France, the Third Republic was founded in 1871 amidst the ruins of Louis Napoleon's popularly-based Second Empire. Its first act was to suppress with the utmost rigour the attempt of the Paris working-class districts to set up a Commune. The effect was to turn the new industrial working class irrevocably against the new Republic. On the right, the Catholics and monarchists failed, despite their initial majority, to capture the state in 1877, and in 1891 the new Pope Leo XIII destroyed their mass basis of support in proclaiming the *Ralliément* of the faithful to the Republic. Under the impact of the scandals that bedevilled the Republic, and the attempt of Republicans to obtain redress for a Jewish staff officer named Dreyfus, wrongfully convicted of espionage by an Army court, the authoritarian element in French politics turned towards a new proto-Fascism of armed street-fighters, the *Camelots du Roi*, and a brilliant anti-Semitic press, the *Action Française* of Maurice Barrés and Drumont, author of *La France Juive*, but failed, through the fundamental individualism of French politics, to produce a leader capable of exploiting it.

Germany herself was no older than France. Proclaimed at Versailles in the aftermath of the Franco-Prussian war, the German Empire was the creation of Otto von Bismarck, the Prussian Chancellor, who had solved the long rivalry for the leadership of Germany of the houses of Habsburg and Hohenzollern, by excluding the Habsburg dominions after defeating them in war in 1866. His action left the Germans of Austria and Bohemia outside the new state which, despite its popularly elected *Reichstag* and its apparently federal structure, remained essentially Prussian in character. The Catholics of the South and West had been reconciled with the new state by the tariffs of the 1880s and the abandonment of the attempt to attack their separate educational systems, but the Prussian state machinery had made no attempt to reach greater agreement with the mass political parties produced by universal suffrage.

The new Italian state was a little older. It had been created with the aid of France in 1859–60 by Cavour, the minister of Piédmont, and Garibaldi, the reckless guerilla leader. But Rome itself had not been freed of alien troops until 1870 at the cost of a feud between the new monarchy and the Pope which was to last until 1929. More serious were the continuing divisions between north and south which the roles of the north in unifying Italy and of the Church in the south perpetuated. Italy remained a political oligarchy.

The state of Austria-Hungary had been remade in 1867 by the so-called 'Compromise' between the Habsburg dynasty and the ruling *élites* of Magyar Hungary. The two states enjoyed a common monarchy, army, financial system and foreign policy but had little else in common, having separate parliaments and separate administrations and having to re-negotiate their mutual trade relations every ten years. Farther east, the states of Greece, Serbia and Montenegro dated back to the early part of the nineteenth century. But each was enlarging itself so much at the expense of the declining Ottoman Empire as to seem in a constant state of creation. The same could be said of the states of Rumania, which took its origin from the end of the Crimean War, and of Bulgaria, set up after the Russo-Turkish war of 1877, and still nominally under the suzerainty of the Ottoman Empire. In the north, Sweden and Norway lived in an uneasy union which had been set up in 1815 and which was soon to be broken. In the east, Russia was ruled by a weak and impulsive Tsar, in a state of impending crisis. The great reforms of the 1860s had freed the serfs and opened the universities. But they had not solved the problem of peasant land-hunger, nor found a place in the Tsardom's structure of social power and status for the new classes produced by these reforms or by the concurrent industrialization which was proceeding so rapidly.

The system which held these states together was also of recent origin. Fundamentally it was the creation of Otto von Bismarck. It rested upon a structure of alliances and conventions. The four continental powers, France, Germany, Austria-Hungary, and Russia, were grouped in two alliance systems each with its commercial and political satellites. The older of the two was that of the Central Powers, based on the Austro-German alliance of 1879, and transformed by the alliance with Italy of 1883 into the Triple Alliance. Bismarck had tied Rumania into this alliance in 1883, and had maintained a strong connexion with Tsarist Russia through the so-called League of Three Emperors of 1882 and the Reinsurance Treaty of 1887. He had also maintained a rather weaker connexion with Britain through the Mediterranean agreements between Britain and his ally, Italy, and by exploiting Britain's need for German diplomatic support in the Egyptian question.[1] His Austrian ally maintained her own control over Serbia through a secret agreement of 1878 by which the ruling family of Serbia, the Obrenoviches, received a secret Austrian subsidy.

After Bismarck's dismissal in 1890, his successors lost touch with Russia and Britain, and allowed Russia to conclude in 1891 a political and, in 1893, a military alliance with France, which Germany imagined to be directed against Britain but which was, in fact, directed against herself alone. Britain had stood off a challenge in the colonial field from France at the Fashoda crisis of 1898 when a French expedition attempted to lay claim to the headwaters of the Nile, had built up a fleet capable of taking on virtually anything Europe could muster against her, and had retreated into a policy of splendid isolation, unsatisfactory in the extreme to her European rivals, who could only wait for the misgivings felt by differing sections of British opinion to bring Britain back to the point where some bargain could be struck with her.

The essence of the Bismarckian system was agreement among the great powers to settle their differences peacefully, and not to allow one country to score gains without the others receiving compensation. This principle had been laid down at the two Berlin congresses of 1878 and 1885 with first Russia and then Britain called to book. These congresses were not repeated, but short conferences, and other devices of cooperation such as international consortia of banks, standing conferences of ambassadors and the like made it possible for the great powers to continue their cooperation and domination of the smaller powers of Europe. Bismarck's dismissal had, however, removed from the scene the one statesman who really understood how the system worked.

THE 'WEAKNESS' OF EUROPE

The new Europe might seem to the outside world to be so strong that its dominance of the rest of the world was unlikely to be shaken for a century or more. But, in fact, it contained a number of fatal flaws, both in its individual states and in the system as a

[1] See Chapter V.

whole, which were to make its period of world supremacy of remarkably short duration. The most dangerous of these was the failure of the European system to accept completely the new principle of nationality. Even in western Europe such obviously 'national' states as Britain and Spain had their problems. The Irish problem bedevilled British politics from 1885 onwards and was in 1914 to bring Britain to the verge of civil war. The twin problems of Catalonia and the Basques introduced extra complications into the tangled web of politics in Spain. In France alone centralist nationalism maintained its sway, and the small revival of enthusiasm for Provençal never translated itself from the cultural to the political sphere. As one moved eastwards so the problems of nationalism became ever stronger and more threatening to the established order. The most dangerous areas lay in the three great multi-national empires of eastern Europe, those of Germany, Austria-Hungary, and Tsarist Russia, and in the marches which separated them.[1]

The two states most endangered were those of Austria-Hungary and Tsarist Russia. The compromise of 1867 had divided the Habsburg Empire along the river Leithen and the Carpathians. Its Hungarian part was the more unified of the two and formed a logical entity dominated by the Magyars of the Hungarian plain. To the north lay the largely suppressed Catholic minority of the Slovaks, to the south the ancient kingdom of Croatia with its own Diet under rigid Hungarian control. The institutions of state employment in Croatia, especially the railways, were potent instruments of Magyarization. To the east lay the province of Transylvania, with Rumanian and German minorities under equally strong pressures to assimilate themselves to the Magyar nation. The so-called 'Austrian' side of the monarchy was far less unified. Magyar Hungary contained only one dominant racial group; Habsburg Austria contained three, and several provinces where no single group enjoyed any domination. The core of the Empire was formed by the German provinces of Austria proper, the Tyrol, the Vorarlberg, Upper and Lower Austria, Salzburg, Carinthia and Styria, the last two provinces extending some way into what is today northern Yugoslavia, and having, as a result, sizeable Slovene minorities. In the north, were the three provinces of Bohemia, Moravia, and Silesia, where Czechs and Germans were locked in bitter contest

[1] See map, European Alliances and Alignments, on page 185.

for dominance over such issues as the language of state and the control of the provincial Diets. Eastwards, lay the province of Galicia where Polish landowners and aristocrats held down a townsfolk consisting of Poles and Jews and a peasantry mainly made up of Ukrainians, especially in the east. Beyond that lay the Bukovina with a mixed population of Jews, Germans, and Rumanians. To the south lay the provinces of Istria and Dalmatia, where the dominant racial group was Italian and the bulk of the population Slovene or Serb; Slovenia where a Slav population managed its own affairs; and the Austrian colony of Bosnia-Herzegovina, placed under Austrian mandate by the Congress of Berlin.

The Habsburg monarchy faced two private nightmares: one was the pull of pan-Germanism exercised on the Germans of Bohemia and Austria by the propagandists of Bismarck's Germany, a pull which expressed itself in such movements as the *Deutsche Nationalverein*, the *Deutsche Schulverein*, and the nationalist anti-Catholicism of Ritter Georg von Schönerer; the other was the growth of a southern Slav or Yugoslav movement which would unite the southern Slav lands of the monarchy around Serbia, as the Habsburg lands of northern Italy, the Milanese, and Venetia, had been lost to Piedmont in the 1860s. The Czech-German struggle in Bohemia and Moravia, which was by far the more immediate and virulent of the racial troubles in the empire, always seemed containable by contrast, since it lacked any real external focus. The continuance of Habsburg control of Serbia thus seemed essential to Vienna as was the avoidance of any serious trouble with Russia in the Balkans. The Austro-Russian agreement of 1897 to preserve the *status quo* in the Balkans was thus of the first importance.

The Tsarist empire was second only to the Habsburg empire in the number of its alien nationalities and greatly ahead of them in the degree to which it sought their assimilation. In the north, the state of Finland annexed in 1805 remained almost totally indigestible, its Swedish aristocracy and its Finnish middle and peasant classes proving equally impossible to assimilate. Along the Baltic coast lay the ethnically-mixed territories of the Estonians, akin to the Finns, the Latvians and the Lithuanians, areas dominated by dynasties of German-Balt nobility from whom in the past the Tsardom had drawn many of its ablest administrators. South of these lay Russian Poland, Byelo-

Russia, the Ukraine, and Bessarabia, each divided between a local peasantry and nobility, a largely Jewish urban middle class, a mixed Jewish-native working class, and a Russian-dominated administration. In Poland the bulk of the Polish aristocracy had gone into exile after the failure of the 1863 risings, without in the least extinguishing the Polish nationalist movement, whose leadership was being taken up by a new university-educated class, a mixture of the rural gentry and the new professional classes. Such elements were hostile to the Tsardom in Russia itself; in Poland they were not only hostile to the Tsardom but to Russian rule as such. In Byelo-Russia, there were only the beginnings of a local nationalism, of lower-class origins, which was still a little unclear as to whether it was Lithuanian rather than Byelo-Russian. In the Ukraine, local nationalism consisted of a combination of regionalist resentment of Tsarist centralism, local feudal antagonism to Russian modernization, cultural nationalism centering on the ancient cities of Kiev and Kharkhov, and general feelings of Cossack solidarity. In Bessarabia, a small element of Rumanian nationalism fed itself on support from Bucharest. All this western belt of the Tsarist empire was undergoing a high degree of industrialization, and showing the first signs of trade union and political labour organization. All these areas had a large Jewish population which the Tsardom was using as scapegoats for its own mismanagements, and repeated pogroms were driving many of the Jewish minority (of perhaps some three million) into emigration westwards.

In contrast with these two empires, Germany faced only one serious racial problem. Of course, there were a Danish minority in Schleswig-Holstein taken over in 1864 after the Prussian war with Denmark and a small Belgian minority in Eupen-Malmédy. There was a very serious problem in Alsace-Lorraine, taken into Germany from France in 1871 and still garrisoned like the conquered enemy territory it undoubtedly was. But the most urgent problem concerned the Poles in eastern Germany, too large and solid a mass to be either assimilated or long dominated, a link with Russia and Austria-Hungary so long as it was in their joint interests to keep the Poles in subjection but a very potent source of subversion if this common interest should cease. The Poles of Prussia lacked leadership outside their Church, being largely agricultural. The working-class politician of Polish origin tended to join the German left rather than to act on his own. The first Polish political representation in the Reichstag was rural in origin.

More serious than the nationalist strains in western Europe were those which came from the industrial revolution, and from the class of industrial workers which that revolution produced. By 1900, this class had passed from industrial organization through the creation of trade unions to direct political activity in most of the countries of western and central Europe. In France and Spain, and to a lesser extent in Italy, their organizations were at such odds with the state that their activity took the form of savage strike action with strong political overtones; in Germany, Belgium and Austria-Hungary they organized themselves into mass parties with a membership well into the millions. Everywhere this political ferment heralded the emergence into political consciousness of two new classes, the educated skilled worker of George Bernard Shaw's *Man and Superman* and the semi-educated industrial worker of large-scale industry. The first provided the leadership and the doctrine, and was joined by the *déclassé* intellectuals from every level of the social scale. The second provided the mass force, the unmoving threat behind the active militants. Neither of these groups had a recognized place in the social hierarchy of any European state, whatever its actual social composition, and their self-consciousness and organization seemed to threaten the fabric of the existing state, based as it still was on what frequently amounted to chattel labour.

An added strain was provided by the emergence of an educated female class which the universities so reluctantly began to admit around the 1890s. Women, however, remained deprived of the vote, treated by the law in the same manner as those men in imperfect command of their reason, and exploited by their employers in the new world of business organization which swallowed so many of them up as secretaries and typists. Feminism was born as a movement among the educated leisured women folk of the upper strata of the *bourgeoisie*, a movement so potentially disruptive of established social mores as to pass easily into the violence of the suffragettes within a decade of its being launched in Britain. To the strains brought by the rapid rate of economic growth through which most European countries were passing was added one which struck at the most basic social institution in European society, the family relationship between male and female.

EUROPEAN POLITICAL EXEMPLARS

To those critics who looked with extreme dissatisfaction at the current political systems in Europe, three distinctive forms presented themselves: constitutional parliamentary democracy of the monarchical or the republican kind; constitutional autocracy of the central European, Prussian, German, or Habsburg variety; and Russian Tsardom. For examples of constitutional monarchical democracy, Europeans turned most naturally to Britain, then to Belgium, the Netherlands, and the Scandinavian states. The basis of these systems was in each case a constitutional fiction by which a cabinet of ministers, representing whichever coalition of political forces could obtain a parliamentary majority in an election, ruled in the name of a monarch whose powers were confined, in Bagehot's classic formulation, to advice and warning. The electoral system in each case provided for universal male suffrage. Parliament was bicameral, the upper chamber normally being hereditary, though in the cases of Belgium and the Netherlands it was of a federal character. France provided the main republican variant, the Third Republic expressing itself through a bicameral legislature, and a cabinet appointed by a prime minister in order to command, as far as possible, a parliamentary majority. The prime minister himself was appointed by the president as the figure most likely at that moment to be able to form such a cabinet. France provided the one exception to the rule that political life in western Europe was dominated by the disciplined mass party. The French electoral system did its best to perpetuate the fractionalism and ever-shifting political alliances which had shown themselves in British politics in the period before the second Reform Bill. But French individualism played an even larger part, and power rested more with the two chambers of the French parliament than with any cabinet or prime minister, however powerful his personality.

In central Europe, constitutional autocracy was the norm. In this system the monarch ruled through a chancellor and a cabinet whose job it was to control and manage a parliament, which, at least where its lower chamber was concerned, stood in somewhat the same relationship to the monarch as Congress does to an American president; that is to say, parliament's role was to approve his legislation and to limit the exercise of his autocracy. Ministers could be, but were not necessarily, chosen from parliament. The orders of the autocracy, to which considerable powers of emergency action were reserved, were executed by a powerful and all-pervasive bureaucracy. The autocrat, like the American president, was commander-in-chief of his armed forces. In turn the military authorities regarded themselves as at least the equals of his civilian cabinet and advisers. As a result conflicts between chiefs of staff and chancellors occurred with some frequency.

Only in Imperial Russia was unbridled autocracy still to be found. The position of the Tsar was strengthened by his quasi-religious role as head of the Russian Orthodox Church in a state whose masses were profoundly devout and acknowledged the authority of the priest almost before that of the policeman. The sole traditional check on the Tsar was his need for the support of the princely families and the aristocracy generally, which gave him his ministers, his senior bureaucrats and his generals and officers. In past history this class had not been above removing individual Tsars who had failed to rule strongly and successfully, so that the Tsarist system had come to be defined as 'autocracy tempered by assassination'. Future events proved that the Tsar still needed this support in times of great stress. But it was already becoming apparent that he needed the approval of a rather larger segment of the ruling classes than before, including the new industrial and commercial bourgeoisie whose power and stake in the state increased *pari passu* with Russia's industrialization.

THE BASES OF SOCIAL AND POLITICAL POWER, TRADITIONAL AND EMERGENT

The fact that even in Russia a public opinion existed, although the 'public' was much less numerous than in the autocracies of central or the democracies of western Europe, shows that the bases and instruments of political power were the same throughout the continent. What differed was the degree to which each was present. One may perhaps distinguish seven different bases of power in the world of 1900. First, came the traditional basis of power, the status, noble and aristocratic, conferred by the ownership of land, which carried with it the triple role of providing advisers to autocrats, an officer class and leaders for agrarian-based political parties in autocracies and democracies alike. Second, came the ever-growing power of the bureaucrat, as the states of the world, both autocrat and democrat, increased radically the scope of state action in industry, in commerce, and in the newly-developing spheres of social insurance. Third, came the power conferred by wealth or the command of wealth, a power which lay with the large-scale investor, the banking house, the brokers and those who controlled the movement of funds and the placing of investments. In an era of such large-scale movements of private capital and government borrowing on the bourses of Paris, Vienna, Berlin, and London, immense power lay in the hands of a Schroeder, a Baring, a J. Pierpont Morgan, a Rothschild. Fourth, was the power of the large-scale industrialist and trader, a Krupps or a Carnegie in steel, a Ballin in shipping, a Mond in chemicals, a Rockefeller or a Deterding in oil, a Rhodes in gold and diamonds, a Nobel in explosives, a Harriman in railways. Fifth, came the power of the democratic political leader in parliament and in the country, the power of a Lloyd George, a Joseph Chamberlain, a Theodore Roosevelt, a Clémenceau or a Poincaré. Sixth, was the power of the new leaders of mass movements, a Jaurés or a Bebel for the social democrats of France and Germany, a Lueger for the Christian Social party in Austria-Hungary, a Kramar for the Czech nationalists of Bohemia. Seventh, came a new group whose influence sprang from the growth of the mass press in Britain and the United States, the newspaper owners and editors, like Alfred Harmsworth in Britain and William Randolph Hearst in the United States. Beyond these, further sources of wealth were to develop, first with new technological advances such as in radio (Marconi) and second, with the development of new techniques in the distributive trades such as the chain store and the department store (Sir Thomas Lipton and Gordon Selfridge in Britain, and the Woolworth family in America).

With the increasing importance of the masses, as consumers,

as tax-payers, and finally as conscripts, there developed out of
the aristocratic traditions of Britain, Prussia, and Austria,
concerned with the link between crown, aristocracy and people,
a new and positive conception of the role of the state as the
purveyor of welfare especially to the urban working classes
oppressed by the appalling conditions in the new towns which
grew up during the industrial revolution. In the regulation of
industry and in the provision of social insurance and medical
services for the poor Bismarckian Germany led the way, to be
followed by the Austrian empire and the monarchical democracies of Britain, the Low Countries and Scandinavia. Such
reforms were anathema to the pure liberal *bourgeois* as interfering
with the processes of the market, but aristocratic benevolence
and the new radicalism were too much for them.

POLITICAL MOVEMENTS: PRO-SYSTEM

The dominant systems in the states of Europe rested upon a
combination of four main political movements. The first of these
was aristocratic conservatism in all its forms, linked in most
countries with the agrarian interests. In Britain, the landed
interest still accounted for much of the Tory party's strength in
Parliament, parson and squire combining to turn rural con-
stituencies into safe Tory seats. In Belgium, in Germany and
Austria-Hungary where aristocracy was far more strongly
entrenched, the parties of this persuasion, the Prussian conservatives and their opposite numbers in German Austria, in
Austro-Polish Galicia, in Magyar Hungary, even in Bohemia,
were the basis of the government's majority in the various
parliaments. Sometimes allied to them, often in opposition, the
national-imperialist wing of the various liberal parties provided
an alternative party in general support of the system. In Britain,
the imperialist wing of the Liberal party, Asquith, Haldane, and
Sir Edward Grey, challenged the Liberal leadership while in
opposition and threw their energies into the development of
Britain's armed forces and international position once they came
into office. In Germany and in Austria-Hungary, the National-
Liberals were in office for most of the 1870s and remained in
general support of their respective autocracies thereafter,

resenting only their refusal to move towards a more parliamentary system of government.

Aristocratic conservatism was informed by a kind of benevolent authoritarianism which looked back in many respects to the ideal of the eighteenth century, of an idealized non-political administrative state opposed to the divisions of mere party politics. Liberal imperialism by contrast looked outwards, reform at home being seen mainly as a means of increasing the efficiency of the state. Liberal nationalists also viewed the world in terms of a historical system in which struggles between states and between social classes were the only roads to progress. Many sought to identify in these conflicts an inevitable historical process, by which class succeeded class or racial group racial group by some 'scientific' law of universal historical applicability. Marx foresaw the rise of the proletariat and the inevitable conflict with the capitalist *bourgeois*. Danilevski, the Russian journalist, writing in 1871 saw the era of the Slav about to supersede that of the German 'cultural-historical type'. More popular than these among the bourgeois were the social Darwinian writers who saw the social process and the relations between states and nations as an extension into human society of Darwin's laws of natural selection, 'the survival of the fittest', 'the struggle for existence', a doctrine which both justified the social groups and nations currently at the top of the existing scale of power-relationships and enjoined upon them the need for continuous exertion to prove themselves worthy of that position. One possible development they foresaw was the merging of racial groups akin to one another into larger political entities, Pan-Slavism among the Slavs of Eastern Europe, Pan-Germanism, Pan-Anglo-Saxonism uniting the British Empire and the United States.

POLITICAL MOVEMENTS: ANTI-SYSTEM

Opposition to the existing systems of government was of two types. In the first place, each system of government bred its own brand of opposition movement. In the second, the growth of imperialism and Social Darwinism was rivalled by the rise of the new universalist movements, socialism, social catholocism, agrarian radicalism and integral or totalitarian nationalism.

In the limited autocracies of central Europe the bourgeois and nationalist parliamentary parties always retained an element of hostility to the *régimes* which denied them real political power and responsibility. Indeed, in all cases there were radical democratic groupings in fairly permanent opposition. Within the western democracies the main division came on the issues of imperialism and social reform, those who opposed the former and advocated the latter often taking their inspiration from a parochial if not isolationist nationalism inherited from the *laissez-faire* radicals of the mid-nineteenth century. The Little Englanders in Britain found parallels in France and in Belgium, in their opposition to overseas adventures as being actions inherently wasteful of the nation's resources and in their belief that the main motive force behind imperialism was corrupt financial adventurism. As such, however, this element only represented one strand in the movement for social reform, which was backed equally by those who felt that radical reforms were necessary to improve the efficiency of the nation-state to fit it for the struggle for international existence. Although divided on most issues, the imperialist and isolationist wings of the British Liberal Party could unite behind an important programme of social and political reform after its electoral victory in 1905. The American movement for social reform, which culminated in the reforms introduced in President Wilson's first two years of office, covered both Theodore Roosevelt and William Jennings Bryan, respectively Republican candidate for the vice-presidency and Democratic candidate for the presidency, in the elections of 1900. And the co-founders of the Fabian Society and the famous London School of Economics in Britain included both the ablest of the younger imperialist Tories, L. S. Amery, and the arch-intellectual reformist radicals, Sidney and Beatrice Webb.

An interesting element in these movements for social and political reform, progressivism in America, Liberal radicalism in Britain and their analogies in France and the other European democracies, was their use of the press to mobilize public opinion against the abuses they sought to reform. The journalism of 'exposure', 'muck-raking' as it was known in America, flourished most, and became for a time extremely profitable in the United States; but it was by no means unknown in Europe where, especially in France, the scent of a scandal was meat and drink to the journalists of the new popular press. Against the sensationalism of much of the popular side of the movement, must be placed the quiet dedication of those actually engaged in work among the poor, the destitute and the forgotten of the nineteenth century, working in the so-called settlements of which Britain's Toynbee Hall was the best known.

Reformist liberalism, however, was essentially a transitory phenomenon, except in the United States and Great Britain. Historically of much more significance at the turn of the century was the growth in strength of the older and the newer universals, Catholicism and Socialism, to which extreme nationalism and the elements which supported it were to prove themselves militantly hostile in the twentieth century. Both social Catholicism and Socialism were mass political movements and as such accommodated themselves a little too easily to the divisions between nations. Neither were to prove strong enough to withstand the outbreak of international war in Europe in 1914. But both were sufficiently moderate, even in a sense conservative in relation to the political institutions and systems of Europe, that they eventually became an anathema to the integral nationalists and proto-Fascists and the totalitarian socialists of the twentieth century.

Social Catholicism had been strong in the 1840s in Germany and France, under Lamennais and Bishop von Ketteler. At that date it had been well in advance of the central direction of the Catholic Church which, it was felt, had identified the Church too closely with those social classes and interests which were being threatened by the processes of social and economic change at work in the early part of the nineteenth century. The advent of Leo XIII and the issue of the Encyclical, *De Rerum Novarum*, in 1891 set the stamp of Papal approval on Social Catholicism. In Belgium, Germany, Austria, the Netherlands, and Switzerland, Catholic parties sprang into existence, or took on a direction which had previously been denied them. In France the Papally-backed movement known as the *Ralliément* ended Vatican support for monarchism and diverted French authoritarianism into proto-Fascist channels. Catholicism entered the trades union and cooperative movements. It took very strong hold among the peasantry of Central Europe, now becoming increasingly politically conscious. The Social Catholic programme included legislation to bar the exploitation of labour, and to foster the growth of small-scale property-ownership both on the land and in industry. Coupled with this programme were attacks on economic and political nationalism, on the concentration of economic power in a few hands through cartels and trusts, and on class warfare. Its leaders were an odd mixture of the aristocrat and the new *petit bourgeois*. In Austria, for example, leadership passed from the aristocratic Baron von Vogelsang to the first of the great modern demagogues, Dr Karl Lueger, three times Mayor of Vienna after 1896, and a violent, if not totally indiscriminate, anti-Semite. In Britain and in America, where aristocratic Catholicism had for obvious reasons never existed as a political force, the movement was much more closely allied with the embryo Labour movement. Cardinal Manning played a major part in this movement in Britain (his intervention in the bitter London dock strike of 1889 is just one example). In America, Social Catholicism was strongly entrenched in the Irish and Central European elements in the trades union movement. As a political force, Social Catholicism was to suffer both from the essentially limited nature of its aims, which in many cases were confined to maintaining the parochial system in education, and from changes in the Papacy itself. Pius X, for example, felt it necessary to keep a tight rein on the movement his predecessor had initiated, and, as a result, the Social Catholic movement in Italy developed in opposition to the Papacy, even to the point, in 1909, when its leader, Dom Romalo Murri, was excommunicated. The conflict between local social idealism and the changes of policy in the Vatican kept it from developing any real international character or organization.

The Social Democratic movement was, in form at least, much more committed to opposing nationalism and developing on an international basis. The First International had been broken in the 1870s in the aftermath of the suppression of the Paris Commune, amidst the bitter quarrels between Marx and Bakunin, the Russian pan-Slav anarchist, who brought into the European socialist movement hostility to the organized state, and an idea of collective freedom of a totally Russian and non-European kind. The First International had acted as a means of inflating the importance of the various national groups, none of which, save perhaps those of France, Switzerland and Belgium, amounted to very much in their own countries. The Second International came only gradually into existence, and achieved formal status with a permanent office and executive in 1900,

after its component national parties had become firmly established in their native political surroundings. The largest single
socialist party was that of Germany, founded in the late 1860s,
and converted, by its experience of Bismarckian persecution,
very firmly to the idea of parliamentary action as a means to
securing the revolution. By 1900, it was a mass party of considerable size with fifty-six seats in the Reichstag, two million or
so voters, and three-quarters of a million trades unionists
supporting it. Its programme centred on the conversion of
Germany to a popular direct democracy, and contained no
explicitly socialist measures such as nationalization for fear of
strengthening the capitalist state. Its dominant theorist, Karl
Kautsky, defended the party's policy with the argument that the
achievement of an absolute majority for the party was historically
inevitable. The revolution would come once such a majority had
been secured. The important thing was to maintain party unity
until that date.

Other important socialist parties were the Austrian socialists
(re-founded in 1888–9) who were dedicated first of all to the
achievement of universal male suffrage and from whose ranks
came the only socialists to attempt to reconcile the growth of
competing national groups with the rigid social categories of
Marxism; the Belgian Labour Party (1885), with twenty-seven
seats in parliament, deadlocked over educational and franchise
issues with Belgian political Catholicism; the Swedish (1889)
equally absorbed in the fight for universal male suffrage; and the
Italian socialists, who elected thirty-three deputies in the 1900
elections in a lower house of 500, despite government repressive
measures against the party and its leadership the year before.
The French socialist movement, characteristically, was divided
into six main groups, not to be unified until 1905 under the
leadership of Jaurés. The British Labour movement was divided
between the Independent Labour Party (1893) with strong
regional, Scots, Welsh and minority elements, the Labour
elements in the Liberal party, the Fabian Society with its middle-
class intellectuals and belief in 'permeation', and the Marxist
Social Democratic Federation. But in 1900 most of these groups
came together with leading trades unionists in the Labour
Representation Committee, with a declared policy of creating a
'distinct Labour Group' in Parliament. However, only two of its
candidates were successful in the 'Khaki election' of 1900 which

was fought in the jingoistic atmosphere induced by the South African War.

In the Socialist International the socialist groups in the two great non-European extensions of Europe, Russia and the United States, played a remarkably limited part, the central role being taken by the German Social Democrats. The comparative impotence of the Russian and American parties stemmed from the very different conditions each faced when contrasted with the parliamentary role of the European Social Democratic movements. But it also underlined the point that in their own countries they only represented one wing of the native radical-revolutionary forces; and that in choosing to embrace the European pattern of social democracy they were in some sense breaking with their own tradition. Both parties, moreover, were very weak in numbers compared with the mass parties of Europe. Neither could accept a parliamentary approach to their problems. Both faced systems of government which seemed at first sight analogous to those of Europe proper but were in fact as profoundly different from those of the European powers as they were from each other.

In the United States the labour movement was divided between the American Socialist party (founded in 1901, its main strength lying among German immigrants) and the various branches of the American trades union movement. The latter was itself in turn divided between the craft unions led by Samuel Gompers, and united into the American Federation of Labour, which concentrated entirely on limiting entry to the labour force as an essential preliminary to the use of economic action to raise the conditions and terms of labour, and the more violent syndicalist advocates of 'one big union', from the Knights of Labour of the 1880s to the International Workers of the World, the 'Wobblies' of the 1905–20 period. The trades union movement, in either of its manifestations but especially in the syndicalist form, was strongly American in ethos and organization, and regarded the intellectuals of the American Socialist party with a contempt tempered only by the personal admiration and adulation all felt for the perennial Socialist candidate for the presidency, the railroad unionist-syndicalist Eugene Debs (1855–1926).

The Russian Socialist movement, like that of America, regarded itself as being part of the European international socialist movement. In America, however, the diffuseness of the political system and the comparative infrequency with which the power of Federal or State governments was used against the interests of the American working classes, made for direct strife between labour and employers and made the capture of the state's machinery by parliamentary means seem impossible because of the other interests involved and irrelevant to the problems faced by the working classes. In Russia, by contrast, the lack of a parliament to conquer, and the omnipresence of the Tsarist system made revolutionary activity inevitable, and only preserved the illusion of unity with the Socialist International by imposing on the would-be leaders of the Russian socialist movement the necessity of living in exile in Europe. The party was officially created in 1898 and its first congress, held that year in Pskov, included delegates from the Polish Socialist party and the Russian Jewish Socialist party, the Bund. When its second party congress met in London in 1903, there occurred the great schism between Mensheviks and Bolsheviks which was to lead to the Bolshevik victory in the Russian revolution of 1917 and the subsequent division of European socialism between democrats and totalitarians from which it has yet to recover.

In Marxist terms, Tsarist Russia had not yet passed through its *bourgeois* revolution, and the time therefore for the replacement in the seats of power of the *bourgeoisie* by the working class lay in the distant future. What then were those who looked for the socialist revolution to do ? Cooperate with the *bourgeoisie* in the overthrow of Tsardom ? Create a mass movement to preach and wait for the time when the socialist revolution could be won by parliamentary means ? Or concentrate on creating a disciplined, single-minded revolutionary *élite* ? Or should they concentrate on the economic struggle, on building up the trades union movement, on strikes to improve the conditions in the factories and legislation to improve the social conditions in which they lived ? Plekhanov (1857–1918) and those who were to be called the Mensheviks wanted a mass movement which would embrace all who called themselves Socialists. Vladimir Ilyich Ulyanov, who took the name of Lenin (1870–1924), preferred discipline and unity, unity in leadership, unity in doctrine, unity in membership. In 1903 at the second party congress in London he split the party over his refusal to behave in a conciliatory manner towards his opponents at a moment when he had secured a majority (hence the title of his section, the Bolsheviks, from the Russian word *Bolshoi*=large, ie, the majority) on the control of the party newspaper, *Iskra*. His minority opponents, the Mensheviks, went ahead with their efforts to turn the party into a mass movement.

The Mensheviks regarded themselves still as part of the international socialist revolutionary movement. But this itself was to be stirred to its roots by the issue which separated both Mensheviks and Bolsheviks from the third group of Russian Marxists. This group argued that the main effort of the Socialist movement should go into the economic front. They were themselves divided into two groups, the Economists arguing for the use of the strike, the Legal Marxists for political pressure for remedial legislation. The issue was formulated most clearly in Germany in the controversy between Karl Kautsky (1864–1938), the party theorist, and Edouard Bernstein (1850–1932), the leading exponent of the theory known as Revisionism. Bernstein argued that socialism could be achieved by an accumulation of piecemeal changes to be brought about by participation in the process of legislation in cooperation with other parties. His view was akin to those held by the Fabian Society in Britain, with their doctrines of permeation, legislation and social reform from above and their belief in the 'inevitability of gradualism'. It was carried to its logical extreme by the independent French socialists, Alexander Millerand (1859–1943) and René Viviani (1863–1925), the first of whom brought on himself the condemnation of the 1900 Congress of the Socialist International for taking a portfolio in the Waldeck-Rousseau cabinet in France the previous year. Millerand and those who followed his example were to be formally expelled by the Socialist International under German insistence following Kautsky's victory over Bernstein. The Fabians, never being affiliated with the International, were able at an early date to convert the British Labour movement to their point of view.

But concentration on economic action could lead those who advocated it to an entirely opposite course, that of the revolutionary general strike, of industrial action to secure revolution, the abolition of the wage system, the expropriation of the capitalists, worker ownership and control of industry, in sum unremitting class war. Those who advocated such doctrines were known generally as Syndicalists. Their main strength lay in

France, Spain and Italy, and, by reason of the diffuseness of government mentioned above, in the United States with the formation of the International Workers of the World, the I W W or 'Wobblies', in 1905.

A strong element in syndicalism was its fascination with violence; from this element was to develop a small but influential school of writers such as Georges Sorel (1847–1922), Vilfredo Pareto (1848–1923), Robert Michels (1876–1936), whose deification of violence, irrationalism and leadership by *élites* was to make the movement from extreme syndicalism to Fascism an easy step for intellectuals to take. Early forms of Fascism were, in fact, developing especially in France and in Central Europe in this period, though it was a Fascism which depended on racialism, the deification of the nation and the organized use of force rather than the ending of social conflict. Its leaders were the brilliant school of French writers grouped around the newspaper *La Libre Parole*; Leon Daudet, Maurice Barrés, Edouard Drumont, Charles Maurras. It expressed itself through organizations such as Deroulede's *Ligue des Patriots*, the young wealthy political hoodlums of the *Camelots du Roi*, the *Action Française* movement, and Drumont's *Socialistes Chrétiens*. In Germany proper, it was much less strong. Anti-Semitism existed, as did the traditions of violence and militarism expressed in the student duelling associations and in the Army. But the various ingredients of Nazism had still to come together. In Italy, where the poet, Gabriele d'Annunzio, and the futurist, Marinetti, were active, there were already groups known as *Fasces*. In Vienna both Czech and German nationalist deputies had discovered the use of violence and rowdyism as a means of political obstruction. Anti-Semitism flourished. Extreme nationalist students organizations had begun to imitate the *Camelots du Roi*. And both in Vienna and in Munich a crop of little-known writers had begun to extol the virtues of Germanism, Aryanism, selective breeding and the extermination of the Jews. But political violence was still the prerogative of the Anarchists. President Carnot of France in 1895 and President McKinley of the United States in 1901, were only the most notable victims of anarchist assassins.

A third type of socialism, apart from that of the Second International and the followers of Lenin, was the peasant agrarian socialism of Russia and Eastern Europe. The most important manifestation of this agrarian socialism was the Russian

Social Revolutionary party which held its first congress in 1898, as a revival of the Russian Populists of the 1870s, under Victor Chernov (1870–1952). A Croat peasant socialist party was founded in December 1904 by Stepan Radić (1878–1928). And ideals of peasant socialism were very strong in the second Zionist *aliyah* leading to the inspiration of the *Kibbutz* movement. A somewhat similar though much less doctrinaire manifestation was the agricultural cooperative movement in Germany and Eastern Europe associated with the name of F. W. Raffeisen (1818–88).

Most of these movements spread only through Europe and overseas on the wings of the great European emigration to the United States. But there were some interesting counter-currents. One, alluded to above, was the spread of Russian peasant socialism to Palestine through a wing of the Zionist movement. A second was the extension of early American syndicalism, embodied in the Knights of Labour, to Canada, Australia, and Latin America, to be followed later by a similar extension of the I W W movement. A third was the counter spread of Ethiopianism and early Afro-American nationalism from the American Negro community to Africa. A fourth was the movement of Islamic and Arab nationalism stretching from India to Morocco. The future shape of the new universalist movements, both genuinely universalist and universalist nationalisms, could be vaguely seen.

In the 1900s, however, the main universalist nationalisms were Pan-Anglo-Saxonism, Pan-Teutonism, Pan-Germanism and Pan-Slavism. Of these, Pan-Teutonism, however, was little more than an emotion, 'a nebulous thing which lent itself admirably to after-dinner speeches'. It inspired the British statesman Joseph Chamberlain in his speech of 1899 in which he spoke of the 'natural alliance' between Germany, Britain, and the United States. It led Cecil Rhodes, the British millionaire visionary, to include Germans and Americans among those eligible for the Oxford University scholarships set up by his will. It played its part in arousing German sentiment in favour of the Boers and against Britain during the South African War. But as a movement Pan-Teutonism never got off the ground. Pan-Anglo-Saxonism was stronger, inspiring neo-imperialists both in Britain and in the eastern United States. It was evident in the works of Captain Mahan, the writer on naval matters, whose books spread the gospel of sea power throughout the world. It inspired such organizations as the Pilgrims, the English-Speaking Union and the 'Round Table' school of neo-imperialists which developed in the British Conservative and Liberal parties after 1906. It is to be found in the thoughts of President Theodore Roosevelt of the United States and in the writings of Rudyard Kipling. Its real influence on the policy of either Britain or the United States is difficult to determine. It did not so much rule out the possibility of war between the two countries as give such a war the added terrors and resentments of a war between brothers, a civil war within the Anglo-American community.

Pan-Germanism was a far stronger movement expressing itself through various organizations in both Germany and Austria-Hungary, of which the German Pan-German League itself was only one among several. To some degree the movement was stronger in Austria-Hungary than in Germany, especially in the areas of Bohemia disputed by the Germans and Czechs. Georg von Schönerer, leader of the Austrian Pan-German party, was elected to the Austrian *Reichsrath* in 1873. In 1882 he united with the future leaders of the Austrian Social Democratic party to advocate a central European customs union between Germany and an Austria divested of her Polish, Rumanian and South Slav provinces. The foundation of the German National Union, *Deutsche Nationalverein*, in 1882 was followed twelve years later by that of the German People's Party, *Deutsche Volkspartei*. That same year the Pan-German League was founded in Germany. It had been preceded by the formation of the German School League, *Deutsche Schulverein*, and the funnelling of German money through the Reich German School League into the maintenance of German schools in Bohemia. Schönerer's nationalism was anti-Semitic, anti-Catholic and anti-Slav. With him and his rival in the German nationalist movement, Karl Wolf, who was elected to the *Reichsrath* in 1897 from the Bohemian constituency of the Egerland, Germanism was on the defensive against the growing strength of Slav nationalism in central and eastern Europe.

The Pan-German League in Germany was most important as an anti-democratic pressure group. With its mere 15,000–25,000 members drawn mainly from middle-class backgrounds, its strength lay in its links with other similar groups and its support in the German press and within the junior ranks of the army. Its

main importance in German politics was to come after the
outbreak of war in 1914.

Pan-Slavism existed both in Russia and among the Slavs of
Austria. The first Pan-Slav organization, the Moscow Slavonic
Benevolent Committee dated back to 1858, the first international
congress to 1867. It was hostile to both Germany and Britain
and deeply opposed to the nationalism of the minor Slav races.
Poland was not a nation but a 'poisoned dagger which the west
thrust into Slavdom's heart'. In 1876, the Ukrainian Uniate
Church was suppressed in the name of Slav unity. In the 1890s
Russification was extended to the Germans of the Baltic provinces, to Finland and to the Caucasus. In the 1880s the first
great pogroms of modern times were launched against the Jews
of Kiev and Odessa. The Czechs were exhorted to embrace the
Cyrillic alphabet and the Orthodox Church. Like the Pan-
German movement, Pan-Slavism was less an outgrowth of the
aristocracy than a movement of the upper *bourgeoisie* and its
loyalty was reserved for Russia rather than to the dynasty ruling
her. Its strength grew as the dynasty weakened. Its enemies were
Germanism, Catholicism, Socialism and Zionism – the other
universals – and of course Britain.

MOVEMENTS WITHIN THE SYSTEM

With the possible exception of the two major ideological movements of Socialism and Social Catholicism, all the political
movements discussed in the two preceding sections were national
before becoming international. There were other movements
which were more genuinely international in character. One could
perhaps even call them intranational in that they operated
among and between the peoples of the individual nations rather
than between their governments. One can distinguish four
important movements which partook of this character: the movement towards intellectual cooperation, the humanitarian movement which expressed itself in the campaign against slavery and
prostitution and in the growth of the Red Cross movement, the
pacifist and disarmament movements and finally in a class of its
own, Zionism.

In the first of these one can distinguish five different fields: the movement towards intellectual cooperation *per se* of which the most significant example was the foundation in 1895 of the *Société internationale d'études, de correspondance et d'échanges*, otherwise known as Concordia, with headquarters in Paris, whose declared aim was to promote good international relations by study of their intellectual, moral and economic 'manifestations'; the movement towards the development of an international language which had by 1900 fathered two main artificial languages, *Volapük* (which had largely run its course by 1900) and *Esperanto*, the creation of Louis Zamenhof (1859–1917), a Jew ... in Russian Poland; the movement towards the development of an agreed body of international law and a community of its practitioners, of which the major figures were Franz von Liszt (1851–1919), a German, and L. Oppenheim (1858–1919), a Briton; the major journals were Belgian, French, and German, and the guiding institutes, the *Institut de Droit International* and the International Law Association, were both founded in 1873, in a genuinely international basis; the movement towards international scientific collaboration which resulted in 1899 in the formation of the International Association of Academics which linked together the principal learned societies of the civilized world; and lastly the organization of international cooperation in the control of epidemic diseases which had resulted by 1900 in the signature of three conventions designed to prevent the spread of cholera from the Asiatic world to Europe along the Arab and Ottoman shores of the Mediterranean.

The humanitarian movement had many aspects, of which perhaps the most important were the campaigns against the slave-trade, and the traffic in women. The first of these had largely been a British campaign until the abolition of slavery in the United States in 1864 and in Latin America in the 1880s and the opening of Africa in the 1880s which united the European powers against the Arab slavers of the Indian Ocean and the Red Sea. In 1890, at Brussels, seventeen powers including the United States, the Ottoman Empire, the Congo Free State and Persia jointly established a code of anti-slave trade regulations and formed international bureaux in Brussels and Zanzibar. The function of the latter was to provide up-to-date intelligence on the movements and activities of Arab slavers. The second took two forms, the setting up of international organizations to protect women against the lures of the pimp and the pander, and the conclusion of international agreements for the exchange of information on the traffic in women and action against those who undertook to conduct the caravans of unfortunate women across Europe's borders to the brothels of Asia and Latin America. (The internal European trade had been largely eliminated by 1899.) A rather different though equally important element was the growth of the International Red Cross after the international Geneva Convention of 1864 had established the principle of the neutralization of ambulances and health personnel. The International Committee of the Red Cross, itself post-dated the formation of more than twenty-two national Red Cross Societies, being set up in 1880 as the successor to the *Comité internationale et permanent de secours aux militaires blessés*, with an entirely Swiss membership. At the Hague conference of 1899 a second convention was adopted extending the provisions of the Geneva conference to war at sea.

The movement towards the 'humanization of war' ran in very close harness with that towards its abolition by the proclamation of pacifism, disarmament and the substitution of arbitration for force as the solution of international disputes. This movement had its religious and economic adherents, but much more important was the growth of such bodies as the Interparliamentary Union (1859) and the Universal Peace Congress (1889), the establishment of the Nobel Peace Prize (first awarded in 1901), and the Hague conference of 1899 on disarmament, arbitration, and the laws of war, which achieved certain very limited successes especially in the establishment of a Court of Arbitration. This movement was to become the forerunner of the far more powerful organizations of the inter-war years.

The last of these international movements was of quite a different kind, that of Zionism, the movement to create a nation for the Jews of the world. Zionism, like other European nationalist movements, began as a cultural and historical force, among philosophers, writers, and historians. The factors which differentiated Zionism from the other submerged European nationalisms of the nineteenth century were the religious system it built on, the long historical self-conscious continuity of the Jewish communities, their differentiation according to the different nations in which the various Diasporae had caused them to settle, the solidarity of the major Jewish communities of Tsarist Eastern Europe, the terrible persecution these communities suffered under Tsarist rule from the 1880s onwards, their great emigration into western Europe and the United States, and, finally, the fact that the geographical area around which they built their national myth had not seen a Jewish political organization for eighteen hundred years.

As a Jewish phenomenon, Zionism depended on the interaction of three elements, the emancipation of the Jews of western and central Europe in the first part of the nineteenth century, the collective consciousness of the Jewish communities in western Russia and Poland, and the fact of Tsarist persecution. The bulk of established western Jewry, in Britain, France, Germany, Austria-Hungary, the Neti... ...ds, and Italy had embraced emancipation as a step towards assimilation. The Jews of eastern Europe reacted in the opposite direction. The Tarist massacres pushed them further. The first Zionist groups, the *Hoveve Zion*, began in western Russia in the early 1880s. Their first president, Leon Pinsker, from Odessa, published his *Auto-Emanzipation*, in 1882. That same year the First *Aliyah*, the first wave of Zionist-inspired immigrants, arrived in Palestine, then under Turkish rule. They were followed by the most idealistic of all the Zionists, the Russian *Bilaim*, who were determined to found Israel's destiny on the land of Israel, as agricultural workers.

The scattered Jewish communities that resulted from this first wave of immigration into Palestine, were kept going mainly by the moneys of the French *Alliance Israelite Universelle*, and their principal banker, Baron Edward de Rothschild of the French branch of that great Jewish banking family. The impetus which built these first stirrings into a major intranational movement and which turned a Messianic dream into an effective political force on the international stage came from Theodore Herzl, a western Jew from Vienna. Like the Rothschilds, Herzl had been reared in the tradition of the *Hof-Jude* (the Court Jew), who protected his interests by the maintenance of good relations and the offer of personal service to the autocratic courts of western and central Europe, rather than in the collective solidarity of the East European ghettoes. In 1896, Herzl, Paris correspondent of the leading Viennese daily, *Neue Freie Presse*, published his appeal for a Jewish state, *der Judenstaat*. In 1897 he summoned the first World Zionist Congress in Basel in Switzerland. In 1901 the Jewish Colonial Trust was established to buy land in Palestine.

And from 1899 until his death in 1904, Herzl paid assiduous court to the rulers of Europe and Turkey. His only offer of aid from those he courted came in 1903 from Britain, when the British government offered him Uganda as a place of settlement. Herzl wished to accept this offer. But it was indignantly rejected by the Russian Jewish delegates to the Zionist Congress. In 1904, the Second *Aliyah*, some fifteen to twenty thousand settlers, nearly all of Russian Jewish origin, left Europe for Palestine. They came inspired by the agrarian socialism of the Russian Social Revolutionaries, and with the aid of the Jewish Colonial Trust, they began to found the socialist land settlements, the *Kibbutzim*, for which Israel was later to become so well known. In addition, they succeeded, over the opposition of French and German Jewry, in making Hebrew their national tongue. Among them was David Grun, the future Ben-Gurion.

INTERNAL POLITICAL AND SOCIAL CRISES

As the nineteenth century ended, each of the major European powers was racked by its own internal stresses and strains. In Britain, the movement for Irish Home Rule was temporarily in eclipse. One generation of leaders had been defeated or disgraced by personal scandal. The Irish parliamentary party had settled down into a respectable parliamentarianism. But beneath the surface a new generation of leaders, poetic extremists, were about to emerge and usher in the bloody series of events by which Ireland was to bring Britain to the verge of civil war and eventually to win independence. In Britain itself, the Whig and radical elements in the Liberal party were beginning to separate, and one could see also beneath the surface a similar parting of the ways between the agrarian radicals of the western Celtic littoral and the new labour movement of the Scottish lowlands and the English and Welsh industrial areas. Enmity for the established Church, the hereditary aristocracy, and the House of Lords acted as a unifying theme, as did the memory of Queen Victoria's Diamond Jubilee and, for all but a courageous few, the hurrah-patriotism of the war in South Africa.

Across the channel, France was bitterly divided by the question of the guilt of the Jewish staff officer, Captain Dreyfus,

wrongly condemned for espionage in 1894. On the one side stood
the radicals and anti-clericals, driven by their desire at all costs
to see justice done, on the other, the traditional patriots, concerned above all to see the Army, in which they felt France's
soul and hope of revenge on Germany for the loss of Alsace-
Lorraine to be incorporated, preserved free of criticism and
denigration. Violence, anti-Semitism and proto-Fascism allied
themselves with the anti-Dreyfusards, Freemasonry, anti-
clericalism and ambition with their opponents. In the meantime,
the French working-class movement remembered the Paris
Commune and listened to the syndicalists who preached direct
action.

In Germany, the system erected by the great Chancellor,
Bismarck, was in steady decline; in election after election the
total votes gained by the Democrats, the Social Democrats and
the other parties hostile to the system increased; the Army
leadership turned more and more in an anti-political direction;
and the power and prestige of the chancellorship and the Kaiser
ebbed away. In Austria-Hungary, Chancellor Badeni's attempt
to solve the language issue in bilingual Bohemia was defeated by
the increasingly intransigent nationalism of both Germans and
Czechs alike. The municipality of Vienna three times elected
the Social Catholic demagogue, Karl Lueger, as its Mayor
against the Emperor's veto. In Italy, thwarted nationalism,
radical anti-Catholicism and suppressed Socialism were building
up slowly towards an explosion. In every country, a superficial
view showed a calm sunset closing the nineteenth century. More
penetrating eyes, however, could see clearly the signs that
portended storm.

Nowhere was this clearer than in the arts. To the contemporary eye, much in the music, printing and literature of the *fin
de siècle* seemed both ethically and aesthetically unsound. The
British academic critic, Ruskin, who died in 1900, could
describe the painter Whistler's work as 'a pot of paint flung in
the face of the public'. But in retrospect his work and that of his
associates in the British literary world seem as romantic as those
of their continental colleagues. In 1898, for example, J. K. Huys-
mans, the French writer whose study of decadent aestheticism,
A Rebours (1884), had had so deep an influence on Oscar Wilde
and Aubrey Beardsley in Britain, was still writing. Wilde, disgraced for homosexuality, published the *Ballad of Reading Gaol*.

The Prince of Wales, visiting an exhibition of the French painter, Toulouse-Lautrec, in London, found the pathetic cripple asleep on a sofa and refused to disturb him. Ravel, the last of the French romantic composers, published his first work, and the great Italian composer, Giuseppe Verdi, had his last work performed in Turin with the young Toscanini as its conductor. The French Impressionists, Manet, Monet, Degas, Sisley, Pissarro, Renoir, were finally achieving the popularity that so long had eluded them.

However, the dominant school in *avant-garde* Paris was that of the post-impressionists, Cézanne, Seurat, van Gogh, the Douanier Rousseau. Gauguin was dying in the Marquesas islands of French Polynesia, Toulouse-Lautrec was to die the following year (1901). And already the younger painters who were to dominate Paris for the next forty years were gathering: Picasso, Fernand Léger, Matisse, Utrillo, Raoul Dufy. All were still painting in what was essentially a nineteenth-century Romantic representational style, concerned above all with colour and light, as the name, Fauvism, soon to be applied to their work, suggests. In sculpture Rodin's romanticized realism dominated Paris. The revolt of the twentieth-century artists and musicians, their obsession with shape, form and architecture, their attempts to demolish existing aesthetics and remake everything from first principles lay some seventeen years in the future with Cubism, Surrealism and Dadaism in painting and Atonalism in music. It was significant, however, that intellectually the separation between them and the aesthetic accepted by the society in which they lived had already been effected. And in their midst lived the two men whose scientific theories were to dominate the first half of the twentieth century, the mathematician, Einstein, and the psychologist, Sigmund Freud, who destroyed traditional physics and psychology to replace them with their exploration of the incomprehensible theory of relativity and the irrational depths of the subconscious.

Beneath the surface, however, the new forces were also at work. The main developments took place in the field of physics and philosophy. As early as 1887 a series of experiments had revealed the inadequacy of the mechanistic view of the physical universe, governed by a consistent and universal body of discoverable principles, to explain the phenomena of light and radiation. In the last decade of the century, scientists investigating radio-activity and nuclear physics were accumulating data of increasing complexity and inexplicability in the terms of existing science. At the same time the dominant schools of philosophy were suffering a series of distinctive attacks from three different directions. In the understanding of the nature of scientific argument, Ernst Mach in Prague and Vienna, Henri Poincaré in Paris, and Hans Vaihinger in Berlin, developing from Kant and the British empiricists, were destroying the idea that the intellectual activity of science consisted in the elucidation of 'laws'. In the examination of the nature and history of society, the position of Spencer, Marx, and the Social Darwinists, had already come under the concerted attack of Emile Durckheim in France who was, with Max Weber, one of the two co-founders of the new sociology, as well as from Vilfredo Pareto, an Italian exile in Switzerland, and Benedetto Croce in Italy. And the whole structure of nineteenth-century thought, with its optimistic belief in moral progress, had already been savaged beyond hope of recovery by the German prophet and critic, Friedrich Nietzsche, writing in the late 1880s. For these writers, the problems of consciousness, of the meaning of time and duration, of the nature of knowledge and reality were all important. Between new philosophers and the natural scientists the 'observed realities' of the common-sense view of the world were to disappear. At the same time Europe's leaders were pulling down the accepted structure of the political world around them. In such a relativist world, it was not to be long before those who despaired of achieving certainty themselves would fall victim to lesser men who had no doubts.

Chapter 3

The Impact of Europe on the External World: The Areas of Activity and Progress

INTRODUCTION

IN 1900, the societies of the non-European world already had four centuries of contact with and conquest by the states of Western Europe behind them. In the process the great native states of America and West Africa had largely disappeared. Settlers had herded the North American Indians into a scattered collection of reservations, occupied the temperate highlands of Central Africa and largely taken over the grazing grounds of the Bantu in South Africa. The Ottoman Empire had been defeated and driven out of Central Europe. The Indian states system had been in a state of decay even during the establishment of the first puny settlements of Portugal, France and the British East India Company. The same processes of disintegration had also been at work in South-East Asia and in the islands of the Indonesian archipelago, and the Moslem Khanates of Central Asia.

But the events of the last quarter of the nineteenth century, with its immense increase in European pressure, had made the divisions in the external world infinitely more apparent. Both among those states which were essentially extensions of the European system, and among those which remained recognizably alien to it, one can detect the existence of a broad gulf between those who were already in the strongest reaction against that pressure, developing their own indigenous nationalisms, seeking solutions to their problems which would be their own and not imposed on them, trying to develop their own strength so that they could stand up to and take their part among the great powers of the European appendix, and those which still lay stagnant and whose major awakening was to come in the future.

European pressures presented themselves in three different

forms. First, there was the pressure of trade, money-lending and investment, an experience which led state after state into bankruptcy and subordination to, if not occupation by, its European creditors. Secondly, there were the varying pressures of European power-politics which led in some cases to direct conquest, in others to situations where it seemed advisable to seek the protection of the strongest, and protectorates, with their apparatus of resident advisers, were established and accepted. Only a small handful of states managed to retain their independence as buffers between the powers, one or two, notably Abyssinia and Afghanistan, proving themselves capable of permanently defeating a would-be conqueror in conditions where its superior military technology could not be brought to bear. Third were the pressures of European population, expanding themselves in an immense wave of emigration, involving something of the order of $55\frac{1}{2}$ million Europeans in the period 1820–1924, the bulk of which emigration was concentrated into the period before 1914. Of the emigrants, nineteen million came from Great Britain, six million from Germany, about the same number of Italians, over a million each from Sweden, Portugal, Austria and Hungary; and about $4\frac{1}{2}$ million Jews came from Poland and Russia into Western Europe and the Americas in the same period. There was also a very considerable internal migration of Russians into Siberia, about $2\frac{1}{2}$ million peasants moving eastwards, between 1891 and 1910. The only comparable movements of non-Europeans were: the emigration of Indians, largely, in the form of contract labour, which led to there being a total overseas Indian population of more than two million by 1924, mainly in Ceylon, Malaya, the West Indies, Mauritius and Fiji; the exodus from China, which by 1924 resulted in an estimated eight million Chinese living overseas, the majority residing in Formosa, Indonesia, and South-East Asia (there was also a considerable Chinese emigration into Manchuria); the movement from Japan, which by 1922 accounted for over half a million Japanese living overseas, mainly in China, the United States, Hawaii, Canada and Brazil; and an unknown volume of African slaves taken by the Arab slavers from East Africa to destinations in Arabia, Egypt and the Moslem Middle East.[1] Within Europe itself, about 600,000 immigrants entered France in the period 1860–1911.

[1] See map, p 7

EXTRA-EUROPEAN EUROPE

At the beginning of the twentieth century, Russia and the United States, the two great super-powers of the mid-century, enjoyed a peculiar status, being both within and beyond the European states system, at once accepting and rejecting the values, ideas and traditions of European culture. Both had been subjected to the pressures of European ideas and culture for at least two centuries, and both had had time therefore to develop their own native reactions to those pressures, including a brand of radicalism which rejected Europe. The parallels which can be traced between the two countries' reaction to and relations with Europe, however, illustrate rather the overwhelming strength of the European impact than any similarity in their historical development, except for the presence of a strong tradition of agrarian radicalism in both. But even there the parallel is in form and not content, save in a common hostility to and rejection of European capitalism in preference to a nativist romantic idealization of the simple virtues of the agricultural community.

Of the two, **Tsarist Russia** was the major survivor of that alternative form of Christianity which grew out of the schism between Rome and Constantinople. It was a state, by this very token, whose rulers had had to force its native nobility into western forms and moulds. In its political system it was a hierarchical and aristocratically-limited absolutism with a strong element of theocracy, in that the Tsar was also revered throughout Russia as the head of the State Orthodox Church, and the 'Father of all the Russias'. In the early nineteenth century, Russia had come to dominate the European scene after the defeat of Napoleon, and to millions of Europeans, Tsarist Russia represented the blackest form of reactionary aggressive authoritarianism. As a great power, however, Tsarist Russia had feet of clay and her major encounters with the western powers in the Crimean War and at the Congress of Berlin in 1878 revealed such internal weaknesses that in each case the Tsardom was driven to attempt to reform itself. By 1900, in consequence of the piecemeal and partial nature of these reforms and the inevitable reaction against them, Tsarist Russia was on the edge of revolution.

In all, eight broad groups can be distinguished as engaged in

the internal struggle for power. At their head stood the aristocracy, educated, cultured, westernized, largely French-speaking,
providing the Tsarist empire with the higher ranks of both it
military and civil bureaucracies. Below them came the country
gentry and the civilian bureaucracy itself. These three groups
alone had some stake in the continuation of the existing system
of authority in Russia. Of the remaining five groups the most
powerful potentially was the capitalist class growing up in the big
cities, in Moscow, Kiev, Odessa and the industrial centres of
Southern Russia. Russian industry developed very rapidly and
on a large scale with the aid of French capital, and the cottage
and small-scale industry phases of industrial organization, found
in Britain's more leisurely industrial development, were largely
avoided or short-circuited. Inevitably, however, the members
of this group tended to a strong identification with the state
which was their major customer and which employed tariffs to
protect them against more efficient foreign competition. It is a
measure of the incompetence of the Tsarist system that this class
was so strongly opposed to its continuance.

Below them came four groups with no stake whatever in the
Russian state. First and most important were the peasants,
emancipated from serfdom in the 1860s but still labouring under
the burden of the redemption dues payable to their former
owners, dominated by hunger for land and the pains and strains of
adaptation to a money economy, without any capital to tide them
over bad harvests or to improve their extremely primitive agricultural methods. Gradually, in the villages, the richer peasants
were separating themselves from the general ruck at one end of
the scale and an agricultural proletariat was also developing at the
other, but it was to be some time before the resultant strains
were to make themselves felt. In 1900 most Russian peasants
were little removed from the kind of despair which can produce a
jacquerie, and their dominant emotions were hatred of the landlords and hunger for land. Second were the industrial workers,
separating themselves since the 1880s from their peasant fore-
bears, especially in Western Russia, Russian Poland and the
industrial areas of the Caucasus and South Russia. Third were
the subject nationalities. For Tsarist Russia, as noted earlier, was
a multi-racial state dominated by its Great Russian element.
Finns, German Balts, Estonians, Latvians, Lithuanians, Byelo-
Russians, Poles, Jews, Ukrainians, Georgians, Armenians,

Azerbaijanis, Kirghiz, Uzbeks, Kalmucks, Tatars, all had come or were coming to hate the Tsarist state and to look on the first sign of its weakening for a chance to assert their independence. Of all these the most striking case was that of the German Balts, imported in the eighteenth century to strengthen the bureaucratic element in Russia, but now moving steadily away from their loyalty to the Tsar as the Tsardom began to take on a Great Russian aspect.

The last group consisted of the intelligentsia, the university-educated class for whom there was no real place in the Tsarist system. This system denied them status, paid them little, and stultified most of their efforts to apply their intelligence to finding new solutions to Russia's problems. Small wonder that their more radically minded elements turned inevitably to assassination and revolutionary activities. As a class their hallmark was that they possessed little apart from their intellectual capital, though their members came from every social level in Russia.

All these groups looked to and at Europe in different ways. The aristocracy embraced French culture but, except for its more idealistic members, shied away from any imitation of European constitutional models. The gentry and the *bourgeoisie* in large measure joined in admiration for such models. The more public-spirited among the gentry had been developing a good deal of ability in the practice of parliamentarianism in the local Councils, the *Zemstva*, set up by the reforms of the 1860s; the industrialist-capitalist class could not but admire a system which, as in France or Britain, would give them so large a share in the political leadership of the state. Within the bureaucracy their viewpoint was shared and protected by the Ministry of Finance.

And yet among the gentry there were many who were disturbed by that competitive commercialism which they believed to be the hallmark of Western Europe. Some no doubt believed their own position would be threatened if the hierarchical system which kept their peasantry subservient was upset. Others embraced a romantic paternalism for which parallels were not lacking in Europe but which they professed to believe to be specifically Russian. Many were suspicious of or hostile to the new industrialist families whose wealth and manner of living offended the more traditionally minded. All these embraced a romantic Pan-Slavism, expressed within the bureaucracy by the police and the Ministry of the Interior, and embodied in Pobedonostsev, tutor to the young Tsar before his accession.

The main division between Europophiles and -phobes, or Westerners and Slavophiles as they were classified at the time, was to be found among the intelligentsia with its revolutionary critique of Russian society. The main point at issue was whether it was inevitable or desirable that Russia's economic and social development should parallel that of the societies of Western and Central Europe. Given their general dislike of the selfishness and individualism of Western capitalist society with its horrors in the exploitation of man by man, its lack either of social conscience or of social justice, its anti-aestheticism, its ugliness, its slums, was there not perhaps, the Russian Europophobes argued, an alternative set of developments, a Russian way to the social millennium. Some of the revolutionary intelligentsia believed in Russian solutions and as a result became preoccupied with the peasant problem, central to considerations of social justice in Russia. Thus, though the first Russian revolutionary outbreak, the Decembrist revolt of 1825, had been entirely western in impulse, the activist wing of the revolutionary movement in the mid-nineteenth century, the so-called *narodniks* who had gone out to live and spread their doctrines among the peasants, had found in the village cooperative, the *mir*, and the cottage industrial cooperative, the *artel*, primitive but purely Russian models for the social organizations they wished to see supersede Tsarist autocracy. Their eclipse, and the subsequent resort of the intellectual revolutionaries to terrorism was also a very Russian phenomenon. But by the late 1880s this in turn had been superseded by the growth of Marxist socialism which marked a return to the revolutionary models of Western Europe discussed in Chapter I. But from the late 1890s onwards the *narodnik* tradition was revived by the Social Revolutionary party, and the single characteristic institution which was to emerge from the revolution of 1905, the *Soviet*, owed nothing to Western revolutionary models.

The **United States** differed from Russia first of all in being an *emigré* state, a society consisting of those whose dissatisfaction with Europe had led them to leave it, where Russia had been forced to join Europe by the admiration and envy of its rulers. Founded in 1776 by the *élites* of the thirteen rebellious British colonies, it had survived the ordeals of the revolutionary wars by adopting a federal structure which prevented centripetal forces from rending it apart in its early days. Thereafter, this new nation had embarked on a policy of expansion westwards across the American continent which, after wars with Britain in 1812 and Mexico in 1846, had carried the Stars and Stripes to the Pacific, the 49th Parallel and the Rio Grande. The Atlantic ocean and the British navy between them had insulated it against any necessity to cramp its society into a military framework as the price of political survival. Without British sea power, the United States' adoption of the policy of avoiding European entanglements and warning the European powers off the Americas, enjoined in its first President's, Washington, Farewell Address of 1796, and embodied in President Monroe's proclamation of 1823, would have been largely pointless. It was doubly fortunate in that for much of the nineteenth century, including the critical period of the 1850s, Europe was absorbed in its own internal conflicts. The only major European intervention, that of France in Mexico in the 1860s, ended in disaster for the French, and the only other European power to make its pressure felt in the Americas was the decaying empire of Spain. Russia abandoned her pretensions in the 1820s and her presence in 1867 when the United States bought Alaska for $7,200,000.

Europe's preoccupation with the problems of Italian and German unification enabled the United States to survive its own moment of crisis without European intervention. But the Civil War of 1861–5 destroyed the socio-economic system of the southern states, and ushered in a period of industrial feudalism both in the north and the west which was to last for more than half a century. The temporary emancipation of the Negroes in political, though not in economic terms, and the break-up of the large estates into sharecropping and crop-lien small-holdings, made the south an agrarian peasant economy dependent on a single crop, cotton, a development which had strong parallels with the state of affairs in late nineteenth-century Russia. However, the creation in America of an agrarian peasant economy was greatly complicated by the Negro question and the absence of a hereditary land-owning class. At the same time, the development of large-scale mining in gold, silver, and copper, and of cattle ranching and, following this, the increasing role of the transcontinental railways as intermediaries between the federal government and the settlers in the distribution of land, introduced the same element of capitalist feudalism into the west. Although the new settlers owned their own land they were still effectively in the power of the railroads, the warehouses and the banks which controlled the terms whereby the produce of their land could be marketed. The latter part of the nineteenth century saw the growth of the great American fortunes and families, the Rockefellers, the Harrimans, the Vanderbilts, the cattle barons, the 'robber barons'. But it also saw the growth of an agrarian radicalism as potent as, and stronger than, the agrarian radicalism of Europe, although it was to be sixty years before the political strength of industrial feudalism was to come under serious assault.

This agrarian radicalism expressed itself in three great waves, the Granger movement which reached its greatest strength in the period 1868–76, the Farmers Alliances of the 1880s, and Populism in the 1890s. Of the three the Granger movement with its strong cooperative aspect was the only one with any element of collectivism. American agrarian radicalism was essentially democratic and individualist. It was also opposed to large-scale capitalism and trades unionism and quite as racialist and nativist as were the radicals of Europe.

Its other major difference from the peasant radicalism of Europe was in its obsession with cheap money, above all, with bimetallism. Bimetallism, the use of both gold and silver to back the currency at a rate of approximately sixteen ounces of silver to one of gold, was normal international practice until the beginning of the 1870s when most of Europe adopted a simple gold standard, and the immense silver deposits of the American mountain states discovered in the previous decade lost any chance of a government market. Silver ceased to be coined in the United States in 1873 and the general effect was to limit drastically the circulation of money, depress commodity prices and raise interest rates. The United States had experimented with a paper currency during the Civil War, the so-called 'green-backs', and the 'cheap money' policy they represented was remembered with gratitude by the farmers of the new west. But at that time, the United States had not been so much a part of the international financial community, and it had been easier to sell American agricultural goods. In the post-1870s the United States was again borrowing heavily from Europe and the tariffs were going up against her agricultural products. Bimetallism in

the United States would have involved limiting or suspending
the international convertibility of the US dollar since there was
far more silver in the world than the United States Treasury
could cope with at the set rate of sixteen ounces of silver to one
of gold. National bimetallism meant economic isolationism.

This was in some sense the greatest strength of the Populist
movement. In 1890 the Populist movement elected four Senators
and fifty Congressmen, ran its own Presidential candidate in
1892 and captured the Democratic nomination in 1896 for
William Jennings Bryan. For the Populists were nativist and
anti-European. The two Satanic forces in their universe were
the Jews and the English. They were aided by a bad financial
panic and widespread unemployment in 1894, and the resultant
election of 1896 was fought out on the issue of agrarian radicalism and bimetallism against the economic and financial forces of
the east and the industrial mid-west. Populism was, in fact, one
aspect of the growth of a native American culture which was
not only non-European but opposed to those elements in
America for whom European mores were all. Its representatives
in American literature at this time were Mark Twain, Stephen
Crane, Frank Norris, Willa Cather and Walt Whitman. Their
opponents were the Easterners, William Dean Howells, Whistler,
Owen Wister (target of one of Mark Twain's most savage essays
in criticism), and the novelist, Henry James, who applied for
British citizenship in 1914. The Populists were defeated in 1896
and again in 1900, but American politics and American culture
have continued to oscillate between their American nativism and
East Coast Europeanism ever since.

The main element in their defeat was the growth of American
nationalism and imperialism. Populism was indeed a part of
American nationalism, and the same men whose Americanism
impelled them to castigate the East for its links with and
dependence on the outside world, were among the first to react
to the cry of the 'nation in danger' or to the idea of an American
mission abroad. Their consciousness of American differences
from Europe was fed in part by glorification of the Anglo-Saxon
element in America, thus echoing the racialist element in other
nationalisms. But it found much stronger fuel in the belief that
the experience of 150 years of pioneering and the democracy of
the American frontier had given the American branch of the
Anglo-Saxon race something lacking to their cis-Atlantic cousins.

While politicians like Senator Henry Cabot Lodge from Massachusetts and writers like Captain Mahan, the naval theorist, lauded the Anglo-Saxon race, the historian, Frederick Jackson Turner, was finding a justification for American national self-consciousness in his famous essay *The Influence of the Frontier in American History*. Together, their sentiments and theories voiced a mood which the mass American press orchestrated and amplified. From 1895 when President Cleveland's message to Congress proclaimed American intervention against Britain in a complicated dispute between Britain and Venezuela over the Venezuelan border with British Guiana; through the issue of orders to the American Pacific squadron to attack the Philippines six weeks before the American declaration of war on Spain in April 1898; to the instigation of a separatist revolution in the Colombian province of Panama in 1903 when Colombia was giving the appearance of dragging her heels over the Panama Canal question; American politics were as much dominated by the ideas and politics of imperialism as those of any European great power. But along with the appeals to national interest and manifest destiny, a different point of view emerged, eventually flowering during the presidency of Woodrow Wilson. For want of a better phrase, it could be called 'educative and liberating imperialism'. This point of view appeared in the American support for the Cuban revolutionaries out of which the Spanish-American war had grown, and in the reasoning behind the annexation of the Philippines. The claim was then made that the Filipinos were not ready for independence and therefore it was up to the United States to 'educate . . . uplift and Christianize them'.

From 1900 onwards, two new elements were added to Populism in the American radical tradition. The first of these was the revulsion against economic and political feudalism on the part of the new professional classes and their followers in the big American cities of the East and the mid-West. The ideas of the Progressive movement, which came to dominate American politics from 1902–16, were a curious mixture of belief in direct democracy, which harked back to some Jeffersonian ideal of small-town politics in the Revolutionary era, and a determination to strengthen the powers of the Federal Government against the 'bosses' of the big cities with their armies of corrupt and ignorant voters and the business barons who financed them. The period of the Progressive attack on concentrations of economic power saw the first great development of the American press aimed at checking, by investigation and revelation, the illegitimate exercise of power. The movement's strength lay in the sophisticated political expertise of the Progressives and the 'muckraking' of American journalism. From their work sprang a doctrine of liberal pluralist democracy through state action to control the abuse of and concentration of economic power which, with the decline of liberalism in Europe after 1900, was to become the main alternative stream to social democracy in the European democratic tradition.

These developments took place against the background of a staggeringly rapid rate of economic growth. The population of the United States rose from 50 million in 1880 to 97 million in 1913, and 35 million of that increase was added between 1900 and 1913. In the same period coal production rose from 64·8 million tons to 517 million tons per annum. (British coal production was surpassed in 1900, when the rate for England was 244·6 million tons.) Similar growth figures were to be recorded in every other industry. With this growth went an immense increase in immigration which ran from 1902 onwards at between 750,000 and one million-plus a year, the previous peak figure (1882) having been 780,000 and that for only one year in a decade in which the normal figure had ranged between 300,000 and 600,000 annually. With all this one must add a stupendous increase in the rate of investment of European capital in the United States and in American indebtedness to Europe, which stood in 1914 at the then astronomical figure of 7·2 billion dollars. The first decade of the twentieth century was to make the United States the major industrial power of the world. By the end of the second decade America would be transformed from the world's greatest debtor to the world's greatest creditor.

In the remainder of the world the only other states which can be discussed under the same heading as the United States and Russia, that is as extensions of the European system, are the **settler states of the British Empire,** the Boer republics of South Africa, and the states of Latin America. Of these the Boer republics came under the category of escapist states and with the Latin American states are discussed in the next chapter. British colonial rule outside the Dominions and India was devoted principally to the maintenance of order, the passage of British trade, and the establishment and encouragement of local economic activity as a means of raising the contributions of local revenues to the cost of administration. German colonial rule lasted for so short a time in Africa that it hardly got beyond the establishment of order and power. Italian colonial rule penetrated just a little more deeply. Only in France can one trace the beginnings of a colonial policy before 1900, and it was to develop as an unstable blending of three conflicting ideas, mercantilism to promote French economic interests, assimilation of the native *élites* through education, and investigation, admiration and preservation of existing cultural and political organizations for all but a handful of the native populations.

The white settler states of the British Empire, Canada, South Africa, Australia and New Zealand all show the development of the same sense of nationalism, of separate identity already traced in the United States. In Canada and South Africa, this was complicated by the existence of a second nationalism, that of the French Canadians and the Boers. In both cases this second nationalism produced difficult obstacles to the achievement of self-government. This phenomenon of double emergence, an emergent nationalism bringing with it another directly opposed to it is to be seen also in the Ottoman Empire after the Young Turk revolution of 1908 and in India. But in neither of these two cases was it to be complicated by white racialism as in the settler states. In South Africa, the whites became very conscious of their own small numbers in comparison with the overwhelming majority of the natives they were displacing. And the white settlers in Australia and New Zealand felt the massive pressure of the surrounding Asian population seeking entry.

Canada was the first of the British settler states to achieve self-government and independence within the general framework of empire; and the present structure of the Commonwealth owes more to Canada than to any other state. Her nationalism developed, as did that of all the white British settler states, by a process of differentiation within a continuing attachment to Britain and things British. But in the Canadian case the differentiation was governed not only by the presence of an open frontier and a constant though never overwhelming flow of immigrants. These factors were present in the development of all the white settler states. Nor was the presence of a long-established European community of great cohesion, with an entirely different language, laws, religion, mores and culture the factor which made Canada the pacemaker in the Empire. A similar factor was also present in South Africa, although in South Africa the ratios between the races were reversed, Boers greatly outnumbering British and non-whites outnumbering both. The factor which made Canadian development unique was the presence and the pull exerted against the normal relationship with Britain by her great neighbour, the United States. Thus though a factor in Canada's history was rivalry between *Canadien* and Canadian with the revolts of 1856, 1870 and 1855 in the Red River area, equally if not more important was the three-way relationship between Britain, Canada and the United States, and Canadian experience, as in the Anglo-American settlement of 1903, that Canadian interests would always have to provide the sacrificial lamb on the altar of Anglo-American unity.

Canada's development, in fact, grew out of an inter-action between the relations between Canadians and *Canadiens* and relations between Canada as a whole and Britain's general external policy. It was British reaction to the rebellions of 1837 inspired by French Canadian radicalism that led to the evolution of the Durham Report: the doctrine of colonial advance towards economic self-sufficiency and political self-government which set in motion the development of the British Empire into the Commonwealth. It was British Free Trade which led to the establishment of the Dominion of Canada in 1867. But it was the Canadian discovery that union could only be maintained if party allegiances ran across the communal boundaries instead of parallel with them which really established Canada; and the principle thus discovered necessitated continuous compromise on external policy between the different communities. Canada could not lean too close to the imperial connexion. Nor could the ultramontane *Canadien* separatists with their *emigré* Royalist clergy altogether succeed in turning Quebec into an eighteenth-century agricultural sanctuary separated from the industrialism and urbanism of the twentieth.

In 1900, it was the Liberals who were in power, led by the French Canadian, Sir Wilfred Laurier. For a time Laurier had ended the control of the separatist *Ligue Nationaliste* in Quebec. And it was Laurier who withstood imperialist pressure in Britain at the Colonial Conference of 1902 to set up a 'real council of the Empire'. But after 1904, when the creation of the new provinces of Saskatchewan and Alberta led to a revival of that perennially disruptive issue in all part-Catholic countries – parochial versus secular state education – Laurier steadily lost control of his ex-*Canadien* supporters. In 1907, Laurier was again successful in imposing on the Colonial Conference the idea of the Empire as a 'galaxy of nations under the British crown'. However, in the crisis year of 1909 in Anglo-German relations, his acknowledgement that 'when Britain is at war, Canada is at war; there is no distinction' was directly challenged by the *Canadiens* in Quebec. In 1910, his nominee was defeated for election in his home constituency by aroused *Canadiens*, though it was his negotiations of a treaty of commercial recipro-city with the United States in 1911 which led finally to his defeat in Canada as a whole. Nevertheless, the long Laurier period of rule had set the pattern for Canadian politics in the twentieth century.

The Conservatives who replaced him in 1911 had in the past found support in Quebec and the other French-speaking areas from the anti-clerical urban elements. It had been Laurier's success in largely reconciling these elements with the Liberal party that had made it possible for him to break the long period of Conservative rule in 1897. In 1911, the Conservatives, the party of the expansionist imperialist English-speakers, descend-ants of the American loyalists, had been chastened by the events of 1903 into viewing the imperial connexion in very Liberal terms. It was therefore easier for them to ally themselves with Laurier's enemies in Quebec in a political *mariage de convenance*: the more so as Canada had generally been doing very well economically in its trans-oceanic trade with Britain ever since the beginnings of imperial preference enforcements in 1897.

The Conservative interpretation of Canadian nationalism was, however, to prove impossible to reconcile with French Canadian isolationism. In 1912, the Conservative leader Sir Robert Borden went to London and, in return for assurances of a Canadian voice in British policy, agreed to raise $35 million to add three Canadian-owned battleships to be part of an Imperial squadron in the British fleet. Although this move was defeated in the Canadian Senate, the onset of war in 1914 immensely streng-thened the whole Conservative position in Canada, and at the same time greatly exacerbated English-French relations. Canada prospered economically, transformed by the needs of Britain to finance not only her war effort but those of her allies from a net borrower to a net lender of capital. By sending nearly half a million men overseas and by suffering 61,000 dead and 175,000 wounded, Canada won a place in the Imperial War Cabinet and separate representation on the British Empire delegation to Versailles. But the political leaders of French Canada largely spent the war years fighting a bitter battle over the use of the French language in the schools of Ontario, and the introduction of conscription in 1917 gave rise to strong separatist manifestations, considerable obstruction, three days of rioting in Quebec itself and wide-scale desertion. Its effects on the Liberal party were to last for another five years or so, and to set a precedent which was to contribute very largely to the *immobilisme* of Canadian foreign policy between the wars.

The early establishment of the Canadian state, and the relatively small number of French Canadians living outside Quebec did at least preserve Canada from the war and civil strife which was to mark the creation of South Africa. But the development of nationalism in South Africa was complicated in a way almost unknown in Canada by the whole question of the non-white majority and of cheap native and immigrant labour. In Canada, the original Red Indian population had been largely ousted and confined to reservations by the middle of the nineteenth century. The importation of slave labour from Africa had never been on a very large scale (though it had created in Nova Scotia for a short time the world's oddest linguistic anomaly, a small group of Negro Gaelic speakers), and the largely short-term immigration of labour from the West Indies left a legacy of goodwill between the British Caribbean dependencies and Canada on which the West Indian members of the Commonwealth still attempt to build a policy. The main problem for Canada was that of cheap Oriental labour from China and Japan, one complicated after 1906 by an Anglo-Japanese commercial convention. But after riots in British Columbia and wild talk of secession to the United States the Canadian authorities, with American encouragement, were able to negotiate a direct agreement with Japan for the voluntary limitation of immigration into Canada by the Japanese authorities themselves, without leaving any legacy of ill-will to complicate later Canadian-Japanese relations. This first Canadian step into the field of external relations was followed in 1909 by the creation of a Canadian department of external relations, marking the first break in the principle of centralized control of foreign policy within the British Empire. The negotiations with Japan also marked the first example of the Canadian preference for quiet negotiations in external matters which was to become the distinguishing mark of Canadian activity on the international scene in the mid-twentieth century.

In **South Africa** the development of a common nationalism was impeded for most of the nineteenth century by the existence of a large non-European population which greatly outnumbered both main groups of European settlers. An added hindrance was the determination of a section of the original Dutch settler community to maintain an eighteenth-, if not a seventeenth-, century separation from the external world, a determination only given temporary quietus by the victory of the British forces in the South African War of 1899–1902. Furthermore, the majority of European settlers were of Dutch not British origin. Schemes of large-scale British settlement never quite succeeded except in the province of Natal. All these factors plus the non-European problem caused the English-speaking settlers to lean more heavily on British colonial rule and to inhibit the growth of the conviction that London neither knew nor cared anything for colonial interests which was the main guiding spirit in the development of settler nationalism in the other parts of the Empire.

Those who administered British colonial rule did their best to apply the principles of the Durham Report to South Africa. But for most of the nineteenth century they had to cope with the problems of a continuous military frontier of a unique type. In the late eighteenth and throughout much of the nineteenth century, the main threat was from the southwards-advancing Bantu tribes whose talent for military organization, developed in the long centuries of movement across Africa from their cradle in the Cameroons, made them formidable opponents. But British colonial rule imposed a theoretical quality before the law for all the Crown's subjects; and insistence on this principle drove a section of the Dutch colonists to trek northwards into Africa, where the Dutch founded Boer republics whose precise degree of independence was a matter of constant dispute with the British authorities. And these republics, with their breakaway Synods and extreme sects like the Doppers, fundamentalist and pro-slavery, developed a degree of military organization and a skill in open warfare which the British underestimated at their peril. In the meantime, those who stayed behind during this period (sometimes called Afrikaners to distinguish them from the Boer trekkers) developed the habit of cooperation with the British colonials: and it was out of the alliance of the Afrikaner leader, Jan Hofmeyr, and the Englishman, Cecil Rhodes, that a Canadian-style compromise began to emerge. But the discovery of gold on the Rand in the heart of the Transvaal, the largest Boer republic, and the development in Britain of a new wave of imperialism in the 1890s made a conflict between Boer and Briton inevitable. And once such a conflict began, Afrikaner and Boer together viewed Britain as the enemy.

The discovery of gold on the Rand brought a flood of British immigration into the Transvaal, and gave British imperialists a lever to move the Boer republics back under imperial control. The Boers did their best to exclude the new immigrants from participation in their own rather simple democratic political system. But nothing could disguise the fact that the new immigrants were paying most of the costs of state while being denied the franchise. Rhodes' attempt to use their grievances to stage a *coup d'état* by his company police, the so-called Jameson Raid, was a miserable failure. Its consequences were to convince both Boers and Afrikaners that Britain was planning to dominate and destroy their nationality.

The Jameson Raid took place in 1896. Three years later the British were at war with the Boer states in an all-out effort to suppress them. The ostensible reason was the position of the British immigrants, the so-called Uitlanders, in the Transvaal, heavily taxed and denied the franchise. The reason widely accepted at the time by radical opinion generally was that the war was fomented by Rand mining interests who wanted to rid themselves of Boer rule. The real reason seems to have been a conviction in the minds of a handful of British imperialists in dominant positions that there was no room in the British Empire for the separatism which the Boers represented and the conflict of loyalties with which they must constantly confront the Afrikaners under British rule. Sir Alfred Milner, High Commissioner in South Africa in 1899, who did more than anyone else to provoke the Boer nationalism which began the South African War, was determined to smash the Boer states and resettle them with a British majority. His scheme was destroyed by the military weakness of the British troops and the incompetence of their leaders. The first few months of war saw nothing but a series of major military disasters for the British.

Thereafter, the tide of war turned, and the main body of armed Boer resistance collapsed. Unfortunately for South Africa that was not the end. The hard core of Boer militants turned to guerilla warfare. And, in the effort to suppress them, the British army authorities used methods of collective punishment, burning farmsteads, and concentrating the families of guerillas and their supporters into hastily improvised camps so unsanitary and poorly supplied with food and shelter that the death rate in some camps rose to 40 per cent or more. By such methods the British alienated not only the Boers of the republics but many of the Afrikaners of the colony; and only exhaustion, war weariness and the fear of a native rising finally brought the guerillas to negotiate with the British. Even then they only came to negotiate and not to surrender. And the negotiations and the subsequent Treaty of Vereeniging (May 1902) confirmed the authority of the commando leaders, the 'bitter-enders', over the moderates, the Anglophiles, the loyalists and the collaborators among Boer and Afrikaner as leaders of the Boer people.

Such a capitulation, for in many respects it was the British not the Boers who capitulated at Vereeniging, made the work of reconstruction in South Africa extremely difficult. A proposal to bring in Chinese coolies to fill the gaps in the labour force in the mines of the Rand brought Britain and Boer South Africa together again. In December 1904, Louis Botha, one of the leading Boer ex-generals, founded *Het Volk*, a new all-Boer party. In 1905, it allied itself with British advocates of home rule for South Africa against the survivors of Rhodes' Progressive party. In 1907, after the Liberal victory in Britain, elections in South Africa gave *Het Volk* with its Liberal allies, and some from a new white supremacist labour movement on the Rand, an electoral victory, with General Botha heading a joint British-*Het Volk* cabinet. The British Liberals saw that their only hope of coping with Boer numbers and reconciling the Boers with the British minority was to bring in the solidly British-settled Colony of Natal. In 1910, the Union of South Africa joined together Natal and the Cape Colony with the two former Boer republics and Botha took his variegated coalition into a new party, the South African National Party. In 1913, an extremist wing broke away to fight against reconciliation of Boer and Britain. And South Africa, like Canada, was thereafter to resist any attempt to bring her into an Imperial Federation. In 1914, extremists led a pro-German rebellion. But Botha put them down and South African forces played their part on Britain's side in the Great War. But there were still two nationalisms, not one, in South Africa, British and Boer; and their only point of union was their common fear of the African, Indian and coloured population in whose midst they lived and whose abandonment by Britain was the price of the Liberal settlement in South Africa.

The two remaining dominions of the British Empire, **Australia and New Zealand**, developed without the complications of double nationalism which so bedevilled developments in Canada and South Africa. At the same time racial issues did exist in each of the Dominions. Resistance to Oriental immigration played a considerable part in the drawing together of the separate Australian colonies. And politics in New Zealand had to take cognizance of the continuing existence of the Maori people and culture. From an early stage New Zealand's history displayed that conflict between the British Colonial Office's commitment to equality before the law for all citizens, whatever their colour, and local white exploitation of the advantage conferred upon them by the fact that the law before whom all were equal was alien to the non-whites, which led to the initial conflict between Boer and Briton in South Africa; only in New Zealand the conflict was on a much less bitter level, since Maori civilization and culture were much less warlike than those of the South African Bantu. In addition, the early settlers did not depend on Maori labour in the same way that the South Africans did. Moreover the Maoris became a minority in New Zealand fairly early in its history so that there was never the sense of being outnumbered which nagged even in their early days at the nerves of Boer and Briton alike in South Africa.

Thus Australia and New Zealand had largely become monoracial societies. Indeed, the original inhabitants of Australia were so primitive in culture and organization and so few in numbers as to have no impact on developments there. Both Australia and New Zealand were settled almost entirely by emigrants from the British Isles, and their development both in internal and external matters was dominated by this fact. Domestic politics became a struggle between the older and the newer immigrants over land ownership long before the issue of labour was injected. Both developed state socialism of a welfare kind and state arbitration of labour disputes long before Europe did. In external matters, both Australia and New Zealand were dominated by their political ties with the 'mother-country' and their economic dependence on the British market, especially after the development of refrigeration. Their economies were essentially pastoral. Both too were recognizably island states. Their defence rested on British sea-power and their trade reached its markets by sea. Both too were Pacific powers who in the 1880s and onwards came into contact with that other great Pacific power, the United States. Their great fear centred around the only Asiatic sea-power, Japan.

In **Australia,** the growth of national feeling was a slow one. There was no external threat of any consequence to bind together the six colonies which developed out of the original scattered settlements or to drive them closer to Britain than normal sentiment would hold them. Nor was there any real conflict with Britain. The process of conjoining the six colonies into the Commonwealth of Australia, which came finally into being in 1901, was a slow one, and a significant factor binding the pro-federal groups together was their common opposition to the emergent labour movement. Even then progress really depended on there being even fewer compelling interests opposed to the process of federation than there were in favour. The process developed therefore into one of bargaining between the colonies.

In foreign and imperial affairs, Australian sentiment was imperialist and racist. Chinese and Japanese labour at first accepted, from the 1890s onwards was rigidly excluded. Australia was 'a white man's country, to be kept that way'. On imperial matters, Australia preferred to control their own armed forces, but regarded Britain's wars as their wars. Towards Britain, Australia developed an uneasy relationship of love and contempt mingled together. Their own country they regarded as a more virile, libertarian and socially egalitarian extension of Britain overseas.

This attitude can be seen very clearly in the doctrines of the Australian labour movement, which after holding office twice on a minority basis after 1907 finally achieved an electoral majority in 1910. Its opposition to large-scale capitalism, its emphasis on redistributive taxation and collective ownership of monopolies were all taken directly from Britain. Its more radical wing was held in check, however, once the party had taken office, by the purely industrial interests of many of its members, by the development of a strong Catholic labour movement, and by its inability to secure the necessary majority for a revision of the federal constitution. Under the leadership of William Morris Hughes, the Australian Labour Party developed therefore into a thoroughly imperialist, not to say jingoist, movement. And in the debates within the Empire on its future constitutional development, which were to take place during and after World War I, Australian spokesmen were to press as strongly for the transformation of the Empire into an imperial federation, as the Canadians and South Africans were to oppose it.

The true nature of Australian nationalism was revealed during World War I. Australia contributed over 300,000 volunteers for overseas service and lost 60,000 dead on Near Eastern and French battlefields. But when Hughes attempted to introduce conscription in 1916 he completely split the Labour Party, as MacDonald was to split the British Labour Party in 1931. Australian labour opinion was thoroughly anti-conscriptionist, and it was overwhelmingly supported by those who had volunteered for overseas service. The rights of labour included, in their view, the right to be free of compulsion. And although Hughes contrived to stay in power by allying himself with his Liberal opponents, who formed a new National party and thoroughly beat Labour in the 1917 elections, the conscription proposals were thrown out by popular referendum. The war was Britain's war and Australia was in it to the hilt. But conscription was accepted only to defend Australia herself, and not to win a war in Europe. Australia was a Pacific power, and her only potential enemy, Japan, was Britain's ally.

New Zealand differed from Australia in three respects. First, it was even more dependent economically on Britain than Australia, especially after the development of refrigeration had opened the British market to New Zealand meat and dairy products. Second, the land ownership issue dominated internal politics since control of land purchase from the original Maori inhabitants rested in the hands of the government. Third, New Zealanders were not possessed by the contempt towards Britain which proved so significant an element in Australian national feeling. Self-governing since 1852, New Zealanders even more than Australians thought of themselves as 'Britons overseas'. New Zealand differed in two other respects: in its pioneering in the field of social legislation and in the existence of the small farmer-labour coalition which made that social legislation possible.

Under this coalition, which was managed by Richard Seddon, one of the outstanding political 'bosses' of the twentieth century, New Zealand initiated a type of egalitarian lower-middle-class mixture of small-scale capitalism and municipal gas-and-water socialism which became the forerunner of much of mid-twentieth-century reformist conservatism in Europe and radicalism in the United States. Its main distinguishing characteristics were land reform, state credit for smallholders, maternity hospitals, a state health service, old age pensions and arbitration with powers of compulsion by industrial courts in labour disputes. It was adopted during a huge agricultural boom which occurred when the introduction of refrigeration opened the British market. Yet even this prosperity was unable to prevent the gradual break-up of the farmer-labour coalition on which the Liberal party was based. Labour moved leftwards as the arbitration courts began to turn against further wage increases; and as labour moved left so the farmers moved to the new conservative Reform Party. For a time Labour itself was divided into two separate and rival trades union organizations – the small craft unions uniting against the large-scale unions of the mining, railway and service industries. This split between the craft and industrial unions was similar to the division between the AFL and the CIO in the United States. In 1916, the New Zealand Labour Socialist party was founded; its first MP was elected in 1918.

In international matters New Zealand outdid Australia in its policies of imperialism, racialism and jingoism. Though always inclined to make a sentimental exception in the case of its own Maori population, New Zealand was thoroughly racialist in external affairs, adamantly opposed to Oriental immigration and anxious about Japan. Indeed, as far as New Zealand was concerned, Britain was her protector in the Pacific. Unlike Australia, New Zealand saw nothing incongruous in contributing funds to the cost of the Royal Navy. By the end of World War I she had enlisted nearly 20 per cent of her male population, 40 per cent of all men between the ages of 20 to 45, to service overseas. Over 50 per cent of these troops were killed, wounded or became prisoners. During most of the war, the country was governed by a national coalition which carried conscription with little or no difficulty. Labour opposition was simply treated as sedition – and such opposition was a factor in the growth of a Labour movement that was to prove much more radical than its counterpart in Australia.

THE NON-EUROPEAN WORLD

The impact of Europe's power, of its military and industrial technology, of its money and its methods of administration, of its ideas and culture on the external non-European world was so overwhelming that none of the non-European empires, states or cultures were able to withstand it. Their reaction usually followed a fairly standard pattern. In the first place came armed resistance, which was overcome by the use of force. Then came adoption of the obvious outward institutions and techniques of western power, military, technical, and educational. To pay for the development of these institutions there had to be trade, which usually meant that the non-Europeans had to borrow European money. For many states, especially those with autocratic rulers, the experience was disastrous. The weak or the over-optimistic rulers plunged into headlong borrowing, which quickly led to bankruptcy and the imposition by the European powers of control over their finances. The ambitious rulers used this access to western military technology to destroy whatever traditional or social restraints on the misuse of autocratic power were indigenous to their society, and, sooner or later, provoked civil or external conflict which led to further western intervention. At the same time, native forces of discontent would borrow ideas from the west, often through missionary channels, to use against their own native overlords.

The second stage of partial borrowing was often followed by an outbreak of atavism, or reversion to whatever was believed to be the innermost essence of the native culture. If the ruling class were alien then opinion would turn against them. In more magic-based societies, the appeal to indigenous magic would be very strong. Dependent on the strength of the native culture and, more importantly, on the political and social strength of the native political unit, one of two reactions would follow the inevitable defeat of the atavist movement. In the weaker cases, there might be total withdrawal into a kind of spirit-religion, as among the Amerinds of North America or, to a lesser extent, the Maoris of New Zealand. In the stronger ones, the westernizing element would come to the fore. Again there might be one of two reactions. In one type, political thinkers would attempt to marry western culture with their own and to find institutions or precepts in their past histories which could be refurbished to seem analogous to the institutions and ideas of the all-powerful west. In the other type of reaction, opinion would turn violently against the native culture and seek to jettison it entirely for a total imitation and adoption of western methods of government and political organization. Either way a process of social change was set in motion which led sooner or later to the rise of new social groups, challenging the authority of those already in power. And these new social groups, paradoxically, would preach or practise a nationalism which, because it inevitably sought to differentiate its nation from the west, would contain atavistic elements and lead to a fresh clash with the powers of Europe. In this process one can find the seeds of the decline of European influence in the later decades of the first half of the twentieth century.

By a curious paradox, the first Asiatic state to react positively to the overwhelming impact of European power was the one which for three hundred years had most rigidly shut its doors to European contacts, the island empire of **Japan.** In 1851, Commodore Perry of the United States Navy, barely forestalling similar Russian action, used a naval demonstration to force the opening of Japanese ports to Western trade. Alarm at the ease with which British and French forces were breaking down their great neighbour, China, had already given rise to a native reform movement, and in the next forty years the reformers remade Japan entirely from a feudal state of the late middle ages into a power capable of challenging and defeating one of the great powers of Europe. The feudal rule of the Shogunate, Mayors of the Palace, who governed in the name of a puppet Emperor, was overthrown, the Emperor restored and his prestige captured by the reformers. The armies of feudal retainers were bought out, and inflation and economic pressure forced them into the armed forces and the kind of administration necessary to run a modern state. Japan embarked on a major programme of industrialization, and deliberately reshaped her government, laws and administration on the most successful models in Europe. By 1896 she had a Cabinet, an assembly, a first-class army and navy. United under an unsteady autocracy based on the Prussian pattern, the armed services held an unusually strong position. In Japan, the ministers of the army and navy had to be serving officers. This meant that the formation of a Cabinet had to be approved by the senior officers of the armed services.

This revolution had not been accomplished without very serious internal pressures and strains. The effect had been to exaggerate the peculiarly Japano-centric nature of Japanese culture, and to turn its settled convictions of Japanese superiority into a dangerously expansionist ultra-nationalism, liable to burst out into aggression which was sudden and violent even by European standards. Japan's foreign anxieties stemmed from concern over the strategic position of Korea, 90 per cent of whose trade was carried on with Japan. At the time, Korea was undergoing her own internal upheaval as her rulers attempted to follow the examples of Japan and China, as Japan and China put increased pressure upon her, and as Tsarist Russian influence spread southwards from Vladivostock. In 1895, the Japanese picked a quarrel with China over Chinese intervention in Korea, and obliterated the Chinese army and navy in a lightning campaign. The peace terms exacted from the defeated empire demonstrated the inability of the Japanese diplomats to control their militarists. Despite repeated warnings of the danger of European intervention, China was forced to cede Formosa, the Pescadores and Port Arthur, to pay a vast indemnity, to recognize Korean independence and to give far-reaching commercial concessions to the Japanese. The Russians did, in fact, intervene to force the Japanese to abandon their claims to Port Arthur, and the stage was set for the inevitable clash between Russia and Japan.

The defeated empire of **China** was perhaps the oldest civilized state in the world. For three thousand years it had been the centre of civilization as far as its experience could reach. It had been repeatedly invaded by barbarians from the north (its ruling Manchu dynasty dated from the last of these invasions), and had always absorbed what it could not repel. Its ruling class was arrogantly and uniquely conscious of its superior virtues in comparison with the new barbarians of Europe who came to the Asian mainland as traders and concession hunters. It was ruled in the last part of the nineteenth century by a young and inexperienced Emperor very much dominated by his mother, the dowager Empress Tsu Hsi. Beneath them, their vast empire was divided into a large number of provincial administrations, each with its viceroy. The empire was held together by a bureaucracy, the mandarin class, entry, training and promotion to which was rigidly controlled from the centre. The mandarins governed China in accordance with a very full and rigid code of conduct, with a very considerable downward devolution of initiative and responsibility.

Imperial China in the nineteenth century was not, however, the stable society it was often represented to be. The dynasty was alien and its control of the loyalties of the Chinese peasantry was not locked in that consciousness of racial identity which enables dynasties to survive foreign defeat. Thus, whereas the Japanese imperial system survived the impact of western civilization, the Manchu dynasty did not.

China had been forced to open its ports to European trade in the 1840s after the so-called opium wars, in which Britain and France forced China to allow the import of opium from their Asiatic colonies as the only means of offsetting a persistently unfavourable balance of trade with China. The price of China's defeat was the establishment of extra-territorial concessions and large-scale European settlements in the main ports and centres of the Chinese coast and rivers, Shanghai, Canton, Hangchow, and Tientsin. At the same time European aid enabled the Manchu dynasty to survive its first reversals. Europeans reorganized the Maritime Customs and so gave China a steady and reliable source of income which made it possible for the Asiatic empire to buy loans on the European capital market. This aid, in turn, helped the Manchus to outlast and eventually defeat the first great anti-Manchu movement, the Taiping rebellions of 1850–64. Meanwhile, European missionaries gave China its first taste of western ideas and education; though the gift was not an unmixed blessing and the attempt to marry it with Chinese traditions and culture a long and weary one. The Taiping rebellion had a strong ideological basis in misinterpreted Protestant Christianity.

The first period of European influence, which followed the second opium war of 1857–60, saw the gradual recovery of control over China by the Manchu dynasty, and the adoption of a number of western techniques, especially in military and naval matters. Armed with moneys from the Maritime Customs, and isolated from further European pressure by Britain, and by the absorption of France and Russia in events in Europe, China began to flex her muscles, extending her control in Manchuria and into Korea. In 1893–4 Chinese forces intervened in Korea after anti-Chinese disturbances. The intervention provoked a rapid and humiliating defeat at Japan's hands, the loss of Formosa and the Pescadores, and the incurment, under the Treaty of Shimonoseki which ended the war, of an indemnity so heavy as to necessitate recourse to the European money market. It brought, too, Russian and German intervention to force Japan to disgorge part of her spoils and stake their own claim on what everyone now took to be the disintegrating corpse of China. In 1895, Russia founded the Russo-Chinese bank and advanced China a loan to pay off the indemnity to Japan. There followed the grant to Russia of railway concessions in Manchuria, obtained by a large personal bribe to the Chinese foreign minister, Li Hung Chang. Not to be outdone, Germany used the murder of two missionaries as an excuse to force China to lease her a base at Kiouchou on the Shantung peninsula. Russia followed with the occupation of Port Arthur, France with that of Kwang-Chou-Wan, Britain with that of Wei-Hei-Wei. The scramble for railway and other concessions in China had begun.

The effect on China was overwhelming. The defeats in the opium wars and the long civil war of the Taiping rebellion had merely resulted in a policy of borrowing some western techniques on a purely practical basis to make up, as it were, some technical deficiencies. The basic confidence of China in the correctness of its own political and philosophical system had hardly been touched. Yet now China had been overwhelmingly defeated by the Japanese barbarians, whom all Chinese affected to despise, as a result of the Japanese adoption of a really far-reaching programme of westernization.

Chinese reaction took two forms. The first was outright westernization by decree. In one hundred days in 1898 no fewer than seventy edicts designed to westernize China overnight streamed from the Imperial palace. They challenged the traditional provincialism of China, and offended everyone. They led the Dowager Empress, Tsu Hsi, to stage a palace revolution and to take the reins of government firmly into her own hands. In the provinces, the stream of edicts had merely strengthened the xenophobic and traditionalist forces which wanted to turn back the clock. These forces expressed themselves through a secret society which the Europeans came to call the Boxers. They sprang from discontent, unemployment, two years of drought, famine, and a disastrous flood of the Huang Ho river in 1898. The targets of their activity were the overt manifestations of Europe in China, missionaries, railways, telegraphs and the like. In 1900, the western powers demanded Chinese action to suppress the Boxer movement. Instead, the Empress allied herself with the Boxer movement and unleashed her troops against the European legations in Peking and the concession in Tientsin. The European powers replied by organizing an international force which occupied Tientsin, marched on Peking, sacked the Manchu palaces and imposed, by the Boxer protocol of 1910, a crippling indemnity on the Chinese state. Russia, acting on her own, occupied Manchuria. Tsu Hsi fled and the Emperor was restored to power. China settled down to a slower rate of westernization, while revolutionary forces continued to seethe below the surface. A new Chinese revolution was not far away.

Like China, the **Islamic world** produced both atavistic and modernistic movements in response to the impact of European power and culture. The eastern wing of the Islamic world, in India, Malaysia, Indonesia, and the Philippines, had passed under western rule or influence before the opening of the nineteenth century. But in these areas Islam was a religion more than a total culture, in that it lacked both the crusading tradition of Arab and Turkish Islam and its embodiment in one Islamic empire. The main strength of Islam lay in the two states of Iran and the Ottoman Empire, embodiments respectively of the Shia and Sunni branches of Islam.

The **Ottoman Empire** of the nineteenth century was only the shell of what it had been in the great days of the sixteenth century. But it was still basically a military-religious autocracy centred around a Sultan who, since the eighteenth century, had also begun to claim and obtain both the status of Caliph, inheritor both of the mystic aura conferred on his successors as heads of Islam to the prophet Mohammed by the prophet himself, and of the mantle of the medieval Arab empires of the Ummayids of Damascus, the Abbasids of Baghdad, the Fatimids of Egypt and North Africa, and the Ummayid survivors of Moslem Spain. As the Ottoman Empire was basically 'an army which had conquered an empire and embraced a faith', the Sultan exercised his power through military and religious organizations and a variety of civil administrations adapted to the peculiar needs of each locality.

By the end of the eighteenth century the military organizations, the Janissaries in the Empire proper and the Mamelukes in Egypt, had got very much out of hand. As a result the Sultan was forced to eliminate the former by massacre in 1826, and to suffer the suppression of the latter by his Albanian officer, Mohammed Ali, and the development of Egypt under Mohammed Ali and his children to the point where it could challenge the Sultan's own power and become virtually independent of him. The religious organization rested as a double structure of schools and courts, the intellectuals, the *ulema* in the schools, the *Qadis* in the courts, instructing in and interpreting the law of Islam, the *Sharia*. At its head was the *Sheikh-ul-Islam*, the Grand Mufti, who, with his supporting muftis and the two *kaziaskers* acted as a kind of Islamic Supreme Court. The muftis would check on whether the Sultan's actions were in accordance with the law of Islam. No legislation could be promulgated without their approval.

The people of the Ottoman Empire fell broadly into two ethnic groups, Turks and Arabs. The language of state was Turkish, that of religion Arabic; but a wide variety of other tongues were tolerated, and many minor linguistic groups were virtually autonomous under their hereditary chiefs. Similarly, the heterodox Islamic sects, such as the Druzes of Mount Lebanon and the Alawis in Syria, were autonomous where they had the strength to maintain themselves. Local chiefs or sheikhs were appointed *qaimaqams* (or governors) while the provinces were each headed by *walis* (viceroys), who acted as chief tax collectors and heads of the local garrisons, and exercised power outside the towns via the local notables and feudatories.

A feature peculiar to the Ottoman Empire was the protection it gave to Jews and Christians, the *Umm' al-Kitab* (the Peoples of the Book). They were organized into autonomous communities known as *millets*, choosing their own head subject to Turkish approval. In all, there were fifteen *millets*, fourteen Christian and one Jewish. Their leaders were functionaries of state, *ex-officio* members of provincial administrative courts, autonomous in matters of spiritual discipline, control of property, education, marriage, dowries, divorce and wills. The sentences of their courts in such matters were executed by the state. This system, in fact, enabled Christian and Jew to play a considerable role in commerce and finance, as well as enabling them to own land.

Under the impact of the French Revolution the Ottoman Sultanate at first attempted to modernize itself from above by the exercise of the Sultan's power on absolutist lines. The process was begun by Mahmud II (1784–1839) who acceded to the Sultanate in 1808. Beginning in 1826, after the elimination of the Janissaries, he raised a modern-style professional army, and set up schools and sent a series of students to Europe to provide himself with an educated officer corps and an efficient civil service. He centralized the administration, abolished the old military system of holding land in favour of leases to tax-farmers, brought the funds of the great religious land-owning trusts or *waqf* under his control and set up western-style ministries. His successor, Abdulmecid (1839–61), continued his work with a series of great reforming edicts, known as the *Tanzimat*. Abdulmecid began by proclaiming the abolition of tax-farming and the equality of all before the law. He also promulgated a new penal code in 1840, re-organized provincial administrations along French departmental lines, introduced commercial codes and a new land law, introducing western-style land-ownership and landlordism, founded an Ottoman bank and experimented with an advisory council of notables.

The effect of these reforms, though they seemed to many western observers the merest window-dressing to give an Oriental despotism a liberal appearance, was to destroy most of the internal checks and balances of Islamic Ottoman society and to accelerate the process of disintegration. The land reforms destroyed the Islamic concept of joint rights in the land shared between tenant tribesmen and their feudal overlords or sheikhs in favour of the western concept of the landlord-tenant relationship. And this institution of European concepts occurred at a time when, in the west itself, it was rapidly becoming apparent that without legislation to protect the tenant, he was open to the grossest kind of exploitation. In the cities many of the rights and

powers of the communities were transferred to the imperial
bureaucracy in the name of efficiency. Most important, as the
reign of Abdul Hamid II (1876–1908) showed, the conventional
limitations on despotic rule itself had been largely weakened.

At the same time the reforms which were introduced, even if
they were only the introduction of western military techniques,
were exposing a small but significant element in Ottoman and
Islamic society to the ideas of western liberalism – and imposing
upon them the task of attempting to reconcile Islamic modes of
thought and the traditions of their own proud society with the
obviously more efficient and more powerful ideas of western
Europe. Abdul Hamid II did his best to isolate the Empire from
such ideas. As a result, many of the most articulate of Ottoman
liberals were driven into exile in Paris. Against them he did his
best to encourage an atavistic reaction against the west and an
upsurge of Pan-Islamic sentiment which he hoped would consolidate the loyalties of his subjects to himself as Sultan and
Caliph. But at the same time he multiplied military and technical
schools throughout the Ottoman Empire to provide it with an
efficient military and bureaucratic *corps d'élite*. By so doing he
increased in number the would-be critics of his own rule.
Within the Ottoman ruling groups he managed largely to divide
and break up the first wave of liberal critics of the Tanzimat, the
so-called Young Ottomans. But he was unable to prevent the
clandestine growth in later years of the Young Turk movement
which was to overthrow him. Finally, by opening these schools
in the provinces he was to raise up an Arab officer class which,
unlike the Young Turks in the Ottoman areas was not drawn
from the traditional ruling groups of the Empire.

A good deal of the trouble lay in the fact that the Ottoman
Empire was more than merely Ottoman and less than totally
Islamic. Ottoman Turkish sentiment thus could always turn
against the Sultanate, even against Islam. (After 1920 Turkey
was, in fact, to abandon Islam officially and embrace even more
extreme a form of imitation of the west than Japan had done.)
In the non-Ottoman parts of the Empire, on the other hand,
those who followed Islam were exposed to currents of thought
which originated beyond the areas of Ottoman control; and the
Christian and other minorities tended to develop a nationalism
which was totally secular and western, either to enhance their
own position within the Empire, or, as with the Greeks, the

Kurds, and the Armenians, to separate themselves completely from it.

The main centres of Islamic thought outside Ottoman control were in Egypt, Persia, and North Africa. Generally speaking, these had been exposed to mild western pressures for some period of time before the 1870s; their reactions tended to follow the path of attempted synthesis of Islam with the ideas of the west. It is only in the less exposed fringes of Islam, in the Sudan, in Somalia and within the Arabian peninsula that one finds examples of atavistic reactions to westernization. And it is significant that in most cases what was being reacted against was not western rule but Islamic rule with western accretions.

Of all these centres perhaps the most important was Cairo where Mohammed Ali had established the virtual independence of Egypt under the rule of his dynasty in the first decades of the nineteenth century. An Albanian by origin, Mohammed Ali had eagerly turned to Europe for modern military, managerial and educational techniques. His successors had followed him by borrowing money and seeing Egypt tied to Europe by the great growth in the cotton market during the Civil War in the United States. The construction of the Suez Canal and the modernization of Egypt under Ismail at a rate too great for its financial strength to bear led, in 1882, to the British occupation of Egypt following closely on an Egyptian nationalist uprising among the army officers, led by Major Arabi Pasha, against the remnants of Ottoman control. The combination of these influences had led to the growth of a school of writers and thinkers who sought in varying degrees to discover in Islam's past parallels for what they took to be the main motives of the west. Their aim was to defend Islam against those who might seek to abandon it entirely in favour of outright westernization. In the main, these writers, such as Rifa Badawi al-Tahtawi (1801–73) and Mohammed Abdu (1849–1905), were Egyptian in origin and their writings tinged with something which was to develop into an Egyptian view of Arab nationalism if not an Egyptian nationalism in itself. A very considerable influence was played throughout the whole Islamic world by the writer Jemal al-Din al-Afghani (1839–97), who was probably born in Persia and who spent his years of greatest influence in Cairo. Al-Afghani worked for a time in India, organized a secret Pan-Islamic society in Paris in 1884 and eventually died in Constantinople as a pensionary of Abdul

Hamid, who had thought to enlist his Pan-Islamist preaching in the service of his own political propaganda.

Al-Afghani's influence spread to North Africa and into Syria and Iraq. In Tunis, a school of modernists had already grown up before the French occupation in 1881. Their influence spread westwards into the last unoccupied Islamic state in North Africa, Morocco, and eastwards into the only area under Istanbul's direct rule, the Beyship of Tripoli. Throughout North Africa, Islam had fossilized far more than in the Near East, and the mystical dervish orders, the *tariqas*, through which popular discontent expressed itself, had become much stronger and more numerous. The reformers, therefore, found themselves obliged, like Luther appealing to the Bible in 1520, to appeal to the *salafa*, the early written sources of Islam, and their movement became known as the *salaffiya*. From it was to spring the early Tunisian and Moroccan nationalist movements of the 1920s and the idea of regional rather than Pan-Islamic nationalism which was to develop with the movement for a unified Maghreb (a unified North-West Africa) in the middle of the twentieth century.

In **Syria** and the **Lebanon** the ideas of al-Afghani and Mohammed Abdu were to find both support and opposition from Christian Arabs for whom the erection of a Pan-Islamic state would mean a continuation of their second-class status. The matter was complicated by the existence of a large number of heterodox Islamic sects, the Druzes of Mount Lebanon and the Alawis of upper Syria being the most numerous. The Pan-Islamists tended to take refuge in Cairo from the excesses of Ottoman rule, when they did not join the growing number of Ottoman exiles in Paris. The Christian Arabs were equally *persona non grata* with the Ottomans; and the intellectuals among them tended to precede the Pan-Islamists in taking refuge in Cairo where the Arabic press was for some time almost entirely under the control of Arab Christian *emigrés* from Syria and the Lebanon. Christian Arabs could support that side of Pan-Islamic writing which emphasized the historical achievements of Islam as a society. But they used these achievements as the historical basis for a secular nationalism in which liberty and equality for all citizens were claimed to be the essential basis of Arab unity. In general these writers spoke of an Arab nationalism, but if they were allowed they would press, as did Khalal Ganem among the 'Young Turks', also for an Ottoman nationalism on a quasi-federal, or, as they put it, 'administratively decentralized', basis. And there were those who spoke of a Lebanese or a Syrian nation. There were even some who preached a Pan-Arab state based on Egypt under the restored rule of the Khedive.

All these were Arabs, drawn mainly from the Maronite or Orthodox communities of the Lebanon and Syria. Other Christian communities, like the Copts and Armenians in Egypt, turned either to cosmopolitanism or to a local nationalism serving whoever happened to be the ruling power in the state. Thus Egypt's Prime Ministers before and during the British occupation included Nubar Pasha, an Armenian, and Butrus Ghali, a Copt. In general, the Christian communities found it easier to adopt western techniques and adapt themselves to western pressures than did the Moslems.

Outside the Ottoman Empire and those areas in direct contact with European influences, the impact of Europe presented itself less as something European than as something alien in the rule of the Islamic state. The reaction to it tended usually to be violently atavistic and puritanical, in the belief that Islam would prevail if it stripped itself of all alien influences. Perhaps the greatest of these movements was *Wahabism* which, under the leadership of the house of Saud, was to conquer all but the eastern and southern extremities of the Arabian peninsula and raid regularly into Egypt, Syria and Iraq until the reduction of the Saudi kingdom by Mohammed Ali's son, Ibrahim, in 1819 to its original small patrimony around the town of Riyadh. Another atavistic movement was that of the *Ansari* in the Sudan, the followers of Mohammed Ahmed, who proclaimed himself the Mahdi (the anointed of God) in 1881, in revolt against the Egyptian rule which had been extended over the Sudan in 1820. The Mahdi's followers controlled what is now the state of the Sudan between 1884 and the British reconquest of the Sudan in 1898. A third consisted of the *Senussi*, founded in Cyrenaica in 1843 by Mohammed Ali el Senussi as a mystical sect with the same mission to redeem and purify Islam from the accretions of Turkish and Tripolitanian rule. Less bellicose than either the *Wahabis* or the *Ansari*, the *Senussi* preferred to consolidate their hold on Cyrenaica by a network of lodges, fortress-monasteries of a non-celibate order, while the leaders of the movement moved their headquarters into the remoter oases of the Sahara desert.

One element which distinguished all these movements is that they occurred largely within that part of the Islamic world which followed the Sunni branch of Islam. The other main branch, the Shia, dominated **Persia** and provided the principal minority group in Mesopotamia; breakaway sects dominated the Yemen (Zaidism), Mount Lebanon (the Druzes), and the state of Muscat and Oman (the Ibadis, though these strictly are neither Sunnis nor Shias). Of these the only one of major political importance are the Imamis, the main branch of the Shia, who dominated Persia.

As a religion Imamism reacted far less obviously to contact with the West than did the Sunni branch of Islam. In part this was due to its strength as an entity separate from the Persian state. Imamism was thus saved from the comparative ossification that attacked Sunni Islam within the Ottoman Empire. A part was also possibly played by the changes in dynasty in the eighteenth century, three separate families occupying the throne between the fall of the Safavids during the Afghan revolt in the 1720s and the accession of the first of the Qajar dynasty in 1779. Whatever the cause, the Persians themselves had little time for the ideas of al-Afghani; and the reaction to western pressure on Persia was to be political rather than intellectual.

This pressure came principally from Russia and Britain, as each sought to extend its power into the lands that lay between the borders of India and Russian Central Asia. By the 1880s Russia had extended her borders up to the northern frontiers of Persia and Afghanistan with the occupation of the last of the Moslem Khanates of Central Asia. Britain in her turn had 'persuaded' Persia to recognize the independence of Afghanistan in the Anglo-Persian war of 1856–57. Both countries were engaged in spreading their activities into Persia itself. Russia acted officially by forming the Russian-officered Persian Cossack brigade as an aid to the Shah, and by founding the Russian-capitalized Discount Bank of Persia in 1891. Britain was represented by individual concession hunters such as Baron Reuter with his Imperial Bank of Persia in 1889 and the tobacco monopoly which was placed in British hands in 1890. It was in the outburst of discontent with this award of the tobacco monopoly to foreign investors and its defeat by a smoking strike, led by the Islamic intellectuals of the Shias, that the Persian nationalist movement was born.

The impact of Europe on **Egypt** came in two forms, the French cultural influence which originated during the brief period of Napoleonic conquest in 1798, and the political impact of Britain after the occupation in 1882. France had done her best to foster Egypt's development as a national state. She had backed Mohammed Ali in his bid to invade Turkey in 1839–40 and she had largely financed the construction of the Suez Canal opened in 1869. Indeed the bulk of the £90 million of Egyptian public debt in 1890 was owed to French bondholders. But in the actual moment of crisis France had held back and British troops had occupied Egypt. British capital had bought 40 per cent of the Suez Canal Company shares in 1874. British ships were by far the most numerous in passage through the Suez Canal. In 1888, France and Russia had imposed upon Britain an international convention for the management of the Canal. But they had also left Britain with no option but to take over responsibility for Egypt's affairs. And under British direction Egypt's army and administration were reformed and modernized and Egypt's finances made secure and efficient. For the Egyptians the experience was both salutary and humiliating. Particularly resented was the sublime assumption of their British overlords that the various racial and religious groups in Egypt could not coalesce to make an Egyptian nation. Britain played, therefore, an important part in the creation of a nationalist movement in Egypt. In the meantime, British engineers and capital presented Egypt with a modern irrigation system which with the aid of fertilizers was to make the Nile valley capable of yielding four crops annually.

The decaying remnants of the Turkish province of **Algeria** fell easily into French hands in 1830. But it was to take another fifty years of sporadic fighting before the French finally pacified the country. During this period the French were bringing in colonists and building up a European settler community, a process which would have been impossible without the removal from its original tribal ownership of millions of hectares of the best arable land. Algeria was administered as a French *département*; and a small educated minority of Arabs was encouraged to see themselves as equal members of the French community. They were not, however, encouraged to become too assimilated unless they were prepared to renounce their religion: they were ruled by a separate Code for the Natives, and they had no political rights as such. French Algeria like Ulster, which in other respects it resembled, became a nursery for generals.

Under Ottoman rule, **Tunisia** had counted officially as a 'regency' with its head carrying the title of Bey. Its ruling *élite* tended to be Turkish, though, in fact, the regency was virtually autonomous. For a time it was in the forefront of the Ottoman reform movement, following the Turkish reforms of 1856 (the Tanzimat), with the issue of a constitution (*Destour*) in 1860. The experiment failed largely owing to the personality of the Bey and his inability to resist foreign loans. In 1869, an International Commission was established to administer its finances and from 1875 onwards the main point at issue was only whether France or Italy would succeed in taking over Tunisia. As the stronger, and backed by Bismarck's Germany, France won, using the pretext of tribal raids into Algeria to occupy Tunisia in 1881. The changing pattern of European imperialism may be seen in the fact that France did not annex Tunisia, preferring to establish a protectorate. Thereafter French colonists poured into Tunisia. To satisfy their desire for self-government they were granted certain representative institutions. A joint Franco-Tunisian Grand Council voted on the budget. A Franco-Tunisian colonialism was being substituted for the nominal sovereignty of the Tunisian Bey. Tunisian resentment was to lead in 1907 to the foundation of a 'Young Tunisian' party to maintain Tunisia's right to manage her own affairs.

The **Moroccan Sultanate** was unique in North Africa in never having passed under Ottoman rule. It was also unique in that its rulers, like the Stuarts in Scotland, rarely succeeded in making their authority felt among the mountain tribes of the High Atlas. Indeed, the area was known officially as the 'Region of Dissidence', the *Bled es-Siba*, the division roughly corresponding to that between the Arabic tribes who acknowledged the law of Islam and, in return for privileges, provided the Sultan with his army, and the Berber areas which, though nominally Islamic, had their own system of customary law and followed various *marabouts* or saints. Throughout most of the nineteenth century Morocco stood off French and Spanish pressure in part with British aid. Towards its end, the last great Sultan, Moulay al-Hassan, began the same process of modernization that Mohammed Ali in Egypt had tried before him. But he died in 1894 before the process could really begin. His successor was only fourteen years of age and Morocco was soon to fall into the hands of the French.

Up to the beginning of the nineteenth century, the north-eastern shores of the **Arabian peninsula** had been the home of a variety of small Arab tribes who lived by trade, piracy and pearl-fishing. The only large states had been the Ibadi state of Muscat and Oman, at the southern end of the Gulf, and the port of Kuwait at the north. The Ottoman Empire claimed a rather vague sovereignty over the central province of Al Hasa which ran down to the edge of the Qatar peninsula. The Wahhabis invaded and occupied much of the province during the first decades of the nineteenth century. The British East India Company had also established trading stations at Bandar Abbas, and later at Bushire on the Persian coast of the Gulf in the middle of the eighteenth century. The threat to its trade from piracy led to the maintenance first of a Company, then of a Royal Naval squadron, to control piracy and to put down the slave trade. By the middle of the nineteenth century Britain had found it necessary to bind all the states of the middle Gulf from Bahrein to the Muscati borders into a network of treaties, to establish peace and to put down piracy; and with these treaties Britain assumed a position as guarantor of political stability in the Gulf which was to endure into the middle of the twentieth century, long outlasting the circumstances in which it had been created. In 1873, the Ottoman Empire reasserted its claims to the al-Hasa province, occupying Qatar too and appointing the head of the sheikhly family as the deputy-governor. The British maintained their protection of the off-shore island of Bahrein, making it by agreements of 1880 and 1892 into what amounted to a protectorate. A political agent was appointed there in 1900. Kuwait did not fall under British influence until the end of the century when, in order to forestall what they believed to be German and Russian attempts to set up a coaling station and a terminus for the Baghdad railroad project, the British extended their protection to the Sheikh of Kuwait. Since the 1780s, Britain had been on amicable terms with the rulers of Muscat; these relations continued after the division of the Omani territories of Muscat and Oman and Zanzibar into their two parts in the middle of the nineteenth century. The entire affair represented the ultimate example of British free trade imperialism. British power was supreme, being maintained against all comers by a naval squadron, and the whole burden of administration in the area, such as it was, was carried by the local rulers with whom Britain had treaty relations.

The British had succeeded to the control of all the **Indian subcontinent** at the end of the Napoleonic Wars. Their victory had been achieved over a collection of mutually warring militarist states and they had inherited a ravaged, exhausted and bandit-tormented countryside. In its pacification and settlement, Britain developed doctrines of administration, reform through legislation and education. Administration was to be thorough and paternalistic, reforms were to create western-style institutions alongside those of India, so that the Indians could be taught to accept or reject them on their own. Education, in the words of Macaulay's famous Minute of 1833, was to produce a 'class of persons, Indian in blood and colour, but English in taste, in opinion, in morals, and in intellect'. The first British evangelical drive along these lines produced what was to be the only major outburst of atavism in the history of Indian contacts with the west, the Indian Mutiny of 1857, a military explosion whose force grew out of the feeling of the traditional Indian military classes that British policy was directed towards destroying the moral, economic and religious basis of their social organization. As such it was essentially anarchic and the attempt of the heirs of the Maratha warrior states, on the one hand, and the last remnants of the Mogul dynasty to cash in on it, on the other, were easily suppressed.

The mutiny had the effect of taking the steam out of the first drive of the early Victorian reformers, and of investing all further reforms with an aura of doubt and uncertainty. The reform of India was still the aim of the British, but it was now seen as a very long-term aim indeed; and the authoritarian ethos of the professional administrators of India became very much stronger, so that the emergence of classes and movements within India which were the direct product of these reforms for a long time went unrecognized. Administration gave India a programme of road, railway, and canal building, of irrigation and public works which first set India's feet on the road of industrial development. More important than this the new communications bound India together and, in conjunction with the use of the English language, made possible the development of a single national movement which cut across the fourteen major language groups and the immense distances of the country itself. This movement developed out of the new class of educated Indians coming from what in old India had been the lower states of society, and largely employed in the lower reaches of the bureaucracy. They were joined by men of the new mercantile and industrial classes, the lawyers demanded by the reformers' introduction of British court procedures and justice, and the journalists and teachers. In 1885 members of these new groups founded the Indian National Congress. It was to act as the spearhead of Indian nationalism thereafter.

Unfortunately, in the foundations of the Congress movement can also be seen the division of India along communal lines. Orthodox Hinduism regarded India as the land of the Aryan Hindus, a definition which made Moslem and outcast into second class citizens. Moslems, centring around the University of Aligarh, watched the Congress movement with suspicion. Within Congress a major split developed between the moderate reformists led by Gopal Krishna Gokhale, who were themselves overwhelmed by the magnitude of the task of westernizing India and were prepared to work with Britain towards this goal, and the extremists led by Bal Gangadhar Tilak, who wanted independence at once and social reform afterwards. The British swung between a cautious policy of introducing consultative and representative councils with Indian participation and a return to the driving administrative paternalism which had produced the Mutiny. The viceroyalty of Lord Curzon (1898–1905) represented the paternalistic policy and led to a complete break between Congress and the British which was to foreshadow the violence and non-violence of the 1930s.

The resignation of Lord Curzon and the Liberal victory in Britain paved the way for the next two great advances towards Indian self-government. The first was the Morley-Minto reforms of 1909 which introduced Indian membership into the advisory councils at all levels and set up an Imperial Legislative Council of sixty members of which twenty-seven were indirectly elected, six of whom had to be Moslem Indians. The second advance was the Montagu declaration of 1917. In this declaration, Britain announced a policy for India aimed at the 'gradual development of self-governing institutions, with a view to the progressive realization of responsible government in India as an integral part of the Empire'. Behind the Montagu declaration lay British recognition of the loyalty of India to Britain in 1914 and the major Indian military effort in the war. But the experience of war was to release Indians from the sense of permanent inferiority to the West that had been built up by one hundred years of subjection to Britain. The year 1919 saw the emergence into the Indian scene of Mahatma Gandhi, the greatest figure of recent Indian history.

Chapter 4

The Impact of Europe on the External World:
The Areas of Reaction and Inactivity

INTRODUCTION

THE previous chapter surveyed the areas of the world where European impact had already produced a significant reaction and rate of development by 1900. This chapter covers rather those areas where this was not yet the case. They fall essentially into four groupings. First, there are the residual empires of the sixteenth and seventeenth centuries, of Spain, Portugal, the Netherlands and France, empires where economic and political stagnation was the rule, where the settlers were too much enervated or economically depressed to indulge in political activity and the natives too much repressed even to envisage such action. Second, are the escapist societies of French Canada and Boer South Africa, societies in deliberate reaction from the pressures of the nineteenth century, seeking to wall off the relentless advance of European liberal urban and industrial society. One could perhaps also class under this grouping the utopian societies of the nineteenth-century United States of which the Mormon settlements at Utah were the most spectacular. By 1900, however, the two republics of the Orange Free State and the Transvaal were the only significant survivors in this category.

The states of Latin America came into a third category, politically independent, economically as much bound into the economy of Western Europe and as much open to its intervention as Egypt, Tunisia, or Iran. The original achievement of independence in Latin America had produced a system of states isolated and insulated from European power politics, and thus free to indulge in the most violent internecine wars without fear of major intervention. But within the individual states the original *élites* had perpetuated the social system of colonial

Spain, with its thin veneer of education and Europeanism. This system dominated and exploited a mass of poverty-stricken, illiterate and superstitious peasants who represented a mixture, here of half-castes, there of Indians, the basic patterns of whose lives, economic and social organization and beliefs had not changed since the seventeenth century. Although the Latin American countries were exposed to great waves of European immigration and were a major target for European and American investment, they remained essentially in a quasi-colonial relationship with Europe that their development of sizeable armies and navies could do nothing to hide.

The fourth great division comprehends the non-European world, or rather those areas where traditional social and political organization had not yet begun to give way to the pressures of westernization. Few political units in these areas had escaped European rule by 1900; only Abyssinia and Liberia in Africa, Siam in South-East Asia, Afghanistan and Tibet in Central Asia eluded or defeated European efforts to conquer and absorb them. In the areas under European control and dominion one can detect two different situations. In some areas the local political organizations, tribes, statelets and principalities were so small as to succumb very easily to direct European rule. Perhaps prolonged war had reduced them to a state of virtual anarchy and weakness. But whatever the particular circumstances the effect of European rule was to obliterate existing political loyalties. And where nationalism was eventually to emerge, it had to create its own political organisms. In the second situation, the European colonial powers found effective large-scale political organizations. In some cases these proved militarily so recalcitrant that they had to be smashed and drained of life. But in many others it was easier, cheaper and administratively more convenient to take over the existing political organization as a protectorate or protected state.

Among the states that fell into this latter category, the greatest single divide lies between the Asian societies which were literate and the African which had no indigenous script. For a state to possess a written language meant that it had records of its history, chronicles, codes of law and works designed to instruct the rulers, and cadres, possibly *élites*, of literates, trained to speculate, philosophize, intellectualize as well as to administer. In non-literate societies, the *élites* tended to be either warriors or magical-artistic in character, prophets, miracle workers or witch doctors. In the former, the native religion was based on scriptures and the body of its faithful remained only marginally open to western missionary activity. In the latter, religion was animistic, tutelary and protective; and its inability to protect its devotees against European power left their culture the more shattered and less able to survive. In the former type of society, the impact of westernizing impulses, as has already been argued in the case of Islam in the previous chapter, meant for the intellectual *élite* an effort to acclimatize and harmonize their own culture with that of the west. In the latter, no such saving process was possible. Native culture was left with only two alternatives, total withdrawal of the type practised by the Amerinds or the Maoris, or disintegration and conversion to the religion of the Europeans.

Westernization came mainly, though not entirely, through missionary education. And the degree to which the process of westernization was slow or fast depended to a great extent on the schools system which existed before western contact. Thus, although there was a high male literacy rate in areas where Buddhism was the dominant religion, the elementary nature of the Buddhist educational system, which concentrated on village schooling, adapted itself only with difficulty to the introduction of western ideas and techniques. The Koranic schools in Moslem areas, on the other hand, and still more the Koranic universities allowed a much faster rate of absorption. In the magical-religious areas of the pre-literate societies of Africa and the Pacific there was virtually no educational system at all before the arrival of the West, and education was taken over entirely by western institutions. At first, almost without exception, these were missionary schools, though after 1903 state educational institutions competed with church schools in French Africa.

The content of this education was mainly modelled on that given in the schools of the colonial powers which, being European, meant that it was mainly designed to produce good servants of the state, lawyers, doctors and administrators. There was at first very little technical or vocational training. These schools tended to produce an educated intelligentsia which was separated from the mass of the native population and 'looked always, even when protesting, towards their rulers'. It was, however, among these *élites* that the new ideas of nationalism first took root.

THE METHODS OF EUROPEAN COLONIAL RULE

The motives which led to the organization of colonies were, as has been argued above, far from simply economic. But, with the exception in part of the settler states, colonies, once acquired, tended to see the development of their administration governed in the last resort by considerations of cost or economic advantage to the colonial power. The dominant economic philosophy was mercantilist. Whatever the pre-colonial pattern of trade the tendency was to tie the colonial economy into that of the colonial power. Where mercantilism gave way, as it did in Britain, to Manchester School liberalism, the overriding question was still that of economic cost. The colony was expected to be as self-supporting as possible. Although mercantilism persisted in the colonies of France, Spain, Portugal and the Netherlands, a colony which failed to produce sufficient raw materials or local revenue to defray the costs of its administration could expect little in the way of a subsidy.

The pressure on colonial governors to produce something that could be turned into profit was, therefore, very strong. Where there existed obviously exploitable resources like gold, diamonds, silver and other minerals then the biggest problem was labour. Where there only existed agricultural resources like rubber, corn, sugar, again the major problem was labour. In a primitive, non-money economy, the inducements to labour were few and the demands of the colonial power inevitably could only be satisfied by heavy taxation, backed by punitive measures to ensure payment, by forced or indentured labour, by slavery or peonage, or by the importation of Indian or Chinese coolies. What developed in many cases was a policy of economic plunder of the existing human and physical resources of the areas brought under colonial rule, a policy of which the most flagrant case was that of the *régime* of Leopold, King of the Belgians, in the Congo.

In the more humane colonies of Britain and France, where public opinion could be mobilized against the grosser forms of exploitation, the emphasis was rather on economy in administration and the encouragement of trade as a source of revenue. The ideal of economy in administration led to the policy of indirect rule through local political organizations, especially in

West Africa and in Malaya. The encouragement of trade led to the development of monopolistic trading companies which in turn stimulated the growth of a class of native agriculturalists, again especially in West Africa, where comparative affluence heralded the growth of an indigenous, property-owning and conservative *bourgeoisie*. This group was complemented by the native professional classes which gradually emerged from the small western educational institutions.

Two factors, however, were always inherent in this system. The colonial governments and western economic *entrepreneurs* usually prevented the retention of much wealth in the colonial territories which produced it. As a result profits and capital appreciation accrued to the benefit of the metropolitan power or to those who originally furnished the capital. Second, the economies of the colonial territories tended to develop essentially on a one-crop basis. Consequently, the economic well-being of such territories became highly vulnerable to fluctuations in world commodity prices, a factor which was to play a terrible role in the world economic crisis between the wars.

EUROPE ABROAD: THE COLONIAL EMPIRES

The main colonial empires remaining, apart from those of Britain and France, were the residues of the old Spanish and Portuguese empires, the Dutch colonies in the East and West Indies and the personal dominions of Leopold, King of the Belgians, in the Congo basin. All of these embodied the crudest kind of exploitation of their colonial territories and in few of them could there be said to be any real attempt at colonial development to compare with the colonies of Britain and France. The exception is provided by the colonial policy introduced by the Dutch in Indonesia after 1900, the so-called 'New Ethical Policy' (see p. 120) with which the colonial power attempted to repair some of the damages done by the policy of the previous century.

As the new century opened the **Spanish Empire** had just lost the Philippines and Cuba to the United States. All that remained were a few small settlements in West Africa to mark the end of an Empire which had once embraced most of the Americas.

The fault was very largely that of the Spaniards themselves who seemed to have learned nothing from the loss of their Latin American empire at the opening of the nineteenth century. For a fresh wave of emigration to Cuba and the Philippines in the 1840s had produced what the Spanish Empire had never known in its hey-day, racial tension between the newly arrived Spaniards and the native-born inhabitants of Cuba and the Philippines, and racial discrimination practised against them.

Spain too sought to recoup her revenues by high imposts on trade with other nations and by heavy taxation, all of which was a great spur to local nationalist movements. In the 1840s and 1850s Spain had also indulged in outbursts of neo-imperialism, especially in relation to Latin America. In 1829, she landed a force at Tampico in Mexico; in the 1850s she menaced Venezuela; in the 1860s her fleet bombarded Valparaiso and Callao, collaborated with France in an effort to coerce Mexico, and her army occupied the Dominican Republic for five years in 1861-5. Thereafter, Spain attempted to rally Latin American opinion to her side by emphasizing their common Hispanic culture, devoting a special effort to the congress held in the 1890s to celebrate the fourth centenary of the discovery of America. An Ibero-American Union was founded and a great revival of interest in the early history and culture of Latin America took place in the Spanish universities. There was a strong element of hostility to the United States in this Hispano-American movement. Its influence in Latin America, however, was of little real importance. Its main role was to salve the wounded pride of Spaniards at the loss of their empire to the United States.

The **Portuguese Empire** was more fortunate. Its main possessions were the settlements in East and West Africa together with a scattering of relics of its former empire in the Indian Ocean, such as the Indian settlement of Goa and the Indonesian island of Timor. In the 1880s a revival of imperial activity in Portuguese East Africa led to conflict with British expansion in Nyasaland and in Mashonaland but in both cases the Portuguese were forced to back down. The Portuguese did, however, establish effective occupation inland from the coast around Mozambique and gradually extended their control over the Arab sheikhs on the coast up to the borders of German East Africa. Internally, Portuguese rule was totally exploitatory. The African colonies

ASIA IN 1900

THE PARTITION OF AFRICA 1870-1900

The Azores 1432

Madeira 1419

Lisbon

Madrid

Constantinople

Rome

Tangier

Algeciras

Oran

Tunis

Bizerta

Tripoli

Benghazi

Beirut

Damascus

Jerusalem

Port Said

Alexandria

Suez

Tehran

Baghdad

Basra

Bahrein 1867 (Br. Pr.)

Kuwait 1899 (Br. Pr.)

Medina

Jiddah

Mecca

ARABIA

Aden 1839

Berbera 1884

Obbia

Mogadishu

Mijertein

SOMALIS

OGADEN

GALLA

SHOA

ABYSSINIA

Addis Ababa

Harar 1887

Gondar

AMHARA

Massawa 1885

Kassala

Suakin

Berber

Dongola 1896

Wady Halfa

Aswan

EGYPT 1871

EGYPTIAN SUDAN 1890/98

ANGLO-EGYPTIAN SUDAN 1899

Omdurman 1898

Khartum 1898

Blue Nile

KORDOFAN 1881/98

Fashoda 1898

BAHR EL GHAZAL

EQUATORIAL AFRICA (1871 EGYPT)

SENUSSI

Cufra Oasis

LIBYA

BORKOU

TIBESTI

L. Chad

Ft. Lamy 1900

Dikwa 1902

BORNU

ADAMAWA 1894

CAMEROON 1884

Fernando Po

TUNIS

ALGERIA 1830/62

MOROCCO

Fez

Rabat

Casablanca

Marrakesch

Agadir

RIO DE ORO 1884

ADRAR

HOGGAR

TUAREG

AIR

Agadès

WEST SUDAN

Timbuktu

FRENCH GUINEA

Conakry

Freetown

SIERRA LEONE 1808

LIBERIA 1822

COTE D'IVOIRE

ASHANTI

KONG

MOSSI

Sokoto 1897

Zinder

NIGERIA

Benin

Lagos

Accra

Porto Novo

THE GREAT POWERS AND THE PACIFIC 1900–1930

had originally been founded to take advantage of the slave trade. Angola went on exporting slaves to Brazil until 1879, and the slave trade from Portuguese East Africa to the French planters on Réunion continued into the 1880s. Even with its nominal abolition the system of forced labour within the two colonies and on the cocoa plantations of the offshore islands of Sao Tomé was virtually the equivalent of slavery. On various occasions it seemed as if the Portuguese Empire was about to break up. And on two occasions Britain and Germany signed or initialled treaties providing for its division between them in the event of such an occurrence.

The Congo provided the worst example of slavery and exploitation. In the early 1880s, Leopold, King of the Belgians, had succeeded in setting up the so-called Congo Free State behind a smoke-screen of geographical and philanthropic sentiment and his dominion was recognized by the Berlin West Africa Conference of 1885. Its occupation, however, absorbed the bulk of his private fortune and to recoup his expenses he was forced to grant a series of railway and other concessions. To secure African labour, his hired mercenaries imposed heavy taxes on the African population which had to be paid in commodities like foodstuffs, ivory and raw rubber and in forced labour. The tribal chiefs were deposed in favour of *capitàs* (headmen) appointed by Leopold's administration, who inevitably used terrorist methods to maintain their power. Native uprisings were ruthlessly put down. The methods of Leopold's agents eventually attracted international notice, and the resultant storm of denunciation forced Leopold to allow the Belgian state to take over his private empire in 1908. By that date he had raised his original private fortune of $5 million to at least $80 million. Belgian rule abolished the worst of the cruelties and barbarities practised by Leopold's agents. But it cannot be said that Belgium made any effort to develop African social and economic advancement or encourage native participation in the colonial government. The large monopolies of Leopold's Congo were left untouched. And, as a result of their efficiency, the general standard of living, including that of the African population, was higher than that of Africans in any other part of Africa. National feeling in the Congo turned to Messianic sects with Christian borrowings to express their own feelings of solidarity and hope.

EUROPE ABROAD: THE ESCAPIST SOCIETIES

Perhaps the oddest forms of European activity abroad were those communities that deliberately tried to remove and completely isolate themselves from nineteenth-century European civilization and advance beyond the frontier of that civilization to establish a state which could somehow be kept isolated from the contamination which they were trying to escape. In many cases such communities were purely religious like the Amish in Pennsylvania or the Mormons who trekked westwards out of the United States in 1846 to build an ideal state in Utah around Salt Lake City. It was anti-urban feelings of an analogous kind that drove many British to settle in Kenya and the Rhodesias and attempt to maintain there an agrarian, individualistic squirearchy of the kind which taxation and the advance of welfare politics were making increasingly impossible in Britain. It is the tragedy of such states that they cannot hold the clock back; although they may advance for a time beyond the advancing frontier of western civilization, i. is bound to catch up with them and engulf them. Only two escapist communities in this century have survived such engulfment to fight back against it, and to attempt to recover their earlier isolation, the *Canadiens* of Quebec in Canada and the Boers of South Africa.

The *Canadiens* differ from the Boers in never having had a state of their own, and in never having tried to trek beyond the European frontier. Rather as the nineteenth century advanced they became the more insistent on preserving the rural ultramontane Catholicism of their seventeenth- and eighteenth-century heritage. They represented France as it had been in the time of Louis XIV before the Enlightenment and before the French Revolution. They drew strength from the anti-liberal mood of the Papacy in the mid-nineteenth century and quietly ignored the modernism of Leo XIII. Their clergy were either native or *emigré* French royalists. And they grew gradually in strength in Quebec despite the success of the Liberals in maintaining themselves in power. They were, above all, protected from extinction by their extraordinary fecundity.

The Boers, by contrast, moved away from British rule in the 1850s in the Great Trek. Where the *Canadiens* were peasants, the Boers were pastoralists and their communities were partially nomadic. They represented an early rural form of Dutch protestantism that had been isolated from the main stream of European development even before emigration to South Africa; like the *Canadiens*, they missed both the Enlightenment and the French Revolution. They were reinforced by Huguenot *emigrés* from France and German protestants from the Rhineland long before English rule was established. And as they moved away from British South Africa so they broke with the synod of their own Church in Capetown which accepted and for a time was dominated by Scottish ministers with an awkward belief in racial equality before God. Eventually, they developed break-away sects like the Nederlands Hervoormde Kirk and the even more extreme Doppers who preached a fundamentalist predestinarian Christianity, believing that the earth was flat and that the Bantu, having no souls, were destined for ever to be 'hewers of wood and drawers of water'. Their republics managed to maintain semi-independent existence until the 1890s. It was their misfortune that the richest gold strike in a gold-hungry world was found in the centre of the Transvaal. The advancing frontiers of British rule had already bypassed them and engulfed them. The inrush of European speculators threatened now to outnumber them in their last reservations. And their attempt to maintain their own power by excluding the new immigrants from citizenship led directly to the war with Britain and their final defeat. (Their subsequent recovery is dealt with in Chapter III above and in Volume II of this series.)

EUROPE ABROAD: LATIN AMERICA

The third and greatest area of Europe abroad where little or no political or social progress was made in the nineteenth century existed in Central and Southern Latin America. The revolutions which established independence were essentially movements against what had become an alien bureaucratic tyranny. No more than the American revolution that formed the United States did the Latin American revolutions against Spanish rule produce any change in the social balance of power in Latin America itself. European Liberalism was imported. But in most cases it degenerated into a sterile and doctrinaire authoritarianism; and the history of the Latin American states in the nineteenth century is one of endless transition from one military dictatorship to another. In part this was simply a product of the immense distances, the poor communications and the thinness of the population in relation to the spaces of Latin America. But it had other causes too. The ruling groups in every state were bitterly divided by Liberal-Clerical conflicts. While they had adopted the trappings of Liberal republicanism from Spain and revolutionary France they only had the long absolutist traditions of Spanish rule to draw on. And when they were not racked by civil war and successive revolutions, they were involved in wars between themselves. Rule varied between authoritarianism with no real tradition of authority to call on and liberalism with no real popular support.

This internal instability prevented any major economic development except in the larger states such as Argentina, Brazil, and Chile; and such economic development as occurred was financed almost entirely by foreign capital of which more than half was of British origin with French, German and United States capital following in that order. There was very considerable immigration from Europe with over three million foreign nationals living in Latin America by 1900. In economic and financial terms Latin America occupied virtually the same position as the European colonies themselves. The bulk of their financial resources and capital assets were in foreign hands and their economies in most cases depended on single commodity crops (as Brazil on coffee and rubber, the Argentine on beef exports, Chile on nitrates) in just the same way as did Britain's colonies in Africa. Latin American states were second only to Egypt and Tunisia in the recklessness of their borrowing, though they tended to default much more often than the Arab states were allowed to. Their defaults exposed them on a number of occasions to coercive action of the type we have come to term 'gunboat diplomacy' and even, on several occasions in the earlier part of the nineteenth century, to actual invasion by European forces. But the combination of European absorption in expansion elsewhere, a certain latent prejudice against imposing colonial rule on people of European descent, and the watchful power of Great Britain and the United States preserved the Americas against any new European colonial ventures.

At the close of the century only three Latin American states,

Argentina, Brazil, and Chile, were beginning to emerge as powers in their own right. Of these, Chile was racially the most homogeneous, Brazil the largest, and the Argentine possibly the most stable throughout the century. But all the Latin American states presented the same picture of violently divided congeries of oligarchic groups with regional political bosses and Army leaders prominently in the forefront. There was also emerging a small educated, Europeanized intellectual class among whom radical and Marxist ideas were beginning to catch hold. On the other side of an immense social abyss could be seen the labouring masses, illiterate, poverty-stricken, and vulnerable to natural disasters. Their mortality rate was high and their expectation of life was brief. Only in the large cities, Buenos Aires, Montevideo, Rio de Janeiro, Valparaiso, did an urban middle class exist. The few signs of new forces coming to the surface were to be found in the growth of anarcho-syndicalism in Chile with the great strikes of 1905 and 1907 and the foundation of the Socialist Labour Party in 1912; in the socialism from above imposed in Uruguay after 1900; and in the growth of the Radical Civic Union, an American-style reform movement, in the Argentine. The reform movements of the mid-century in Mexico and Colombia seemed to have fizzled out. Everywhere else army rule, local bossism, civil war or demagogic government was the order of the day.

The exposure of the Latin American countries to European coercive measures had led early in the nineteenth century to a number of weak and tentative movements towards some kind of Pan-American solidarity. Successive conferences, at Panama in 1826, at Lima in 1847–8, at Santiago in 1856, at Lima in 1864–5 and at Mexico City in 1896 had produced a number of collective agreements, but most of these pacts proved worthless almost at the moment they were signed. American influence led to the summoning of the first Pan-American Conference in Washington in 1889, but suspicion and fear of the United States made its deliberations fruitless. Moreover, Latin American opinion in general became profoundly alarmed over the course American policy took after 1898.

NON-EUROPEAN STATES: AFRICA

In the medieval and early modern period in European history, Africa had witnessed a series of remarkable empires both in east and west Africa. In **East Africa**, most remarkable was the Shona kingdom associated with the city of Zimbabwe, the remnants of which were destroyed in 1834 by breakaway Zulu rebels coming from southern Africa. At the time of the last great European scramble for Africa the main states were, firstly, the Arab Sultanate of **Zanzibar**, relic of a wave of expansion in the 1830s from the Arab kingdom of Oman on the southern shore of the Persian Gulf; and, second, the inland states of Buganda, Ruanda and Urundi lying in a belt from the eastern shores of Lake Victoria Nyanza down to the shores of Lake Tanganyika.

Buganda was entirely a Bantu kingdom, which had succeeded early in the nineteenth century to the primacy of the region when the much larger kingdom of Bunyoro broke up. It was being challenged by a revival of political activity in Bunyoro when the Europeans first arrived. In 1875, the Kabaka Mutesa of Buganda invited Christian missionaries to counter the infiltration of Islam and Arab slave traders from Zanzibar and the Sudan. But his kingdom was speedily threatened anew as schism and civil war developed between the converts of Catholic and Protestant missionaries. Only British intervention and the establishment of a protectorate over all of present-day Uganda saved the Bugandan states from disintegration. Thereafter Britain's need to have some firm authority on which responsibility for minor matters could be devolved and with whom issues of land tenure and purchase could be negotiated preserved the kingdom of Buganda under British rule.

Ruanda and **Urundi** were multi-racial states where the more recently-arrived Nilotic *emigrés* from the Ethiopian highlands, the Watutsi, ruled as an aristocracy over the earlier Bantu immigrants, the Bahutu and the aboriginal pygmies. They fell nominally into that part of East Africa which was awarded to Germany at the Berlin West African Congress of 1884-5. But in fact, German influence had hardly made any contact with Ruanda and Urundi before the outbreak of war in 1914; in 1919 they passed under Belgian mandate since they adjoined the Belgian Congo.

In **Western Africa**, the Negro empires of the early modern period had been larger and more powerful than the states of East Africa. In succession, Ghana, Mali, and the Songhai empires had ruled the savannah country south of the Sahara Desert. The Songhai were overthrown in the sixteenth century by invasion from Morocco and the *entrepôt* trade on which its wealth rested ended by the arrival of Europeans on the coast. The European arrival on the coast seems to have been preceded by a considerable movement of native tribes out of the reach of the savannah empires through the rain forests to the African coast, and a fresh growth of Negro states at Benin and in Dahomey and, inland along the Niger river, the formation of sizeable city states among the Hausa. In west Central Africa, a large nation appears to have developed in the Congo basin around the Meni Congo tribe. But the advent of huge markets for slaves in the New World stimulated a state of continuous warfare and slave raiding among the African states themselves which over the three centuries it raged reduced all but a few states to disintegrated tribalism. Those which survived turned into militarist confederacies, such as that of Dahomey with its Amazon corps of virgin women.

When the last phase of European expansion in Africa opened, the main African states consisted of military autocracies in the interior, the Tucolor in Senegal, the Mandingoes in the upper Gambia, the Ashanti Confederacy with its capital at Kumasi and the state of Dahomey, already mentioned, and a chain of Moslem emirates among the Fulani and Hausa on the savannahs, of whom the Sultan of Sokoto was the nominal overlord. The coastal tribes were subdivided into hundreds of petty chiefdoms. There were something like eight hundred alone in the area lying to the east of the Niger delta.) The British penchant for indirect rule, using the local political structures to do most of the work of maintaining local law and order and collecting taxes, easily preserved the larger political units in the West African interior. But on the coast the political units were so small that de-tribalization began with the establishment of colonial rule. And the West African coast was to prove one of the earliest stamping grounds for Pan-Africanism.

In **South Africa**, the largest African political units at the time of the collision between the advancing Boers and the Bantu tribes were all more or less organized along military lines, since they had been the spearhead of the Bantu migrations and the instrument used to roll up the Hottentot aborigines before them. Of these militarist states by far the most remarkable was that of the Zulus in what is today Natal, built up out of a group of tribes by Chaka Zulu, who became great chief in 1818, into one of the most effective military machines in history. Some of his regiments broke away from his control and fled his wrath in two directions. One wing under Mzilikasi moved deep into the Transvaal before swinging northwards into what is today Rhodesia where they set up the Matabele State. Others moved directly northwards, destroying the last shadow of the Zimbabwe empire on the way, and ranged north as far as Lake Victoria before settling along Lake Nyasa. Their murders and raids laid waste much of Central Africa; and what destruction they had begun, the Arab slave raiders from Zanzibar completed. Apart from the Bechuana and the Basuto, whom Matabele pressure forced to band together for their own survival, the whole of southern and central Africa presented no political system capable of standing up to the advance of European influence and settlement apart from the Zulu whose military power was finally broken in 1879–80.

By 1900, there were only two independent African states south of the Sahara, Ethiopia and Liberia. **Liberia,** like its neighbour the British colony of **Sierra Leone,** was originally founded as a settlement for Negro slaves liberated by emancipationists in the New World and 'repatriated' to Africa. Of the two, Sierra Leone was the older, having been founded as a refuge for Negroes who remained loyal to the Crown during the American revolution and deportees from the great Negro rising of the 1790s in Jamaica. To these were added slaves seized by the British naval anti-slavery patrol. The first Sierra Leone settlements were made in 1787–91 and a distinctive Creole culture developed there.

Liberia was the product of American emancipation in the 1820s–30s, and, unlike Sierra Leone, gained its independence (in 1841). Both faced the same problems, the impossibility of re-uniting the Europeanized culture of the former slaves with the tribal structure among the natives. British rule in Sierra Leone preserved the two cultures side by side and developed a distinctive 'Creole' culture, as it was called, among the ex-slaves and their descendants, with Creoles associated with the executive and legislative councils of British rule and the first West African institution of higher education at Fourah Bay. In Liberia, an adroit policy of balancing between Britain and the United States preserved its independence. But the ex-slave element, modelling themselves on the ante-bellum South, created what was, in fact, a totally colonialist *régime*, and between 1914 and 1919 accepted American military aid as the only means of suppressing a succession of native uprisings.

Ethiopia was a very different matter. The Ethiopian Empire traced its independence and civilization back to pre-Christian times. It embraced Monophysite Christianity as the state religion in the fourth century AD. It had survived the onset of Islam, mainly because of its geographical isolation, though on one famous occasion only the providential arrival of a ship-load of Portuguese soldiers saved the day. In the late nineteenth century it was preserved mainly by the infusion of energy from the frontier kingdom of Shoa. The last emperors of the old Ethiopian empire, Theodore II and John IV, had in turn been killed, the one in conflict with Britain which led to a British expedition against his capital, Magdala, the other while fighting with the Mahdist forces in the Sudan. John's death made it possible for Menelik II of Shoa to claim the title of Emperor and to extend his rule outwards from Shoa's capital of Addis Ababa. Not only did Menelik II take over the traditional centres of the Ethiopian empire in Gondar and Tigré, but he also acquired the Moslem kingdom of Harrar to the south and a congeries of petty kingdoms to the west. He accepted some aid from France and Russia, and allowed his territory to be used by French expeditions against the headwaters of the Nile at the time of the Fashoda crisis. Even more significant was his crushing defeat of a major Italian invasion at Adowa in 1896, the first defeat inflicted by a non-European state on a European power since the days of the Ottoman invasions of Europe.

The state he attempted to rule was largely feudal. The barons of the north, especially the hereditary princes, the *Ras* of Tigré, were bitter enemies of the house of Menelik. The annexationist policy he pursued brought under Shoan rule not only members of the dominant Amharic race but also Galla and Danaquil tribesmen of Moslem and pagan faiths. The task of integrating the various aristocracies into the Ethiopian system was long and difficult and Menelik's need of western capital, if only to pay for

the arms used to maintain his position, always left him vulnerabl
to a repetition of the British expedition which had overthrow
Theodore II.

By 1906, the three powers which had established themselve
around the Horn of Africa, Britain, France, and Italy, signed
treaty agreeing to maintain the integrity of Ethiopia, but at th
same time providing for its division among them in the event c
its breakdown. The death of Menelik in 1913 and his successio
by an unbalanced Emperor who shook Ethiopia to the core b
embracing Islam, the faith of his mother, could very well hav
led to such a division. However, Ethiopia was saved by the fac
that the European powers were absorbed in the Great War,
its survival owed more to the balance of interests between th
European powers than to any inherent ability on Ethiopia's pa
to repeat the victory of Adowa. In 1900, Ethiopia, in comparativ
terms, was barely entering the sixteenth century.

REVOLTS AGAINST THE WEST

The imposition of colonial rule over the better organized an
more selfconscious African cultures and states was not an eas
process. In some cases the impression of western power was s
great that it was accepted passively as a kind of divine imposition
This was especially the case where European occupation ha
followed or taken advantage of a long period of chaos or civil war
In other situations, wise and intelligent colonial administrators
particularly those who employed the methods of indirect rul
first developed in Nigeria by the British, were able to obtain th
active participation of the traditional leaders of the local Africa
political units. In still others, passive opposition was the initia
reaction. But in a very large number of instances the impositio
of colonial rule was followed within at most two decades by
violent revolt led by the traditional political and religious Africa
leaders.

The occasions for these revolts were numerous and varied. I
a great many cases it was simply harsh and unimaginative
colonial administration that was at fault. Brutality by nativ
police and violence directed against native women figured high
on the list of accepted explanations for these uprisings. In othe

instances there was a definite clash of interpretations of the existing *status quo*. In the hut tax war in Sierra Leone in 1898, for example, the chiefs of the inland protectorate regarded the imposition of a levy on them by the colonial government as derogatory to their sovereignty, which they did not feel they had surrendered simply by signing a treaty of protection with the colonial power. The Matabele and Mashona risings of 1896 in Rhodesia, like the Herero risings of 1904 in German South-West Africa, seem to have arisen from a conflict between European ideas of ownership as applied to their cattle herds, and the much more complex concepts of their own society. The Ashanti revolt of 1900 arose from a total misconception on the part of the British Governor of the nature of the Golden Stool, the mystical symbol of Ashanti unity, which led him in public council to offend grossly the deepest feelings of the Ashanti people. Other uprisings, as for example, the Maji-Maji rising in German East Africa in 1905, the Zulu rebellion in Natal in 1906, and the Makombe rising of 1917–20 in Portuguese East Africa, arose from protest against the draconian invasions of local tribal authority by the representatives of the local colonial power, invasions which included loss of lands, the imposition of heavy taxation and the introduction of severe labour laws, if not of forced labour as such.

The violence with which so many of these rebellions were conducted and the central role played in so many cases by witch-doctors, spirit-mediums, semi-mystical secret orders and charms supposed to protect the wearer against European bullets reveal the atavistic religious convictions of the rebels who believed they were fighting to preserve the very essence of their culture. And the violence and bloodshed with which they were so often put down reveal an equally strong, if more racialist, conviction on the part of the Europeans that it was the authority of their culture, their *mana* as the Maoris of New Zealand would say, which had been attacked. In South-West Africa, over 90,000 natives, 80 per cent of the Hereros and about half the other tribes drawn into the revolt, were killed. In German East Africa, an estimated 120,000 natives died from bullets or starvation. And the defeat and destruction of tribal authority in most cases only speeded up the process of pauperization and detribalization which the intro-duction of western rule, the western money economy and western systems of employment brought with them.

THE BEGINNINGS OF AFRICAN NATIONALISM: PAN-AFRICANISM AND ETHIOPIANISM

The atavistic revolts of the tribes represented only one form of African reaction to the European conquest, and one that was only possible in the rural areas where the traditional political structure was not immediately affected by western industrial civilization. But where that civilization struck roots in Africa, in the seaports, in the industrial towns and in the mining areas, there was an insatiable demand for labour. Africans were lured, bribed, shanghaied and conscripted to work in the new centres, and, once engaged as workers, came to stay and live where they worked. The experience was in most cases a traumatic one, since the labour forces were a mixture of many tribes and deprived of all traditional patterns of religious or political leadership and authority. The process of detribalization was a long and painful one. But, generally, among the detribalized, especially among those exposed to European education through mission schools and the like, there began to develop a new feeling, one of African nationalism, of a separate African identity.

As South Africa was the most advanced area in the continent in 1900, these new feelings showed themselves there first. But they were also to be found in British West Africa, where Fourah Bay College in Sierra Leone had been producing a small number of university-educated Africans since the middle of the nineteenth century. The new feelings showed themselves first of all in two different forms, in the preaching of Pan-African sentiments by a few intellectuals, with the development of an African press, and in the formation of break-away African churches. In the early stages, those responsible were profoundly influenced by contact with Negroes from the more advanced cultures of the United States and the British West Indies. The American influence showed itself mainly in the religious field, the West Indian in the political. A major role in the political field was played in South Africa too by the half-caste Cape Coloureds and by the Indian community.

Ethiopianism, that is the foundation of African Negro churches, originally struck root among the freed slaves of the American South in the decades after the American Civil War.

n the 1880s, the first of a number of American Negro mission-
ries from these churches came to Africa to play their part in the
great missionary effort all the Christian churches in Europe and
America were devoting to the new-found continent. The first
Ethiopian churches as such developed in Nigeria in 1891. But
South Africa had already seen the break-away of individual
African Negro priests from the Anglican communion, to be
followed by a similar break-away from the Wesleyans in the
Transvaal. In 1896, Bishop H. M. Turner of the African
Methodist Episcopal Church in the United States sponsored the
union of these groups into the African branch of his own church.
But more Ethiopian churches continued to form and by 1918
there were more than 76 in South Africa alone. These Negro
missionaries took a number of Africans back to the United States
to be educated before returning to Africa to continue in the
mission field. John Chilembwe, who led the Nyasa revolt of 1915,
was one such.

Political Pan-Africanism came first of all from the British
West Indies. One of its earliest propagandists was E. W. Blyden,
a West Indian who emigrated to Liberia in 1850, whose books
asserting the existence of a unique African personality had a
profound influence both in West Africa and among the educated
Negroes of the United States. From Liberia, John Payne
Jackson came to Lagos in 1891 to found the first pan-African
newspaper, the *Lagos Weekly Record*, in 1891. The first Bantu
language newspaper, *Llanga Lase Natal*, was founded in Durban
in 1902. That same year a leading Moslem in Capetown,
Abdullah Abdurahman, founded the African People's Organization to work for the extension of the rights enjoyed by the Cape
Coloured community or coloureds in other parts of South Africa.

A second wave of Pan-Africanism originated in the United
States in 1905 with the rallying of the leaders of the American
Negro community against the spread of 'Jim Crow' segregationist
legislation in the American Southern states after 1900. In 1905,
a number of prominent American Negro leaders, including the
historian W. E. B. du Bois, set up the Niagara movement, which
was to develop five years later into the National Association for
the Advancement of the Coloured People.

In 1908, the two strands of West Indian Pan-Africanism and
American Ethiopianism came together with the organization of
the first Pan-African Conference by a West Indian barrister,

H. Sylvester Williams, who had developed a legal practice in London based in part on representing African chiefs negotiating with the Colonial Office and other organizations, and Bishop Walters of the African Methodist Episcopal Zionist Church in the United States. Du Bois produced a memorial of this conference. Later he became editor of the NAACP journal, *Crisis*, which was to develop a significant circulation in Africa. But the outbreak of war in Europe prevented the holding of any further conferences until 1919, though the Great War was largely responsible for developing African political consciousness and diminishing the European *mana* in Africa.

NON-EUROPEAN STATES: ASIA AND THE PACIFIC

The principal independent or semi-independent states in Asia still surviving in 1900 were the Kingdom of Siam, the States of Malaya, and the theocracy of Tibet. **Indo-China** finally passed under French rule in the 1880s, although the French allowed a shadowy existence to continue for the Kingdom of Cambodia and Laos within the *Union Indochinoise* which they set up in 1887. **Siam** managed to avoid a similar fate despite a major crisis with France in 1895 which involved the loss of one-fifth of her territory, largely because Britain and France were agreed for most of the latter part of the nineteenth century on the desirability of maintaining Siam as a buffer state between their respective possessions in Burma and Indo-China. A very considerable role was played in maintaining Siamese independence by the long and liberal rule of King Chulalangkom (1868–1910), who used his semi-divine status and his traditional powers and prestige as the legal owner of all land to carry through a great many reforms. He bound the best of the military class to him by setting up Councils of State to advise him, made much use of foreign technicians and advisers and made considerable administrative reforms. He was aided by the opening of the Suez Canal in 1869 which linked the Siamese economy more closely to the European market. He avoided, however, a lavish commitment to public investment, and the tight money policy practised by his advisers, while preventing Siam from running up the kind of debts which would inevitably have brought European intervention, put a damper on economic expansion at a rate which would upset the normal tenor of Siamese life.

Malaya presented a rather different picture. In the south, Singapore had been entirely created by the British as the greatest commercial *entrepôt* for all South-East Asia, its population consisting largely of *emigré* Chinese. To Singapore were added, in 1826, other British trading settlements at Penang and Malacca, the whole being known as the Straits Settlements. In up-country Malaya, the latter half of the nineteenth century saw an immense development of tin-mining by European and Chinese capital with the growth of a large and rowdy Chinese labour force. By 1900, Malaya was producing half the world's supply of tin and the various sultans of the Malay states were rich enough to be able to give a battleship, H M S *Malaya*, to the Royal Navy in 1911. To all this was added the cultivation of rubber which enjoyed a fantastic boom in 1910–12. By 1914, Malayan rubber had captured the world market from Brazil.

From the 1850s then, developments had been casting an increased strain on the relations between the various Malay sultans; piracy, inter-state war, faction fights between Chinese secret societies, pressure from the Netherlands in the south and Siam in the north led to the gradual extension of the British residential system, first introduced into the state of Perak in 1874. Under the residential system each Sultan's position was guaranteed by the British, who undertook to help maintain order. In return, the Sultan accepted a British resident, whose 'advice' had to be asked and acted on in all administrative matters, and who became responsible for overseeing the collection and control of all revenue. By 1895, British residents were installed in all the central and southern Malayan states except Johore. In 1895, four states in central Malaya were persuaded to come together into the Federated Malay States with a common administrative structure, and a capital at Kuala Lumpur and a resident-general. There followed an immense economic development, revenue tripling itself in ten years. In 1909, the Sultans formed a Federal Council to advise the resident-general. That same year the four northernmost Malay states were ceded to Britain by Siam in return for a £4 million loan and the abandonment of British extra-territorial rights. They preferred, as did Johore, to remain outside the Federation and to accept a British adviser rather than a resident. Johore did not even accept an adviser until 1914.

The advance of rubber cultivation brought a fresh wave of immigration from Southern India, and by 1911 Malays themselves constituted a bare 51 per cent of the population. But whereas the opposition of capital to labour divided the Chinese and Indian communities, Malay society showed itself remarkably resistant in the face of this invasion. The sultans and the Malay peasantry remained dominant in the general fields of agriculture and fishing and proved able to expand the food supply in step with the increase in population. Islam gave them its remarkable powers of cohesion. But, above all, the main force in preserving the traditional structure of Malay society was the rule of Britain, whose overriding concern for the maintenance of law and order here as in India preserved the structures it found on conquest virtually unaltered, like flies in amber, until the moment of its withdrawal.

In **Burma,** British rule was not so beneficent in its effects. The three British wars in 1826, 1852, and 1855, were to destroy entirely the traditional system of divine royalty and the authority which went with it. The five years of anarchy, dacoity and piracy which followed necessitated military action and the introduction of direct British rule down to village level. The degeneration of Burmese society was accelerated with the introduction of large numbers of Indian coolies to aid in the commercial development of agriculture to serve the Indian market. The Burmese authorities gradually lost control of their land to Indian capital. There was a rapid rise in crimes of violence and xenophobia. Burmese opinion took added exception to being governed as a province of India, even though Burma benefited from the general advance of India towards self-government. An advisory Legislative Council was set up in 1897 and a Burmese civil service on Indian lines developed slowly thereafter. The ascent from the depths of 1900 was a very slow one, greatly retarded by the decline in native monastic culture and the absence of any significant European educational effort to replace it.

Tibet was the most remote of all Asian states, isolated both by geography and by an inward-looking religion whose principles left its devotees largely uninterested in the outside world. It was a theocratic state, governed for two hundred years by regents from the nobility chosen by the lamas (the monks of Tibet). A peculiar amalgam of Mahayana Buddhism with Tibet's own magical-mystical shamanism, Lama rule, had been finally established in the seventeenth century AD by Mongol princes from Central Asia, under the head of one of the competing lama sects to whom a Mongol prince gave the title of Dalai Lama. Although the Chinese intervened to expel an invasion from Central Asia in 1720 and remained in active occupation of Tibet until the middle of the eighteenth century, their withdrawal left Tibet autonomous again under the religious hierarchy and until the advent of the thirteenth Dalai Lama in 1895, the Dalai Lamas were mere figureheads. The thirteenth Dalai Lama, however, was determined to make Tibet completely independent. But his attempt to achieve independence by playing off the British in India, the Russians and the Chinese against one another proved disastrous. His entertainment of a Russian agent in 1903 caused the Indian government to take up traders' complaints and launch an expedition which reached Lhasa in 1904, and led to his temporary deposition by the Chinese. Reinstalled, he appealed to Britain for aid against China in 1909, only bringing down on his head a Chinese expedition, from which he fled to exile in India in 1910. Tibet remained under direct Chinese occupation for two years until the Chinese Revolution of 1911 so weakened the Chinese authority as to enable the Tibetans to expel the Chinese garrison. The Dalai Lama returned to independent rule even though he received British aid in the reorganization of his armed forces.

THE BEGINNINGS OF NATIONALISM
IN SOUTH-EAST ASIA

The **Philippines** were the scene of the only major nationalist movement in South-East Asia before 1900. Its causes can be traced to the wealth that flowed into the islands, after nearly three hundred years of stagnation under Spanish rule, with the opening of the Chinese ports to European trade in 1840. At the same time, friction gradually developed between the native Filipino clergy and the large Spanish monastic orders which, having originally converted the Philippines to Catholicism in the sixteenth century, had come to own large quantities of land on the islands. There were clergy-led rebellions in 1843 and 1872 and a Messianic break-away movement, the Colorum movement in the 1840s. By the 1890s, a new movement had grown up which represented a coming together of three separate groupings, a gathering of native magical traditions in a secret society, the so-called *Katipuran*, led by one Emilio Aguinaldo, of a schismatic religious movement, such as the Independent Filipino Church, and of European liberal anti-clericalism represented by José Rizal who founded the *Liga Filipina* in 1892. In 1896, these various forces revolted against Spain. Rizal was executed and in 1897 the Spanish bought off the rebel leaders with 800,000 pesos. It was at that moment that the outbreak of the Spanish-American war led the Americans to enlist Aguinaldo's support against the Spanish garrison of the islands. When Spain withdrew nationalist leaders raised the flag of independence. But neither their Catholicism nor their easy corruptibility convinced the Americans that they were 'fit for self-government'. Commercial strategic and imperialist reasoning reinforced this basically Protestant Anglo-Saxon conviction of the backwardness of the Catholic Hispanicized Malay-Moro-Chinese population of the Philippines, and the islands were duly annexed to the United States in the sacred name of the American mission to 'uplift them and civilize them and Christianize them' (the words were those of President McKinley). There followed two years of bloody rebellion as violently put down. American opinion, however took its mission seriously. In 1903, local elections were held and in 1907 the Philippines were given a general assembly on a restricted franchise. By 1918, the Philippines were well on their way again to self-government.

In **Indonesia,** the nationalist movement took much longer to develop than in the Philippines, and when it came it was Islamic rather than Catholic. In other respects, however, it represented a similar admixture of western and indigenous ideas. Dutch economic exploitation in the nineteenth century had created a large and restless labour force. Dutch control had also destroyed much of the authority of the traditional rulers, while at the same time producing a population increase in Java on such a scale as to outstrip the rate of expansion of agricultural production. The main resistance to Dutch rule in this period came from the *ulemas* the intellectual leaders of Islam. In 1900, the Dutch reversed their stand to introduce the so-called New Ethical Policy. It aims were to expand and develop a new educated Islamic *élite* and to improve the social services and welfare of the islands. But the Dutch were unable to overcome the opposition of the resident European population who were unwilling to curtail their economic privileges. And administrative convenience dictated the continuation of direct rule through local sultans throughout all but the principal islands of the Indonesian archipelago. The effect of the New Ethical Policy was to create a semi-educated group not easily disposable into a system of administration dominated either by the Dutch or by local sultans. At the same time Chinese merchants were invading Java and establishing a stranglehold on the rural economy.

The combination of Islamic resistance to Dutch rule, European liberal ideas expressing themselves through the products of the New Ethical Policy and Javanese economic grievances led in 1906 to the establishment of the 'High Endeavour' Society, the aim of which was to establish schools and regenerate Javanese culture and in 1911 to the establishment of *Sarekat Islam* (the Islamic brotherhood), which at first was supported by Dutch officials. At its second conference in 1916, the first to be held on a nation-wide basis, the leaders of *Sarekat Islam* passed a resolution demanding Indonesian self-government. At the same time, Dutch socialists were beginning to proselytize in Indonesia, and after the Russian Revolution of 1917 Indonesian nationalism was to pass through a predominantly Marxist phase.

THE DECLINE OF POLYNESIAN SOCIETY

Worst hit by the arrival of western ideas and influences were the island cultures of Polynesia, the Maori states of New Zealand and the kingdom of Hawaii. At the time of the first contacts with European culture in the Pacific, Polynesian political organization was based on decentralized tribal kingdoms with a considerable record of internecine war. The introduction of European firearms only made these wars more bloody. At the same time the isolated Polynesian communities proved highly vulnerable to European diseases.

Thus, in **New Zealand,** the first of the large Polynesian-inhabited areas to fall under European rule, eighteen years of tribal warfare and epidemics (1821–38) reduced the population of North Island from 200,000 to 100,000. At first, European occupation did not bring a unified resistance until European encroachment on Maori-held lands had already become irreversible. Maori opposition ranged from a relatively benign attempt to achieve Maori unity in the 'King' movement to the racial-magical fanaticism of the *Hau-hau* movement with its attempts to appropriate the magical element in Christianity which the Maoris thought to be the secret of European strength. Maori resistance, however, was easily defeated. Thereafter, despite the British policy of attempting to draw the Maoris into the economy by the construction of railways and the appointment of Maori members of the New Zealand parliament, the Maoris withdrew into isolation within their communities and by 1896 their numbers had dropped to a mere 42,000. At this point the white New Zealanders spoke of eventual disappearance of the Maori people.

After 1896, however, a new leadership, based on the Maori seats in the New Zealand parliament, stemming partly from half-caste Maoris like Sir James Carroll, partly from missionary-educated Maoris, began to bring about a revival. In 1897, the formation of the Young Maori party began to replace the declining traditional leadership. And its rediscovery of Maori language and culture through the methods of western ethnology led to a revival of pride in the Maori national heritage and the growth of a sense of Maori unity over and above tribal differences. The population trend was very slowly reversed. And Maoris began to work for a synthesis of European knowledge, ideas and practices which was made the more difficult for the lack of any but oral Maori traditions.

The state of **Hawaii,** by contrast, managed to maintain its independence until the end of the nineteenth century. In part, this was due to the achievement of Kamehameka I who, by the close of the eighteenth century, had managed to unify most of the islands under his rule prior to all but the first European landfalls. Hawaii, however, remained open to trading and missionary contacts, and indeed by the 1860s had adopted Christianity on such a vast scale that it no longer constituted a field for missionary activity. The islands had also accepted American and British settlers and American, French and British consuls. And periodic descents on the islands by warships of these three powers in pursuit of national aims and a short period of British occupation led in the 1840s to a joint Anglo-French guarantee of Hawaiian independence. Thereafter, British and French activities gradually declined and Hawaii became economically dependent on the United States, particularly after the Reciprocity Treaty of 1876. But with the increase in commercial wealth came an invasion of American, Chinese and Japanese settlers, smallpox and the decline of the native population from 200,000 in 1800 to barely 40,000 in 1890. In 1884 in order to secure extension of the Reciprocity Treaty a coaling station at Pearl Harbor on Oahu Island was ceded to America. In the effort to assert their sovereignty the monarchs of Hawaii inevitably came into conflict with the American settlers, and from 1887 to 1891 there were a series of political disturbances in the islands. In 1892, the white residents finally revolted against Polynesian rule, and set up a temporary government and applied for annexation by the United States, which followed, after an initial rebuff, in 1898 in the wave of imperialism fostered in America by the Spanish-American war.

THE WEST INDIES

Nowhere did the impact of European colonial rule and European mercantilist policies produce a political pattern more contrary to geography than in the islands of the Caribbean. Few areas showed less signs of economic, social or political progress at the opening of the twentieth century. The interaction of Spanish, French, Dutch, British and United States imperialism produced a chain of islands divided from one another by language, culture, political system, religion, trade and finance, and even by racial composition. Indeed, each was tied so firmly to its metropolitan economic system that neighbouring islands might well have been on separate continents for all the intercourse between them. The British-owned Bahamas lay next to Cuba, which was to win its independence from Spain in 1898, only to pass at once under the equally unwelcome protection of the United States. South of Cuba lay British Jamaica, east the independent Negro republics of Haiti and the Dominican Republic, the American colony of Puerto Rico, taken from Spain, and the American Virgin Islands.

Next came the long chain of Leeward and Windward Islands with French, British and the occasional Dutch islands interspersed with one another, British-held Trinidad and Tobago, the Dutch Curaçao and the three Guianas, one British, one French and one Dutch (Surinam).

Throughout the area, the largest population group was made up of descendants of the African slaves brought there in the sixteenth, seventeenth and eighteenth centuries. The next most numerous group was that composed of the products of union between slaves and European settlers. In the nineteenth century, the British brought in Chinese coolies and Indian indentured labour to British Guiana and to Trinidad and Tobago, and the Dutch imported both Indians and Javanese to Surinam. Cuba and Puerto Rico contained large colonies of Europeans of Spanish origin, and there were British, French and Dutch planter minorities in the remaining islands. American rule brought in American businessmen, some planters and technicians for the American-owned and controlled fruit-producing plantations. The largest single crop was sugar, followed by coffee, cocoa and, in the south, oil and bauxite. The single most important reason for the stagnation of West Indian society for the first three decades of the twentieth century was the decline in the world price of sugar.

The **French West Indies** were largely governed in the nineteenth century according to the general pattern of French colonial practice. French slaves were emancipated in 1848, and in 1875 the islands were permanently incorporated as departments of Metropolitan France. The inhabitants were assimilated into France; adult male suffrage was introduced and the French educational system imposed as an inevitable accompaniment to the incorporation of the islands into the departmental organization of Metropolitan France. Yet sugar, the main product of Martinique and Guadeloupe, competed on the French market with French-produced beet-sugar, the production and marketing of which was heavily subsidized in France by the French government. France's West Indian colonies became a permanent drain on the French economy and as a result economic and social development in the colonies stagnated for lack of funds.

The **Dutch West Indies** suffered equally from the slump in world demand for cane sugar, and the economies of Surinam and Curaçao were also run at a loss to the metropolitan exchequer. Dutch rule, however, was more paternalistic than that of France, though Surinam had a legislature of thirteen members, nine of whom were elected, left over from the days when it was run by a Dutch Chartered Company. An Assembly whose members were nominated rather than elected was set up to rule the Dutch island possessions in 1865. Such a system was not designed to stimulate political activity among the local inhabitants, and in 1900 the Dutch West Indies showed even less signs of any social or political ferment than the French colonies.

The **British West Indies** had enjoyed representative institutions at the beginning of the nineteenth century, though the only interests represented were those of the planter oligarchy. The Negro uprisings in Jamaica in 1865 led, however, to the abolition of the old assembly and the adoption of the standard British policy of Crown Colony rule. However, British opinion prevented an extension of the franchise to cover the illiterate and propertyless Negro masses. The Governor ruled through a legislative council, a number of whose members were, after 1884, elected on a property-owning basis which let in the small property owners of Negro or Creole blood. The effect was to destroy the political power of the small white oligarchy and to remove from the West Indies the prospect of racial strife. The Crown Colony system spread to the other British West Indies with the exception of Barbados and the Bahamas which preserved their eighteenth-century assemblies. But any chance of social or political progress was destroyed by the drastic slump in the world price of cane sugar with the invasion of the British market by European-produced and subsidized beet sugar. By 1900, only 2·5 per cent of British sugar consumption came from the West Indies and the concurrent outbreaks of disease among Trinidad's cocoa and Jamaica's banana plantations left the islands virtually destitute.

West Indian labour emigrated to New York and the United States generally, and political consciousness tended to manifest itself among the *emigrés* in the form of Ethiopianism. Educated West Indians came to Britain and played their part in the early stages of the Pan-African movement. In their culture, the masses of the people reverted to a more primitive form of Africanism, with *obeah*, spirit worship, the Shango cult, pocomania and other degenerate forms of half-remembered, half-invented African-type superstitions taking hold. Destitution was their lot and a high birth rate produced a level of over-population which made the alleviation of poverty quite beyond the resources of the colonial power. Only among the small middle class could the first stirrings of a distinctive West Indian political consciousness be found. Otherwise, the West Indian remained proud to be British, and it is significant that only one out of four of West Indian immigrants to the United States chose to take out American citizenship, to the disgust of the American Negroes among whom they lived.

Cuba provided the real exception to this record of stagnation, though the revolutionary forces in the island were essentially those that had succeeded in casting off Spanish rule on the American mainland in the period after 1800. The revolutionaries were an admixture of Hispanic and Creole elements determined to free themselves and their island from a rule at once paternalistic, inefficient, corrupt and dictated by metropolitan considerations quite alien to Cuba. They resented the heavy Spanish taxation, the huge imposts on Cuban trade with the United States, the biggest market for Cuban sugar, and the discrimination practised against the Creoles by the new wave of Spanish immigrants in the 1850s. The conspiracies of 1848–51 were followed by the ten-year war of independence in 1868–78 in which over 200,000 lost their lives. It was a fresh Cuban rebellion in 1895 which did so much to turn American opinion against Spain in the period before the outbreak of the Spanish-American war in 1898. But when the war was over, Cuba had achieved nominal independence only to pass under the domination of the United States. The energies of the Cuban revolution seemed to have been dissipated, and Cuba, having fought for a century, only managed to achieve the status and ambitions of a Latin American *caudillo*- and army-ridden oligarchy.

Section Two

The Breakdown of the European System

Chapter 5

The Nature of the European System

CENTRIPETAL FORCES

BY 1900, the European great powers had managed to survive eighty-five years without a major war, though there had been numerous crises, minor wars, and war-scares; especially in the middle of the century after Louis Napoleon had succeeded in breaking the old ties between Austria and Russia, and initiated a succession of small but violent wars, which were to end with his own defeat at the hands of Bismarckian Germany in the Franco-Prussian war of 1870–71. Thereafter, Bismarck had succeeded in re-establishing much of the old ethos of cooperation between the European powers established in 1815, the idea of the 'Concert of Europe' as it has been called, to deal with the strains consequent on the increasing disintegration of the Ottoman Empire, and with those arising from the scramble for territory in Africa.

The basic idea underlying the concept of the Concert of Europe was the principle of the balance of power and the maintenance of parity of force between the Great Powers. Its motive force was fear of a major disturbance of the *status quo* that would raise any one of the powers to a position of such quasi-Napoleonic supremacy over its rivals that only a costly and long-drawn-out major war could restore the balance. The Concert of Europe therefore called for cooperation to prevent disturbance of the *status quo* by the smaller powers. It also provided agreed compensation to the other great powers, in those instances when one great power enlarged its area of dominion to a degree which the others found excessive. Thus, at the Berlin Congress of 1878, Tsarist Russia was forced to revise the peace terms it had imposed on Ottoman Turkey after the Russo-Turkish war of 1877. At the Berlin West Africa Congress of 1884–85, British claims to exercise a Monroe Doctrine over the African continent were set aside in favour of the doctrine of effective occupation. Another case in point was the joint intervention of Russia, France and Germany in Tokyo in April 1895 to secure modification of the Japanese peace terms at the end of the Sino-Japanese war. At the same time, in 1880, 1886 and again in 1897, international naval demonstrations and, in the last case, a blockade, were used to enforce the position of the great powers against Greece and Turkey.

An element in the Concert system was the negotiation of agreements to maintain the *status quo* or, failing that, to reach prior agreements to change it. The two agreements of February and December 1887 on the maintenance of the *status quo* in the Mediterranean and the Austro-Russian convention of April 30th, 1897, on the maintenance of the *status quo* in the Balkans are examples of this kind of cooperation. The instruments of the system included also Congresses and councils of ambassadors. Such councils were called into session repeatedly at Constantinople to control and intervene in the process of disintegration of the Ottoman Empire. They drew up or approved numerous schemes for the reform and modernization of the Ottoman administration, none of which, it is true, proved capable of covering the basic problem of reconciling that empire with the rise of Balkan nationalism, but which were continuously successful in restraining the rate of its disintegration and in preventing the outbreak of a major war.

A major factor in this process was the authority and control of foreign policy enjoyed by the various foreign ministries of the major powers and the secrecy in which the processes of their diplomacy were carried out. Bismarck affected to distrust the British government as a partner in negotiations because British governments insisted that treaties had to be disclosed to and ratified by Parliament. But British governments could play their cards in negotiations as close to their chests as any one else. It was only treaties they insisted on publishing. British foreign secretaries and British diplomats could and did hold their own with the diplomats of the Quai d'Orsay, the Wilhelmstrasse, the Ballhausplatz or the Tsarist Foreign Ministry. And the British cabinet system, so long as it was secure in its command of a majority in Parliament, proved no more (and no less) apt to dither when it was undecided than the chancelleries of any continental power. In France, the impermanence of individual cabinets was compensated for by the continuity of ministers in the same office in one cabinet after another.

Elements in the maintenance of the balance of power were the armed forces of the great powers and the commanding position across the European exits to the oceans of the world exercised by British bases. British naval superiority was often threatened during the last decades of the nineteenth century, but never challenged. And it proved adequate in times of crisis, as for example, during the Boer War, to prevent any question of European intervention.

While the British fleets confined the major play of international power politics to Europe, the balance inside Europe was maintained by the institution of large conscript armies, with reserves rapidly mobilizable by means of the railway networks laid down in the 1860s–70s. The conscript armies gave the military leaders of the eastern autocracies equal say in the formulation of foreign policy with the foreign ministries, and their tendency to think at times in terms of a quick *coup d'armes*, especially in Tsarist Russia, added a note of peril to the formal manoeuvres of the diplomatists, though it was really only after 1900 that they began to play a major part in the formulation of foreign policy outside Tsarist Russia.

A second element of instability was provided by the growth of a nationalist public opinion in most of the great powers, and a press which could be muzzled and advised, 'inspired' even by government direction, but which could also sit in judgement on governments which it felt had betrayed the national interest. The press, unfortunately, fed on its fellows in other countries, and came to act as an echo chamber for rumours and an instrument for inflaming opinion against potential enemies. A 'press war' or a war of insults between the newspapers of two countries, each repeating accusations made by its opponents prior to returning them with interest, could, if left unchecked, bring public opinion to the verge of war. The continental autocracies tended to keep their press in line by censorship and subsidy. Much of the French and Italian press was open for sale to all comers. The British press fell into two parts, the quality press which was not unamenable to the quiet appeal to the national interest, and the more popular press which could in some instances be managed by the judicious distribution of honours. It was the heyday of the great editor and the great foreign correspondent. But it is difficult to argue that the role of the press was not that of a peril rather than a support to international peace; though public opinion, even in Tsarist Russia, acted as an effective brake against the more outrageous forms of horse-trading.

An essential element in the international scene too was the ubiquity of royalty and its tendency to be related to the English Crown. In the autocracies, the person of the Kaiser of Germany, the Austrian Kaiser Franz Josef, or the Tsar, was of extreme importance in the dual role of head of state and commander in chief of the armed forces. Bismarck's strength lay in the unbroken faith placed in him by the Kaiser, William I. He did not long survive his master's death. Kaiser William II was a very different figure, irascible, impetuous, often silly, arrogant and hasty in his judgements and obsessed by power. His cousin, Tsar Nicholas II of Russia, was a weak and ambitious man, open to bad counsellors, fervently anti-British, determined to hang on to power, and a bad judge of men, preferring the second-rate and the sycophant to the few first-rate officials in his service. In Austria, the aged Kaiser acted always as a brake on adventurism, his main discoverable emotion being a conviction that he was himself the Austrian state. Even in Britain the personality of the Crown counted for a good deal, especially when the cabinet was hesitant or divided. Nor were any of the monarchs and emperors beyond personal diplomacy from time to time.

Great power cooperation in the political sphere was paralleled very often by similar cooperation in the financial sphere. This was especially the case when one of the smaller powers threatened to default on her debts, or, in the resultant action to prevent such default, one power seemed likely to obtain an advantage the others regarded as excessive or offensive.

Perhaps the first instance of the establishment of an international financial administration was the creation of the Chinese Maritime Customs after 1853. This was a Chinese institution with a British Inspector-General and a partly European staff which collected dues from all European merchants in the Chinese treaty ports and paid the revenues direct to designated Chinese banks. The British were able to gain international acceptance for the Inspector-General remaining a British subject so long as Britain retained the dominant position in European trade with China. A second instance was Anglo-French cooperation in the late 1870s to enforce on Egypt a government willing to give the first priority to the service of Egypt's debts to British and French creditors. And after the British occupation of Egypt in 1882,

Germany joined France and Russia at London in August 1884 to insist on the principle of international agreement to any British proposals to re-organize Egypt's finances. Similar action was taken in 1880-1 with the establishment of an international Council of Administration of the Turkish debt with seven members named by foreign banks or groups of bondholders with the presidency of the Council alternating between the French and British representatives. And when in 1898 an inter-national Financial Commission was appointed on German initiative to control the servicing of Greek foreign indebtedness, three governments, Russia, Austria and Italy, were invited to nominate representatives to the British, German and French organized council although little or no share of the indebtedness was held by their nationals. Banking syndicates and international consortia tended to be run on similar lines.

The most far-reaching, though not necessarily the most successful, of these joint international actions involved the Mürzteg programme for reform in Turkish Macedonia. This programme, begun in 1903, called for the division of Macedonia into five police districts, under Austrian, Russian, Italian, French and British command, with the *gendarmerie* directed by an Italian officer. Austrian and Russian civilian officers were also to be attached to the staff of the Turkish Inspector-General for Macedonia. In May 1905, the ambassadors of these powers were joined by the German ambassador in demanding that this *régime* should be tightened up by the appointment of four Financial Delegates to be attached to the Inspector-General, the Delegates to be appointed by France, Germany, Great Britain and Italy, and to cooperate with the Austrian and Russian Civil Agents. When the Turks refused, an international squadron under an Italian admiral occupied the Turkish customs house on the island of Mytilene, and the Turks accepted the new proposals.

CENTRIFUGAL FORCES

Beneath this surface appearance of cooperation lay those long-standing rivalries and enmities between the great powers which made its continuance so important. Some of these rivalries dated back to the three crucial events of the mid-century: the defeat of

Russia in the Crimean War of 1854–6 by Britain and France; the Italian use of the Franco-Prussian war of 1870–1 to end the French occupation of Rome and to isolate the Pope in the Vatican City; and the German defeat of France in that same war and the annexation of Alsace and Lorraine. Between Austria and Russia there lay Austria's failure to support Russia in the Crimea and the question of who was to be dominant in the Balkans. Between France and Britain there lay since 1882 the British occupation of Egypt and the French determination to end it.

After 1871, Bismarck had used these enmities to keep Europe divided and peaceful. At first he had relied on the hostility to republican institutions common to the three eastern autocracies, united in the League of the Three Emperors, to keep France isolated. He engineered French expansion in Africa and pressure on Egypt as a means of embroiling France with Britain. After 1878, he built up a structure of alliances, first with Austria in 1879, then with Austria and Italy in 1882 (the Triple Alliance), then with Austria and Rumania in 1883. In 1884–5, he taught Britain the need for German support to counter-balance French pressure on the international control of Egypt's finances. The two Mediterranean agreements of 1887 between Britain, Austria, and Italy, were made with his encouragement as the best way of tying Britain into his alliance system, which he crowned that same year with the negotiation of the Reinsurance Treaty with Russia. The Reinsurance Treaty, in turn, put him in the position of being able to maintain the balance between Austria and Russia, since in each case the question of whether his alliance with Austria or his guarantee to Russia became operative depended on him alone.

His successors in 1890, not perceiving the decisive position these treaties gave to Germany, allowed the Reinsurance Treaty to lapse. Bismarck had already allowed France and Russia to meet on the common ground of their enmity to Britain over Egypt and the British support for Ottoman Turkey. In 1891 and 1893, political and military conventions were signed between France and Russia (the Dual Alliance) which bound the two nations to support one another if either were involved in Europe. With this guarantee of their position against Germany in Europe, each felt free to pursue their respective colonial policies, France against Britain in Egypt, Russia against Britain in central Asia and in northern China. Bismarck's successors, misunderstanding the position, believed the Franco-Russian alliance to be directed against Britain. Indeed, they congratulated themselves that their central and neutral position would enable them to extract advantages from either side in return for diplomatic and military support in whatever crisis might ensue. But, in truth, their policy of the 'free hand' left them little chance of success, since they had little or nothing to offer either France or Britain, or Russia or Britain in the event of a conflict between them. In its search for links with France and Britain, Germany accepted, in 1893 and 1894, frontier settlements in Africa which cut off the colonies of the Cameroons and German East Africa from further expansion into the African interior. And such concessions as could be wrung from Britain simply irritated successive British governments into thinking Germany to be an incompetent and annoying blackmailer.

The Franco-Russian alliance showed its strength in the Near Eastern crises of 1895, when for once the British did not feel free to send a fleet to the Dardanelles. But the upshot of the crisis was the abandonment by Britain of her own efforts to find an amenable way of withdrawing from Egypt. There followed the direct confrontation of French and British troops at Fashoda on the Upper Nile in 1898 from which France had to retire ignominiously. The crisis was provoked by the arrival of a French expedition, which had set out from West Africa the preceding year, at Fashoda, on the Upper Nile. Its dispatch was inspired by the idea of obtaining a pledge which might be used to secure a British evacuation of Egypt. But by the time it arrived at its destination, the international position had changed. A British army had invaded the Sudan and stood ready to arrest the French expedition. France herself was in the grip of the Dreyfus scandal. And France's Russian ally was unwilling to support her. In a conflict with Britain, France could do nothing without the support of another major naval power and in 1898 the German fleet was, in international terms, a negligible quantity. Nor could Germany offer Britain any real support against Russia in the Far East. There was no German interest there adequate to recompense Germany for the risk of a war on her eastern frontiers with Russia. Nor were Bismarck's successors the least sure of what they wanted out of the mediatory role they hoped to play.

Lacking any decisiveness in Berlin, the Bismarckian alliance system was perceptibly weakened. In the Near Eastern crises of 1895-7, Austria found herself without German diplomatic support and therefore virtually powerless. Thus, it is hardly surprising that in the latter stages of the crisis provoked by the revolt in Crete in 1896 the Concert of Europe functioned fairly well, or that in April 1897 Austria and Russia agreed to respect the *status quo* in the Balkans. And if Austria felt weakened Italy felt still more weakened. In the 1894–6 period, Britain was grateful for her support against French pressure towards the upper reaches of the Nile. Britain encouraged Italian activity in Eritrea and in Somalia as a means of countering French attempts to find a route towards the headwaters of the Nile from Djibuti on the Red Sea coast. But in 1896 the Italians met disaster at the hands of an Abyssinian army at Adowa, and Britain's decision to bid for control of the whole Nile valley herself and the subsequent diplomatic defeat of France at Fashoda meant that Britain also no longer had any real need of Italian support. The Italians, isolated and weak, began to make their peace with France. In 1896, Italy recognized the French position in Tunis, and two years later a ten-year-old tariff war between the two countries was ended.

The outcome of the decade of diplomacy following Bismarck's dismissal had been to destroy the balance of power which he had given Europe, and to leave Europe divided into two alliance systems, the Triple Alliance of Germany, Austria and Italy with Rumania as an appendage, and the Dual Alliance of France and Russia. In Bismarck's system, Britain was tied to Germany by her need for German support on the question of Egypt's finances, and through the joint interest she shared with Austria in resisting Russian expansion in the Balkans. After Bismarck's fall, both these ties disappeared. In 1895–6, she abandoned her old policy of opposing Russian expansion in the Balkans. And from this followed the decision to remain in Egypt, one which greatly diminished her need for German support in the administration of Egypt's finances. Britain had, in short, reverted to the isolated role which had so defeated Bismarck after 1870, before Disraeli's intervention in the Near Eastern crisis of 1877 and British involvement in Egypt had given him a means of pressuring her. As a result, Austria had virtually retired from international politics, and Italy, Germany's other partner in the Triple Alliance, had felt obliged to edge towards France. The Triple Alliance was in disarray, and Germany's international position was isolated and without influence commensurate with her military and industrial strength and her central position in Europe.

Chapter 6

The Diplomatic Revolution. Stage 1: The Isolation of Germany, 1899–1904

INTERNATIONAL politics in the last decade of the nineteenth century were dominated by the colonial rivalries of France and Russia with England, and governed by the Franco-Russian alliance. For its two signatories the Franco-Russian alliance had the effect of strengthening each of them and freeing them from any fear of a European attack. For France, it was a protection against Germany and for Russia a shield against Austria. It enabled France gradually to wean Italy away from the Triple Alliance, since it made her almost strong enough to challenge Britain in the Mediterranean. And by freeing Russia of direct anxieties in the Balkans it converted the Tsar's advisers to the view that it would be better to attempt to keep the Ottoman Empire a going concern rather than allow the European complications which might follow its break-down to distract Russian energies from expansion in Korea, Manchuria and North China, and in Persia. The Tsar's advisers toyed with the idea of seizing the Dardanelles by force if the collapse of the Ottoman Empire seemed inevitable. But they preferred to cooperate with the other members of the Concert of Europe to prevent such an event from taking place. The Austro-Russian convention of 1897 led logically to the cooperation of the two powers in attempting to find a solution for the spread of nationalism to Turkish Macedonia, where widespread disturbances broke out in 1902.

As Russia turned to expansion in China and to pressure on Persia, and France to a decade of attempts to secure either an end to the British occupation of Egypt or compensation elsewhere for acquiescence in its continuation, both parties came inevitably into conflict with Britain, the one true imperial power. The British reaction, first of all, was to strengthen the fleet, which Gladstonian economizing and hostility to expenditure on

armaments had gravely weakened. Then, once the naval pro
gramme initiated in 1895 had begun to remedy the deficiencie
and restore the British navy to the two-power standard (by which
Britain's naval strength was to be kept equal to the combined
fleets of the next two largest sea-powers), the British governmen
made strenuous efforts to find some kind of a *modus vivendi* with
each of its two challengers. Of the two, France was the easier to
stand off. And the French bid for the Nile headwaters wa
forestalled by the occupation of the Sudan and the defeat of th
Mahdi, and went off at halfcock in 1898 at Fashoda, when Franc
herself was bitterly divided by the Dreyfus affair, and ha
made no diplomatic preparations whatever to face a crisis with
Britain.

Russia was a more formidable proposition, since the Russia
empire was by no means as defenceless in the face of Britis
seapower as France seemed to be. It was true that until th
Trans-Siberian railway was completed, Russia's military positio
in the Far East was at least in part dependent on the sea-route t
China. But Britain was also vulnerable to Russian overlan
pressure in Persia and on the Indian-Afghan border. Th
Salisbury government attempted, therefore, to reach an under
standing with Russia over the Far East. In 1897, a joint Anglo
Japanese naval demonstration prevented the Russians fron
occupying a port in Korea. But after the Russian occupation o
Port Arthur in the same month, Salisbury proposed an agree
ment on spheres of preponderance in the Chinese and Ottoma
Empires. In April 1899, agreement was, in fact, reached o
railway concessions in China, using the Great Wall as th
division between the areas within which each country woul
seek railway concessions. But the Boxer risings proved too grea
a temptation for the Russian administration, and the Britis
government was forced to look elsewhere for an ally to restrai
Russia.

Britain's need for an ally seemed the more necessary at th
end of the nineteenth century in the light of the trouble Britai
was facing in the South African war, the challenges issued to th
British position in North and Central America, and the begin
nings of German large-scale naval construction. British govern
mental opinion at the end of the century was an odd mixture o
arrogant and self-confident isolationism and strained nerves
There can be no doubt that the ignominious military failures i

South Africa which marked the second week of December 1899 shook British self-confidence badly. The steady development of American pressure in the Caribbean, when coupled with the major development of the American navy, combined sentimental and strategic reasons for reaching agreement with the United States. Involvement in South Africa meant that Britain could spare only a handful of troops to take part in the relief of the Peking legations during the Boxer risings. And, on June 12th, 1900, the German *Reichstag* voted the second navy law in three years, providing for the construction of a fleet of 38 battleships over the next two decades. The vote was taken amidst a storm of anti-British oratory and press comment following on British interception of the German mailship S S *Bundesrath* on suspicion of carrying contraband to the Boer republic in January 1900.

Since the early 1890s, the Kaiser's advisers on foreign affairs had been conducting a foreign policy which, being embarrassed by the difficulty of choice between the various colonial contestants and restrained by the Franco-Russian alliance, had given Germany various small colonial prizes, but had gained her nothing of importance. But more significant was the lack of any real thought among the Kaiser's advisers on what Germany's objectives should be. By 1895, Germany had sacrificed any chance of a large colonial empire in Africa by the agreements of 1890, 1893 and 1894 which delimited the frontiers of her African colonies so as to cut them off from the still-unclaimed interior of the continent. The agreement with Britain of August 30th, 1898, on the reversion of the Portuguese colonies in the event of a break-up of Portugal, briefly promised the chance of more colonial expansion. But the next year Britain concluded a direct agreement with Portugal which secured that small state from the dangers which had seemed to threaten it. Once again the Germans found themselves in the cold. The *condominium* with the United States in Samoa which Germany extracted from the agreement with Britain of November 1899 was hardly adequate compensation.

Germany's aims had to be European, since the balance of power was tilted against her by the Franco-Russian alliance. This implied one or two alternative courses, either the attraction of Britain to the side of the Triple Alliance, or the offer of a German alliance to France and Russia against Britain, in return for a formal French recognition of the loss of Alsace-Lorraine.

But the unfortunate truth was that to attract Britain to the side of the Triple Alliance meant Germany had to be willing to fight Britain's battles against Tsarist Russia; while to join France and Russia against Britain was to offer France a strength she did not need, in return for Alsace-Lorraine which she could not abandon.

Thus when British statesmen approached Germany for an alliance as they did in 1897, in 1899 and again in 1901, the negotiations failed essentially for want of any real meeting of minds and interests. On the other hand, when Germany made gestures designed to convince France and Russia of their mutual hostility to Britain, as for example in the dispatch of a congratulatory telegram to President Kruger, the Boer leader, after the collapse of the Jameson raid, the effect was to exacerbate British feelings without making any real impression on France or Russia. Nor were British statesmen thoroughly convinced Germany had anything to offer. As Lord Salisbury commented in 1901: 'It would be hardly wise to incur novel and onerous obligations to guard against a danger (that of isolation) in whose existence we have no historical basis for believing.' The point had already been made in 1897 when the British reply to the German telegram to Kruger had been to mobilize a 'flying squadron', a move which made any talk of German intervention in Africa seem stupid.

It was hardly surprising, therefore, that the Kaiser's advisers should have concluded that only a large fleet could improve the German position, one big enough to make it too risky for Britain to challenge Germany and at the same time make it worthwhile for France or Russia to offer concessions to secure either Germany's neutrality or its support in the event of their finding themselves at war with Britain. Thus, successive German Navy Laws in 1897 and 1900 projected a force divided into three fleets, Home, Foreign and Reserve, comprising no fewer than 38 battleships, 14 large cruisers and 38 small cruisers to be built by 1920. Between 1900 and 1905, 12 battleships were laid down, and 14 launched.

The creation of a large German navy, when taken with the pre-eminence of the German army in Europe, could not but be taken in Britain as a direct threat to British security. And the British Admiralty, in fact, began quiet preparations to build up to a three-power standard, and to shift the principal home fleet bases from the English Channel to the North Sea coast where they could guard against Germany. The most dangerous situations, however, were in China and Persia where events were getting out of control. In Persia, the Russians secured in 1900 a virtual monopoly of all Persia's foreign loans for ten years. There was also talk of a Russian-Persian railroad with a terminal on the Gulf, and Russian ships actually appeared in the Persian Gulf itself. In China, the Russians used the excuse of the Boxer rising to send 100,000 troops into Manchuria and to use their position there to secure a monopolistic position in Manchuria, Mongolia and Central Asia, and railway concessions south of the Great Wall as a price for their withdrawal. Still worse by Japanese standards was the appearance of Russian ships at the South Korean port of Masampo, where they hoped again to set up a coaling station. The Tsar's entourage was coming to be increasingly dominated by a group of senior army commanders and concession-hunting adventurers, known as the 'Korean group'.

The British tried direct negotiations with the Russians and a new approach to the Germans, but both were in vain. They, therefore, took up the offer of an alliance made in the summer of 1901 by the Japanese. The signature of the Anglo-Japanese alliance on January 30th, 1902, struck the British as providing at last the diplomatic stop against Russia they had so long been seeking. Moreover, London felt it gave England control over Japanese policy, as it was believed to be impossible for Japan to defeat Russia in war, but not impossible that Japan's naval hotheads might involve Japan in a war in which Russia might well defeat her. The Germans took the signature of the alliance as indicating that Britain had broken from the policy of splendid isolation. In this they were mistaken. The signature of the Anglo-Japanese alliance marked not the ending of British isolation but its reinforcement; and a very welcome reinforcement it was to those whose nerves, unlike Salisbury's, were becoming a little strained. The British also gained confidence from the way in which Canadians and Australians had come to Britain's aid in South Africa and in the vision they derived of the new nations of the Empire reinvigorating Britain herself and lifting some of the burdens of imperialism from the shoulders of what Chamberlain in 1902 called 'the weary Titan'.

At the same time, the British felt impelled to settle matters in the western hemisphere, especially in relation to the outstanding issues connected with the Canadian frontier with Alaska and the question of the concession to build a canal through the isthmus of Panama. In the British approach to the United States, three elements were prominent. The first was a pan-Anglo-Saxonism which persisted in thinking of the United States as still being part of the colonial domains of Britain, and in putting its inhabitants, especially its *élite*, in the same category as the *élites* of the emergent Dominions, Canada, Australia or New Zealand, rather than in the category of aliens and foreigners. This sentiment, imperialist, jingoist, and essentially racialist, had been increased by a vicarious pride in America's display of strength and ruthlessness during the Spanish-American war. It made disputes with the United States of a different order entirely from those with European powers. Thus, President Cleveland's message to Congress over Venezuela struck British opinion as surprising but not outrageous; whereas the Kaiser's telegram to President Kruger struck that same opinion as outrageous but hardly surprising.

A second element in the British decision to reach a *modus vivendi* with the United States was a cold military calculation of the same type which had impelled the British government to attempt to settle its differences with Russia in the Far East. The Admiralty's view was that Britain could probably defeat the United States in war, but that such a war would bring with it a dangerous weakening of Britain's position *vis-à-vis* Europe. In fact, the Admiralty, as part of its advance preparations against the development of German sea-power, was gradually weakening the West Indies squadrons. The Government's advisers had no desire to suffer from a revival of the Continental League of the War of the American Revolution. Third, the issues involved with the United States were comparatively unimportant for Britain (though not for Canada).

The United States was already flexing its own muscles. In the Presidential election of 1900, the Democratic-Populist candidate, William Jennings Bryan, was defeated by the incumbent President McKinley, in a straight fight over imperialism. In March 1901, the United States Senate, under the Platt amendment, agreed to an American withdrawal from Cuba on terms which turned Cuba virtually into an American protectorate. In September 1901, President McKinley was assassinated by an anarchist and Theodore Roosevelt (for all his Americanism, the most European of American presidents save only John Kennedy) succeeded him. In December 1901, the Senate ratified a very much revised Hey-Paunceforte Treaty between Britain and the United States. The treaty called for American construction of a canal through the Isthmus of Panama, and at the same time abrogated an agreement of the 1850s which provided that any such canal should be run jointly, and be left unfortified. In November 1903, losing patience over Colombian delaying tactics, Roosevelt assisted a revolt of the isthmian part of Colombia, and set up the Republic of Panama, in what must have been one of the most flagrant examples of imperialist intervention in this century.

Roosevelt's leadership in foreign affairs was established in what was to become a twentieth-century tradition of diplomacy by rhetoric and well-publicized gesture. But behind this rhetoric was a careful appreciation of the balance of strength and the need for quiet negotiation. And he was to display this combination of *fortiter in modo, suaviter in re* (of violence in rhetoric and caution in action) in his domestic policy, as he was also to demonstrate his dislike of being coerced. This aversion to being coerced was illustrated by his reaction to the miners' strikes of 1902, and in his revival of the anti-trust legislation of the 1890s in prosecuting the Harriman railway empire in the Northern Securities case of 1902. In his more general approach to the problems of the United States he was at this stage so cautious, that an American historian has written of him 'the straddle was built, like functional furniture, into his thinking'. But his indecisiveness reflected that of American opinion generally, unable to decide whether the massive concentration of economic power into trusts or controls was bad in itself, or merely abominable when misused.

Roosevelt was, however, an excellent associate for Britain, even if his behaviour in appointing politicians rather than legal assessors to the commission of arbitration set up in 1903 to settle the disputed Alaskan-Canadian border was regarded as rather sharp practice. Britain needed a strong friend. This need was the more apparent as the Conservative leadership in Britain, the senior military and naval advisers and the inner circle of informed lay opinion began to reflect on the appalling revelations of British military incompetence and of the politician's ignorance of military matters experienced during the South African war. The outcome of the Esher commission set up to investigate and report to the Cabinet on the lessons of the South African war was the foundation in 1904 of the Committee of Imperial Defence, in which civilian political and military personages were united with the responsibility of overseeing Britain's readiness to meet force with force and of maintaining a balance between Britain's foreign policy and her military strength. A parallel search for the improvement of the nation's efficiency underlay in part the great Education Act of December, 1902, which marked not only the nationalization of Britain's primary education system, but the invasion by the state of the field of secondary education.

The failure of the negotiations for an Anglo-German agreement, the Anglo-Japanese alliance and the limited Anglo-American *détente* all increased Britain's freedom of action and marked the defeat of the German hope that Britain would eventually come to Germany cap in hand. But their combined effect on the diplomatic balance was less than that of the virtual defection of Italy from the Triple Alliance, thus weakening the other two signatories, Germany and Austria. The causes of Italy's defection were part diplomatic, part internal, but there can be no doubt that, of the two, internal weakness was the more important. This weakness stemmed from the Italian failure to carry through an economic and social re-organization of Italy to correspond with the political re-organization involved in unification. Its effects were, on the one hand, to give politically conscious Italians an unrealistic conviction of the importance of Italy on the world scene, a conviction which rested essentially on a fiery national egotism that made no real calculation of strength. Its other effect was to accentuate the poverty of the Italian south and Sicily. In the mid-1890s, the two strands came together. Strikes and minor agrarian risings in Sicily caused the dispatch of 50,000 troops, the proclamation of martial law and a state of siege. Crispi, premier and strong man, pushed the interpretation of a treaty with Abyssinia to claim an Italian protectorate and drove the Italian commander in Eritrea, under charges of lack of initiative, into a rash and ill-considered advance into Abyssinia, which ended in the disaster of Adowa. Eight thousand dead and five hundred million lire spent, and nothing to show for it, caused Crispi's downfall, but the social disorders in Italy increased and multiplied. By 1898, order was only being maintained in Italy's main cities by the use of the

my and martial law. Eighty people were killed in Milan in
May 1898, when the army turned cannon and grape-shot against
the crowd. In 1900, the Left and the Left Centre in the Italian
parliament walked out rather than vote the government quasi-
despotic powers. The same year the King himself was assassinated by an Italian anarchist.

This internal weakness was complemented by a similar weakness in Italy's external position. The defeat of Adowa at the
hands of the 'savages' meant that Britain no longer needed
Italian support. Without Britain, Italy was isolated and the
Triple Alliance useless to her as a means of resisting French
pressure. After 1894, the French position in the Mediterranean
had been much strengthened by the alliance with Russia. And
unable to stand off French pressure, Italy felt herself obliged, in
1896 and 1898, to recognize France's position in Tunis, and end
the ten-year tariff war with France. In 1900, an agreement was
reached on the French interest in Morocco, and Italy's ambitions
in Tripoli. In 1902, the Triple Alliance was renewed, but five
months later, on November 1st, 1903, a secret note to France
reassured the French government that Italy would remain
neutral in any war in which France was involved. The Triple
Alliance was virtually at an end.

For France the Italian defection from the Triple Alliance
represented the accidental achievement of something which ten
years earlier would have represented a major gain. But at least
since the death in 1894 of the Sultan, Mouley Hassan, who was
the last strong ruler in Moroccan history, French eyes had been
turned on the idea of rounding off their North and West African
possessions by obtaining a protectorate over Morocco. After the
humiliation of Fashoda, the acquisition of Morocco as compensation for the loss of Egypt became the main aim of French
foreign policy. The experience of Fashoda made it seem essential
to the new French foreign minister, Delcassé, to make the
diplomatic preparation for a move against Morocco as thorough
and meticulous as possible. Thus, when the time came for
French action, France would have the equivalent of a mandate
from the majority of the interested European powers. These
powers included Italy, Spain, Germany, and Britain. Of the
four, Britain was the most important, since the young Sultan
leaned heavily on British advisers. There were also considerable
British economic interests in Morocco, and local British influence

was being placed behind the idea of reforms in Morocco on lines
similar to those introduced into Egypt.

Delcassé's method was gradually to tackle the less important
of the powers concerned and to reach an understanding with
each of them until Britain could be dealt with in isolation. The
agreement with Italy was achieved on December 14th, 1900. At
the same time the French initiated approaches to Spain and
began to encroach from the south-east into the tribal areas of
Morocco which no Sultan had ever entirely succeeded in pacifying. In 1901, they secured an agreement with the Sultan on
French control of the police on the frontier with Algeria. In
1902, the tribes, incensed by the Sultan's well-meaning attempt
to introduce a European system of taxation, rose under a
pretender. That November, the French got as far as drawing up
a draft agreement with Spain, but found themselves stymied by
a Spanish refusal to sign unless their own international situation
was improved either by their admission to the Franco-Russian
alliance or by a British guarantee of Spain's Moroccan claims.
So far as Germany was concerned, German spokesmen repeatedly declared that her interests in Morocco were trifling and
insignificant. Germany seemed more interested in the Russian-
English confrontation in the Far East, and at one time negotiating
with Britain for an agreement on a projected railway to Baghdad
from Constantinople, and at another approaching Russia with an
offer of aid against Britain.

The approach of a seemingly inevitable clash between Britain
and France's ally, Russia, in the Far East and in Persia added
urgency to the French schemes. The outcome of the Boer war
had done nothing to abate the hatred for Britain dominant among
the Tsarist administration. Its members were still preoccupied
with Manchuria and Korea, and with their desire for a warm-
water port on the Persian Gulf. Within the Russian administration the conflict raged between Count Witte, the Minister of
Finance, who favoured a policy of peaceful penetration of China
by diplomatic and financial methods, and the Ministries of War
and the Interior who thought in more militant terms. In 1902, a
new element was added to their internal struggle. An aristocratic
adventurer, an officer in the Tsarist guards, Bezobrazov by name,
had captured the Tsar's mind in 1898 with a scheme for exploiting the timber resources of the Yalu river valley which
divided Korea from Manchuria. A concession had been obtained

from the Korean court in 1899. However, during that same year, Witte and Lobanov, acting for the Tsar's Foreign Ministry, had succeeded in burying Bezobrazov's Yalu scheme, while substituting a plan calling for the penetration of China proper by economic means.

Since 1900, however, Witte's own position with the Tsar had been growing steadily weaker. The Ministries of War and the Navy despised the commercial nature of his imperialism and hankered after more direct methods. They were able to argue, too, with some effect, that this was a game at which Russia was always grotesquely handicapped in contrast with Britain. The Boxer uprisings had enabled them to convert the Tsar to the more direct policy of force and the occupation of Manchuria. But again Witte and the Foreign Ministry were able to argue that to provoke a conflict with Britain and/or Japan would be unnecessary folly as long as the double-tracking of the Trans-Siberian railway was not completed. The Alexeiev-Tseng agreement of November 1900 on Manchuria, which restored its administration to China in return for extensive concessions to Russia in the matter of railways, represented a victory for their school. But Russia found herself under continuous diplomatic pressure from Japan and Britain to withdraw her troops from Manchuria.

Such pressure defeated its own purposes. The Alexeiev-Tseng treaty was followed by the negotiation of a draft Russo-Chinese agreement reflecting the demands of the Russian military, providing for the retention of the Russian forces in Manchuria indefinitely, and granting a monopoly of concessions in Manchuria to Russia in direct contravention of the doctrine of the 'Open Door' principle propounded in 1900 by the American government. At the same time came the Russian naval attempt to seize a base at Masampo on the tip of the Korean peninsula, a move which led to a direct Japanese naval demonstration and a Russian withdrawal. The European crushing of the Boxer rebellion, and the humiliating terms demanded by the European powers for the indemnity, had made the Chinese authorities anxious to do anything to evade too great a surrender to the 'barbarians'; they, therefore, took advantage of the Japanese intervention to publish the draft of their second agreement with Russia, and to plead Japanese pressure as a measure of avoiding the necessity of accepting it. There followed direct negotiation between Japan and Russia, in which the Japanese, conscious of their own weakness *vis-à-vis* Russia, proposed a division of Korea into spheres of influence and the application of the 'Open Door' principle to Manchuria, in effect its neutralization between Russia and Japan.

The Japanese intervention and the rejection of the draft Russo-Chinese agreement represented a defeat for Witte and his policy, and was followed by a marked revival of Bezobrazov's influence. A temporary coalition of the three Ministries of Finance, Foreign Affairs and War, of Witte, Lamsdorff and General Kuropatkin, held him in check long enough to secure the signature, in April 1902, of a second Russo-Chinese agreement which provided for the evacuation of Manchuria in three six-month stages. But the succession of shifts and compromises to which Japanese pressure was driving the Russian ministers was beginning to grate on the nerves of the Tsar and his military advisers. Bezobrazov succeeded in capturing the support of Admiral Alexeiev, the principal naval adviser, for a hare-brained scheme to use the existing forestry concessions on the Yalu river as a screen for a Russian military advance into Korea, the Russian troops being disguised as foresters. In November 1902, Admiral Alexeiev was dispatched to the Far East to develop the scheme. In the meantime, although the first stage of the Russian evacuation of Manchuria was completed on schedule, no attempt was made to put the second into operation, and by April 1903 it was clear that the Russians were in breach of the 1902 Agreement.

The Russian government had not in fact abandoned their ultimate intention to evacuate Manchuria. They now advanced seven further conditions for the continuation of evacuation, conditions which would have established a Russian commercial primacy, if not a virtual commercial protectorate over Manchuria. Much to Russia's surprise, the Chinese rejected these conditions as the result of Japanese and American pressure. This rejection, when coupled with the increase in peasant disorders in Russia, the growing strength of the Russian liberal constitutional movement and the increasing activity of the Social Revolutionary terrorist wing, greatly weakened Witte's position. The Tsar felt increasingly oppressed by the various challenges to the absolute exercise of his powers. At the same time he was being seduced by the vision of a new Tsarist empire in the East, an Asian empire, which would emphasize Russia's rejection of Europe. In these views he was greatly encouraged by the Kaiser, and by those advisers who felt, like Count Plehve, the Minister of the Interior, that Russia needed a 'little victory now to stop the revolutionary tide'. A Japanese proposal in July for direct negotiations was therefore left unanswered for three months.

The turning point came in August 1903, when Admiral Alexeiev was appointed Viceroy in the Far East and Count Witte was dismissed and ordered to hand over control of the railways in the Far East including the Chinese Eastern Railway, to Bezobrazov. In September, a special committee for Far Eastern affairs was set up and General Kuropatkin joined the 'Koreans'. After all, they argued, the South African war had revealed the military weakness of Britain, and the Japanese were beneath contempt. A regiment of Tsarist cavalry could sweep the Japanese army aside. Even the belated collapse of Bezobrazov's financial schemes and his flight to Switzerland could not disturb their determination to descend upon Korea, consolidate the Russian position in northern China and put an end to Britain's humiliating obstruction of their plans.

The French, appreciating the urgency of the situation, did what they could. In July 1903, therefore, direct conversations were opened with Britain, after a much publicized and highly successful visit by King Edward VII to Paris. Pressure on Britain's exposed nerves in Egypt proved an infallible weapon in securing British concessions in Morocco, although final recognition of Britain's position in Egypt was a difficult pill for the French to swallow. The Anglo-French *Entente* was duly signed on April 8th, 1904.

It was, in essence, a settlement of differences between the two powers, of a sort Britain had often attempted to get but had hitherto failed to secure for want of an equal will on the side of the French. It was secured at a sacrifice of British interests in Morocco and a recognition of the impending Franco-Spanish agreement, actually concluded in October 1904, on the eventual partition of Morocco. In return, Britain secured French support for her position in Egypt and her schemes for a reform of Egyptian finance and administration. And a number of minor disputes on Madagascar, Siam and the New Hebrides were adjusted. It was the kind of settlement Britain had desired for years as a diplomatic way to end the pressure from both ends of the Franco-Russian alliance. It was Germany who turned the *Entente* into an alliance directed against herself.

By 1900, the Kaiser's advisers were beginning to be a little impatient with the failure of the policy of the free hand to show any results. The concessions wrung from Britain in the colonial sphere represented only a minor gain when compared with Britain's decreasing need of Germany and refusal to get involved in a continental alliance except on terms which would have benefited Britain but involved Germany directly with Russia. And every German attempt to secure a continental league with France against Britain broke down for lack of any real gain to France from such an alliance. The French defeat at Fashoda and the obvious approach of conflict in the Far East turned German attention to Russia, and between 1897 and 1903 there were a number of German attempts to get an agreement with Russia; but again the Germans wanted the one thing the Russians could not concede, either Russian abandonment of her alliance with France or pressure on France finally to abandon her claims on Alsace-Lorraine. In the meantime, the Germans were careful not to alienate either of the two partners in the alliance. France was given a free hand in Morocco and Germany was careful not to become involved in the attempts and rivalries of Britain, Russia and Austria over the reform of the Turkish administration of Macedonia. Germany had an added inducement to keep out of the Macedonian problem in that, since 1897, she was beginning to win a favourable position within the Ottoman Empire itself. In October 1898, the Kaiser had toured the Empire from Constantinople to Jerusalem and had proclaimed his affinity for Islam. The following year German interests had secured the initial concessions on the Berlin to Baghdad railway, and German banks were moving into the Ottoman Empire.

The signature of the Anglo-Japanese alliance in 1902 was therefore welcomed in Berlin, as a sign that German policy was on the right track. There would soon be a direct conflict between Russia and Britain, both would turn to Germany for support and Germany would then be able to make her own terms.

Chapter 7

The Diplomatic Revolution. Stage II: The Weakening of the Franco-Russian Alliance, 1904–6

THE signature of the Anglo-French *Entente* marked, though its signatories would have denied this, the first great step in the realignment of Europe. But in itself it was only a partial step, and by itself it contained a contradiction, since it left France united with two powers, Britain and Russia, who were virtually at war with one another, in Central Asia and the Far East. The victory of the Korean school in Russia made a clash between Japan and Russia seem virtually inevitable. The prospect of such a war was viewed with barely disguised alarm in Britain and the United States, who together shared the universal conviction of Japan's inability to stand up to Russian military force. But their efforts to restrain the Japanese and to secure the conclusion of some kind of agreement were frustrated by the arrogance of the Russians and the Japanese capacity for rapid decision once negotiations had proved fruitless. The Russo-Japanese negotiations collapsed on February 5th, 1904. Five days later the Japanese fleet staged a surprise attack on the Russian squadron at Port Arthur.

The military odds in the Far East were heavily weighted in Japan's favour, once the universal illusion of Japanese military backwardness had been exposed. The Japanese Navy, officered and trained on the British model, was more than a match, both in morale and in the modernity of its vessels, for the Russians. The geographical position of Japan enabled it to control the Russian access to the open seas both from Vladivostok and from Port Arthur. The Russian Far Eastern squadron was easily bottled up in Port Arthur, once its flagship and commander had been blown up by a mine on April 13th. On land, the Japanese army disposed of some 270,000 men with the colours and some

200,000 more in reserve. The Russian forces in the Far East
numbered a mere 80,000 men, and their reinforcements from
European Russia were limited to 30,000 men a month by the
carrying capacity of the Trans-Siberian railway, whose double
tracking was not yet completed. The first engagement, at Kurak
on the Yalu river, in May 1904 resulted in a major victory for
Japan, the Russian armies losing over one-third of their effective
strength. A second Japanese victory at Liaoyang in August
isolated Port Arthur and drove the main Russian forces northwards in retreat to Mukden. In July 1904, Port Arthur was
surrounded, and a grisly war of siege, bombardment, mine and
counter-mine began to which there could only be one ending
unless a Russian relief force could break through.

In October 1904, the Russians took the decisive step of dis-
patching their Baltic fleet on a long and, as it transpired, disastrous voyage to the Far East. Before the Baltic fleet could reach
the scene of action, Port Arthur surrendered in January 1905.
In February and March, the long and desperately fought battle
of Mukden, with over 300,000 men engaged on each side,
resulted in a further Russian defeat and withdrawal. And on
May 27th, 1905, the Russian Fleet, tired, disorganized, and
demoralized by its long voyage round the world, met the flower
of the Japanese Navy under Admiral Togo in the Tsushima
Straits, and was obliterated. For the first time since the sixteenth
century a European power had been decisively defeated in war
by an Asiatic. Not that the Russian commanders in the field
accepted this. Russian reserves were still filtering along the
Trans-Siberian railway, and Japan's resources both in manpower
and money were being steadily exhausted. But at home, in
European Russia, the steady succession of defeats had destroyed
whatever credit the decaying Tsardom possessed, and revolution
was in full swing. The Tsar was driven to accept an American
offer of mediation made in June 1905, and Russian and Japanese
emissaries met thereafter under American supervision in
Portsmouth, New Hampshire.

The task of making the two combatants accept a reasonable
settlement was not an easy one. The Japanese, flushed by victory,
were inclined to push their claims beyond what Russian opinion
could be brought to accept or Britain and America to condone.
Neither of the two latter powers wished to exchange the threat
of a Japanese hegemony in Asia for that of Russia. Britain's

effectiveness was reduced by her anxiety that Russia, defeated in the Far East, would recoil on to India and Persia, where revolution was imminent. Britain's statesmen saw themselves impelled to re-negotiate the alliance with Japan, hitherto conceived of as being confined to the Far East; moreover, it only came into operation if a second non-signatory intervened in a war in which one of the signatories was engaged, so as to cover a Russian attack on India. The spectre of an Anglo-German war had begun to form on the horizon, and the British were concerned with the threat of a Russo-German alignment or of a Russian exploitation of Britain's increasing preoccupation with the balance of naval and military power in Europe. The growth of German naval power was beginning to necessitate a concentration of the Royal Navy in European waters. At the same time the Japanese victory had fired the Japanese with the idea of establishing direct control over Korea where the United States had certain entrenched rights and interests and raised the dangerous possibility of conflict between Japan and America.

The deadlock was broken by two moves. In July 1905, Roosevelt's Secretary of War, William Howard Taft, visited Japan, which then agreed that its suzerainty over Korea would directly contribute to the maintenance of peace in the Far East. In return, the Japanese declared that they had no designs on the Philippines. The Japanese also gave Britain assurances that they had no plans which would bring them into conflict with the United States and that the Alliance would not operate in the event of a conflict with the United States, arising out of a violation of the latter's rights in Korea. On August 12th, 1905, the Anglo-Japanese Alliance was formally renewed, and Britain was free to turn her attention to Europe.

The task of getting the Japanese to see reason over the exaction of a large indemnity from Russia was more difficult. For a time, Britain acted as a go-between, but President Roosevelt's personal impatience with the British ambassador in Washington led to a break between London and Washington. Instead Roosevelt exerted direct financial pressure on Tokyo by withholding action on Japanese requests for a loan, desperately needed to repair the country's financial exhaustion by the war. As a result of this pressure, the Japanese demand for an indemnity was withdrawn, and on September 5th, 1905, the Treaty of Portsmouth was signed. Southern Sakhalin and the Liaotung peninsula were added to Japan. Korea was identified as being within the Japanese sphere of influence despite Korean protests. And the Russians undertook to evacuate Manchuria.

The Treaty represented a major success for President Roosevelt. At no real cost to America, and in a position where American opinion would certainly have made the use of American force virtually impossible, he had secured the establishment of a balance of force between Japan and Russia which thwarted the previous attempts of both powers to establish commercial monopoly and political domination in the Far East. What he had not guarded against and what the future was to hold was a combination of the two powers to exploit Manchuria and north eastern Asia, one in which Britain's increasing preoccupation with the balance of power between France and Germany in Europe would force her to acquiesce, and which diplomatic pressure from America alone would be inadequate to prevent.

The effects of the Japanese defeat of Russia were far-reaching throughout the Asiatic world. In China, the Japanese victory confirmed the reformers in their pressure to modernize the empire, and the revolutionaries in their determination to overthrow it and purge China of the alien, Manchu, dynasty. Steps were already under way to modernize the Chinese army, and two of China's future leaders, Yuan Shih-kai and Hsu Shih-ch'ang, were engaged in building up an *élite* force of six divisions called the Peiyang army. Major efforts were undertaken to modernize the Chinese educational system. The classical examination system was abolished in 1905, and command of the 'new learning' became the essential to advancement within the bureaucracy. Increasing numbers of Chinese students were going abroad to Japan, Europe, and the United States, to study. These students developed various movements aimed at transforming the empire into a constitutional monarchy, the erection of a republic and the destruction of the system of land-ownership from which Chinese conservatism drew so much of its strength. In 1905, Sun Yat-sen, a political *emigré*, organized the Alliance Society (T'ung Men Hui) among the Chinese community in Tokyo. Its fourfold aim was to overthrow the Manchu dynasty, restore a Chinese national state, establish a republic, and equalize the system of land ownership. But the effect of these developments was to lie in the future. Far more serious for the balance of power in Europe was the outcome of the internal revolution in

Russia and the development of a direct Franco-German confrontation in the first Moroccan crisis of 1905–6.

One of the pressures under which the Tsardom had laboured before the outbreak of the Russo-Japanese war and which had contributed to its intransigence was a constant and continuous current of dissatisfaction with the Tsarist system as such. Tsardom was viewed as being incompetent, inefficient and above all unenlightened. The factors and events which had brought Russia to a situation where the least false step would entirely destroy the Tsardom's credit in the eyes of the Russian people included: its inability to deal with the causes of peasant unrest, or to suppress effectively the widespread peasant disturbances of 1902–3; the constant threat of Social Revolutionary terrorism culminating in the assassination of the repressive Minister of the Interior, Count Plehve, in July 1904; the overthrow of Count Witte, and the snub to the aspirations of the increasingly wealthy industrialist and commercial classes of St Petersburg, Moscow and South Russia; the senseless nationalist repression of the minority nationalities of Finland, Georgia and the German Baltic, and the fresh outbreaks of anti-Semitism embodied in the Kushynov and Crimea pogroms of 1903; some forty-five Jews were killed, which was small-scale by Nazi standards, but frightening in 1900, when a state's total abandonment of a section of its citizenry to the baser passions and hatreds in man's breast was considered alien and revolting.

The assassination of Count Plehve had already led to a marked loss of Tsarist courage. Censorship was relaxed, state workmen's insurance on the German model was introduced and the Zemstvas' jurisdiction was enlarged. But all this was not sufficient. In November 1904, a great congress of Zemstva representatives in St Petersburg demanded the convocation of a representative assembly and the granting of civil liberties. Pressure was building up and with it the nerves of the police and repressive forces in the Tsardom were stretched taut. On January 22nd, 1905, the so-called 'police' trade unions got out of hand. These unions were founded with the secret acquiescence of the Ministry of the Interior as a means of limiting the threat from the trades union movement, and at the same time preventing their employers, the industrialist class, from turning against the state. In January, the St Petersburg union, led by Father Gapon, a priest in police pay, was permitted to demonstrate against the rising price of food brought about by the inflation caused by the war with Japan. Troops sent to keep order panicked and fired on the crowd, wounding or killing over three hundred people. Protest strikes spread in all the big cities. A month later the Tsar's uncle, the Grand Duke Sergei, was assassinated by a Socialist Revolutionary.

In March 1905, under the continuing stress of defeat in the Far East, the Tsar announced his intention of constituting a 'consultative' assembly. Various concessions were made to the minority nationalities, especially to the Jews and Poles. But the Tsar still dragged his feet on reforms and such concessions as he made could only be interpreted by Russian opinion as the occasion for more pressure. In May, Prince Miliukov brought together all strands of liberal aristocratic and *bourgeois* opinion into the 'Union of Unions' with a programme calling for universal suffrage and a Russian parliament. In the meantime, strikes and insurrections multiplied throughout Russia. In Finland, a nation-wide general strike paralysed the Russian administration. A full-scale revolt broke out in Georgia. Peasant disturbanecs spread throughout the Ukraine, White Russia and the Baltic in a curiously similar pattern, which seemed to indicate Social Revolutionary influence. The crew of the battleship *Potemkin*, stationed at Odessa, mutinied. In August, the Tsar recalled Count Witte to office and published a manifesto creating a national assembly with deliberative powers only and elected by a rigidly limited property franchise, but this move failed entirely to stem the upsurge of revolutionary activities. In October, a nation-wide general strike and the setting up of the first Soviet, a council of workers which claimed sovereign powers, in St Petersburg paralysed the government and forced the Tsar to yield. The 'October Manifesto', issued over the Tsar's signature on October 30th, appointed Count Witte prime minister, and set up a Russian parliament, the Duma, to be elected on a wide franchise and with real if limited legislative power (very far-reaching powers, it developed, were to be reserved for the Tsar).

The effects of the October Manifesto when coupled with the breakdown in economic activity produced two conflicting groups. On the one hand, there were the liberals and, on the other, the more conservative elements drawn from the aristocracy, the gentry and the *bourgeoisie*. Two parties emerged from Miliukov's Union of Unions, the more conservative Octobrists and the Liberal

Constitutional Democrats or Cadets who still pressed for a constituent assembly. The Social Democrats and the St Petersburg Soviet, led by Trotsky, rejected the October Manifesto as a whole and fought back with strikes and an insurrection in Moscow. On December 16th, the entire St Petersburg Soviet were arrested. In the meantime, Witte floated a new foreign loan of about $400 millions, so that the government would not have to depend upon the Duma for funds. With this loan Count Witte had outlived his usefulness and the Tsar dismissed him in May 1906, shortly before the first meeting of the Duma.

Four days before the Duma met, Nicholas II promulgated the so-called Fundamental Laws, which proclaimed the Tsar to be the supreme autocrat and which permitted him to resume complete control over the armed forces, foreign affairs and the executive branches of the government. An upper house was created, half of whose members were to represent various corporate bodies throughout the country, half to be appointed by the Tsar. The elections to the lower house of the Duma had made the Cadets the largest party, with 179 out of 497 seats, but their hopes that the setting up of the Duma would lead to the adoption by Russia of a genuine parliamentary system of government had been bitterly disappointed. They devoted most of their time to criticizing the government and on July 21st the new Prime Minister, Peter Stolypin, dissolved the Duma and arrested several of the Cadet leaders. The remainder adjourned to Viburg in Finland, which, though part of the Tsar's empire, was not strictly under Russian jurisdiction. There, they issued a manifesto calling on the Russian people to refuse to pay taxes. But their appeal fell largely on deaf ears. The effects of the peasant and working-class risings of 1905–6 had only frightened the bulk of the *bourgeoisie* who again supported the Tsarist state. In the countryside, the more right wing among the gentry had organized their own strong-arm groups, the so-called Black Hundreds, against peasant disturbances. Stolypin was left to clean up the mess.

Meanwhile, the outbreak of the Russo-Japanese war roused the German government once more to hopes of an Anglo-Russian confrontation. It was not long in coming. In October 1904, the Russian Baltic fleet, while passing through the North Sea, mistook a group of English trawlers off the Dogger Bank for Japanese torpedo-boats and fired on them, sinking one of the trawlers. The Germans immediately offered the Russians a draft treaty of alliance against attack by a European power. The Russians accepted this alliance in principle but refused to sign before they had consulted with their French allies. The Germans refused this demand. They also turned down a Russian attempt to secure German aid against Japan which would have brought the Anglo-Japanese alliance into action. This attempt broke down on the German conviction that Britain was only waiting for an opportunity for a pre-emptive strike against the German fleet. Once again the Germans found themselves confronted with what was to be their dilemma until 1907; there was nothing they could secure from the colonial powers of Britain, France and Russia which would compensate them for the fact that in any colonial war Germany would have to fight on her land and maritime frontiers. The Germans returned to the charge in July 1905 when the Kaiser met the Tsar at Björkö in the northern Baltic. But the Tsar had second thoughts on his return to St Petersburg and repudiated the draft agreed on at Björkö, thus bringing to nothing yet another German scheme for a triple alliance against Britain (in which the Germans had even briefly hoped to enlist the United States).

The weakness of Russia revealed by the Russo-Japanese war and the 1905 revolution left France desperately exposed to German pressure. The Third Republic was still a long way from recovering from the strains of the Dreyfus affair. The Dreyfusards, Radical, Radical Socialists, Independent Socialists, supporters of the Republic, had been shaken by the strength of political Catholicism revealed in the French officer corps. But this had been nothing compared with the hostility aroused in republican circles by the activities of the religious orders which had sprung to the support of the Army in its battle with the Republic. The Waldeck-Rousseau government of 1900–2 had taken the initiative in legislation for the protection of the Republic against these religious orders. Waldeck-Rousseau himself had wanted all associations to be registered and supervised by the state. But he had been overruled by the radical anticlericals and the law of July 1901 had required special legislation by the French parliament to authorize the formation of any religious order in France. And the attempt by the existing orders, the 'congregations' as they were called, to fight the 1902 elections on the basis of reversing this legislation resulted in a last resounding defeat for the French Catholic right. Waldeck-Rousseau resigned in June 1902 before the new Chamber met and was replaced by Emile Combes.

Combes applied the Law of Association against the congregations with extreme rigour. More than this, in 1904, the new Pope, Pius X, chose the occasion of an official visit by President Loubet to Rome to protest to the European powers that such a visit was an offence to Papal dignity. As a result, the majority in parliament created by the 1902 elections turned even against the Catholic church as such, and a bill was introduced ending all connexion between the French state and the church, including appointments and payments of salaries, and transferring control of all church property to special private corporations at the parish level. But before this law could be enacted, the parallel attempt to purge the Army backfired. General André, Republican Minister of War since 1900, had turned to the Masonic lodges for information on the political sympathies of the officer corps as a means of producing a General Staff loyal to the Republic. In the process, he had built up a system of spying and witch-hunting which shocked France when it was exposed. The Combes government fell in January 1905, to be replaced by one under Rouvier, and a new bill of separation had to be steered through the Assembly by the former Socialist, Aristide Briand. The law separating church and state was finally promulgated in December 1905. These developments did nothing to sweeten French political life, and the years 1900–5 saw a great upsurge in the political strength and effectiveness of the extreme French right, the *Action Française* and the *Camelots du Roi*, forerunners of Fascism with their virulent anti-Semitism, their violence in the streets and in Parliament, and their denigration of everything connected with the Republic.

The increasing bitterness of French political life made it the more important for successive Republican governments to avoid charges of incompetence and neglect of the national interest in their conduct of foreign affairs. Delcassé, French Foreign Minister since 1897, thought he had avoided such charges. Although Delcassé himself could never be described as a friend of Germany, a considerable section of the French republican left were, by and large, well disposed towards Germany. Many of their more *bourgeois* elements came from the *milieu* of French commerce and finance (as did Rouvier himself), which infinitely preferred combinations and consortia to conflict. Moreover, these same French financial groups were greatly interested in persuading Germany to let them take a share in financing the Baghdad railway. The French socialist left, united in one party in 1905 under the leadership of Jaurés, were equally anti-nationalist and inclined to trust the country which produced the largest Social Democrat party in the world. The general attitude of both groups to super-patriotism was reflected by the passage in 1904 of a bill reducing the period of service in the army to two years.

Ever since 1900, Delcassé had been preparing the ground for a French take-over in Morocco. After the conclusion of the Anglo-French *Entente* in April 1904, he had returned to his courtship of Spain, and in October of the same year had signed a secret convention which provided for the eventual partition of Morocco between the two countries, Spain taking part of the Mediterranean coast of the Sultanate. In January 1905, every-thing seemed ready. A French emissary was dispatched to Tangier to put before the Sultan a programme of reforms which would have given France a protectorate over Morocco.

It was at this stage that the German government chose to intervene. What seems to have irked the Kaiser's advisers was a feeling that here was yet another colonial division which would give them no profit. The Germans also were alarmed by the closeness of Franco-Italian relations displayed in President Loubet's visit to Rome and angered by the failure of their first attempt to secure an alliance with Russia during the Dogger Bank crisis of October 1904. On March 31st, 1905, the German Kaiser disembarked from his yacht at Tangier. There he publicly asserted German interest in Morocco, insisted on the full inde-pendence of the Sultan of Morocco, and demanded an inter-national conference. Rouvier and Delcassé, concerned and touched at their most vulnerable point, attempted to buy off the Germans with assurances of France's willingness 'to dissipate any misunderstandings', but in vain. Delcassé tried to interest the French Cabinet in an alliance with Britain, a possibility which he professed to discover in British proposals for 'full and confidential discussions'. Again he failed and his resignation followed. But Delcassé's fall had no effect on German pressure on France, which continued unabated. French opinion, aroused at last, began to harden. Rouvier was forced to accept the demand for a conference. But the conclusion of the German-Russian treaty at Björkö on July 24th, which the Germans hoped would lead to a continental alliance, and the consequent German *volte-face*, the relaxation of pressure on France, and recognition of French 'special interests in Morocco' came too late. France set herself steadily against the Björkö Treaty and the Tsar was forced to abandon it.

The Conference itself met at Algeciras in January 1906. But by the time it gathered, Europe as a whole had taken a look at the prospect of a European war for the first time since the 1880s and had not liked it. No one wanted war less than the high command of the German Army. The Franco-Russian alliance faced them, in military terms, with a war on two fronts against numerically far superior forces. The only solution they had found to this military problem was the use of Germany's interior lines of communication, the speed of her mobilization and her excellent railway system to concentrate the bulk of their armies against one of their two enemies so as to knock her speedily out of the war. This done, the German armies could be reconcentrated against the surviving enemy. The slowness of Russian mobilization and the sheer distances involved before any major Russian cities could be reached by a German offensive in the East made France the obvious first target. The knock-out blow would have to be delivered in the first six weeks of war; otherwise, the Russian armies would be free to strike for East Prussia or Berlin. In the 1890s when this scheme was first elaborated, the German war plan called for a break-through at the southern end of the Franco-German frontier through the Belfort gap. But in 1905–6, in the aftermath of the Moroccan crisis, this plan was changed. The main weight of the German attack was now to be placed in the north and the southern flank would be deliberately weakened to draw the French armies away from the areas of German concentration. The French would be out-flanked and the road to Paris would be wide open. In military terms, the need to out-flank the French required that the great fortresses of the north, such as Verdun, would have to be circumvented. Military logic led to the conclusion that to be really effective the German offensive would have to go through Belgium. And the final orders so provided, embodying the Schlieffen plan, named after General von Schlieffen who drafted it.

The other power to be shaken by the Moroccan crisis was

Britain. The dismissal of Delcassé disgusted British opinion and alarmed it as to the state of French military strength and morale. The unprovoked nature and the intensity of the German pressure on France was added confirmation of Britain's own incipient anxieties over Germany. The growth of the German navy had continued unabated, and the Admiralty was steadily changing the worldwide dispositions of the British fleet to match this new threat. The design of the German battleships, with their heavy armour and short cruising range, struck naval observers in Britain as peculiarly suspicious. The naval display staged by the Germans in 1904 on Edward VII's state visit to Kiel caused an outbreak of anxious comment in the British press. In 1904, Admiral Fisher became First Sea Lord, and introduced sweeping reforms in naval organization. Even then Britain's military and naval authorities felt the balance of power all over the world swinging slowly against them.

The resignation of the Conservative government in Britain in December 1905 brought into office a Liberal cabinet, which represented an alliance between imperialism and social reform, with the latter element predominating. The general election of January 1906 which followed gave the Liberals a landslide majority and launched them on a programme of political and social reform which was to preoccupy the energies and interests of all but a few imperialists. The bulk of Liberal opinion was suspicious of France, violently hostile to Russia, once the wave of revolution had begun to subside, and friendly towards Germany. However, the handful of imperialists were able to use Britain's power to bolster the ailing position of France and to oppose the growing strength of Germany, without their cabinet colleagues really being aware of what was happening. The personality of the new Foreign Secretary, Sir Edward Grey, with his strong respect for international law and morality and his intense Francophile sentiments, was particularly important. His conservative predecessor, Lord Lansdowne, had been inclined to give the Germans the benefit of any doubt. Grey was not so inclined, and the first action he and his few imperialist colleagues undertook was to authorize the opening of military staff talks with France as a means of reassuring French morale against Germany. The Foreign Office were now preoccupied with the balance of power in western Europe in a way they had not been since the 1850s.

The steady withdrawal of British naval strength from the rest of the world was accompanied by a steady and on the whole welcome increase in American strength under Theodore Roosevelt and a willingness to use it on the world scene in a way utterly without precedent in American history. Roosevelt had begun by the consolidation of the American position in the Caribbean noted in an earlier chapter. Indeed, he became even more determined to resist further European encroachment in that area. The joint Anglo-German naval action in 1903 against Venezuela in the name of debt-collection proved particularly unwelcome. The threat of a similar situation in the Dominican Republic the following year led Roosevelt to formulate what came to be known as the 'Roosevelt corollary' to the Monroe Doctrine. Chronic violations of their international obligations by powers in the western hemisphere, he said, would compel the United States to intervene as the only alternative to a European intervention to enforce recognition of those obligations. Under this doctrine, US Marines were sent into the Dominican Republic in 1904, despite Congressional opposition, and the Customs administration of the Republic was taken over to service its international debts. Similar intervention was to follow in other countries in the Caribbean in the years to come.

On the domestic front, Theodore Roosevelt's strength was greatly enhanced by the 1904 Presidential elections which for the first time made him President in his own right with a majority of over two and a half million votes over his conservative Democratic rival, Judge Alton D. Parker. This victory gave him the confidence to move to embrace with greater enthusiasm the doctrines and policies of the Progressive movement. The anti-trust legislation was more strictly enforced, and the powers of government to regulate and inspect inter-state commerce were greatly increased, especially in the fields of railway rates, food and drugs. Also the first steps were taken to conserve American natural resources against the wasteful, inefficient rapacity of those who were exploiting them.

Roosevelt then was busy building an image of America which would be recognized by Europe as a strong and capable power. His rewards came in the manner in which European opinion accepted his intervention in the Russo-Japanese war and in the Moroccan crisis of 1905–6. Germany particularly went out of its way to secure his participation in the critical Moroccan situation. And it was American assurances of support against unreasonable demands which played a crucial part in persuading the French government in July 1905 to accept the proposal for an international conference. But the strength of Roosevelt's position in these years lay in his intelligent use of what was still disinterested isolationism. He could intervene in European problems and causes because of the combination of strength and non-involvement in his position, secured by the exclusion of European influence from the New World, the 'Roosevelt Corollary', his own personality and reputation and the size of the American navy, which by 1906 was the second largest in the world. So soon as the United States became drawn into international politics by its own actions or interests, to that extent America became vulnerable and her strength the more easily discounted. And the years 1904–5, in fact, mark the highest point American influence in Europe was to attain for a good ten years to come.

A noticeable feature of these years of Roosevelt's Presidency was the growth of the Progressive movement throughout the United States. Progressive machines were built up in state after state, paving the way for the great Progressive election of 1912. It seemed that America was following the example of Europe in building a Socialist party and a trades union movement which was made up of conservative craft unionists and a radical anarcho-syndicalist movement. As usual in American politics though, the similarities with European developments had significant differences. As noted in Chapter II above, the craft unions in the United States were conditioned by the flood of immigrants to restrict entry and unionize only those industries where casual labour was the exception rather than the rule. The masses in the large-scale industries, especially the miners, were left on their own. It is significant in this context that the one big union which represented the miners of the west, the Western Federation of Miners, formed in 1893, broke away from the American Federation of Labour in 1897 and changed its name in 1902 to the American Labour Union. In 1905, the American Labour Union formed the basis of the main American contribution to the anarcho-syndicalist movement, the International Workers of the World (the IWW), nicknamed the 'Wobblies'.

Despite its name, the only international element in the IWW was the ethnic origin of its members. Its only international action

was to spread across the 49th Parallel into Canada. Besides the
WFM, three other groups were represented in its formation;
the American Socialist Labour party of Daniel de Leon (1852–
1914), which from its formation in the 1890s opposed the AFL,
with its unionist wing, the Trade and Labour Alliance; Anarcho-
Syndicalists, mostly recent immigrants from Russia, followers of
Bakunin and Peter Kropotkin, their aim the destruction of all
government and its replacement by the communal organizations
of workers which they expected to spring up spontaneously in
its place; and, finally, emotional Socialists attracted by the
personality of the main Socialist Presidential candidate, Eugene
Debs. The main force in the IWW, however, was 'Big Bill'
Haywood of the Western Federation of Miners. His version of
syndicalism concentrated on industrial action as the most important, though not the only, weapon to achieve labour's aims
and he preached the formation of 'one big union', centrally-
directed and disciplined, to be the main planning agency for the
new proletarian society. But the main characteristic which
distinguished the IWW from the other branches of the labour
movement (from which both the WFM and de Leon broke away
in 1907–8) were its tactics which involved the mobilization and
concentration of union members wherever there was trouble.
Its main influence lay among its migrant miners, loggers and the
seamen of the middle and far west. It was to reach its greatest
strength in 1915.

The course of the diplomatic revolution of 1899–1906 had
resulted in a complete change in the alignments of the Great
Powers, an alignment which was rapidly approaching bi-polarity.
The old division at the centre between the Austro-German
alliance and France and Russia was confirmed by the course of
the Moroccan crisis and the failure of the German attempts to
seduce Russia and persuade France into a continental union.
Instead Russia, defeated in the Far East, was on the road to
settling the outstanding issues between herself and Britain and
her Japanese ally. The three oceanic powers, Britain, Japan, and
the United States, had achieved a temporary understanding with
one another. Britain had achieved a stronger understanding, one
which continued to approach the reality, if it avoided the
appearance, of an alliance with France. And France, in her turn,
had succeeded virtually in detaching their ally, Italy, from the
Central Powers and, by the making of the Mediterranean an

Anglo-French lake, still further confined German ambitions to the European mainland. The German action at Tangier had, in fact, ended the period of European pressure on the external world and marked the first real shot in a European civil war which in its turn was to make inevitable the decline of European power and the revival of the rest of the world.

The division of Europe into two major power groupings was to be accompanied by a further division, the gradual separation of the Scandinavian powers into what was eventually to become a neutralist, social democratic, anti-colonialist bloc north of the Baltic. The process was to be a long and devious one, which, for most of the decade before 1914, was in fact to bring Denmark and Sweden closer to Germany than to neutralism. It was initiated, however, by Norway, with the break of the Norway-Sweden Union in 1905. The two countries had been united under one crown, that of Sweden, in 1815, Norway retaining its own Parliament, the *Storting*, and armed forces, but with control of foreign policy, as a monarchical prerogative, being exercised by the Swedish foreign office. During the mid-nineteenth century, successive Swedish monarchs had considered creating a Scandinavian League of Neutrals, even of a union of Denmark with Norway-Sweden. Sweden had intervened in the first Schleswig-Holstein crisis in 1848 and had, in fact, formed in 1853 a League of Neutrals with Denmark during the preliminaries to the Crimean War. By a treaty of November 1855, France and Britain had guaranteed Norway-Sweden against Russian attack, and for good measure had included in the treaty which ended the Crimean War a clause demilitarizing the Aaland Islands. Thereafter, Sweden drifted away from this kind of pan-Scandinavianism, and indeed it was by repudiating rash promises made by Charles XV to Denmark in 1863 that the Swedish Council did away with direct monarchical rule and established itself as a proper Swedish cabinet. The unfortunate Danes were left alone to face Prussia and Austria in the war of 1864 over Schleswig-Holstein.

The essence of Scandinavianism was an attempt to take Scandinavia and the Baltic out of the clash of the Great Powers. Before German unification in 1871, the two Great Powers most concerned with the Baltic were Britain and Russia, and Scandinavianism represented a revulsion against Russian pressure. After the advent of Germany, the Swedish government began to move towards Germany and abandon the old connexions with Britain. In part, their actions reflected the internal struggle for power through which Norway and Sweden were now passing. In Norway, this struggle lay essentially between the large land-owners and the peasants, fishermen and *petit-bourgeois* of the towns who were united in the Liberal party. It was complicated by the Swedish issue, with the land-owners leaning more and more towards Sweden, their opponents experiencing the revival of a specifically Norwegian nationalism, expressed in the growth of a major Norse school of literature. This revival of Norwegian cultural nationalism included the playwrights Ibsen and Björnson, and the composer Grieg, and expressed itself in the revival of the local dialect, the *landsmaal*, which in 1884 was made equal with the Swedish language in the schools and in official usage. In 1884, the Swedish king was forced to accept the Liberals as the dominant party in Norway and appoint a Liberal cabinet which would be responsible to the Norwegian *Storting*.

Sweden had had her constitutional revolution in the 1860s when the Council had taken over the management of foreign affairs from Charles XV, and the old *Riksdag*, divided into four Estates, had been replaced by a bicameral legislature. But it had been a conservative revolution, carried through under conservative auspices, and the electorate for the new lower house was severely limited by the imposition of a property qualification. The revolution had serious consequences for the union with Norway. While the conduct of foreign affairs was the prerogative of the Crown, foreign policy could be represented as the affair of both countries. But now the conduct of foreign affairs was clearly in the hands of a Swedish ministry and cabinet. Conflict between the two countries inevitably developed, with the Norwegians, convinced that their widespread maritime and commercial interests were being neglected by the aristocrats of the Swedish foreign service, pressing for the introduction of a separate Norwegian consular service. Matters came to a crisis in 1895, and only the setting up of a Union Committee could postpone the inevitable clash.

An element in Norway's withdrawal was fear of Swedish military force. Between 1896–1904, the Norwegian cabinet bought four new ironclads and modern artillery, strengthened the voluntary rifle clubs which had come to form a substantial 'Black' army, and built fortifications to defend Oslo from

Swedish overland attack. In 1904, the negotiations on the Union Committee broke down. Norway announced the formation of its own consular service which was vetoed by the Swedish King. The Norwegian cabinet promptly resigned as a body, and the *Storting* passed two resolutions dissolving the union and declaring Norway to be an independent monarchy. The Swedish cabinet decided not to use force and approved Norwegian independence on September 23rd, 1905. The throne of Norway was offered to the Danish prince Charles, who accepted it, taking the title of Haakon VII after a plebiscite had confirmed his popular support.

The Norwegian action introduced a new element into an already complicated situation. The rise of German naval power had already upset the whole Anglo-Russian balance in the Baltic, and German policy joined that of Russia in wishing to exclude British influence permanently from the Baltic. As negotiations opened for a new international guarantee for Sweden and Norway, Sweden began to suspect that British influence had been behind Norway in the dissolution of the union. For a time, it seemed that Swedish suspicions played into German and Russian hands. A guarantee treaty for Norway was in fact signed, but the Swedes refused to have anything to do with it, maintaining that it was directed against them. For a time, the Germans hoped for a Baltic *entente* with Russia and Sweden which would exclude Britain completely from the Baltic, but a Russian attempt to write into the draft treaty a clause allowing the remilitarization of the Aaland Isles belatedly awoke Swedish suspicion of Russia. The Germans proposed separate North Sea and Baltic conventions guaranteeing the *status quo*, which were eventually signed in April 1908. That same year the pressure of the Swedish radical forces finally broke through and universal suffrage was introduced in Sweden. Even then the conservatives scored a victory by writing into the new electoral laws a provision for proportional representation. On the outbreak of war in 1914, Sweden reverted to Scandinavianism, aided by a British failure to stage the naval break-in to the Baltic which their regular summer naval manoeuvres in the Baltic had previously foreshadowed, and a German decision that their purposes were best served by Danish neutrality and by using Denmark to bar the Baltic entrances. The Norwegian revolution thus foreshadowed a great decline in British influence in the Baltic, which was only to be restored after Germany's defeat.

Chapter 8

Europe turns on itself: the weakening of the Dual Alliance, 1906–9

THE beginning of 1906 ushered in a period of four years during which European affairs increasingly dominated world politics. Over these years the position of the Central Powers, Germany and Austria-Hungary, deteriorated markedly both in domestic and foreign affairs, and both absolutely and relatively in relation to their opponents, Britain, France, and Tsarist Russia. No sooner had the Algeciras Conference on Morocco met on January 16th, 1906, when it quickly became evident that the German bid to turn the Moroccan issue to their favour had boomeranged. The German delegation found itself faced with a permanent line-up of Britain, France, Russia, Italy and the United States, and supported only by its Austrian ally. Some German leaders, notably Baron von Holstein of the foreign ministry, wanted to use force to obtain their ends; but the Kaiser and the Chancellor, Bülow, refused to countenance war, and von Holstein resigned in disgust. The final act of the Conference, signed on April 7th, 1906, gave France and Spain substantial control of Moroccan reforms, but still left intervention by the Great Powers a possibility.

The internal situation in Morocco deteriorated under the French pressure, and, after French occupation of the whole Atlantic coast in August 1907, civil war broke out between the Sultan and his brother Moulay Hafid which only ended in December 1908 when, on German initiative, Hafid was recognized as Sultan. This German intervention proved no real advantage. In 1909, Germany was forced to sign an agreement recognizing French primacy, and in 1910 Moulay Hafid was forced to ask for French assistance against another claimant to the throne.

The German position was further weakened by the progress

of Anglo-French and Anglo-Belgian staff talks. Even though the British emphasized the absence of any treaty commitment, and the bulk of the British cabinet remained uninformed, the knowledge of British support made the government of Clemenceau in France, who succeeded Rouvier as premier in 1906, strong enough to ride out all the German pressure, despite the growth of extremism both on left and right after 1906. The unification of the various factions of the French socialist movement in 1905 under the leadership of Jaurés had been followed by a considerable increase in the parliamentary strength of the Socialists in the 1906 elections in France. This growth in socialist representation had aroused the advocates of direct action, who feared that socialism was about to become a parliamentary movement which would collaborate with those they should be preparing to overthrow. The inclusion of Briand and René Viviani, both former independent Socialists, in the Clemenceau cabinet added fuel to their fears. A wave of strikes led by the militants of the Trades Union movement, the *Confederation General du Travail*, followed through the years 1906–10, splitting the Socialist party again at the Limoges conference of 1906 on whether to attempt to reconcile the party with the CGT. Nevertheless, Clemenceau was able to weather these strikes without difficulty.

France's ally Russia was similarly experiencing a revival of governmental strength and stability. Peter Stolypin, prime minister since June 1906, dealt easily with the first Duma in July. In August, he instituted severe measures to suppress the continuing peasant disorders. The Tsarist Army commanders were virtually given a free hand in suppressing the nationalist risings in the Baltic, in the Caucasus, and in Siberia, and new anti-Jewish pogroms were now instituted.

In October-November 1906, Stolypin promulgated a series of decrees designed to strengthen peasant ownership of land and weaken the old system of communal ownership. The pattern of consolidating individual land holdings in the villages was begun under the supervision of Land Commissions. In October 1906, Stolypin instituted conversations designed to form a new parliamentary ministry. But the second Duma elected in February 1907 was even more extreme than the first; the Social Democrats and Socialist Revolutionaries, having ended their boycott of the elections, won a total of 99 seats, the Octobrists and the extreme right 95 seats, and the Cadets 92 seats.

In June 1907, Stolypin demanded that the parliamentary immunity of the Social Democrats be cancelled on the grounds that they were implicated in a plot against the Tsar's life. He then dissolved the second Duma. Fresh elections were held on a much narrower electoral law which weighted the representation of the land-owners and wealthy industrialists much more heavily than anyone else. To elect a deputy it took only 230 landowners, compared to 1,000 wealthy business men, 15,000 *petit bourgeois* townsfolk, 60,000 peasants or 125,000 workers. The new Duma was heavily dominated by the right with 127 Rightists, 154 Octobrists and 54 Cadets. Only 33 deputies representing the left were elected. In foreign relations the new parliament was to prove violently anti-German and excessively, indeed embarrassingly, nationalistic.

Thus, Germany found herself confronted with much stronger governments in both France and Russia. And this happened after it had already proved impossible for Germany to divide them even at the moment of Russia's greatest weakness.

Russia's position in the Far East was greatly strengthened by the Russo-Japanese agreement of 1907, which marked out spheres of influence in Korea and Manchuria. More important, however, was the conclusion of the Russian *Entente* with Britain in August 1907. For the British government this was definitely an anti-German move. Stolypin's Russia, with the Dumas suppressed, had little popularity in Britain in contrast to Germany and Austria-Hungary, where parliamentary forces seemed to be in the ascendancy. But the increase in German armed strength, and, in the eyes of the British, the irresponsible manner in which the Germans were prepared to use it, made it desirable to end the obvious causes of friction between Russia and Britain. Actually, the *Entente* itself was entirely concerned with Central Asia. Persia was divided into British, Russian, and neutral zones of influence. Russia recognized Britain's primacy in the Gulf and in Afghanistan and Britain made encouraging noises about revising the Dardanelles agreements in Russia's favour.

For Russia, paradoxically, the main aim of the *Entente* was to regain a certain freedom of action in the Baltic and in the Balkans and Izvolski, Russian Foreign Minister since May 1906, went to considerable pains to reassure the Germans that it was not directed against them. Despite these reassurances the *Entente*, by ending British and Russian anxieties in Central Asia, could only strengthen their positions against Germany in any future crisis.

This was the more unfortunate in that, in Britain, opinion in the armed services was now thoroughly convinced of German enmity. In 1906, the British Admiralty initiated a fresh wave of naval competition with the launching of the Dreadnought, a new type of battleship which carried ten heavy guns in its main battery, in contrast to the four guns found on all previous battleships. At one stroke the value of all existing battle-fleets was reduced to nil, and a new and highly expensive form of competition, both in quality and in quantity, instituted. So rapid was the technological revolution in both the size of capital ships and in the calibre of the guns they carried, that by 1914, the Dreadnought itself was unable to take its place in the first line of Britain's battle fleet. The 1905–6 naval construction programme contained one Dreadnought and four battle-cruisers of an equally revolutionary type. Thereafter, the official programme envisaged the construction of four of these capital ships annually.

The advent of the Liberal government brought into power a cabinet, part of which greatly objected to diverting monies from social reform to arms production. With the Admiralty's reluctant approval they dropped one ship from the 1906–7 programme and planned to drop two from the programme of 1907–8. This decrease in ship construction accompanied proposals that the Second Hague Peace Conference, due to meet in June 1907, should consider disarmament on land and at sea. The British gesture went unanswered in Germany. The German Chancellor denounced disarmament proposals as impractical in a speech in April 1907. The Conference itself proved largely abortive, save for reaching a number of minor agreements on the laws and conduct of war. None had been completely ratified by 1914 and most were ignored by the belligerents during the 1914–18 war.

In October 1907, therefore, the British restored one of the two Dreadnoughts dropped from the 1907 programme. In November, the Third German Navy Law was published. It provided for the construction of four capital ships annually in place of a previous rate of three and projected a fleet of 58 capital ships for 1917–18. There was considerable alarm in Britain. But the Admiralty kept its nerve. Indeed, it only secured the cabinet's agreement to a programme of one Dreadnought and one battle-cruiser for 1908-9 after a major cabinet crisis.

None of these developments could be at all welcome to the German government, whose position in internal affairs was weakening steadily with the growth of the parliamentary forces in the *Reichstag*. In the 1898 elections, the balance of forces in the *Reichstag* had been roughly equal, 138 Prussian Conservative and National Liberal deputies facing 102 in the Centre Party and 139 on the left, including 56 Social Democrats. But the 1903 elections had seen the forces of the left rise to 152 deputies, with 81 Social Democrats, while right and centre remained virtually static, save only that the balance within the Centre Party was slipping towards the left. This became evident in December 1906 when the Centre joined the left to defeat a government bill calling for the re-organization of the Colonial Office and the provision of funds to help the suppression of the Hereros rising in South-West Africa. It was true that the subsequent dissolution of the *Reichstag* produced, after fresh elections in 1907, a reversal of the 1903 results with 159 deputies on the right to 121 (with only 43 Social Democrats) on the left. But the victory was of little advantage to the *régime* when compared with the growth of parliamentary sentiments among the National Liberals.

The real state of affairs was revealed in 1908 when the Kaiser published an interview with the British newspaper, *The Daily Telegraph*, in which he boasted of the part he had played during the Boer War in preventing the formation of an anti-British coalition. The *Reichstag* exploded in a storm of criticism in which only the Prussian conservatives remained silent. The Kaiser was forced to issue what amounted to a public apology, in the form of an announcement that he would respect his constitutional obligations. Chancellor Bülow was able to govern for a time as the virtual parliamentary head of a democratic coalition, but the episode, while discrediting the Kaiser, did nothing really to strengthen the Chancellor's position or to introduce a genuine parliamentary coalition. Bülow fell over a minor defeat in the *Reichstag* in 1909, and his replacement, Bethmann-Hollweg, was, as usual, the Kaiser's nominee. In the long run, the episode shook the credit of all three institutions, Kaiser, Chancellor, and *Reichstag*, and only served to increase the tensions between German authoritarians and parliamentarians.

The steady deterioration in the position of the Austro-Hungarian government was more marked in foreign than in domestic affairs. The years 1903-7 were, it was true, years of considerable crisis in Austria-Hungary's internal politics, involving not only further strains in Czech-German relations in Bohemia, but also a major crisis in relations with Hungary, a crisis moreover which involved the resurrection of the South Slav movement.

In 1897, the Austrian Prime Minister, Count Casimir Badeni, had attempted to solve the Czech-German struggle in Bohemia and Moravia by making knowledge of both languages obligatory for all members of the government service. But the Germans throughout Austria had raised such disorder that the Emperor dismissed Badeni and rescinded the offending legislation. This action only embittered the Czechs and made a settlement of the language issue virtually impossible. Dr Koerber, appointed Premier in 1900, attempted to solve the nationalities problem by a progressive economic policy. But the elections to the *Reichsrath* in 1901 greatly strengthened the Pan-German and Young Czech parties, and national rivalries broke out equally strongly between Poles and Ruthenians in Galicia, and the Italians of the southern Tyrol and the German majority in the whole province. Riots in Innsbruck over the proposal to establish a separate Italian-speaking law faculty at the university caused Koerber to resign. His successor, Baron von Gautsch, was successful, however, in securing a compromise between Czechs and Germans in Moravia in 1905, which divided the province between the two nationalities. But an attempt to negotiate a similar compromise in Bohemia broke down again in riots and obstruction at the provincial Diet.

Austria's relations with Hungary were governed by the rise of separatist sentiment in the so-called Independence party led by the son of Kossuth, the rebel leader of 1848 who had died in 1894. The decennial negotiations of the quotas for common expenses, and of the customs and commercial treaties were already exacerbating relations between Vienna and Budapest, when, in 1902, the Kossuthists introduced a bill increasing the Hungarian contingent in the common army and chose at that time to stage demands for the total Magyarization of the language, officers and flag of the Hungarian regiments. They were backed by the strongly Catholic and aristocratic National Party. Their demands were flatly rejected by the Emperor himself, and in November 1903, Stephan Tisza, leader of the Liberal Party, was appointed by Franz Joseph to drive a compromise bill through the Hungarian parliament. In 1905, Tisza finally dissolved parliament and called for elections. Stimulated by the example of Norway's secession from the union with Sweden, Kossuth's party, linked with a large anti-Tisza coalition, swept to victory with 163 seats against 152 for Tisza's Liberals. On Tisza's resignation, the Emperor adjourned parliament and appointed his own premier. In addition, he threatened the Kossuthist coalition with the introduction of universal suffrage, a device which would have destroyed the strength of the Kossuthites and greatly increased that of the non-Magyar minorities, Croats, Rumanians and Slovaks, whose combined strengths in the Chamber had already risen from 8 to 24 in the 1905 elections. The Slovak nationalists had already thrown up Dr Milan Hodza, a future premier of Czechoslovakia, and the extremist Catholic nationalist, dictator of the German puppet state of Slovakia from 1939-44, Father Hlinka. Six Slovak deputies and eight Rumanian nationalists, demanding autonomy for Transylvania, were among the twenty-four victors of 1905. In Croatia, in the meanwhile, the South Slav movement had been revived and strengthened by the formation of the Peasant's party of Stepan Radic. In 1903, peasant risings had expressed their discontent with their Magyar overlords, and in the following year deputations from Croatia joined deputies from the Austrian provinces of Istria and Dalmatia to complain to the Emperor, but were barred by the intervention of Budapest. In 1905, at the Congress of Fiume, the advocates of a union of Dalmatia and Istria with Croatia in a third, south Slav, member of the Dual Monarchy, on a level of equality with Austria and Hungary, offered their aid to the Kossuthite coalition, if the latter would accept the separation of Croatia from Hungary and its union with Dalmatia.

Nothing was less welcome in Kossuthite circles. In February 1906, the lesson was brought home when the reassembled parliament was closed with the aid of a battalion of Rumanian soldiers from the Bukovina. The coalition yielded at once. Internally, the 1906 elections strengthened their position, giving Kossuth's Independence party alone an absolute majority, although the election of twenty-six minority deputies, sixteen from the Rumanian nationalist party, contained its own warning. The Hungarian quota of common expenses was raised by 4·9 per cent to 36·4 per cent, and the extremists' demands for the

Magyarization of the Army were quietly buried. So too were the proposals for universal suffrage.

The mere discussion of universal suffrage in Hungary, however, left the way open for its introduction into the Austrian provinces of the Dual Monarchy. In court circles, many saw in such revolutionary action a means of breaking the strength of the middle-class nationalists and of advancing the Christian Socials and the Social Democrats, mass parties both committed in theory to a multi-national approach, and both devoted to the survival of the Habsburg State. The first elections to the *Reichsrath* on a basis of universal male suffrage came in May 1907, and resulted in the reduction of the middle-class nationalist parties to approximate parity with the Christian Socials and the Social Democrats.

The electoral reform of 1907 did not however produce the expected result in Bohemia. The cabinet of Baron von Beck, appointed by the Emperor to introduce universal suffrage in Austria, had a considerable success in other fields. It succeeded in carrying through new compromise negotiations with Budapest, in carrying the budget through the *Reichsrath*, in securing an increase in the Austrian armed forces and in legislating for the nationalization of the Austrian railways. But Beck himself was accused by the heir-apparent, the Archduke Franz Ferdinand, and his circle of having betrayed the interests of the monarchy in his negotiations with Budapest; and his attempt to negotiate a Moravian-style compromise in Bohemia broke down entirely. In November 1908, Beck resigned. From 1908, the internal cohesion of the Empire entered a further stage of disintegration.

Beck's resignation, which came at the height of the Bosnian crisis of 1908–9, made apparent to all the deterioration in Austria's international position since 1900. This deterioration had begun with the military nationalist *coup d'état* of June 1903 in Serbia, in which King Alexander and his Queen had been brutally murdered by a group of young officers, and Peter, heir of the rival Karageorgovich dynasty, had been elected to the Serbian throne in his place. In December 1904, the extreme nationalist Pan-Slav Radical party had won command of the Serbian Assembly and its leader, Nicholas Pasic, became Premier. Austro-Serb relations deteriorated. Serbia awarded a large arms contract to French rather than Austrian interests, and turned to preparing for a customs union with Bulgaria. Austria

:cured its abandonment; but her attempt to use a tariff boycott
⟩ re-establish her position of commercial and political domi-
ance in Serbia – the so-called 'pig war' (Serbia's exports to
ustria consisted largely of pig-bristles, leather and pork
roducts) – proved a failure.

The issue of Serbian independence seemed particularly
angerous to Vienna because of the link between Belgrade and
ie Serbo-Croat elements in the southern Austrian provinces, in
Croatia and in southern Hungary, and the 'South Slav' move-
ient which sought to bring them together. Both the Habsburg
Monarchy's anxiety over Serbia and the temptation to assert
rong leadership in foreign policy combined to produce a course
f action which was to end in disaster. The two main figures in
iis *débâcle* were Conrad von Hötzendorff, the Chief of the
ustrian General Staff since 1906, a violent anti-Slav, and Baron
ehrenthal, the new Foreign Minister, who succeeded Count
ioluchowski the same year. Aehrenthal began, it is true, by
nding the 'pig war' with Serbia. Yet he was very soon driven to
ie conclusion that nothing could be done with Serbia, and he
gain tried to modify Serbian policy by diplomatic means.
lthough some anxiety had been caused in Vienna in 1902 by
ie conclusion of a secret Russo-Bulgarian military agreement,
ustro-Russian cooperation in the Balkans, especially over the
Macedonian issue, had gone very well. In the summer of 1907,
ierefore, Aehrenthal played with the idea of reducing the
ix-power control of Macedonia virtually to a two-power Austro-
Russian control by excluding Britain. In October 1907, Aehren-
hal and Izvolski, the Russian Foreign Minister, discussed a
Russian proposal to revise the Straits convention in Russia's
avour and Aehrenthal obtained Izvolski's support for a projected
ailway through the Sanjak of Novibazar, which lay between
ierbia and her fellow Slav monarchy, Montenegro, to Salonika.
n February 1908, the two countries combined to block a British
roposal for a six-power note to the Ottoman sultan demanding
idicial reform in Macedonia. The Concert of Europe was for
he moment at an end.

Aehrenthal unveiled his Novibazar railway project in January
908. It was at once denounced by the Serbs as designed to split
ierbia from its fellow Slavonic kingdom of Montenegro. Serbian
rotests were taken up in Russia, where the third Duma was
trongly Pan-Slav in sentiment and the Russian press even more

so. Izvolski was forced to protest publicly, although he was a
pains to control the protests of the Russian press as soon as h
could. But the reception of the railway project in Europe wa
ominous for the future. In France and Britain, it was seen, quit
unjustly, as inspired by Berlin and even welcomed, as a revival o
Austro-Russian rivalry in the Balkans. In Serbia, it reinforce
the enemies of the Dual Monarchy, already doing their utmos
to spread subversion in the twin provinces of Bosnia-Herzego
vina, Turkish in their nominal sovereignty but under Austria
rule since 1878. Together with the rejection of the British pro
posal in Macedonia it marked the end of European cooperatio
in the Balkans for the moment and cleared the way for the majo
crisis over Bosnia-Herzegovina which was to begin later in th
year. It played a major part in the Russian move towards Britai
after the Anglo-Russian *Entente* of the previous year, and th
crucial meeting of King Edward VII and the Tsar at Reval i
June 1908 at which Russia agreed to new British proposals fo
the extensive reform of the Macedonian administration and fo
the strengthening of their mutual position in Persia.

Russian pressure had already produced an explosion in Persia
as the news of the Reval meeting was to do in Ottoman Turkey
The Persian revolution, which broke out in 1906, was essentiall
Shi'ite in character, the Messianic nature of this branch of Islam
making a direct assault in the name of the Sharia on the Shah'
exercise of his despotism, the vehicle for expressing Persian dis
satisfaction with a Shah whose insensate profligacy was misusin
the national treasury and delivering Persia over to Russia
control. The revolutionary movement organized itself in
number of semi-secret associations, the so-called *anjumen*, whic
united merchants and professional men, with ideals culled from
the western liberal tradition, with the *ulemas*, religious intellec
tuals. In 1905–6, their agitation broke out into the open, and th
attempt of the Shah's advisers to suppress them led many o
their number to seek religious sanctuary in the shrines of Quum
and, more sensationally, in the British Embassy.

The Shah found himself forced to grant a constitution, and t
summon a national assembly, the *Majilis*, in December 1906
Shortly thereafter, he died, to be succeeded by his despoticall
inclined brother, Mohammed Ali Shah, and a long struggl
ensued between the *anjumen*, which had now shed their secre
character, and the new Shah, in which the latter twice, i

December 1907 and again in June 1908, suspended the constitution. The subsequent disturbances revealed the *anjumen* to be
well established in the country. The *anjumen* in Tabriz led a
revolt against the Shah in July 1908, and were able to resist
efforts to suppress it until Russian troops intervened in April
1909 to raise the siege. In the meantime, the association in
Isfahan, which had gone underground in 1908, had opened
negotiations with the powerful Bakhtiari, the greatest of the
Persian mountain nomad tribes. In January 1909, tribal forces
drove the Shah's troops from Isfahan, and in July entered
Teheran, and the Shah took refuge in the Russian legation. The
nationalists deposed him and set up a Regency for his twelve-
year-old son.

The events of 1906–9 had shown the strength of the *anjumen*
against the Shah. They had not, unfortunately, revealed any
constructive ability on the part of their leaders, nor any agreement, or even any clear views as to the *régime* which they wished
to see established, after the overthrow of the Shah's despotism.
The result of their revolution, despite its origins in injured
nationalism, was to weaken rather than strengthen Persia against
foreign intervention. And the introduction of American financial
advisers in 1910 was to prove an inadequate substitute for a
properly worked out scheme of reform with public support
behind it.

The weakness of the Persian revolution stands out the more
strikingly when contrasted with the success of the Turkish
revolution of 1908. The revolutionaries in Persia were an amalgam of the wealthy merchant classes with western contacts and
Moslem intellectuals of the reformist variety. As such they had
far more in common with the Arab nationalists of Syria and
Egypt at this date, than with the revolutionaries of the Committee of Union and Progress. In part, this was due to the fact that
the ruling *élite* of the Ottoman Empire had kept the unique
system of recruitment by talent which had been the secret of
Ottoman success in the greatest days of the Empire. Abdul
Hamid, normally represented as the most reactionary of Sultans,
had in fact outdone his predecessors in opening schools throughout the Empire. The revolutionaries in Ottoman Turkey were
drawn from the ruling *élite*, in revolt against a system of despotism which prevented them from ruling effectively. They were
patriots for an Empire with a religious, not a racial basis,

nationalists for the Ottoman state, and constitutionalists becaus
the old controls on Ottoman despotism had broken, and constitu
tions seemed to work in the West. Their nearest parallel can b
found among those groups who took Japan from isolation t
world power in two generations. It was the Japanese defeat o
Russia which fired their imaginations. And in the future the
were to prove second only to the Japanese in their imitation an
adaptation of European models.

Their greatest strength developed from 1908 onwards, no
among the exiles in Paris but among the officer groups i
Macedonia and Anatolia. For these the Anglo-Russian meetin
at Reval in June 1908, which seemed to foreshadow a nev
Entente at the expense of Turkey, was the breaking point
Already a number of young officers, feeling the Sultan's polic
on their trail, had preferred to go into hiding in the hills c
Macedonia. On July 4th, mutiny broke out among units of th
Third Army Corps in Macedonia and spread rapidly to th
Second Army Corps in what is still today European Turkey. O
July 21st, 1908, under the threat of a march on Istanbul, th
Sultan gave way and proclaimed the restoration of the consti
tution of 1876. The way now seemed open for the liberalizatio
and democratization of the Ottoman Empire. The reason suc
reform failed to materialize was largely due to the Europea
powers for whom the prospect of a revival of Ottoman strengt
was so unwelcome as to call for immediate action.

Five powers were involved, Russia, Austria, Serbia, Bulgaria
and Greece. The main blow to Turkish democracy was struc
by Austria in October 1908 with the annexation of Bosnia an
Herzegovina. The decision had been taken as a result of a
Russian initiative in July proposing discussion of the Novibaza
issue, and Bosnia and the Straits. Aehrenthal felt this mov
would prove an essential counter to the growing Pan-Ser
propaganda organized in the two provinces by emissaries from
Belgrade. It was discussed between him and Izvolski in Sep
tember 1908 at Buchlau in Bohemia, at a meeting in whic
Izvolski failed to grasp the imminence of the Austrian action
believing he had been promised Austrian support for his am
bitions for a revision of the Straits agreements. Neither mar
seemed to have realized that the action they were discussing wa
contrary to the spirit of the Concert of Europe in that it was no
being done with the agreement of the other powers, and n

question of corresponding compensation to them was suggested. Only Ferdinand of Bulgaria, as a result of a meeting later that month with Aehrenthal, grasped what was going on. Izvolski, in the meantime, continued his long planned visits to Rome and Paris, London and Berlin, to organize support for his claims.

Ferdinand's intuition (for he does not seem, as was believed at the time, to have been in collusion with Aehrenthal) enabled him to anticipate the Austrian action by one day and proclaim the independence of Bulgaria from the Ottoman Empire. Aehrenthal's action came on October 6th. The next day Crete proclaimed her union with Greece, thereby adding to the crisis.

Izvolski's reactions were governed by his belief that he had been deceived by Aehrenthal and by the intensity of Pan-Slav reaction in Russia, an element he had misjudged, as before over Novibazar. The Austrian action included a declaration of withdrawal from Novibazar. But this was by no means adequate to appease Russian opinion, and his own schemes for the Straits were defeated by British insistence that Turkish agreement was essential. And Aehrenthal now refused Izvolski's call to attend a conference to discuss Bosnia, which he affected to believe to be a *chose jugée*. Izvolski had nothing therefore to defend himself with against charges that he had been out-manoeuvred by Austria, and had agreed to sell the interests of a fellow Slav state (Serbia) down the river. It seems doubtful whether he had obtained the prior backing of his cabinet and prime minister for his schemes. Aehrenthal, in his turn, had secured the assent, but by no means the support, of either his premier in Vienna or the cabinet in Budapest. The German Kaiser rejected his action as contrary to Germany's interests in Turkey, while Britain and France regarded the whole affair as a total departure from the rules of the game.

The strongest reactions came from Italy and Serbia. Italian opinion regarded the Austrian action as an unwarranted increase in Austrian power. The Serbs saw it as virtually an act of war. Guerilla bands were organized, Austrian goods boycotted. The Serbian government, backed by the assurances of the pan-Slav Russian press, demanded compensation in the strongest terms. Serbian military strength was built up until the Serbian army was virtually in total mobilization. These manifestations were viewed with growing rage in Vienna where pressure grew in turn for a preventive war against Serbia. In Germany, these

manifestations strengthened those who had welcomed the
Austrian action against the Kaiser. Assurances were given to
Aehrenthal, notably by Bülow, the German Chancellor, which
amounted to an unconditional promise to restrain Russia in the
event of an Austro-Serbian war.

On the other aspects of the crisis, Germany did her utmost to
be conciliatory, especially in relation to Turkey. By February
1909, Austria and Bulgaria had agreed to pay financial compensation to Turkey. But Russian support still enabled Serbia to
threaten Austria and to run the danger of provoking an Austro-
Serbian war. Germany, therefore, first assented to an Austrian
proposal for military staff conversations and then in March
forced the Russians to abandon support for Serbia and declare
their formal acceptance of the annexation by threatening to let
'matters take their course', that is, to allow an Austrian invasion
of Serbia which Russia was not prepared militarily to resist.
Serbia, isolated, was forced to back down and promise to check
anti-Austrian propaganda in a note of March 31st, 1909.

The effects of the Bosnian crisis were principally in the psy-
chological field. It was easy to argue that Aehrenthal had no
more acted against the spirit of European cooperation than
German, French or Russian statesmen before him; that he could
not have acted as he did without a concomitant eagerness on
Izvolski's part for a major *coup* which would establish his own
position, and that of his government, after the decline of Russia's
position among the Great Powers. But the fact remains that
Aehrenthal had acted without any consideration for the interests
of the other European powers, and had subsequently managed to
avoid paying any compensation other than to Serbia and Turkey.
He had bitterly offended Russian, Italian and Serbian opinion,
and left Britain convinced of his dependence on Germany. In
fact, this was the exact opposite of the impression he had wished
to convey. The German intervention in March 1909, designed
as much as anything to demonstrate Germany's commanding
position, offended everybody without any gain to herself.

The diplomatic consequences of the Bosnian crisis were,
therefore, far-reaching. Italy and Russia drew together, and
concluded at Racconigi in October 1909 a secret understanding
designed to preserve the *status quo* in the Balkans; and, failing
this, to favour the division of Ottoman Turkey on a basis of self-
determination, with Italian support for Russian ambitions in the

Straits; and Russian support for Italian claims in Tripoli further began a long-term military build-up of her position on Austria's southern borders. In France, the first Briand cabinet, which succeeded Clemenceau in 1909, began long-term consideration of the improvement of France's military position, as did Russia. The Russian government, in fact, turned to diplomacy in the Balkans, to the encouragement of Balkan nationalism against Austria and the attempt to create a Balkan alliance which would bar Austria's way to the Balkans.

Perhaps the most serious consequences were to be felt in Austria and in Ottoman Turkey itself. The Bosnian action gravely exacerbated both German-Slav relations in Bohemia and Carniola, and Hungarian relations with the Croats. In 1909, the Hungarian Governor-General in Croatia placed more than fifty Croats and Serbs on trial in Agram on charges of treasonably plotting with Serbia, and condemned thirty of them to hard labour on evidence so patently inadequate that a higher court annulled the sentences. Still worse, in March 1909, at the height of the Bosnian crisis, the Austrian Foreign Minister allowed the publication of an article by the historian, Friedjung, which accused Croat and Serb leaders of trafficking with Belgrade. At the subsequent libel trial, the documents he had used were shown to be blatant forgeries. In Hungary, the Independence party continued its pressure for still greater devolution of powers, and when Kossuth tried to be conciliatory, his radicals repudiated him. Fresh troubles broke out in Galicia in 1908 with the assassination of the Polish Governor-General by a Ruthenian nationalist. And, at the height of the Bosnian crisis, the Prime Minister's disagreement with Aehrenthal's foreign policy brought down the last strong cabinet to hold office in Austria before 1914.

The strongest effects were felt in Ottoman Turkey. The immediate loss of territory and prestige to Austria underlined the position of the liberals and would-be parliamentarians in Istanbul, and, on the one hand, enhanced the position of the committee of Union and Progress which now emerged as the power behind the liberal statesmen, and, on the other hand, caused a revival of extreme Moslem reaction. In April 1909, the First Army Corps mutinied under the influence of Moslem propaganda and marched on the Turkish Parliament, affording the Sultan the opportunity to rid himself of the Committee's nominee as Grand Vizier and replace him by a more pliable man.

Modernism in the provinces was halted by a circular instructing provincial governments to safeguard the law of Islam, the *Sharia*, and outbursts of Moslem extremism culminated in large-scale massacres of Armenians in the province of Adana. The Committee's reaction was swift. From Salonica, troops loyal to the Committee of Union and Progress marched on Constantinople, deposed the Sultan, appointed his brother to replace him, and in August reduced his constitutional powers to those of a French president, able to appoint the Grand Vizier but no more. The Vizier with his cabinet was supposed to be responsible to parliament, though the maintenance of military rule until 1911 made this position largely academic.

The manifestations of Serbian, Greek and Bulgarian nationalist aggressiveness from the time of the Russian crisis onwards convinced the extreme leaders of the Turkish revolution, especially the leaders of the Committee of Union and Progress, that the liberal Turks' hope of creating an Ottoman Empire on a basis of equality between Christian and Moslem, Turk and non-Turk was an illusion. A ruthless policy of centralization and Turkisation was the answer, one which, as events in the external relations of the Ottoman Empire sharpened the lesson, gradually alienated the new *élites* of the Arab and other non-Turkish communities in the Asiatic empire. From 1909, Arab nationalism in the *vilayets* (provinces) of what were to become Syria, the Lebanon, Palestine and Iraq, previously concealed between the twin currents of the Liberal Islamic movement and hostility to Hamidian despotism, begins to emerge in its true colours. On their side, the Turks began to exalt their Turkishness, expressed in organizations such as the Society 'Turkish Hearth', founded in 1912, and in the rise to prominence of the writer, Ziya Gökalp, with his gospel of Pan-Turanianism, of Turkish kindom with the Turkic-speaking peoples of the Crimea, the Transcaspian emirates, Iran, Afghanistan, and Chinese Central Asia.

The Turkish *élites* under the Young Turk movement were basically those of the old Ottoman Empire. But Hamid's educational reforms, especially his wide scattering of military schools, was producing by the turn of the century a new educated Arab group of young officers and intellectuals not necessarily drawn from the old land-owning families of the Arab provinces of the Empire. These young men eagerly greeted the 1908 revolution and embraced the Ottomanism of the Liberal Turks. But even

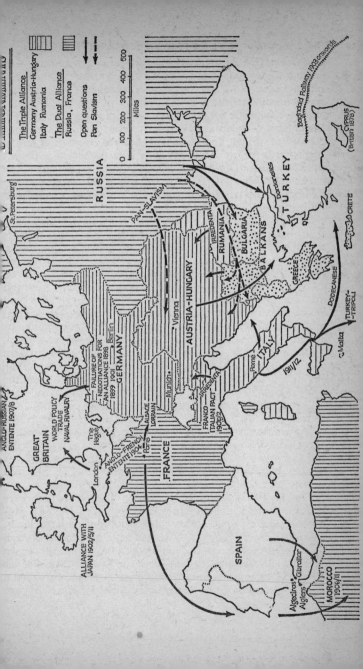

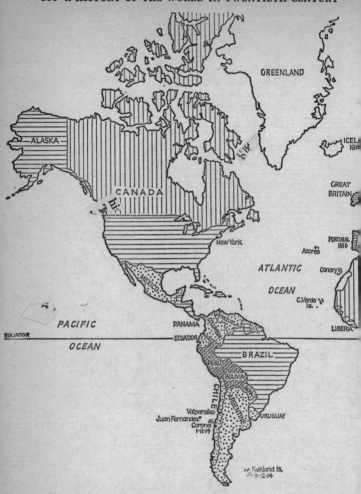

GREENLAND

ALASKA

CANADA

New York

MEXICO

PACIFIC

OCEAN

EQUATOR

PANAMA

ECUADOR

COLOMBIA

VENEZUELA

PERU

BOLIVIA

BRAZIL

CHILE

ARGENTINE

URUGUAY

Valparaiso

Juan Fernandez

Coronel
1·11·14

Falkland Is.
8·12·14

ATLANTIC

OCEAN

ICELAND
1918

GREAT
BRITAIN

PORTUGAL
1916

Azores

Canary Is.

C. Verde
Is.

LIBERIA

WAR AT SEA AND WORLD
IN AUTUMN 1918

Murmansk

FINLAND

RUSSIA
(SOVIET REPUBLIC)

Leningrad

•Moscow   Omsk   Irkutsk

CIVIL
WAR   MONGOLIA   MANCHURIA

USTRIA-
NGARY   CHINA   Kiou   JAPAN
3-11-18   TIBET   Chou 7-11-14

TURKEY
30-10-18   PACIFIC

LYA   BRITISH INDIA   Hong Kong   OCEAN

EGYPT   ARABIA

ABISSINIA   SIAM

BELGIAN   BR.I
CONGO   EAST
               AFRICA   INDIAN   Padang   NEW GUINEA
               (GER.)   OCEAN   Singapore
GOLA   E.AFRICA
               14-11-18   DUTCH
                                                     EAST INDIES

                    MADAGASCAR
                    (Fr.)   AUSTRALIA

UNION OF
S.AFRICA   NEW
                                                                    ZEALAND

Central Powers
German Colonies
Areas under occupation
by central powers   Allies & Associates
                                     of Entente 1917/18
Entente & Allies 1914/18   Broke Diplomatic relations
Dominions & Colonies   with Central Powers
of Entente   Areas of Russia under
                                     occupation by Allies or
Neutrals   White Russian troops

                    Fronts & lines of Intervention

AUSTRIA - HUNGARY
POLITICAL & ETHNOGRAPHICAL 1900

in the first election to the Ottoman Chamber of deputies they found themselves prejudiced against. Between them the new intellectuals and the western-educated Arabs of the Lebanon (see Chapter III) only secured 60 seats to 156 for the Turks in the Chamber of Deputies and a mere three seats out of 40 in the Senate. And after the 1909 *coup*, the Committee of Union and Progress banned all non-Turkish political organizations and began to tighten the powers of the central administration. Arab nationalism thereafter went underground or into exile. In Syria, the only overt manifestation was the Arab Literary club which came to act as a kind of demi-official intermediary between the Committee of Union and Progress and Arab leaders. The most important of many secret societies was *Al Qahtani*, founded in 1909, with the declared aim of turning the Ottoman Empire into a dual Arab-Turkish monarchy, with an Arabic language state with its separate parliament and administration. Its strongest adherents were among the young Arab army officers. However, this secret society was soon penetrated by the Turkish police.

More important were the two organizations formed in exile. The first of these, *al Fatat*, or the Young Arab Society, was founded in 1909 by a group of Syrian Arab Moslems in Paris with aims roughly similar to that referred to above, of Arab independence within an Arab-Turkic monarchy. A more overt group, since, though it operated in exile, it cultivated contacts among the members of the Turkish governments of 1909-12, was that which came together in the so-called Ottoman Decentralization Party, founded in 1912 among Syrian *emigrés* in Cairo, in contact with the leaders of the Islamic Liberal movement among the Egyptians such as Mohammed Abdu. Prominent among these Syrians were Rashid Rida, who was to follow Abdu as the leading exponent of Islamic Liberalism, and the Emir Shekib Arslan, a Druze from the Lebanon, who, from his exile in Switzerland, was to become one of the most prominent figures in the Pan-Arab movement, his influence spreading from Morocco to Palestine in the decade before World War II. Perhaps most significant were the conversations opened in 1911 between a group of thirty-five of the Arab deputies in Constantinople and the newly appointed Sharif of Mecca, Hussein ibn Ali, in which the Arab deputies promised Hussein their support if he rose against the Turks, and recognized him as 'Caliph of the prophet, the one man responsible for the interests of all the Arab countries'.

The Arab nationalist movement, as it was to manifest itself in the twentieth century, had at this time two other important elements, the Egyptian nationalist movement and the Arab sheikhs of the Arabian peninsula. It was in the years 1906–10 that the Egyptian nationalist movement began to separate itself out from the early development of Arab Liberal and nationalist thought, and to develop along purely Egyptian lines. In so doing, it was following the logic of Egypt's separate position in the Arab and Ottoman world, a position which could be dated back to the middle ages, but which took its modern form from the work of Mohammed Ali. The separation of the Egyptian movement from the mainstream of Arab Liberalism is at first sight odd in view of the presence in Cairo of the main figures in the Arab Liberal movement at this time, the *Salafiya* leaders Mohammed Abdu, Rashid Rida, and the Syrian, al-Kawakibi, and the Christian nationalists Shummayil, Faris Antun and Negib Azoury. The difference sprang from the British presence in Egypt. Without that presence, Cairo could hardly have become the centre for Arab nationalist exiles from the Ottoman Empire. But to the Egyptian nationalists, Britain appeared as the mainstay of the rule of the Khedive, and the supporter of that oppressive oriental despotism against whom Arab liberal writers preached resistance.

Two events led to the estrangement of the young Egyptian national movement from British rule. The first was the British refusal to restore the Sudan to Egyptian control after the British reconquest in 1898. The unity of the Nile valley became an essential element in the nationalists' programme. The second was the Denshawi affair, in which the murder of a British officer after a shooting incident was made the occasion for a Draconian visitation on the inhabitants of the village in which the incident had occurred. In 1907, Lord Cromer retired, his policy of ruling Egypt on strict administratively imperialist lines in ruins. His successor, Sir Eldon Gorst, attempted to create a coalition of moderate opinion behind the Khedive, and did his best to divide the nationalist movement. In this he was greatly aided by the death in 1908 of Mustafa Kemal, the young nationalist leader (who should not be confused with the Turkish dictator of the same name). Those Egyptians who followed the *salafiya* for a time cooperated with the new Governor-General, and he was successful also in splitting away from the nationalist movement the leaders of the Coptic minority and the 'party of nobles', the mainly Turkish members of Cairo's ruling classes. Cromer had already shown the way by appointing Sa'd Zaghlul, one of Mohammed Abdu's pupils and friends, as Minister of Education in 1906.

In 1908, Sir Eldon Gorst appointed Butrus Ghali Pasha, the principal political figure among the Copts, as Prime Minister. There were then three main political parties in Egypt, all founded in 1907, the People's Party which followed Abdu, the Kemalist National Party, and the Khedive's party which was the party of Constitutional Reform. Only the Nationalists remained anti-British. But Gorst, in turn, succeeded in alienating the moderates as well as the nationalists. The moderates hoped for a continuation of Liberal reform in alliance with the British. Instead they saw British support given to a Khedive who seemed to want to restore the absolutism they regarded as an alien accretion on Islam. And, in 1909, the British ruined all chances of a successful outcome to their policy by forcing Butrus Ghali's government to propose a revision of the Suez Canal Company's concession, due to expire in 1968, to make it run a further forty years. There was an outburst of nationalist agitation, public order declined terribly and Butrus Ghali was murdered by a fanatic. His successor allowed the Assembly to throw the bill out. Sir Eldon Gorst died within the year from cancer, and Lord Kitchener came to replace him. After a period of repression he was able by 1913 to restore good relations with the moderate nationalists by introducing a revision of the constitution, giving the Legislative Council of the National Assembly the powers to suspend and initiate legislation. Sa'd Zaghlul resigned his ministry and was elected vice-president of the new Assembly.

In these years, too, the Arab monarchies of the twentieth century first began to take their shape. In 1908, under pressure from the Ottoman Liberal Turks of the revolution, the Sultan released from captivity in Constantinople Hussein ibn Ali, the head of one of the two branches of the house of Beni Hashem, the direct descendants of the Prophet Mohammed, from which families alone could be appointed the Grand Sharif of Mecca. At this date the position was largely titular, since Mecca, the holy city of Islam, was the capital of a Turkish province, with a Turkish Governor-General and garrison. Nevertheless, the claims of the Grand Sharif to be head of Islam could technically be considered strong. And, in securing his own appointment as

Grand Sharif, Hussein was responding cannily to the pan-Islamic currents which were then sweeping the Middle East. On arrival in Mecca, he took steps to reassert the temporal position of the Grand Sharif as Amir of Mecca, soliciting the support of the *bedouin*, rebuffing a Young Turkish delegation, quarrelling with the Turkish governor of the Hejaz, and defeating a Turkish proposal to destroy the special status of the Hejaz as exempt from taxation and conscription. At the same time his youngest son, Abdullah, future King of Jordan, was elected deputy for Mecca to the Turkish parliament, and made it his business to build up contacts with the Arab nationalist societies of Syria. It was probably Abdullah who secured the opening of contacts with the Arab deputies in Constantinople mentioned above. And it was in these years that Hussein and his family began nurturing plans for an Arab kingdom independent in all but name of the Ottoman Empire.

On the other side of the Arabian peninsula, in the country then called Nejd, another future Arab monarch, Abdul Aziz ibn Saud, had recaptured his ancestral capital, Riyadh, from the Rashidi of Hail in 1901, and beat them in battle in 1903. He was faced in 1904 with an attack by Turkish troops called in by the Rashidi to restore their position. After an initial defeat he succeeded in obliterating the Turkish army. But he nevertheless felt it safer to sue for formal submission to the Sultan. This submission did not prevent him catching and killing the Rashidi sheikh in April 1906; and thereafter the Turks withdrew their troops from the Nejd. From 1906–10, ibn Saud was gradually consolidating his desert realm, terrorizing the minor sheikhs into acknowledging his supremacy and putting down uprisings against him with a severity beyond the normal practice of *bedouin* politics. In 1913, he began to use the Wahhabi faith of his followers to settle them in religiously-governed settlements, gathering them together in a kind of religious brotherhood known as the *Ilkhwan*. In 1911, he contacted the British in Kuwait and proposed an alliance to expel the Turkish garrison from the Hasa, the coastal province south of Kuwait. His proposal was turned down. In May 1913, he undertook the conquest of Hasa himself. But after expelling the Turkish garrison in May 1914, he again insured himself against the possibility of Turkish support for his tribal rivals by accepting the nominal appointment of a Turkish Governor-General of Nejd.

The third of the Arab rulers to assert himself in this period was less successful. This was the Imam Yahya of the Yemen, who, in 1911, with Italian encouragement, rose against the Turkish garrison on the coast. The rising provoked full-scale Turkish intervention and the capture of his capital, Sana. A treaty re-established his rule as a Turkish agent in the highlands, but left a Turkish army of some 14,000 men in the coastal strip. Further north, the Asiri tribes under that now-vanished dynasty the Idrisi, also rose against the Turks and managed to establish some degree of independence, which they were to maintain until their absorption by ibn Saud in 1925.

Chapter 9

Europe turns on itself: the Anglo-German Crisis, 1909–12

BY 1909, the pattern of events which was to lead the European powers to mutual self-destruction was already beginning to be established. In the Bosnian crisis can be seen the first of the three elements in that pattern which played the largest part in the outbreak of the war in 1914, the attempt of the Habsburg monarchy to stifle Balkan nationalism, its inevitable enemy, before the monarchy itself began to fall apart; and a second element, the challenge of Imperial Germany to Russian Pan-Slavism in the Balkans and at the Straits had also made an appearance. The third element, that of Germany's challenge to Britain, underlay and antedated both of these. With the intensification of Anglo-German naval rivalry and the second Moroccan crisis of 1911 it was now to emerge as the most significant element on the international scene. For the first time since the Kaiser's telegram was sent to President Kruger in 1897, British opinion beyond the closed circle of the Foreign Office, the Admiralty, and the War Office, the Cabinet and the few journalists in the know began to echo the wondering words of the Liberal Premier, Asquith, who told his chief Conservative opponent Balfour in 1908: 'Incredible as it might seem, the Government could form no theory of the German policy which fitted the known facts, except that they wanted war.'

The main elements in this change of opinion were the growing realization of German naval strength coupled with the increasingly assertive role played by Germany in European politics. Of these, by far the more important was the naval issue. Agitation began at the time of the publication of the British 1908–9 naval programme in February 1908, a programme which seemed absurdly small in relation to German construction. It was fanned by a highly imprudent personal letter addressed by the Kaiser to the First Lord of the Admiralty, Lord Tweedsmouth, attempting to reassure Lord Tweedsmouth that the German programme was not directed against the British. In April 1908, Tweedsmouth's successor as First Lord, Reginald McKenna, was persuaded by the Admiralty that the next annual programme should include no fewer than six Dreadnoughts, the Kaiser's letter having played its part in converting the Admiralty to the policy of laying down two keels for every one laid down by Germany. This proposal was fought bitterly by the advocates of economy in the Cabinet, of which the two strongest were Lloyd George, the Chancellor of the Exchequer, and Winston Churchill. In June 1908, Churchill was the Kaiser's guest at the German Army manoeuvres, and returned to Britain convinced of Germany's pacific intentions.

That was not the conviction which their meeting with the Kaiser at Kronberg in August 1908 left on King Edward VII and Lord Hardinge, the permanent head of the Foreign Office. The Kaiser refused point-blank to consider any reduction in the German naval programme, which was, he said, a point of honour with Germany. He would rather go to war than submit to British dictation. Thereafter, navalist agitation increased in Britain. It fed on the Kaiser's *Daily Telegraph* interview, and the Anglophobe reaction in Germany that followed, and was compounded with rumours that the Germans were planning a secret acceleration of construction so as to give them in 1912 not the projected thirteen Dreadnoughts built and building, but on some estimates seventeen, on others twenty-one to the British figure of eighteen. The British Cabinet compromised on this news, by laying down four Dreadnoughts in the 1909–10 programme with four more to be laid down before April 1910 if the necessity was proven. In March 1909, the Cabinet revealed its estimate of German naval strength to a hushed and shocked House of Commons. There followed a major outburst of public opinion in support of an eight Dreadnought programme for 1909–10, an outburst compounded by the news which broke in April 1909 that Germany's two allies in the Triple Alliance, Austria and Italy, were each about to lay down four Dreadnoughts. In July 1909, the Cabinet decided to lay down all eight Dreadnoughts.

The British decision, in turn, resulted in a major Cabinet crisis in Germany between Chancellor Bülow and the Chief of

T–H

the German naval staff, Admiral von Tirpitz. It was the latter who was the main driving force behind the German programme. A convinced navalist, he had evolved a variation of the Mahan thesis as to the connexion between seapower and great power status. According to Tirpitz's theory all that was necessary was to build a fleet sufficiently large as to make it too dangerous for the larger naval powers to attack, since their resultant naval losses would leave them weaker than their more immediate rivals. This so-called 'risk theory' was conceivably valid in a polycentric, multi-polar, great power system. But such a system, even if it had existed in Bismarck's day, was beginning to disappear at least five years before Tirpitz began to formulate his theory, with the conclusion of the Franco-Russian alliance and the gradual bi-polarization of the great power system into two alliance systems. And nothing, so it turned out, was more calculated to accelerate this process of bi-polarization than German naval construction, since British opinion gradually took on the conviction that the German fleet was directed solely against Britain.

Bülow did his best, therefore, to persuade Tirpitz and the Kaiser of the need to reduce naval construction in the interests of an Anglo-German *rapprochement*. He failed completely and resigned in July 1909. His successor, Bethmann Hollweg, was if anything more anxious for agreement with Britain, but negotiations, which began in October 1909, were hampered by the German insistence that a naval agreement could only be accompanied by a political agreement which would bind each to benevolent neutrality, if the other were attacked by a third party. The aim was clear, to disrupt the Anglo-French *Entente*, which British official opinion was coming increasingly to see as essential to the balance of power in Europe. The British government could only counter this German thrust by postponing negotiations until after the 1910 General Election. The 1910–11 naval programme introduced into Parliament in May 1910 included five Dreadnoughts and provoked a fresh outburst of opposition from the radicals in the cabinet led by Churchill. Australia and New Zealand each volunteered to pay for an additional capital ship. A further five capital ships were to be included in the programme for 1911–12.

A second German overture to Britain had been made in June 1910, and a further eighteen months of negotiation followed. It broke down again because of the conflicting aims of the two sides. Britain wanted an *Entente* on the lines of those concluded with France and Russia which would put an end to the existing sources of tension between the two countries, of which the naval issue and the Baghdad railway line were the most important. The Germans wanted to detach Britain from the Franco-Russian alliance. Nothing less would compensate them for agreeing to modify their naval plans. The British entered the negotiations with little hope of their success and great suspicion of their opponents. The Germans entered with an entirely exaggerated idea of Britain's willingness to negotiate and of her vulnerability to economic considerations. Even then there was a chance that German pressure might have been partially successful but for Germany's own action in July 1911 in provoking the second Moroccan crisis.

The British Liberal government, on whom the German pressure was to be exerted, were, as had been earlier remarked, an odd mixture of conservatism in world affairs and social reformism at home. That minority element in the cabinets of Sir Henry Campbell-Bannerman, and his successor, Herbert Asquith, who were interested in foreign affairs, are normally described by historians as imperialists: but they had little of the aggressive drive for annexation which is regarded as essential in imperialism. Theirs was much more the imperialism of the satisfied, and their aim in international affairs was to preserve the *status quo*. What offended them most and also aroused their suspicions, in German and Austrian actions, was the lack of respect they felt was so often shown by those two powers for the interests of the other European powers and for the conventions of international intercourse. In the pattern of European politics, they were the conservative element, Aehrenthal, Bülow, Izvolski even, the radicals. They were, however, only one element in a party which included many much more genuine radicals than these foreign statesmen, men fairly and squarely in the English radical tradition of resentment of externally-imposed limitations on national freedom of action in domestic affairs, simplists who saw the task of British foreign policy to be that not of maintaining the checks and balances of the international power system, but of finding some once-and-for-all solution to all international problems which would enable them to return to the serious business of pressing for internal reform and lambasting as reactionaries those who opposed them.

As a result, the British government felt unable to play as determined a hand as they might otherwise have done. And a great many of the more vital issues and decisions were never thoroughly discussed by the Cabinet. Instead, the bulk of British energies were concentrated on those internal battles which by 1914 were to bring Britain to the verge of civil war. The roots of these lay in the determination of the Liberal movement in 1906 to secularize the education system, introduce a system of redistributive taxation, grant a degree of Home Rule to Ireland, reform the system of land revenue and taxation, reduce the political power of the brewery and drink interests and protect the position of the Trades Unions, a programme which involved tackling head-on the power of the main corporative organizations which had hitherto dominated those large areas of governmental activity in which previous governments had been content to devolve responsibility upon private persons and voluntary organizations. Many of these organizations were well represented in Conservative circles. The Liberals' reforms would have greatly reduced their power; indeed, the main Liberal objection to most of them was that they represented undemocratic concentrations of power. And the permanent Conservative majority in the hereditary House of Lords remained determined to obstruct and thwart all the Liberal reforms which were intended to serve this Liberal purpose. Thus, the 1906 Education Bill was reduced to such a travesty of itself in the House of Lords that the Commons refused to proceed with it. Only the Trades Disputes Bill and a Workmen's Compensation Act of the major programme of 1906 went through without emasculation. In 1907, the Irish Devolution Bill and two bills designed to deal with the land problem in Scotland were defeated. In 1908, the Budget and the Old Age Pensions Bill got through the Lords in deference to the constitutional convention in which matters of finance the Commons were sovereign. But the principal bill of this session, one designed to reduce progressively the number of public houses and a new education bill, were again thrown out by the Conservative majority in the Lords. Talks designed to reach a *modus vivendi* between the two Houses seemed to be getting nowhere. And greatly to the alarm of the Liberal Party, there seemed to be no very great public outcry among the electorate at this wanton thwarting of the democratic process.

It was in these circumstances that the new Chancellor of the Exchequer in 1909, the Welsh radical, the one-time small-town lawyer, David Lloyd George, came to draft the 1909 Budget. He needed to increase the Budget by £14 million, about 10 per cent on its 1908 level, to cover the cost of the eight Dreadnoughts to meet the German challenge, and to build up the revenue to finance the schemes of social insurance on the German and Continental model under discussion in Liberal intellectual circles. His task was made to seem much more difficult by the fact that a trade recession had actually reduced the revenue from Customs and Excise by 15 per cent of the total Budget. He chose to use his need to raise more revenue both for social and defence purposes to attack the main interests behind the Conservative opposition in their weakest position, their liability to taxation. Not only did he penalize the brewing interests for their opposition to temperance reform by a six-and-a-half million pound increase in duties; he also raised Income Tax progressively and introduced a supertax on incomes of £5,000 and over for that portion which exceeded £3,000 per annum. Most daringly, he introduced four taxes on increases in land values, and a capital gains tax confined to gains in the capital and rental value of land. Together, these constituted a direct attack on the principle of property and the position of the hereditary land-owning peerage and gentry, on which so much Conservative support in the rural areas was based. In November 1909, after six months of heightened tension, the House of Lords broke the precedents of 250 years and rejected the Budget. The Liberal Government at once dissolved Parliament and were returned with a majority of 124 including 84 Irish Home Rulers.

The Budget was presented again to the new Parliament, and duly passed by the House of Lords. But the Liberals were now determined to democratize the House of Lords, and break the corporative powers which in their view stood behind it. Their ultimate weapon was to be the power of the Crown to create a sufficient number of Liberal peers to swamp the Conservative majority in the House of Lords; but they were bound by the King's belief that he would only be correct in doing so if a second General Election had given the Liberal Party a specific mandate for such a step. At this critical moment King Edward VII died and was succeeded by his son, the 46-year-old King George. For six months a last attempt was made to reach agreement between the two Houses, or to find a way out of the *impasse* by the creation of a new Centre Party; but these manoeuvres were in vain. In December 1910, a second General Election confirmed the Liberal majority, and left the way open for a new Parliament Bill linking the powers of the House of Lords to a suspensory vote which could only delay a Bill for three sessions before it should finally become law. When the House of Lords realized that the Liberals had secured the new King's consent to a mass creation of peers, the majority gave in, leaving a die-hard minority of just under a hundred irreconcilables to record their votes against the government.

The Parliament Act of 1911 had broken the power of the House of Lords to obstruct the Liberals' reform programme. It had by no means crushed the resistance of the British right to what they regarded as subversive and socialist doctrines, inspired by the spirit of class warfare rather than of public service. The Liberal Party programme of 1911 included the major schemes of sickness and unemployment insurance foreshadowed by Lloyd George in 1909. That of 1912 included a major measure of Home Rule for Ireland and the disestablishment of the Anglican Church in Wales. If the land taxes of 1909 were considered subversive, these were regarded by the Conservatives as positively revolutionary. They had already turned on their leader, Arthur Balfour, and forced him to resign, replacing him with a Canadian Scottish business man, Bonar Law. Their decision ushered in what was to be perhaps the greatest crisis in British politics since the Jacobite Revolt of 1745, a crisis which began with the arming of Conservative Unionists in the six Protestant counties of Northern Ireland or Ulster and the raising of a volunteer force of 100,000 men. This was essentially a political move designed to force the Liberal Government to think again – but it was accompanied by alarming and unscrupulous invocations of physical force. What transformed their move from a reckless game of bluff to a preparation for civil war and insurrection was the parallel growth of extremism in the South of Ireland, where volunteers were also being raised and drilled, and arms collected. Most of the major powers in Europe stood on the edge of civil strife in the decade before 1914. But not even Austria-Hungary, only Russia in fact, had reached a state of disorder and division similar to that of affairs in Britain.

Nor was this the only source of disorder in Britain. The

Trades Union movement, like its opposite numbers in France and elsewhere, had embarked on a programme of militant industrial action which threatened to paralyse the country. The most discontented were the railwaymen and the miners, followed by the dockers. Then there was the movement to secure the suffrage for women, which in 1905 had abandoned ordinary methods of propaganda for the use of publicity and violence, its supporters chaining themselves to railings, invading Parliament, assaulting Ministers and even breaking shop windows and burning down country houses. Nor were there lacking charges of corruption, charges which publicly crystallized in 1912 around Ministers' dealings in the American Marconi Company's shares, at the very moment its British parent company was concluding a large and lucrative Government contract. The scandal was somehow smoothed over by the Liberal Party leadership, but it shook the position of the Liberal Government severely, and did much to exacerbate feelings on both sides of the party division.

These internal developments greatly undermined Britain's international position which was being weakened in other directions. The two most serious developments were the breakdown of the Anglo-Russian understanding on Persia and the increasing threat of serious trouble between Japan and the United States, trouble which could disrupt the settlement in the Far East and face Britain with the impossible choice between her Japanese ally and her 'cousins', the Americans, with whom it was axiomatic now that war was unthinkable.

The breakdown in Anglo-Russian understanding in Persia was partially connected with the Russian fear that the constitutional revolution of 1909, which overthrew the Shah, was basically directed at them, and was favourable to Britain. In 1908, Russian troops had intervened in the disturbances and occupied Tabriz, one of the revolutionary centres. Although they evacuated Tabriz at the end of the year, the subsequent hostility of the population to the Russian colony in the city drove them to a second occupation in May 1909, and, in October, Russian troops invaded Persian Azerbaijan in force, making little effort in the field to hide their annexationist intentions. An element in the Russian action was anxiety over the growth of German influence in Persia, over the activities of the German bankers with whom the concession for a German bank in Persia was under discussion, over reports that Germany was about to ask for a railway concession in Persia, and over the increase of German arms trade with Persia. Britain reacted by pressing for closer cooperation with Russia in Persia, especially in a joint Anglo-Russian loan to the new Persian Government. In May 1910, the British and Russians together demanded that Persia submit any European requests for concessions in the English or Russian zones of influence in Persia to the power concerned for its advance approval.

This move provoked such strong German pressure on Russia (the Germans having again perceived a chance of using the Persian issue to pry open the Anglo-Russian *Entente*) as to bring the new Russian Foreign Minister, Sazonov, on a visit to Potsdam with the Tsar. During the visit, the inexperienced Sazonov, led by his desire to reduce German-Russian tension, verbally promised Germany that Russia would not support Britain in an anti-German policy, in return for similar German reassurances regarding Austrian policy towards Russia. The two countries further agreed to link the Berlin-Baghdad railway to a projected Russian railway system in Northern Persia, and Germany gave assurances that she would not intervene in the Russian Zone in Persia. Sazonov retreated very rapidly from the most far-reaching of these reassurances, which somewhat naturally caused considerable alarm in Britain and France when they became known. But the appointment of Shuster, an American financial expert, as adviser to the Persian Government in 1911, and his appointment in turn of a British officer to command the *Gendarmerie* in northern Persia caused a fresh crisis, which was not ended until the threat of a Russian invasion of Central Persia caused Shuster's dismissal, something in which Britain was forced to acquiesce, albeit with very bad grace. The conclusion in August 1911 of a German-Russian agreement on the railway issue in Persia, at a time when the Agadir crisis was at its height, did nothing to ease Anglo-Russian relations.

Britain's position in the Pacific was equally precarious owing to the development of major tension between Japan and the United States; tension in which the British Pacific Dominions were also closely involved. The conflict sprang in part from the growth of anti-Japanese feeling on the west coast of the United States and in Canada, which expressed itself both in opposition to fresh immigration from Japan and in measures designed to make the position of immigrants as difficult as possible. Japanese emigration to the United States and to Canada began in the late 1890s. In 1907, no fewer than 30,000 Japanese arrived in the United States from Japan, and in the period 1902–6, about the same number of immigrants, most of whom were Japanese, came from Hawaii to the United States. The number of Japanese residing in the US rose from 2,000 in 1890 to 24,000 in 1900, 72,000 in 1910, and 111,000 in 1920. The immigrants were mainly males and employed as labourers, but once established they sent back to Japan for brides. In October 1906, the school board in San Francisco acted to segregate the Japanese children in the city's schools. In effect, they were only transferring to the Japanese the anti-Oriental racialism from which the Chinese had suffered since the 1880s (see Chapter III above). The Japanese had not failed to observe the troubles of the Chinese in the United States, and had tried discreetly to discourage immigration from Japan to America by controlling the issue of passports. But they were unable to stop the migration of Japanese labour from Mexico, Canada and Hawaii to the United States, and there had already been vain attempts by Californian interests to influence Congress to restrict Japanese immigration. The action of the San Francisco school board followed the frustration of this pressure for action on a national scale by the Federal authorities.

The school board's action caused a considerable exacerbation of Japanese-American relations. President Roosevelt, however, realized the dangers in the situation and brought extreme pressure to bear on the San Francisco school board to rescind their order. While discreetly preparing the American fleet, he was able to negotiate an agreement with the Japanese, the so-called Gentleman's Agreement of February 24th, 1907, by which Japan bound herself not to issue passports to would-be immigrants to the United States. At the same time he acted on his executive authority to exclude from the United States all immigrants who held passports not valid for the US, thus shutting off immigration from Hawaii. On March 13th, 1907, the school order was rescinded. But before his retirement from the Presidency in March 1909, he was forced to intervene on several other occasions to scotch further Californian anti-Japanese legislation.

The crisis had however been an alarming one, and led Roosevelt to attempt to enlist the support of Canada (where anti-Japanese riots had broken out in Vancouver in September

1907) to bring pressure to bear on Britain, Japan's ally. His efforts were negated by the action of the Canadian Government in sending an unofficial emissary to Japan to negotiate an agreement by which the Japanese Government would restrict immigration to Canada on its own. For at least a year Roosevelt was partially convinced of the imminence of a Japanese-American war; and his convictions led him to order the US Fleet to the Pacific as the first stage in a world cruise which demonstrated to the world the position of strength the US Navy had come to occupy. In October 1908, at Japanese invitation, the fleet visited Tokyo; in November the Root-Takahira agreement pledged both powers to maintain the existing *status quo* in China and the Pacific. The conclusion of the Root-Takahira agreement greatly eased American-Japanese relations, and the US fleet was moved back to its Atlantic bases. But the agreement bound only the Roosevelt administration; and his successor, President Taft, was to institute a forward policy in China and Manchuria which was difficult to reconcile with the spirit of the Root-Takahira agreement.

The main element of this new policy was the active encouragement of American overseas investment, dollar diplomacy, as it has been called. In 1908, American investment in the Far East was generally made in Japan, and not in China. The appointment of the former American Consul in Manchuria, Willard Straight, as head of the American State Department's Far Eastern Division, began a deliberate attempt to reverse this trend. Straight was perhaps the first of the American ideological China lobbyists. His most important field at first was railways, where his ally was the American railway tycoon and millionaire, Harriman. In 1905, Harriman had attempted to buy the South Manchurian railway. In 1909, he joined with Kuhn, Loeb and Co, the American bankers, to persuade Straight to leave Government service and to act as their chief negotiator. Their aim was to force the Japanese to sell the South Manchurian railway, by purchasing from Russia the Chinese Eastern railway, and building on to it a line which would run parallel with the South Manchuria railway from Chinchow in the south to Aigun on the Siberian border. These were tactics of the sort which Harriman had used to create his American railroad empire. In this instance, they received the full backing of the United States Government, which approached Britain in November 1909 with a proposal to effect the complete neutralization of the Manchurian railways, or failing that to support jointly the projected Chinchow–Aigun line; in other words to join in a dubious commercial manoeuvre, the aim of which was to injure the principal Manchurian interests of Britain's ally, Japan. This gratuitous attempt to drive a wedge between Britain, her Japanese ally and her Russian partner in the *Entente* was supported only by Germany, as another move in her constant struggle to break up the alliances and understandings which Germany believed kept her from playing her proper part in world affairs. A similar approach to Russia only provoked the Russian and Japanese Governments, with British and French acquiescence, to conclude in July 1910 an agreement which resulted in the practical closing of Manchuria and Mongolia to all but Japanese and Russian capital. Thus, Roosevelt's policy of maintaining a judicious balance between Japan and Russia, while never offending Japan, was in ruins. Inevitably, the Americans heaped on Britain much of the blame for the failure of this ingenuous, unnecessary and ill-considered manoeuvre.

A similar effort was made by Straight to force American participation in the Anglo-French-German consortium engaged in 1909 in negotiating a loan for the projected Hukuang railways from Hangchow into the Kwangtung and Szechuan provinces of China. Failing to make any impression in London the American Government turned to direct pressure on Peking. By means of using this pressure to block a Chinese grant of the Hukuang concession, the American Government was able to force the three European Governments to admit the American banks to the consortium. The main effect of the pressure was to contribute greatly to the sequence of events which led to the 1912 Revolution in China.

This course of events was the most embarrassing to the British Government in view of the need to renew the alliance with Japan which was due to expire in 1915. The renewal of the alliance in 1905 had enabled the British among other things to withdraw all their capital ships from the Far East to face the rising menace of Germany. By 1910, the Japanese Navy had become so powerful as to make Japan wholly unassailable. Whereas, in 1905, Japanese strength was a useful means of restraining Russia from any attack on Britain's Asiatic possessions, by 1910 Britain could not afford to risk a break with Japan unless she was quite free of any anxiety as to her naval position in Europe. The anxieties aroused by this growth of Japanese seapower among the British Dominions in the Pacific, whose policy of Oriental exclusion rendered them easy victims for Japan to pick a quarrel with, were she so inclined, reinforced this argument. The breakdown in Japanese relations with the United States caused by the racialism of the Californian state legislature and the dollar diplomacy of the Taft administration made it essential for Britain to renew the Anglo-Japanese alliance only on terms which would effectively prevent its ever becoming operative against the United States.

The British thought they had found a means of securing these safeguards when President Taft publicly proposed the negoti-ation of a universal arbitration treaty, or, failing that, a series of bilateral arbitration treaties. Negotiations were taken up simultaneously in Washington and Tokyo, and an Anglo-American arbitration treaty was signed in August 1911, less than a month after the conclusion of a revised version of the Anglo-Japanese alliance, which specifically excluded it from operating against any nation with whom Britain had an arbitration treaty. The American Senate's failure to ratify the arbitration treaty was dealt with by a British declaration that they would still continue to act as though it were in force. This face-saving device concealed but did not eliminate the fundamental depen-dence of the British position in the Pacific on Japan and the United States, neither of whom Britain could afford to offend. This was to be a major source of anxiety, weakness and dis-traction to Britain in the post-war years.

The dilemma faced by the British Government was underlined by the effects of Japan's growing power on the British Pacific Dominions, Australia, New Zealand and Canada. Since the Dominions' participation in the South African war, a strong current of opinion in Britain had pursued the idea of creating out of the Empire a kind of super-confederation, and of enlisting the aid of the Dominions to lighten Britain's increasing burden of defence. At the 1902 Colonial Conference, the then Colonial Secretary, Joseph Chamberlain, had appealed for aid to the Dominions, depicting Britain in harsh tones as a 'weary Titan', bowed down under the 'too vast orb of its fate'. His reward was a slight increase in the subsidies paid by Australia and New Zealand for the auxiliary squadron maintained by Britain in their waters, and their reluctant agreement to British control of these forces. The growth of Japanese strength after 1905 was viewed in Australia and New Zealand with great alarm, amounting on at least one occasion to near panic, and the US fleet was given a tumultuous welcome on its visit to Sydney in 1908.

The increasing of the German threat to British security was marked principally by the removal of the British battle squadron from Chinese waters in 1905, and it was only in 1909 that the naval agitation in Britain made a real impact on the Dominions. The result was the undertaking by Australia, New Zealand and the Federated Malay States each to provide one Dreadnought or battle cruiser for the Navy. The Admiralty, then suffering from a double anxiety as to the forthcoming end of the Anglo-Japanese alliance, argued that each Dreadnought or battle cruiser should form the nucleus of a battle squadron, of which, in all, four were contemplated, respectively for the East Indian, Australian, Far Eastern and Canadian Pacific stations. The creation of separate Dominions fleets, however, only enhanced the need for Britain to secure agreement on a unified imperial foreign policy, and in May 1911 the British Foreign Minister, Grey, made a general *exposé* to Dominions delegates of British policy and the menace Germany was felt to constitute to the heart of the Empire; he obtained their wholehearted support for the renewal of the Anglo-Japanese alliance. This consultation marked a major stage in the evolution of the old relationship between Britain and her colonies towards the modern Commonwealth. There is no necessity to consult colonies.

The renewal of the Anglo-Japanese alliance and the signature of the Anglo-American arbitration treaty relieved Britain of a pressing extra-European anxiety at precisely the moment at which Germany chose to provoke a fresh crisis with France. The occasion for this crisis was the steady disintegration of the Sultan's *régime* in Morocco, where the increasing resentment of the inland tribes against the growth of French influence in the country had led them into revolt against the *régime*. In 1910, Sultan Moulay Hafid appealed to the French for military assistance. However, the organization of this assistance had not ended the revolt, and in the spring of 1911, Moulay Hafid found himself besieged by tribesmen in Fez. His appeals to the French resulted in the organization of a French relief column which raised the siege of Fez on May 21st, 1911. The French Government was aware that this action was difficult to reconcile with the terms of the Algeciras agreement of 1906 which had reaffirmed the independence and integrity of Morocco. The central figure in the current French Cabinet, the Finance Minister, Joseph Caillaux, was an advocate of economic cooperation between Germany and France; and the French Government, under his prompting, did its best to appease the Germans in advance of the relief of Fez. But their slowness in producing serious proposals, and the parallel action of Spain in occupying two towns in the zone secretly allocated to her in the Franco-Spanish agreement of 1904, led the Germans to overplay their hand out of a mixture of suspicion, misunderstanding and over-confidence. On July 1st, the German gunboat, *Panther*, arrived in Agadir, a port on Morocco's Atlantic coast, with the declared aim of protecting German interests there. This somewhat forceful statement of German interests was followed on July 15th by a demand for compensation, in the shape of the cession to Germany of the whole of the French Congo, in return for the grant of a protectorate over Morocco to France; the pill was sweetened by the offer to throw in German Togoland with Morocco as France's share of the deal.

By contrast with the crisis of 1905 the Agadir crisis provoked by these demands caused little panic in France. The Caillaux government met them with a firm refusal to cede the whole Congo, but with an apparent willingness to haggle over a detailed agreement. But in London the sheer scale of the German claims raised fears not only that Germany would secure a naval base at Agadir, but, much more seriously, that this was yet another German attempt to humiliate France and destroy the *Entente*. These fears were instrumental in bringing over to the side of the Germanophobes in the Cabinet, David Lloyd George, the most powerful and controversial figure in British domestic politics. In a speech at the Mansion House on July 21st, 1911, he issued a warning that Britain would prefer war to a European pacification achieved at the cost of her national honour. The German-French crisis in fact passed off quite smoothly with a minor Franco-German exchange of territory, and German recognition of a French protectorate over Morocco in November 1911. But its effects in Europe were quite different. In France, the French nationalist and colonialist right wing raised charges of timidity against Caillaux and secured his replacement in January 1912 by the right wing chauvinist anti-German Lorrainer, Poincaré, who was determined to strengthen France against Germany.

In Britain, the crisis had revealed a lack of preparation for war and a total disagreement between the Admiralty and the Army authorities on the strategy to be followed should war occur. In October 1911, Winston Churchill was appointed to the Admiralty, and thus the other great opponent of an Anglo-German naval race was converted to the need to outbuild Germany. The moment was significant. The British intervention in the Agadir crisis had enabled the German navalists to argue that a larger German fleet would have restrained Britain; and in the autumn of 1911 discussions began on a new German navy law, the *Novelle*, designed to provide Germany with a fleet two-thirds the size of the Royal Navy. Advocates of economy in both countries were able to secure one last attempt at an Anglo-German agreement before the *Novelle* was submitted to the German *Reichstag*. But the conversations held during the visit of Lord Haldane, the German-educated, Scottish-born War Minister, to Berlin in February 1912 broke down again on Germany's refusal to modify her building programme except in exchange for a British guarantee of neutrality in any war in which Germany might be embroiled. Churchill, at his most bellicose, announced Britain's intentions of building Dreadnoughts so as to maintain a superiority of 60 per cent over the German Navy, and laying down 'two keels for one', for every supplementary ship Germany might lay down.

At the same time, measures were taken to counter the other alarming element in the *Novelle*, its intimation that the vast bulk of these ships would be immediately available for action throughout the year. When taken with new increases in Austrian and Italian Dreadnought construction, the new German naval construction faced Britain with the necessity of so concentrating her battle fleets against Germany as to leave an inadequate margin of strength against Germany's allies in the Mediterranean.

The British chose to deal with this new menace in four ways. First, they appealed to the Dominions, and succeeded in persuading the Canadian Government to offer the construction of three new battleships to play the main part in an Imperial squadron to be stationed at the western mouth of the Mediterranean at Gibraltar. Secondly, they increased construction with the aim eventually of providing a Mediterranean fleet capable of matching the Austrian and Italian fleets. Thirdly, they did their best to build up the Turkish fleet, for which they had already laid down two Dreadnoughts in 1911. And finally, and most significantly, as an interim measure, they concluded in November 1912 an agreement with the French, by which the French fleet would take over the defence of the Mediterranean. As a further element in strengthening the British position the Admiralty decided to increase substantially the speed of their latest battle-ships by converting them from coal to oil. To secure fuel supplies, the Admiralty in 1914 bought a controlling interest in the Anglo-Persian Oil Company, formed six years earlier after the discovery of oil in commercial quantities in South-West Persia, and forced a partial agreement between Anglo-Persian and its main competitor, Royal-Dutch Shell. Their action involved Britain much more seriously in Persian politics than before, and necessitated an agreement between Britain and the South Persian tribes over which the Persian Government's control was sketchy at best, which further weakened the Persian Government's position.

These years 1910–12 were marked also by the advance of liberalism in the Iberian Peninsula. In Portugal, republicanism had fed on the contrast between her mighty imperial past and the pitiful showing made by Portugal during the last stages of the scramble for Africa. As a last resort to avoid the establish-ment of a republic, King Carlos, in 1906, had come to entrust Franco, the strong man of the Regenerationist Party, with quasi-dictatorial powers. His rule had been brought to an end in 1908 when it was beginning to show signs of success, by the assassi-nation of the monarch. He was succeeded by his son Manuel, a weakling of nineteen. Two years later, in October 1910, the Republicans staged a *coup d'état*, and King Manuel took refuge in Britain. Royalist uprisings followed in 1911 and 1912; but the absence of any encouragement from the exiled King made it impossible for the rebels to win the necessary public support. The revolution was, in fact, the last result of a political struggle for power which had by 1911 largely lost its *rationale*. The new Republican *régime* was challenged almost at once by the nascent Portuguese labour movement. The ensuing labour troubles revealed the lack of any popular basis for the rather Victorian parliamentary system the Republicans now introduced. Inevit-ably, Portuguese republicanism degenerated towards a new dictatorship.

Chapter 10

The Breakdown of the System, 1912–14

FROM 1909–11, the Committee of Union and Progress had remained in virtual control of the Ottoman Empire. In 1911, however, the longing of the intellectuals and would-be parliamentarians in the movement for a more constitutional *régime* threw up an opposition group, the New Party, within the Young Turk Movement. A Party Congress failed to thrash out the differences within the movement and in November 1911 the malcontents linked with other Parliamentary figures to create a separate party, the Liberal Union. At the same time, venerable survivors of the Parliament of 1878 raised their voices against the Committee. The Committee's action in virtually suppressing the parliamentary opposition by calling a General Election in January 1912 and so arranging the election so that all but six of their opponents lost their seats only threw opposition back into the complicated byways from which they had themselves emerged. Young officers in Rumelia took to the hills, and a secret committee, the 'Saviour Officers', was formed in Istanbul with the aim of overthrowing the CUP and calling new and free elections. In August 1912, they ousted the Committee from power and formed a new parliamentary *régime*. But by January 1913 the *régime* had slipped so badly in resisting European pressure that the officers of the Committee were able to stage a new *coup d'état*. From June 1913 until 1918 Turkey was governed by a military *junta* headed by three men, Enver Pasha, Talat Pasha and Cemal Pasha.

Despite these internal struggles for power, the Ottoman Empire had been showing considerable signs of life and reform in the years 1909–11; so much was this so, when taken with the progress of the French occupation of Morocco, that the Italian Government, which had long had designs on Tripolitania and

Cyrenaica, was gravely alarmed. In September 1911, Italy picked a quarrel with Turkey over the treatment of Italian interests in Tripolitania and declared war on her. At the outbreak of the Italo-Turkish war, an Italian invasion force landed on the coasts of the two Ottoman provinces, and in November 1911 claimed Libya to be annexed to the Italian crown. However, Italy failed to beat the Ottoman forces in Libya, which were strongly supported by the local Arab population. The Italians chose, therefore, to widen the war. In April 1912, an Italian squadron bombarded the Dardanelles, and the following month, Italian troops occupied the Dodecanese islands off the Aegean coast of Turkey. The Ottoman position in Europe, meanwhile, was steadily deteriorating. Clandestine negotiations with Italy, ------ed in July, resulted on October 18th, 1912, in the signature of the Treaty of Lausanne, by which the Turks agreed to withdraw their forces from Libya and Cyrenaica on the understanding that, once the withdrawal was complete, the Italians would withdraw from the Dodecanese.

It was, however, already too late to save what remained of Turkey in Europe. Rebellion in Albania, the increasing activity of Serbian and Bulgarian *comitadjis* in Macedonia, the ambitions of Serbia, Bulgaria, Montenegro, and Greece, all combined to make the end seem imminent. The only thing needed was agreement on action against Turkey between the would-be successor states. Occasion and encouragement for this was provided by Russia, intent on repaying Austria for the humiliation of the Bosnian crisis of 1908–9 by encouraging the formation of a Balkan alliance to bar further Austrian expansion into the Balkans. The Russian Foreign Minister, Sazonov, was apparently convinced that only in this way could stability be achieved in the Balkans and a further deterioration in Russia's position in Europe be avoided. In fact, his conviction that the disintegration of the Ottoman state was only a matter of time can be seen in his disavowal of a proposal made by the Russian ambassador in Constantinople in October 1911 to secure from the Ottoman state Russian control of the Dardanelles in return for a Russian guarantee against any attack on them or adjacent Turkish territories.

Thus, when Serbia and Bulgaria concluded in March 1912 an alliance against any Great Power intending to invade or attack Ottoman territories in Europe, which included secret provisions

for the partition of Macedonia between them and for mediation
by the Tsar in the event of any dispute, Sazonov accepted this
agreement in the belief that it would act as a stabilizing factor in
the Balkans. In June, an alliance between Greece and Bulgaria
followed, though without any secret clauses. In August 1912,
Austria and, in September, Sazonov, who suddenly panicked,
asked Constantinople to accept concessions in Macedonia in
order to avoid a Balkan war, but the Turks refused to make the
concessions. That same month Bulgaria and Serbia decided on
war, in order not to miss the favourable advantage conferred by
Turkey's preoccupation with Italy. On October 8th, in a last
effort to avert war, a joint Austro-Russian note was presented to
the Balkan governments promising Great Power intervention to
secure reforms in Macedonia. But this proposal, the last thing
the Balkan states desired, came too late. The same day Montenegro jumped the gun and declared war on Turkey. Bulgarian,
Serbian and Greek declarations followed ten days later.

The armies of the new Balkan states proved infinitely more
effective than either European or Turkish opinion had expected.
A month after the outbreak of this first Balkan war, Serbian
forces had reached the Adriatic, and the Bulgarian armies closely
invested the Chatalja line, the last Turkish lines of defence
before Constantinople. An Albanian assembly proclaimed
Albania's independence at Valona on November 28th. On
December 3rd, Turkey, Bulgaria and Serbia signed an armistice;
the Greek and Montenegran forces continued hostilities however, the Montenegrans besieging Scutari, the Greeks Janina.
The disappearance of all but the residual extremities of Turkey
in Europe confronted the Great Powers with the most serious
upset the Concert of Europe had yet experienced. Before it was
clear that the Turkish lines of Chatalja would hold, Russia was
constrained to warn the Bulgarians against any occupation of
Constantinople on pain of being fired on by the Russian fleet.
But Pan-Slav sentiment in Russia was such that the Russian
Government felt obliged to support the Serbian claim for an
outlet to the Adriatic. To this the Austrians, with Italy's support,
remained adamantly opposed. The Austrian Government began
preparatory military moves, and the Russians retained certain
troops due for demobilization.

Peace was maintained by the good sense of all the powers
confronted with the possibility of war. At Russia's suggestion,

Britain called a Peace Conference; and a conference of the ambassadors of the Great Powers in London met to discuss the territorial changes which the final defeat of Turkey in Europe would involve. Austria insisted on the rights of the newly-proclaimed Albanian state to full control of all the Adriatic coast between Montenegro and Greece. In the face of this insistence, British, German and French advice was able to secure Russian abandonment of her support for the most far-reaching of Serbian claims. But the Peace Conference proved unable to reach agreement on a settlement agreeable to Turkey, for whom the mere discussion of surrender of Turkish claims on Adrianople sufficed to provoke the *coup d'état* of January 1913 by the leaders of the extreme nationalists, Enver Pasha, Cemal Pasha and Talat Pasha.

The *coup d'état* in Constantinople was followed by a renewal of the war. But the new Turkish rulers were no more successful than their predecessors, and a new armistice was concluded at the end of April 1913. The Peace Conference re-opened in London on May 20th, 1913. As before, the main difficulty proved to be restraining the victors. A naval demonstration was required to secure Serbian evacuation of Durazzo and Montenegran evacuation of Scutari, two cities which Austria regarded as essential to Albania's existence. On May 30th, 1913, the Treaty of London brought to an end the first Balkan war, Turkey ceding to the victors all her European territory except a strip of about thirty miles north of the Straits, and abandoning all claims to Crete.

The division of the spoils among the victors was to lead in less than a month to the second Balkan war. The central issue was the division of Macedonia. Baulked in the Adriatic, Serbia now demanded more compensation in Macedonia than Bulgaria, dominated and terrorized by the terrorist International Macedonian Revolutionary Organization, was in any mood to grant. At the same time, Greece refused to evacuate Salonica, which the Bulgarians also claimed. Rumania claimed Silistria, awarded to her by an ambassadors' conference in St Petersburg on May 9th. On June 2nd, Serbia and Greece concluded a new Treaty of Alliance against Bulgaria. Encouraged to excess by Austrian attempts to build up Bulgaria against Serbia, the King of Bulgaria ordered his troops to attack both Greece and Serbia on the night of June 29th, without the knowledge of his government. This foolhardy action exposed Bulgaria to the full onslaught of all her neighbours. Rumania occupied the Dobruja. Greek troops cleared most of the Aegean littoral. Serbian troops occupied all the territory Bulgaria had gained in Macedonia. And Turkey re-entered the lists to recover her former territory up to and including Adrianople. Defeated on all sides, Bulgaria was forced to sue for peace. The Treaty of Bucharest, signed on August 20th, 1913, deprived her of the major part of her gains in Macedonia and in Thrace as well as all the Dobruja. A separate Treaty of Constantinople, signed on September 29th, 1913, with Turkey, confirmed the Turkish re-occupation of Adrianople and set the frontier on the Maritza river.

There followed a similar period of megalomania on the part of Serbia and Greece in connexion with their continuing occupation of Albanian territory. Serbian intransigence on the frontiers when set against the mildness of Serbian reassurances to Austria provoked the gravest of suspicions in Vienna, and led, in October 1913, to the dispatch of a direct Austrian ultimatum to Belgrade demanding the evacuation of Albania. Faced with this direct threat, Serbia withdrew her troops, but it was to take another six months to settle the Albanian frontier with Greece, and even then the dispute over the Aegean islands remained unsettled.

This series of defeats at the hands of their former subjects could only enhance the tendency of the new Turkish *régime* towards centralism and Turkism noted in Chapter VIII and increase the strain on relations between the dominant Turkish *élite* and the other races of the empire. The worst sufferers were to be the Armenians whose own reliance on terrorism was to make them only too vulnerable to similar methods. In brief, their presence in villages inextricably interwoven into the Anatolian heartland of Turkey made their nationalist claims, their Christian faith and their links with the west insupportable to the Young Turks. From 1912 onwards, the Turks embarked on a policy of deliberate repression of the Armenians, which was to culminate, under the spur of war, in the terrible massacres of 1915-17 in which an estimated million and a half Armenians perished.

With the Arabs, the Young Turk leaders had to be more subtle. Various abortive military measures, as described in Chapter VIII, were undertaken to deal with the peripheral chiefs of the Yemen, Asir, and the Nejd. Negotiations were opened through his son Abdullah, one of the surviving Arab delegates to the

Turkish parliament, with Hussein, the Sharif of Mecca. In April 1914, Turkish pressure drove Abdullah to approach the British Governor-General of Egypt, Lord Kitchener, to ask, unsuccessfully, for arms for defence against the Turks. This pressure eased somewhat the same month when, in a scene reminiscent of Canossa, the Turkish governor of the Hejaz, being under instructions from the Turkish government who did not wish to alienate Hussein entirely, was forced to kiss the Sharif's robe. But the Turkish determination not to tolerate Arab pretensions was shown by their stiffening attitude to the Arab nationalists of Syria, the Lebanon and Palestine and of the Arab exile.

In January 1913, immediately before the Young Turks' *coup d'état*, a Committee of Reform was formed in Beirut to demand both the recognition of Arabic as a language of state for the province of the Lebanon and a high degree of decentralization to the provincial level. Similar demonstrations elsewhere in the Arab provinces led the new leaders of the Turkish government to announce various decentralizing measures in May. In June 1913, an Arab Congress met in Paris under the auspices of the Decentralization Party, and the secret society, *al Fatat*. The Turkish junta immediately entered into negotiations with the Arab Congress leaders, offering to include three Arab ministers in the Cabinet, to appoint five Arab governors of provinces and to concede the use of Arabic as a language of instruction in the elementary schools. Once the leadership had been won over, however, these concessions were withdrawn, and a decree of August 1913 scaled down or rescinded all the promised concessions.

In the international field, the new Turkish junta's resentment of their defeats turned them to further measures of modernization of their armed forces. In the naval sphere they turned to Britain, the leading naval power, who had in fact been maintaining a naval mission in Constantinople, at their request, since 1908. In 1911, two Dreadnoughts were to be built for Turkey in British yards, and in early 1913 a project of selling Turkey two pre-Dreadnoughts of the *Royal Sovereign* class was discussed between the two countries.

In the military field, the Turks naturally turned to the leading power on land, Germany. In June 1913, General Liman von Sanders was named head of a military mission of forty-two

German officers to train the Turkish army. The Turkish government chose to appoint him a member of the Turkish War Council, to grant him the rank and powers of a general in the Turkish army and to give him command of the First Turkish Army Corps which was guarding Russia's Black Sea life-line to the outside world, the Black Sea Straits. In November, the news of his appointment became known to the Russians. Protests couched in the strongest language were made in Constantinople and Berlin. For a time, military measures were apparently contemplated; but milder counsels prevailed, which was just as well for Russia as her army turned out to be unprepared for hostilities. In January 1914, Germany and Turkey agreed to promote Liman von Sanders to Field Marshal in the Turkish army and thus remove him from direct command over the Straits. This brought the crisis to an amicable end. The incident, however, left a lasting impression of German enmity on the mind of the Russian Foreign Minister, Sazonov, an impression which was to play its fateful part in the events of July 1914.

Nor was this the end of the deplorable consequences of the second Balkan war. Rumania had been bound to Germany and Austria-Hungary by a secret alliance since 1883, and the alliance was in fact renewed in February 1913. But the role of Germany and Austria in supporting Bulgaria during the second Balkan war had caused a great deal of annoyance and resentment in Bucharest. In the autumn of 1913, at the instance of the Austrian heir-apparent, Count Czernin was sent as ambassador to Rumania to attempt to win her support against Serbia. But Czernin found himself confronted with a series of complaints about the treatment of the Rumanian minority in Transylvania by the Magyars; the King of Rumania proved unwilling to acknowledge the secret alliance in public or to lend himself to Austrian schemes for a Rumano-Bulgar-Greek coalition against Serbia. Instead, he laid himself open to encouragement from the French and Russian ministers, encouragement which culminated in a visit by the Tsar to Constanza in June 1914 and discussion of a possible marriage of one of the Tsar's daughters to the Rumanian Crown Prince, Carol. Rumania's adherence to the central powers was clearly one of form only. The unhappy Austrians also managed at this time to offend their Italian allies by announcing measures designed to strengthen their own position in the Mediterranean as well as that of their new creation,

Albania. All in all the Balkan wars had been an unmitigated disaster for the Habsburg monarchy.

The events of 1912–13 had, on the whole, responded remarkably well to the procedures of the Concert of Europe. But 1914 was to prove that its fundaments had been shaken beyond hope of their functioning again. Austria-Hungary felt herself encircled by enemies intent on disrupting her internal order. Germany revealed a growing anti-Slav feeling and an increasing readiness to back Austria-Hungary against Russia without inquiring too closely into the merits of any particular issue. Britain still seemed capable of playing a mediator's role, but only when no direct quarrel between France and Germany was involved, and there had been no diminution in French suspicion of Germany, rather the reverse. Perhaps the worst feature of the Balkan crisis was the increasing difficulty the civilian elements in the three eastern empires were having in controlling their military commanders. They were to prove incapable of resisting the demands of the military for more armaments. In January 1913, a new arms race began on the European continent.

Once again the prime offender was Germany, or rather the German General Staff. In 1911 and again in 1912, they had insisted upon a larger German army. In January 1913, they demanded the formation of three new army corps. Although this demand was resisted on financial grounds, legislation passed in the *Reichstag* in July 1913 increased the peace-time army by 100,000 men at once, a figure which was to rise to 150,000, giving a total of 810,000 men by October 1914. The strain on Germany's financial resources was such that her naval construction programme had to be drastically cut, and Admiral Tirpitz attempted to make a virtue of necessity by offering to accept the ration of sixteen capital ships to every ten German ships proposed the previous year by Winston Churchill.

But Britain, now worried over Austrian and Italian construction, was in no mood to accept a proposal made *before* the passage of Germany's 1912 bill and based not on post-Dreadnought construction as Tirpitz made it, but on a figure which included Britain's overwhelming superiority in pre-Dreadnought ships. Britain's programme for 1913 added five new super-Dreadnoughts to the Fleet, the ill-fated *Royal Sovereign* Class. In addition, Churchill announced the formation of an Imperial squadron formed of the New Zealand, the Malayan and the three projected Canadian battleships. As an alternative, Churchill renewed his proposal for a 'building holiday' in capital ships, a sop to the radicals in his party. However, the proposal was indignantly rejected by Germany. The German rejection led Churchill to warn in October 1913 that the naval estimates for 1914 would have to be markedly increased (the Canadian Senate had meanwhile rejected the proposal to build three Canadian Dreadnoughts). And a bitter battle ensued both within and outside the Cabinet. As a result Churchill only succeeded in securing the four battleships of the 1914 programme by greatly cutting the light cruiser construction, creating a deficiency in this class which was to show itself markedly once war had begun.

More serious for the peace of Europe were the repercussions of the German army increases. In Russia, under the additional impact of the Liman von Sanders crisis, the Tsarist government adopted at the end of the year a vast new army programme, designed to make good the deficiencies revealed in munitions and artillery and to add half a million men to the one million three hundred thousand already under arms.

The reaction to the German army increases was faster in France than in Russia. In July 1913, the new French President, Poincaré, called for a credit of five hundred million francs and an increase in the length of army service from two to three years as a means of matching the lower French birthrate of the classes of 1895 onwards, now being called to the colours, with the intake of conscripts from the same classes in Germany. The increase gave France 790,000 men under arms on January 1st, 1914. It was bitterly fought in the French parliament and press and opened the way for a pronounced movement of French opinion towards the Radical and Socialist parties, united, as they were, on an anti-militarist platform. In December 1913, the patriotic Barthou ministry was overthrown and replaced by a middle of the road ministry including Caillaux, who had voted against the three-year term of service.

Austria-Hungary followed the Russian increase in armaments in March 1914, raising her annual intake from 175,000 to 200,000 men. In 1912–13 staff talks also began between the High Commands of the Triple Alliance. A naval agreement was reached between Austria and Italy in June 1913 on operations against France. Italian anxieties in Libya delayed the conclusion of a military agreement, and one was still under consideration in June 1914. But in the course of the discussions the German and Austrian Chiefs of Staff agreed in May 1914 that 'any procrastination' in the opening of a war against the Triple *Entente* 'led to a lessening of our chances'; they also expressed a good deal of scepticism of Italy's readiness to march, correctly as it happened, since the Italian Chief of Staff proved totally ignorant of the foreign policy position then being occupied by Italy's political chiefs. The increases in the effectiveness of the Russian army were agreed by the Italian Chief of Staff as well as his allied partners to increase the chances of defeat every year. And it was he, in fact, who in these conversations first voiced, in April 1914, the idea of a pre-emptive strike against the Triple *Entente*.

The increasing intransigence of the militarists in the Great Powers was in part a consequence of, in part given the lie by, the immense growth in strength of the radical, conciliationist internationalist, often anti-militarist forces in each country. There is a good deal to be said for the view that the principal cause of the tragic European breakdown in July 1914 was the inability of the democratic forces in central and eastern Europe to establish control over the militarist elements in their society, and the abdication of the autocrats not to their loyal democratic subjects but to their irresponsible military advisers. Under the French and British systems, the soldiers were at least formally under the control of the civilian cabinets and parliaments, though even here the events of 1914–18 were severely to try that control. The main danger came from an alliance of soldiers with the political nationalists of the right. In Italy, as we have seen, the Italian Chief of Staff was kept totally in ignorance of his government's foreign policy. In the eastern autocracies, the control of the armed forces was vested in the position of the autocrat alone, who could back Chancellor against Chief of Staff or *vice versa*, providing he had the personality to remain in control. In 1914, to Europe's eternal loss, neither the Kaiser nor the Tsar possessed that degree of personality, and the oldest of the three, Franz Josef, no longer cared.

This does not mean that the democratic anti-militarist reaction was without interest. It was certainly strong enough to preclude in every power save Austria-Hungary the idea of pre-emptive war. Its growth was, in fact, impressive. In France, the appointment of the Doumergue cabinet and Caillaux did not stem the lood. The general elections of April–May 1914 produced an increase in Socialist strength of 34 seats to 102 and a Radical party of over 160. President Poincaré's efforts to keep a ministry committed to the three-year term of service were ignominiously defeated and on June 14th, the ex-socialist, Viviani, took office with a compromise cabinet. On June 28th, the murder of Franz Ferdinand was to render his efforts superfluous.

In Italy, events were following a parallel course, though with much more violent reactions than those in France, owing to the weaker state of Italy's liberal-radical constitutional parties of centre and left. In 1911, Giolitti, the veteran radical leader, had increased the electorate from three to eight million, by introducing what was virtually universal male suffrage for all above the age of thirty. As in France, the previous years had seen the growth of an extreme Right dedicated to the ideas of violence, authoritarianism and expansion abroad. And as in France, the years 1911–12 produced a great rise in jingoist nationalism throughout Italy. This expressed itself not simply in support for Italian participation in the arms race but also for the Libyan adventure, and this manifestation of imperialist nationalism on the right was to produce an equally violent reaction among its opponents. The Socialist party swung violently to the left, rejecting any collaboration with a parliamentary system that could so easily be won for *bourgeois* imperialism; so violently that the reformist wing was expelled, and the young revolutionary, Benito Mussolini, was pitchforked into the editorship of the party newspaper, *Avanti*.

In 1913, therefore, the elections in Italy were to produce a rise in the Socialist vote so as to give the party 78 seats and a full quarter of the total vote cast. The middle-class radical vote rose proportionately, forcing the dominant liberal leadership under Giolitti into a coalition with the clericalists to maintain themselves in power. This coalition broke down in February 1914 with the withdrawal of radical support, and in June 1914 popular discontent broke out in a wave of violent strikes and peasant risings. Bologna, Ancona and other towns declared themselves independent communes and a republic was declared in the Romagna. Violence bred violence and the new cabinet of Salandra put down the risings with great severity. It was to prove even more nationalist than the coalition it had superseded.

In Germany, the introduction of the armaments programme

of 1912 in the *Reichstag* had been accompanied by elections which made the Socialist party with 110 seats the single largest party, and in the subsequent election of a President and Vice-President for the new assembly, a Progressive was elected President, and for a brief period a Socialist was elected Vice-President with some National Liberal support. In November 1913, an incident between the military garrison of the Alsatian town of Zabern and the civilian population produced an outburst of indignation against the Army, the officer Junker class and the system they embodied, which showed how desperately devoid of support they were in Germany as a whole. By a majority of 293 to 54, the *Reichstag* censured the actions of the Government. Only the onset of war was to rally the nation to the support of Imperial Germany again.

Even in Russia a similar reaction against the system could be traced. By 1914, nearly one and a half million industrial workers were on strike. A growing Great Russianism in the Dumas and in the administration and a relentless rise in Russification led to an increase in anti-Russian sentiments among the subject nationalities. The election of the fourth Duma in 1912, despite gerrymandering and widespread corruption, saw a growth in the Cadets and the left from 87 seats to 123, and a corresponding growth in the nationalist Right from 127 to 145 seats. The victims of this squeeze were, as in Italy, the conservative centre, the Octobrists whose vote fell from 154 to 121 seats. The Social Democratic share dropped slightly from 17 to 13 seats.

The growth in the extreme right was due in part to heavy Tsarist subsidy. But the extremists were far from being creatures of the *régime*, being as or more radical in their nationalism as the Social Democrats were in their socialism. Loyalty as such figured far lower on the rightists' scale of virtues than among traditional conservatives, and failure or defeat remained as dangerous for the Tsar and the *régime* as ever. Among the aristocracy an additional factor augmented the opposition to the *régime*. This opposition stemmed from the increasing dominance exercised over Tsar and Tsarina by the drunken and lascivious peasant monk, Rasputin, through the effectiveness of his unusual hypnotic powers on the haemophilia of the Tsarevich, the heir to the throne.

In Austria-Hungary discontent with the system expressed itself as always in a sharpening of the demands of the various national groupings. In the 1911 elections, the ministerial parties.

specially the Christian Socialists and the Poles, sustained severe losses. The Social Democrats saw the virtually total secession of their Czech wing and showed themselves as violent as any once the new *Reichstag* met. The German *National Verband*, a coalition of nationalistically inclined parties, saw a considerable increase in their strength. Italians, Slovenes and Ruthenes displayed increasing resistance to the Habsburg *régime* and there was an ominous growth among the Ruthenes of secessions from the Uniate Church, which though orthodox in rite, acknowledged the supremacy of the Pope, and was therefore in some way identified with the Habsburg monarchy, to the Russian Orthodox Church. In late 1913, the police of Austria and Hungary arrested a considerable number of Ruthenes on charges of conspiring to unify the Ruthenian areas with Russia.

Among the Czechs there was a marked growth in neo-Slavism, a version of Pan-Slavism which saw Austria's Slav population as the leaders of the Slavs against the German menace. Kramar was the uncrowned leader of Slav Bohemia. The realist, western-looking Masaryk was important only in the effectiveness of his own personal interventions into Habsburg politics, his party being a comparatively minor splinter group. Yet, apart from Masaryk, no section of Czech opinion took seriously the idea of secession from the Habsburg state. Among the southern Slavs, secessionism and union with Serbia were sentiments often encountered, but the dominant opinion sought a Trialist solution, a separate Slav kingdom within the Empire, which would transform the Dual into a Triple Monarchy.

In Hungary, the 1910 elections had brought to power a revived and reconstituted Liberal party under the title of the party of National Work. Its directing genius, Count Tisza, who became premier in June 1913, was determined to maintain the link with the Habsburg crown and restore the dominance of the Government over Parliament. The Magyar separatists were routed in debate, their filibustering tactics effectively ended. Though the franchise was extended, it was done so on a combination of educational, occupational and property qualifications which still disenfranchised the labouring and artisan classes, small farm-owners and traders and the lowest levels of the salaried class and this prevented the non-Magyars from effectively challenging Magyar supremacy. But despite Tisza's victory over the separatist elements in Parliament, separatism and Hungarian nationalism remained as sentiments so deeply rooted in the Hungarian people that Tisza could not afford to ignore or contravene them.

In Croatia, the era of the Balkan wars saw a new outbreak of separatist nationalism, after the passage of a bill widening the franchise slightly in 1910. In April 1912, the constitution of Croatia was suspended by the Magyar viceroy, in the face of a two-thirds majority in the Diet hostile to the administration. Extremists, one a Bosnian student, in contact with a Serbian secret society, the *Black Hand*, twice attempted to assassinate the Viceroy. But Tisza, replacing their target by a new Viceroy (who was himself gravely wounded by an extremist shortly after taking office), managed in the last months of 1913 to assuage Croatian feelings sufficiently to make it possible for the constitution to be restored and new elections for the Diet held. Despite a further attempt, again by a Bosnian student with connexions in Belgrade, on the Viceroy's life, Croatian opinion was much quieter in the first months of 1914. Count Tisza did not, however, feel strong enough to make any real concessions to the Rumanian and Ruthenian minorities in eastern Hungary, and the state of agitation and suppression in the Rumanian inhabited areas of Transylvania did a good deal to influence the *rapprochement* between Rumania and Russia mentioned earlier in this chapter. Tisza's skill, ruthlessness and courage were capable of controlling the nationalist fervour of his own and the other national groups under Magyar rule, but not of reconciling them to it. There were those who believed that with time this could be achieved, but time was the one element Tisza could not dispose of.

The tides of liberal reformism and countervailing nationalism were at their strongest in Britain, where, by June 1914, the nation was on the edge of civil war and its army had been shaken by mutiny. The Liberal programme of 1912 had included a bill setting up a Parliament in Dublin to be entirely responsible for Irish domestic affairs, including those of the six largely Protestant counties of Ulster. The bill, vigorously fought by the Conservatives in the Commons amidst scenes of near-riotous disorder, was passed in January 1913 and was sent to the House of Lords where it was inevitably rejected. Under the new Parliament Act it needed therefore only to be passed again by the Commons in the sessions 1912-13 and 1913-14, that is, without any new General Election having to be called, to become law.

In July 1913, the new leader of the Conservative and Unionist party, a Scots Canadian, Bonar Law, who had succeeded Balfour in 1912, promised Conservative support to any measure of resistance Ulster might take. In September 1913, a mass meeting of Ulster supporters near Belfast signed a 'Covenant' pledging themselves to use 'all means which may be necessary to defeat the present conspiracy to set up a Home Rule Parliament in Ireland'. Steps were taken to raise, drill and arm the 'Ulster volunteers', a force of about 100,000 men. And the War Office and the officer corps of the Army generally, where Ulstermen had always played a disproportionately large role, saw themselves faced with a situation in which they might have either to enforce Home Rule and shoot down their fellow countrymen or refuse to obey orders and commit mutiny. In March 1914, as the Government felt it wise to take precautionary military dispositions against a possible rising in Ulster, the large majority of officers of the 3rd Cavalry brigade, already in Ireland at the Curragh, replied to questions put by the Army Commander in Ireland that they would sooner be dismissed from the Army than take part in operations against Ulster. The question was hypothetical, as no orders for operations against Ulster had been issued or drafted; but the subsequent parliamentary and cabinet crisis gravely shook the morale of both army and country alike.

The new King, George V, brought the political leaders of both parties together, but was unable to make any headway against those on the Conservative side who saw their task not so much as that of preventing Home Rule coming about as that of using the issue to overthrow the Liberal party and reverse the course of the parliamentary revolution the Liberals had set in motion. The counter-revolutionaries, led by two prominent lawyer-politicians, Sir Edward Carson and F. E. Smith, used conciliatory language in Parliament. But in April 1914, they ran into Ulster a large consignment of arms purchased from Germany, the country which they professed to believe the biggest threat of all to Britain's imperial position. Talks continued, on the basis of a temporary exclusion of Ulster from the terms of the Home Rule Bill (which was in the course of passage through the Commons for the crucial third time, after which it would become law despite the veto of the House of Lords), but the Conservative and Unionist leadership only supported such a solution in the expectation that it would be rejected by the Irish nationalists, and the bill therefore would become void. On the day the news of the Austrian ultimatum to Serbia was received, the Cabinet were still earnestly debating the Irish issue, and civil war in Ireland still seemed only a hair'sbreadth away. Irish opinion was moving steadily away from the parliamentary nationalist party and towards those extremists who since the 1860s had been asserting that only violence and murder would rid Ireland of Anglo-Saxon rule.

The growth of the Home Rule crisis, with its increasing evidence of Army support for the Conservative-Unionist position, was accompanied by a parallel growth in strength of the radical, anti-militarist, anti-imperialist wing of the Liberal party. As noted above, the naval estimates of 1913 and 1914 ran into considerable opposition both inside the Cabinet and parliament, led by the radical Chancellor of the Exchequer, Lloyd George. There was a corresponding easing of Anglo-German tension as a result of the revived cooperation between Britain and Germany during the Balkan crisis of 1912–13. In this atmosphere, a new Anglo-German colonial agreement on the future of the Portuguese colonies in Africa was initialled in October 1913, in view of the expected break-up of Portugal's colonial empire as a consequence of the revolution in Portugal. Negotiations for a settlement of the long-standing dispute over the German-planned Baghdad railway took longer to conclude, but they too were brought into an agreement in June 1914. Most important for the European balance of power, however, was the thwarting by parliamentary opposition of a Russian move to conclude a naval staff convention with Britain similar to that concluded between France and Britain. In July 1914, the bulk of Liberal opinion in Britain was as pro-German as it was anti-Russian.

These movements of liberal-radical opinion against militarism and imperialism in Britain, France, Germany and Italy were paralleled by the growth in activity and concern with the avoidance of war on the part of the Socialist International. Since its foundation in 1900 the Socialist International had gone through two successive stages. In the first, from 1900–6, it had principally been concerned with the fight against party disunity, that is against revisionism and reformism in Germany and for a unification of the various socialist parties in France. With this achieved in 1906, and under the shock of the first Moroccan

crisis of 1905–6 with its threat of war in Europe for the first time
in thirty years, the Socialist International turned to discovering
ways and means of preventing war. At the Stuttgart conference
of 1907 and again at Copenhagen (1910), Basle (1912) and Berne
1913), there were repeated discussions of proposals for calling
an international general strike, the moment any power began to
mobilize its forces. The main resistance to such proposals came
from the German leadership, who, while agreeing with their
opposites in France, Britain and the western democracies that
war in Europe could only be imperialist in origin, had distinct
reservations on the subject of war with Tsarist Russia, the
embodiment in their eyes of autocracy and barbarism. Such
resistance delayed the passage by these conferences of resolutions
which would unequivocally commit the constituent parties to
industrial action to thwart war; but the Basle conference passed
a manifesto of action against the Balkan wars, and at Berne the
French and German delegates discussed a settlement of the
Alsace-Lorraine question.

The years 1910–13 saw similar movements for progressive
reform, if not revolution, in the United States, in Mexico and
in the Chinese empire. In each case, however, their effect was,
in international terms, to reinforce their differences, their
separation from the main stream of European civilization. In
America, the Progressive movement had been markedly growing
in strength since the Presidency of Theodore Roosevelt. As
noted in Chapter III, it combined in its beginning two potentially
contradictory strands in American political thought, a belief in
direct' democracy, which inevitably made its protagonists
suspicious of too great a growth in the powers of the central
government, and a conviction that in the strengthening of the
powers of a democratically-elected government and the capture
of the legislative power from the alliance of corrupt politicians
and large-scale business interests lay the only hope of a preservation of American democracy against the growth of a capitalist
oligarchy or plutarchy. The Progressive's belief in direct democracy was expressed in the evolution of various devices such as
the referendum, the initiative, the recall, direct primaries to
elect political candidates and direct election of Senators,
designed to bring back to politics the direct contact between
political leaders and the citizen body of the town meetings of
evolutionary America. By 1914, over twenty States had adopted

the initiative and the referendum, and ten the recall. Two-thirds
of all the States had adopted the direct primary in State elections
and in 1913 the Seventeenth Amendment made direct election
of Senators part of the American Constitution. Increasing
numbers of posts in the Civil Service were being put beyond the
scope of political appointment; municipal home rule and
commission government were placing city government beyond
the reach of corruption.

In 1910, however, the conflict between this belief in direct
democracy and the concomitant drive to strengthen the powers
of the Federal Government as the only means of taking progressivism from the state to the national level, broke into the
open. The leadership in provoking this conflict was taken by
Theodore Roosevelt, who, in the two years since his resignation
of the Presidency to Taft, had evolved a long way from his old
hesitancy. He allied himself that year with the progressive wing
of the Republican party in proclaiming what he called the 'New
Nationalism', the essence of which was a wholehearted use of
central government powers to serve social justice and alter
existing economic relationships. His intervention was never
supported by the Republican rank-and-file and was bitterly
opposed by the party bosses. And failing to capture the party's
nomination for the Presidential election of 1912, he broke away
and founded his own, the 'Bull Moose' party, taking with him
most of the out-and-out Progressive wing of the party. The
Democrats, themselves divided between a party machine candidate and the perennial candidate of the Populists, William
Jennings Bryan, adopted as their compromise candidate, the
democratic conservative, Woodrow Wilson, Governor since 1910
of New Jersey. An electoral minority (42 per cent) gave him and
his party all but eight States in the Electoral College, 290 to 145
seats in the House of Representatives, 51 to 49 seats in the Senate
and 21 State Governorships; and once in power he initiated a
campaign of major reforms comparable in American terms only
to that of the British Liberal party between 1909 and 1912.

As a reformer, however, Wilson was hampered by his respect
for the rights of the States and his belief in the essential rightness
of the normal processes of American politics, providing they
were used in a democratic way. He distrusted the new nationalism of Theodore Roosevelt as being essentially paternalistic; and
his remedy for the concentrations of economic power against

which Roosevelt had campaigned was not to develop the powers of government on a comparable scale but the more traditional American approach which called for the dispersal of power and reduction in size through anti-trust legislation. He believed in the 'organization of the common interest', 'the people' against the 'special interests' who were corrupting American democracy; and the two themes of respect for States' rights, and belief in the unalterable virtue of the common people given strong executive leadership were central both to his domestic and his foreign policy.

His reform programme consisted essentially of four proposals, the reduction of tariffs, the reform of the banking system, the introduction of income tax and the regulation of business. The first he carried by a bold campaign of public oratory against the pressures of all those special interests which had grown up behind the tariff barrier. But to reform the banking system was much more difficult. The issues involved did not lend themselves easily to being dramatized in public, and his own dislike of centralization of economic power restrained him from the radical reforms really required to make the system effective and invulnerable to panic. A casualty in his banking legislation was the easing of farm credit, so much a part of the agrarian programme; he did not feel strong enough for the head-on collision with the banking interests necessary to force this through. In the regulation of business the main items on his programme were the establishment of the Federal Trade Commission in 1914 to prevent unfair methods of competition, the Clayton Anti-Trust Act, and the Rayburn Securities Act, defeated in the Senate and not reintroduced. To carry these proposals through he felt obliged to make his peace with the machine politicians. The principal figure in the Progressive wing of the Democratic party, Louis Brandeis, the natural candidate for the Secretaryship of Justice, was therefore excluded from office.

Comparison with both the reform programmes of European liberal and radical movements and with the platform on which Theodore Roosevelt had campaigned underlines the gap which divided Wilson's reforms from the mainstream of European radicalism at this period. Wilson used the language of radical anti-capitalism in Europe; but his programme displayed none of its concern for social justice, none of its determination to attack the economic foundations of capitalism, none of its identification with the organization of the working class. Government in Wilson's view should be concerned with regulation. Individuals rather than institutions were to be penalized for the infliction of social injustice. Liberty rather than equality was his concern. And his views on tariffs and trade struck European observers as being those of a mid-nineteenth-century Liberal. In this, Europeans were mistaking the basis on which his position had been attained. He shared with the Manchester School their belief in the essential pacifying nature of free trade. But his objections to tariffs and to trade subsidies were less economic than political, being directed against the distortions of power that were introduced when the Federal government became the tool of particular interests. His foreign policy like his trade policy stemmed essentially from his belief in the rightness of the common people if given strong and disinterested leadership. It was in this field that he was to suffer his worst defeats and disappointments.

The greatest disasters of his career in foreign affairs were to be deferred until the year 1919 towards the end of his second term. But they were foreshadowed in his Mexican policy, where he came for the first time into conflict with radical nationalism. Revolution had, in fact, broken out in Mexico in May 1911, nearly two years before Wilson came to power. Its origins were complex, its occasion, a loss of nerve and judgement on the part of the dictator, Porfirio Diaz, too simple; the revolution swept away the dictatorship without offering anyone of real strength to put in his place. Those who made the revolution, and made the Liberal, Francisco Madero, President, came at first, almost without exception, from that small property-owning class which Diaz himself represented but barred from power. But the forces they used: the discontent of the copper mine and mill workers, whose strikes had been so bloodily repressed in 1906–7; the land-hunger of the peasants; the ambitions of the discontented and underpaid military; the resentment of the Mestizos and the Indians against the Church and the Creole aristocracy which oppressed and exploited them; these proved far more than Madero could control. What began virtually as a palace revolution among the dominant social *élite* swiftly developed into a prolonged civil war. This conflict was greatly complicated both by the interventionist anxieties of the major foreign investors, who wanted to find and back some strong man, capable of reimposing order and national stability, and by the traditions of brigandage to which agrarian rebellion so often turned once its chances of success had disappeared. Almost immediately, agrarian risings broke out in the south, of which the most famous was led by Emiliano Zapata. Madero himself was compromised by the greed of his relations, who took the adage 'to the victors belong the spoils' only too seriously. And in February 1913, General Huerta, Madero's senior officer, seized power for himself and had Madero executed.

It was at this moment that Woodrow Wilson took office as President of the United States. The Huerta *régime* was immediately accorded recognition by Britain and most of the other military powers. But Wilson, revolted by the judicial murder of Madero, refused recognition to Huerta's *régime*, on the grounds that Huerta's claim to represent Mexico's legitimate government rested on force and not on the consent of the governed. Huerta, however, obstinately refused to fall, and in considerable exasperation, Wilson eventually, in April 1914, provoked an incident in the port of Vera Cruz and landed marines. From this *impasse*, he was rescued by the mediation of the three major South American powers, Argentina, Brazil and Chile. And a deal concluded with the British government the previous autumn secured the gradual withdrawal of British support from the Huerta *régime*. In August 1914, Huerta fled Mexico, and the vacant reins of power were seized by the American candidate, a landowner from the north, Venustiano Carranza. But this was far from the end of this troubled chapter in American-Mexican relations. It is worth noting that Wilson's determination, in his own words, 'to teach the South American republics to elect good men', led him, despite his denunciation of dollar diplomacy, and his desire, proclaimed in March 1913, to 'cultivate the friendship and deserve the confidence of our sister republics of central and south America', to a much more far-reaching policy of intervention in the affairs of the Caribbean and Central American republics than that practised by his predecessor. The virtual protectorate over Nicaragua was continued. In the Dominican Republic, American intervention to secure free and democratic elections led eventually, in 1916, to a military occupation of the island which was to last eight years. At the other end of the island, American warships and troops intervened to keep order in Haiti in January 1914, and, the following year intervened again to establish by treaty what was in all but name a protectorate over the island. Their intervention was to give the island fifteen years of comparatively efficient and orderly government.

But these blessings are more normally used to defend colonial rule of the kind the Wilson administration usually denounced as 'interested and self-seeking' when practised by the colonial powers of Europe. Wilsonian interventionism was more high-minded than that of his Republican predecessors – and in many ways was probably in the best interests of the populations of the weak, ill-governed and poverty-stricken states on whom it was practised. Only it was difficult to reconcile with Bryan's and Wilson's view of international justice and impossible to reconcile with the aspirations and anxieties of the Latin Americans. Nor was it in the long run effective in solving the internal political difficulties of the Caribbean and Central American states. As an instrument of progress colonialism has to be full-blooded, generously and forcefully applied over a prolonged period of time. Otherwise, it is apt to secure order not by removing the internal causes of disorder but merely by putting them into suspended animation, to revive when the source of external control is removed.

Mexico was not the only state to slip at this time from the control of the Great Powers into a civil war which was to lead at length to its standing on its own feet. A similar case, that of China, proved to be far more decisive in its long-term implications for the world balance of power. By 1912, the effects of the reform programme undertaken by the Manchu emperor in 1905 had begun to make their mark. In 1908, one of the last acts of the emperor before his death had been to issue a decree outlining a proposed constitution including the introduction of parliamentary government in China by 1917. The emperor was succeeded by his three-year-old nephew, the Regency being exercised by the new emperor's father, Prince Ch'un. The next year, provincial assemblies were convened, and in 1910, the proposed National Assembly was called in its turn, with half its delegates elected, half appointed by the Prince Regent.

The new National Assembly's main role was to oppose further Chinese involvement with European finance and to urge the participation of Chinese finance in the development of the Chinese railway system. In 1911, the central government nationalized the main Chinese-owned railway running into Szechwan as a preliminary to its development with funds provided by the European Consortium. Risings followed in Szechwan, where local feeling was inflamed against further European investment, and on the middle Yangtse, and the Prince Regent in despair turned to the principal military reformer, Yuan Shih-kai, to re-establish order. Yuan, a man of devouring ambitions, used the invitation of the Manchu court to establish himself as Premier of the provincial Parliament, and to seize full powers from the dynasty, while at the same time opening negotiations with the rebels. In February 1912, he forced the abdication of the Manchu dynasty and his own appointment as President of the new Chinese republic; a representative of Sun Yat-sen's T'ung Meng Hui was appointed as Prime Minister.

At this stage, the control of China was divided between three main forces. In the south, especially in the maritime provinces, control was exercised by followers of Sun Yat-sen, or by military leaders sympathetic to him. In the north, Yuan Shih-kai's control was nearly absolute. In the western provinces, power lay in the hands of the provincial military governors who tended to exercise it as they saw fit. At this stage, the leaders of the T'ung Meng Hui, now transformed into the Kuomintang (Nationalist) party, came to regret their first backing of Yuan Shih-kai. After the elections of the winter of 1912-13 had made the Kuomintang the majority party in both Chambers of the main Chinese parliament, Yuan viewed the Nationalists as the strongest enemy to his own autocratic ambitions. However, Yuan was fortunate early in 1913 in negotiating from the European consortium a new loan of over $100 million. In March, therefore, he had the parliamentary leader of the Kuomintang assassinated. In mid-July the pro-Kuomintang generals in the south rose in revolt. They proved unable to stand up to Yuan's superior military and financial resources. In November 1913, Yuan outlawed the party, and in January 1914 dissolved parliament. In May 1914, he introduced a new constitution which, by purporting to model itself on that of the United States, established Yuan as virtual dictator in China. He had achieved the recognition of the Great Powers. But this was not to prove of much avail to him after August 1914 had concentrated their attention on Europe, and left him alone and weak to face the anxiety-prompted imperialism of Japan, for whom a strong and united China would mean an end to her hopes of pre-eminence in the Far East.

Section Three

The War of 1914–1918

Chapter 11

The Onset of War

THE MOOD OF EUROPE IN 1914

SINCE the early years of the new century, the intellectual and philosophical movements dominant in 1900 had been challenged by a whole cluster of new movements which stressed all that those they challenged had suppressed. As argued in Chapter II, those movements dominant in philosophy and intellectual life in 1900 had been rationalist and positivist, while those dominant in music, art, architecture and literature had been romantic and intuitive. There was now to be a curious reversal. Rationalism and positivism were to be challenged by pragmatism and intuitive philosophy, while in the arts the great romantic traditions were to be challenged by the restoration of an intellectual aesthetic interested first of all in form and formal relationships. These challenges were to lead, especially among the arts, to a half-century of internecine warfare, in the course of which the gap between the participants on both sides and their public was to widen to an almost impassable chasm.

The origins of these challenges lay in the decades before 1900. The critical developments in many fields seem to cluster around the years 1905 or later. It was in this year that Sigmund Freud published his *Three Essays on the Theory of Sexuality*, perhaps the most effective embodiment of his exploration of the unconscious, outlined in his earlier *Interpretation of Dreams*, and his consequent emphasis on the pre-eminence of pre-rational sexual drives in the explanation of human motives and behaviour. That same year the amateur German mathematician, Albert Einstein, by publishing his famous *Theory of Relativity*, pulled together all the various developments and discoveries of the previous two decades in physics and mathematics, and provided them with a new basic theoretical matrix to replace that which had been destroyed in 1887. The effect of his work was to re-establish the scientist's faith in the ability of man's mind to comprehend the nature of the physical world; though the physical world as hypothesized by Einstein bore little or no relation to that experienced by the senses of the ordinary man or to the matrices into which he fitted that experience. The divorce between intellect and science and the perception of the average man widened rather than narrowed as a result of Einstein's work, and even sixty years later, very many educated men could not either comprehend or expound his theories so that others would comprehend them. There was more than a little justice in the doggerel rhyme,

> Nature and Nature's laws lay hid in night;
> God said, 'Let Newton be', And all was light.
> It did not last. The Devil, shouting 'Ho,
> Let Einstein be', restored the *status quo*.

But for the world of science, Einstein's work was to provide a basis for new progress, which has still not proven outmoded.

The revolt against positivism took place less from any appreciation of the physicists' earlier destruction of their own previously held view of the universe, than from a discontent with mechanistic theories of volition and the physicists' attack on religion which had turned philosophers and psychologists to examining and considering the nature of the religious motive as such. It is curiously significant that of the two most dominant figures in the revolt against positivism, one, the American, William James, was a psychologist who had written on varieties of religious experience and the other, Henri Bergson, began by studying unconscious memory through speech defects, thus following the same route that Freud did. In philosophy, the central years of the new challenge were thus 1906, the year in which William James published his *Pragmatism*, and the following year in which Bergson propounded his theory of the *élan vital, Creative Evolution*.

In the worlds of painting, architecture, and music, the most critical period seems to have opened in 1906. In painting, Europe was divided between the two great schools of Paris and Central Europe, schools with hardly a single point of intellectual or other contact with each other, yet moving from opposite ends to a similar meeting ground. In 1900, Germanic painting, divided

as it was between Berlin, Munich and Vienna, was dominated by
the first great revolt against the art of the academic, the *Sezession*,
a Central European equivalent to *Art Nouveau*. In 1904, the
group, *die Brücke*, in Dresden, launched itself into a decade of
the most violent experimentation with the architectural balance
of simplified forms and violent colours. Their nearest equivalent
in Paris was the *Fauve* school, following the Post-Impressionists.
For them the great year was 1907, the year of the Cézanne
memorial exhibition. The introduction to the catalogue enunci-
ated two great precepts, which had come to Cézanne only a year
or two before his death: 'To paint is not solely to copy an
object; it is to seize a harmony between the numerous relationships' and 'Everything in nature models itself upon the sphere,
the cone and the cylinder.' The first of these led Henri Matisse
to the exploration of rhythms in colour, and to the development
of an architectural treatment of colour analogous to the work of
Nolde, Kirchner, Schmidt-Rottluff and Mueller, in Germany.
(A minor member of *die Brücke*, Hans Purrmann, actually
studied for some years in the school Matisse founded the previous
year in Paris.) The second principle led Picasso and his friend,
Braque, into Cubism and beyond. Both lines of development
saw the painter progressively detached from the object painted.
And in both, the painter was becoming more and more interested
in imposing a form, a structure on his work. The first line of
development, that followed by Matisse, can perhaps best be
distinguished as the exploration of decoration, of visual sensation,
the second, followed by Picasso and the Cubists, that of design.

   In architecture, meanwhile, the main departure from *Art
Nouveau* (*Jugendstil* in Germany) was being taken by a German
school of designers and architects, intent on returning to simple
unornamented design which would be relevant to the purpose
for which the artifact was designed (*Sachlichkeit* was the German
catchword), based on modern materials and techniques with its
individual parts in harmony with one another. In 1907, they
founded the *Deutsche Werkbund*, to promote *Sachlichkeit* and
Qualität (quality). And the *Deutsche Werkbund* was followed by
the foundation of similar *Werkbünde* in Austria in 1910 and
Switzerland in 1913. The movement culminated in the Cologne
exhibition of 1914 at which for the first time the full genius of
Walter Gropius, founder of the principal seminal centre of
modern architecture, the *Bauhaus* (1919), first attracted the

public. In painting, however, the Central Europeans continued to reject the machine for an ever increasingly violent exploration of colour. In Munich, in 1912, a group of painters founded the *Blaue Reiter* school which included Franz Marc, August Macke, the Russian Wassily Kandinsky. The Swiss surrealist, Paul Klee, was to exhibit in this school in the early 1920s.

The virtues which Gropius preached – simplicity, science and technique, hard struggles and no personal security, the architecture of the machine – carry a curiously positivist ring about them; although what the modern German architects were interested in was to come to grips with modern engineering techniques rather than with science itself. Among them the greatest controversies raged on the issue of standardization or individualization. In their interest in new and imaginative forms they were close to the intellectual approach of French Cubism, which following Cézanne's seminal aphorism broke the multifarious shapes and outlines of the observed world into the simple cones and cylinders of three-dimensional geometry. In their attempt to reconcile art with the machine they parallel the Italian Futurists, whose first manifesto was issued in 1909. But here again the Italians introduced a third approach to the intellectualism of Gropius and Picasso. The Futurist manifesto of 1909 deified the violence as well as the clean lines of the automobile: and geometry expressed itself in a temporary obsession with its instruments such as the set square and the T square in the so-called 'metaphysical' phase of Italian surrealism, of which di Chirico was perhaps the best-known painter; this was, however, a wartime development.

In France, surrealism, that of Odilon Redon, the Russian painter Chagall, James Ensor and others seemed to belong to the less intellectualized line originated by Matisse. It was greatly enhanced by the terrific impact of Russian ballet, which began with the first season of the Diaghilev company in Paris in 1909, the decor of which, by Benois and Bakst, highly coloured, often semi-oriental fantasy, had an overwhelming impact on popular taste. The extraordinary combination of violence and delicacy which distinguished the choreography of the Diaghilev company and its principal dancers was highly characteristic of the last years of European culture before 1914. That same year, 1909, saw in Paris the first outbreaks of *apachism*, an unbridled, underworld violence of a type new to Europe.

In social philosophy and in literature, one can trace a new irrationalism developing after 1905. Here the influence of Freud and Einstein is unimportant. Those involved were often followers of Bergson. But the crucial event was the first Moroccan crisis, which for the first time since 1870 confronted the young with the possibility of war in Europe. In France, this expressed itself in a revival of intellectual Catholicism, of which the writers Charles Péguy and Alain Fournier, prophets of a return to the medieval order of the city or the idealized innocence of youth, are perhaps most significant. In Italy, it led to the violence of the Futurists, and the flamboyant heroism of the poet, Gabriele d'Annunzio. In Germany, one can trace a rather similar development which, however, began earlier and was not so clearly a reaction to the events of 1905. This was the development of the cult of youth by youth in the *Jugendbewegung*.

The central element in this movement was a reaction against the close intellectual discipline of the German home and school, a reaction towards an indefinable sense of freedom; but it was a freedom within a small group of peers with a chosen or recognized leader. Its main manifestation was the institution of the *Wandervögel*, hiking and rambling groups rediscovering the beauties of the countryside and the simplicities of folk-song. But it was also intensely nationalist in sentiment, and upper *bourgeois* in origin, and the freedom it sought had no political or parliamentary content. Its intellectual mentors were a curious duo of political and cultural critics of Bismarckian Germany, Paul de Lagarde and Julius Langbehn, its main literary voice the poet of the aristocratic *élite*, Stefan George. War came to it as to Péguy and Alain Fournier, and the young poets of Britain, Rupert Brooke and Julian Grenfell, as the final, only too easily welcomed, challenge and release from their earlier hesitations.

These poets, indeed the whole youth itself, operated as a far shallower level of literary consciousness than those two writers from Austria-Hungary, offspring of the great and still not thoroughly understood centre of culture which was Habsburg Austria, who explored most fully the new depths of the unconscious to which Nietzsche and Freud had pointed. These were the poet, Rainer Maria Rilke, and the writer, Franz Kafka. Not that either of them was deliberately impelled to his choice of subject by his philosophical analogues. Far from it. Rather that their inspiration led them into these realms of the unconscious.

For Rilke, insulated by the aid of a circle of well-to-do friends from the grosser necessities of economic man, the task he set himself was primarily one of reconciliation with and acceptance of the ancestral terrors of these new depths, a task brilliantly achieved in his ultimate work, the *Duineser Elegien* (1922). For Kafka the terrors themselves had to be charted. That itself was almost more than he could tolerate. And he left behind him two nightmare accounts of the terrors of a world in which all seemingly settled points of reference failed to provide the individual with anything to which he could relate, of which he could actually make sense. These two works, *The Castle* and *The Trial*, were written during the period after 1913, and only published after the author's death. They were to outdo even the horrors of the totalitarian states of the 1930s.

The achievement of these writers must not, however, be allowed to obscure the continuance of the older rationalist-humanist tradition of the late nineteenth century. A link is perhaps provided between them by the French novelist Proust, whose major investigation of the nature of time and continuity, *A la Recherche du Temps Perdu* (Remembrance of Things Past), was conceived and in part written before 1914 (the first of the ten volumes, *Du Côté de chez Swann* was published in 1913). They were concerned with the predicament in which Kafka found himself, with the problem of reorientation to a world where, as the physicists had discovered a generation earlier, nothing was as it seemed, and intellectual truth was difficult to recognize. And, driven like the physicists to the recognition that relative truth is all that could be discovered, they found a certain security, as the physicists had done, in the process of intellectual activity itself, providing this activity was itself honestly practised. Perhaps the most significant examples of this approach, which was to produce some of the greatest figures of Europe in the 1920s, were the early work of André Gide, the French writer who founded the *Nouvelle Revue Française* in 1908 and the publishing house of Gallimard in 1911, which were to become the literary academy for modern writers in France, and, in Germany, of the novelist, Thomas Mann.

In the field of music, events and ideas were to turn away from the Romantics' preoccupation with the totality of experience. In Italy, the followers of '*verismo*' began, even before the turn of the century, to seek to relate their post-Verdian music dramas to

the common and the contemporary. Mascagni and Leoncavallo
turned to the life of the Italian village, Puccini, the last of the
great Italian opera composers, to Paris (*La Bohème*), to Japan
(*Madam Butterfly*), even to the American Wild West. Among
the Germanic and French composers, romanticism was, however,
still burning itself out in the work of the post-Wagnerians in
Germany and France, with Richard Strauss and Hugo Wolff, in
Gustav Mahler's immensely over-orchestrated all-embracing
symphonies, and lastly, perhaps the final lunacy of the post-
Wagnerian Romantics, in Arnold Schönberg's *Gurrelieder*
(completed in 1911 and orchestrated for ten different violin
parts, eight different parts each for violas and 'cellos, three four-
part male choirs, one eight-part choir, and, as well as immense
wood and brass sections, a percussion section which employed
thirty-two performers including six tympani and an iron chain!).
A third school, in revulsion to this, grew up in France in the
Impressionism of Débussy, Ravel, and Fauré.

An interesting separate element is the development of various
national schools of music, or rather of composers in individual
national traditions other than those of France, Germany and
Italy which make up the main-stream of European classical
music. The most important single national tradition was that of
Russia. Moussorgsky's songs played their part in the development of Débussy's impressionism. More important was the work
of Rimsky-Korsakov and of the principal Russian recruit to the
new music of twentieth-century Europe, Stravinsky, whose music
for the ballets *Firebird* (1910), *Petrushka* (1911) and the *Rite of
Spring* (1913) added immeasurably to the impact of the Diaghilev
ballet. Bartok and Kodály in Hungary, Manuel de Falla in Spain,
Sibelius in Finland, Janacek in Slovakia, Nielsen in Denmark,
Vaughan Williams in Britain were all experimenting with a
tonality which owed as much or more to the folk music of their
own countries as to the main schools of European music.

These various strains were, however, all running out by 1914,
as composers turned to the exploration of form, reverting, as
Ravel did in 1911 with *Daphnis and Chloe*, to a new classicism,
or moving on to atonalism, as Schönberg did with his *Erwartung*
(1909), and *Pierrot Lunaire* (1912), and to the twelve-tone row
of Josef Hauer, propounded in Vienna in 1914, and followed by
Schönberg's two best-known colleagues, Anton Webern and
Alban Berg.

It is, perhaps, still too early to bring all these various intellectual movements under one theoretical roof. What is noticeable and significant at this time is the gulf which divided the culture based on Paris from that based on the cities of Central Europe, a gulf of considerable ignorance despite the opportunities for contact which were available. The culture of Paris remained virtually untouched by the movement in architectural design which was to eventuate in Gropius and the *Bauhaus* school. The painters of Central Europe visited Paris and saw the preliminary exhibitions of Impressionist and Post-Impressionist art which visited Munich, Stuttgart and Vienna – yet there seems to have been little or no contact between the giants of the Central European and Parisian schools of painting, and such contact as there was was all one way, towards Paris.

A second point to notice is the degree to which art and music, and, to a lesser extent, literature, from the peripheral states of Europe, came to play a fertilizing role in the two European cultures of Paris and Central Europe. The theorist and publicist of the *Blaue Reiter* group was the Russian painter, Kandinsky. Diaghilev and Stanislavsky came to dominate the stages of Europe in ballet and acting style. Chaliapin, the great Russian bass, bestrode the operatic stage, and a generation of dancers, Nijinsky, Pavlova, Karsavina, Lopokova, and their stage designers were to pass into legend. From Scandinavia, the dramas of Ibsen and the writings of Strindberg swept the theatres of Europe. In literature, Dostoevsky and Tolstoy were the principal Russian influences. In philosophy, William James's pragmatism has already been mentioned. And, in the realm of popular culture shortly before the war, ragtime, the first great innovation in popular music and dancing since the waltz and the polka, invaded Europe from the United States, a forerunner of the true American jazz and folk music which was to make so profound an impact in the 1920s.

These influences were only a symptom of the growing eclecticism of much of European culture. More significant perhaps of the gradual damming up of some parts of the stream of European creativity, or perhaps, of the dissatisfaction of Europe's artists and musicians with inherited forms and ideas, was the eagerness with which they turned to the African and Oriental for models. Not that at first sight there was anything new in this. Eighty years earlier Ingres, Delacroix and the French romantic painters, had turned to the scenes and colours of North Africa, to escape the *bourgeois* classicism of their predecessors. But the painters of the new century were finding more than models from the Japanese, Javanese, Negro and Polynesian art which influenced them so profoundly; they were borrowing ideas of form and balance from the Japanese, themes and motifs from the Negro art of West Africa. At a different level, a dreadful mish-mash of misunderstood Buddhism and Yoga was invading the salons of London and Paris, fads and fashions to some, but to others signs of a lack of confidence and security in the continuity and fertility of European thought and philosophy, an ironic and revealing sidelight on the apparent serenity, security and unshakability of the European way of life in 1914.

These movements, outlined in the foregoing passages, with the single exception of the youth movement, took place and hold only among a series of intellectual and academic *élites* who were becoming progressively more and more isolated from the main body of educated opinion in Europe. At this latter level the main conflict was between the irrational nationalism and love of violence originally propagated by Nietzsche, and the continuing belief in scientific progress and social improvement of the positivists. Neither Freudianism nor the seething intellectual chaos out of which the theory of relativity was to emerge had begun to filter through to the great middlebrow mind, which can be seen perhaps at its clearest in Britain, convulsed between the pseudo-scientific optimism of H. G. Wells and G. B. Shaw, whose play *Man and Superman* was a kind of bowdlerized Nietzsche for the intellectual nursery, and the gentle romantic corporativism of G. K. Chesterton and Hilaire Belloc. The pernicious Oxford school of Platonic anti-democratic corporativism of Bosanquet and Jowett was translating itself into the neo-imperialist collectivism of the Round Table group. In France, Bergson and Sorel were influencing the dominant school of military theorists into the belief that France's *élan vital* in attack would outweigh Germany's superiority in men and materials. In Germany, the popular philosophy was nationalist and patriotic, if not chauvinist, in its attitude to non-German ideas, peoples and culture. Nationalism, historicism, anti-modernism were everywhere strong. They were opposed by a growing consciousness of what was common in European culture, strongest among the university-educated of Europe, and an equal consciousness of the way in which economic forces were tying Europe together so that war in Europe would come close to economic suicide. When, at the end of July 1914, the outbreak of war seemed inevitable, those nationalist patriots in every country who gave the war an enthusiastic welcome were opposed by those who thought war was stupid and suicidal. A group of British liberals protested to *The Times* that if Britain fought on Russia's side against Germany, she would be embracing the cause of barbarism against civilization. It was indeed the end of a Europe.

THE IMMEDIATE CAUSES OF THE OUTBREAK OF WAR IN 1914

In the controversies which have raged around the origins of the 1914–18 war and the responsibilities of the various belligerents for its outbreak, it has not often been recognized that there were not one but three wars which broke out in that year, and that each school of national historians has tended only to focus on that in which his own country was first involved. Of these three, the first was that between Austria and Serbia, the second that between Germany and her Austrian ally on the one hand, and Russia and France on the other, and the third that between Britain and Germany. The first followed on the Serbian failure to accept the Austrian ultimatum provoked by the assassination of the heir to the Habsburg throne, the Archduke Franz Ferdinand, by one of a group of terrorists trained in Serbia and armed and organized by a nationalist secret society run by the head of the Serbian Army intelligence service. The second followed on a German ultimatum to Russia demanding the cessation of Russian preparations for mobilization, begun as a means of diplomatic pressure on Austria to abandon her punitive war on Serbia. The third followed on the German violation of Belgian territory in the course of an offensive designed to knock Russia's ally, France, out of the war, before Russian military strength could be completely mobilized and hurled against Prussia's eastern heartlands. What needs to be explained are the links between these three wars.

These links were provided almost exclusively by military considerations. The Tsar and the Russian Foreign Ministry, concerned to save Serbia from the consequences of her folly, only intended to mobilize on their frontiers with the Austrian empire. Their military advisers said that to confine mobilization to the Austro-Russian frontier was impossible, and perilous if it were possible, in view of Germany's alliance with Austria. More disastrous for the peace of Europe, however, were the war plans of the German military. Obsessed since the conclusion of the Franco-Russian alliance with the peril of war on two fronts, they had concluded that Germany's only hope of evading simultaneous invasion and defeat was to take advantage of Germany's internal lines of communication, her strategic railway system and her speed of mobilization. Germany could mobilize in thirty-six hours, France in forty-eight. Russia needed nearly three weeks. In these three weeks the bulk of Germany's armed forces could be thrown against France, the French armies overwhelmed by superior numbers, France defeated and Russia confronted with a reconcentrated and victorious German army on the east. The time limits set by the plan were impossibly slender. Their effect was to make of Russian mobilization the signal for a German attack on France. Every hour wasted in diplomatic contacts thereafter brought the Russian armies an hour nearer to East Prussia and Berlin and gave the German armies in the west an hour less in which to achieve victory, the French an hour more in which to prepare their defences. The whole German war plan was based on the idea of a pre-emptive first strike against France.

But there was more to it than that. The French frontier with Germany was defended for much of its length by difficult hilly country, by the Rhine and by a series of fortresses. And classic German military doctrine called always for a victory through encirclement of the enemy. The original German plans of the 1890s envisaged a breakthrough in the south, through the so-called Belfort gap. But in the aftermath of the Moroccan crisis of 1905 the scheme was revised. France's great eastern chain of fortresses was to be circumvented by a drive through the plains of Belgium and Luxemburg, a drive which would give the Germans still more room in which to deploy their extra man-power and divisions. The consequent violation of Belgian neutrality of which Germany and Britain were guarantors by a treaty of 1839 was to the military not their affair. It was a political matter on which they did not feel competent to pronounce. The effect of this military decision was to confront Germany's political leadership in the hour of crisis with no choice but defeat or the acceptance of a plan for victory, called the Schlieffen Plan after its drafter, which would violate what they were pledged to honour.

The German violation of Belgium in its turn brought the possibility of war with Britain into account. The German military had largely discounted this possibility. The record of the British army in the Boer War was not such as to earn it the respect of the foremost military power in Europe. The reforms of the Haldane *régime* went unnoticed or were dismissed as not having been tested in battle. In any case, the British army was a minute professional force compared with the great conscript armies of Central Europe. The six divisions of the British Expeditionary Force were a drop in the bucket by comparison with the eighty odd divisions which the Germans proposed to throw against France. In any case, there was a good deal of reason to doubt how seriously Britain would take a treaty that was seventy-five years old at the time of its violation. Moreover, all of Germany's plans were predicated on a victory so quick that British strength would simply come too late to be of any military use to France.

In this, the Germans were making two serious mistakes. The first was to misunderstand the contingent nature of the British staff arrangements with France. They were, as has been seen, the product of divided counsels and interpretations as to the ends of German policy. One section of the Cabinet, a minority, but a consistent and well-organized one, believed that Germany was intent on the hegemony, not only of Europe, which she had when she chose to exert it, but also of the outside world. An equally small minority, as doctrinaire in its beliefs but less well organized, was composed of out-and-out pacifists and isolationists who saw no useful purpose to be served by intervention in Europe's quarrels. The floating middle was inclined by ideological conviction to the latter point of view, or could be expected to be so inclined, unless its members could be shown that international justice and Britain's vital interests were both involved. The German invasion of Belgium was admirably designed to combine both these issues; being unprovoked aggression at once against a small power of which Britain was a guarantor, and against a strategically important area which British policy for the last four hundred odd years had insisted should not fall under the dominance of a Great Power. The German invasion of Belgium was to destroy Germanophilia in Britain for three generations.

These military plans and attitudes were important, especially in the three autocracies of Germany, Austria-Hungary, and Russia, because of the dual role of the sovereign as head both of the civilian and the military sides of the state, and the consequent unstable nature of civil-military relationships. In Germany and in Russia, the autocrats, Kaiser and Tsar, were adolescent, unstable personalities, and felt themselves as much soldiers as civilians. Their openness to military advice and the degree to which they shared their generals' dislike of their civilian ministers was greatly to weaken the effectiveness of the civilians' advice. In Austria, the aged Franz Josef saw events not in nationalist but in dynastic terms – and he was, therefore, the more amenable to the arguments of the military. In both Germany and Austria the military classes were convinced of the inevitability of a war and the advantage of staging one before Russian strength was really built up. In Russia, the military were convinced of the duplicity of Germany and deeply suspicious of German intentions. In every case, there was an element of deceit in the arguments used to secure from the autocrat the orders to mobilize.

The immediate occasion for the Austrian attack on Serbia was provided by the Serbs. It is now established beyond a peradventure that the assassination on June 28th, 1914, of the Archduke Franz Ferdinand and his wife during an official visit to the provincial capital of Bosnia Herzegovina, was organized by a Serbian secret society, the Black Hand, whose effective head was Colonel Dragutin Dmitrievich, the head of Serbian military intelligence; and that the Serbian government, at least in the person of the Premier, N. Pasic, had foreknowledge of the plot. Indeed, Pasic made an attempt, albeit a remarkably feeble one, to warn the Austrian authorities in Vienna in advance. The assassins were all recruited from the disaffected student youth of Bosnia. The aim behind the assassination plot will probably always be unknown. This much is clear, that Franz Ferdinand was regarded in Belgrade as the most dangerous man on the Austrian side, since his dislike of the Hungarians had led him to support the idea of making the Habsburg dual monarchy into a triple monarchy by the erection of a third, Slav, state. But the possibility cannot be excluded that it was Colonel Dmitrievich's scheme to provoke a war between the Habsburg monarchy and Serbia in which Russia would be forced to come to Serbia's aid. He was in regular touch with the Russian military attaché in Belgrade from whom he had received explicit assurances of Russian support in such an event. Whatever the truth of this, 'the shots which echoed round the world' were fired by a tubercular student below the age of twenty-one, fired with the ideals of Pan-Serb nationalism to whom the disruption of European peace was of little consequence compared with the advancement of his ideal. And he was incited by a man who was himself an assassin (he had taken part in the bloody murder of the Obrenovichs in 1903), a barbarian of intrigue, violence and terror himself, to whom peace was a meaningless and unwelcome abstraction, a man only one step removed from the professional bandits and brigands for which the Balkans were then infamous.

The murder caught the Austrian administration at its weakest point. Not that there was much love lost for Franz Ferdinand himself; indeed, the comparative obscurity of the funeral arrangements scandalized all Vienna. It was immediately assumed that Serbia had a hand in the assassination and all Europe united to condemn Serbia for allowing its territory to be used by terrorists for attacks into Austrian territory. Under any circumstances a *prima facie* case existed for the Austrian state to take the severest police measures and demand far-reaching guarantees of Serbian good behaviour. Unfortunately, for the peace of Europe, this was not enough for the Austrian government and military. Moreover, the investigating judge was slow at getting the conspirators to confess, and the part played by Serbian officials did not emerge immediately or in such a way as to carry conviction and stifle opposition. The result was to delay Austrian action against Serbia, so that the first flush of anti-Serbian feeling in Europe was weakened, Russian Pan-Slavism was aroused, and opinion in Europe saw instead of the chastisement of a nest of terrorists and brigands, an assault on Serbian national independence.

The root of the trouble lay in Vienna. The years of the Balkan wars, especially the months following the second Balkan war in which the Austrian authorities had striven to prevent the increase of Serbian territory at the expense of Albania, had convinced the Austrians of Serbia's fundamental hostility. An ultimatum had already been necessary in October 1913 to secure the withdrawal of Serbian troops from Albania's territory. The Austrian Chief of Staff saw the assassination as a declaration of war by Serbia. Count Berchtold, the Foreign Minister, was converted to the military view of the need for a preventive war against Serbia, and the Emperor wrote to the Kaiser that 'the continuation of the situation is a chronic peril for my House and my territories'.

The first task was to secure German support lest Russia intervene to prevent the chastisement of Serbia. Assurances of German support were obtained from the Kaiser and the German Chancellor on July 5th–6th, and the terms in which these assurances were expressed suggest that the Kaiser and the Chancellor did not believe the danger of Russian intervention to be very serious. There followed a period of a week in which Berchtold had to meet and overcome the severe opposition of Count Tisza, the Hungarian premier, anxious not to add to the Empire's internal Slav problem. The visit of the French President to St Petersburg further delayed matters. The Austrian demands were not in fact presented in Belgrade until the evening of July 23rd. Their terms amounted to the establishment, at pistol point, of a police protectorate over Serbia. And they were to be accepted or rejected within forty-eight hours. Their tenor did more than anything else to win support for Serbia as the gallant little nation being bullied by her over-mighty neighbour, where she had previously been seen as a backward and near anarchic state whose territory was a nest of bandits, brigands, terrorists and would-be assassins.

The Austrian ultimatum caught the Serbian government in an unresolvable dilemma. To yield was impossible on a variety of counts. Serbian nationalist opinion very largely approved of the assassination. The *Black Hand* was well organized among the Serbian officer corps. The Serbian government, moreover, had very good reason not to wish to see the question of links between those who plotted the assassination and themselves subjected to any real investigation. On the other hand, they faced for the first time an obviously aroused and militant Austria. In their dilemma, they had already appealed to Russia on July 22nd. On receipt of the ultimatum, they directed a fresh appeal to the Russian government.

In St Petersburg, the reports of impending Austrian action against Serbia had already caused a good deal of alarm. The

Serbian appeal of July 22nd caused Sazonov, the Foreign Minister, to wire a warning to Vienna not to address unacceptable demands to Serbia. The Austrian ultimatum itself was greeted with shocked horror. Russia immediately appealed to Britain and France. A Council of Ministers, convened in the afternoon of July 24th, decided on a partial mobilization of the Russian army and a full mobilization of the Black Sea and Baltic fleets. The Serbian government was advised to give a moderate answer; and every Russian diplomatic effort was bent to securing a withdrawal of the time limit in the Austrian demands; an especial appeal was directed to Britain to make her position plain.

On the evening of July 25th, the Serbian reply was handed to the Austrian Minister in Belgrade. With a great show of moderation it accepted all the Austrian demands save those involving Austrian participation in the investigation of the conspirators' connexions in Serbia. The Austrians had not expected their demands to be accepted; and the Serbs did not expect their reply to satisfy them. The Serbian army was, in fact, given its orders to mobilize three hours before the delivery of the reply to the Austrians. The Austrian Minister broke off relations and asked for his passport. Three hours later the Austrian emperor ordered the mobilization of eight army corps against Serbia, to begin on July 28th.

The events of July 24th–25th in Vienna and St Petersburg mark the link between the Austro-Serbian war and the Russo-Franco-Germano-Austrian war. The actual linking event was the combination of miscalculations in the two capitals. In Vienna, Russia's reactions had been taken for granted. Germany was relied on to give Russia pause in 1914 as she had during the Bosnian crisis. In St Petersburg, Sazanov apparently hoped to produce a diplomatic line-up which would isolate Vienna. Germany's possible action in support of her ally does not seem to have been given much thought at this stage. Sazanov's hopes were pinned on a hostile demonstration by Britain, perhaps another Mansion House speech. This he soon found was unattainable. The main idea in the British mind was mediation Britain and France would restrain Russia, and Germany would restrain Austria. With this aim, on July 26th the British proposed a four-power conference, Italy, Germany, France and Britain to meet in London immediately.

This proposal was the product of the British Foreign Secretary's knowledge of the divisions in his own Cabinet, where an influential section were for neutrality on all issues. With it, the scene of miscalculation shifted to London. The British plan depended on the ability of Germany to hold Austria, and Britain and France to restrain Russia. In fact, neither Austria nor Russia could be restrained. Although Germany, in the person of her Chancellor, backed the British plan for a conference, the Chancellor's hand was weakened by the military anxieties of the German General Staff lest the European war they dreaded should open before Germany could strike the pre-emptive blow on which German strategy rested. And the Austrian authorities proved unwilling to pay any attention to representations. On July 27th, they declared the Serbian note totally unsatisfactory. Russia in her turn accepted the British idea of a conference. But this acceptance was vitiated by the Tsar's telegram to the King of Serbia promising support. The only method of restraint which would now have worked would have been a declaration from one or more of Austria's or Russia's allies that they would *not* support them in the event of war. No such statements were forthcoming. On July 28th, the Austrians declared war on Serbia, the Emperor being induced to sign the declaration by a false report of Serbian firing on Austrian troops.

The next two days were crucial, and provide a clear demonstration of the strength of the two forces which brought Europe to ruin, the Russian drive into the Balkans and Austria's reaction to it, and the failure of the civilians to control the military in Berlin. The news of the Austrian declaration of war on Serbia, and still more of the bombardment of Belgrade the following day (July 29th), provoked a crisis in St Petersburg. The Foreign Minister, Sazonov, decided that partial mobilization was what was called for, but the War Minister and the General Staff were so convinced that war with Germany was inevitable that they persuaded the Tsar to order general mobilization. A warning from the German ambassador that mobilization would mean a general European war only confirmed them in their views; but at the last moment an appeal from the Kaiser induced the Tsar to recall the order for general mobilization and substitute only partial mobilization against Austria.

During this breathing space, the German and British governments each did their best to work out a compromise. On the

evening of July 28th, the German Chancellor had done hi
unavailing best to restrain the Austrians, but without success
the German *démarche* not taking place in Vienna until after th
Austrian declaration of war. The German proposals envisage
the Austrian troops halting in Belgrade, and made their occupation of the Serbian capital the gauge for Serbian good behaviour. On the 29th, the Germans were impelled to repeat thei
proposals by a series of events which greatly weakened their ow
position. During the course of the day, it became obvious tha
neither of their two remaining allies, Italy or Rumania, woul
support them, and for the first time it became clear that Britai
would in all probability back France and Russia. The probabilit
of British action in this sense was made clear to the Germar
ambassador in London in the afternoon of July 29th, as ar
accompaniment to the proposal that Germany should mediat
with Vienna perhaps on the basis of an Austrian occupation o
Belgrade. The German Chancellor reacted during the night o
July 29th–30th by bombarding Vienna with telegrams threatening German inaction if Austria refused to enter into conversations with the Russians.

The German Chancellor seems, however, to have been already
convinced of the inevitability of war. On July 29th, the draft o
the ultimatum to Belgium demanding the passage of Germar
troops through Belgium was sent to the German embassy ir
Brussels. And that evening the Chancellor made a first bid fo
British neutrality, saying that in the event of a victorious wa
Germany did not aim at any territorial acquisitions from France
He was unable to give similar assurances about the Frencl
colonies and he prevaricated over Belgium. And his control ove
his military was slipping, as Moltke, the German Chief of Staff
took the opportunity on July 29th of hinting strongly to the
Austrians that they should answer the Russian partial mobili-
zation by a general mobilization

On July 30th, in fact, independently of each other, Germany
and Russia both decided on general mobilization. The Russian
decision was an agonizing one for the Tsar to take, and he wa
only induced to take it by allegations, quite untrue, that the
German measures of preparation for mobilization were already
secretly in a very advanced position and that Russia was ir
serious jeopardy of surprise attack. The Russian Army and
Foreign Ministry were of one mind on the desirability of and the

nevitability of war with Germany. The German decision was
not so immediate, in that the Crown Council of July 30th after
lengthy argument decided to issue the preliminary order for
mobilization, the notification of a so-called 'threatening danger
of war', by noon on July 31st. The Chancellor fought a losing
battle against the Kaiser and his military advisers, who were
convinced that mediation was pointless, and themselves alarmed
at the evidence of French and Belgian preparations for war,
preparations which could well put the whole German war plan
in danger. That same evening the Austrian government also
decided on general mobilization. Their decision was greatly
influenced by two telegrams from the Chief of the German
General Staff urging them to mobilize against Russia and ad-
vising that such action would bring the German alliance into
operation. 'Every hour of delay makes the situation worse. . . A
European war offers the last chance of preserving Austria-
Hungary. Unconditional support by Germany.' The Austrian
government had already rejected the proposals for a halt in
Belgrade, as had the Russians. War was now inevitable.

News of the Russian mobilization reached Berlin on July 31st.
It made any further resistance by the German Chancellor to the
military impossible. That afternoon the Germans addressed an
ultimatum to Russia demanding the suspension of all military
activity on pain of German mobilization and war. At the same
time the order 'threatening danger of war' was issued. Almost
simultaneously the French were given a time limit to say whether
they would stay neutral in a Russo-German war. If they were to
declare themselves neutral, then they were to be requested to
surrender to German occupation the fortresses of Verdun and
Toul as guarantees of their neutrality. The Schlieffen Plan would
only work if France entered the war at once and the Germans,
by advancing these totally unacceptable terms, made sure of her
entry. Belgium issued the order for general mobilization that
evening, and a French decision to mobilize was also taken at that
time, though the order was not issued until the afternoon of
August 1st. With this, war became for all the powers a matter of
waiting for the ultimata to expire.

For all the powers, that is, except Britain. Since July 27th, it
had become apparent that the Liberal Cabinet and the country
were deeply divided. Over half the Cabinet were against British
involvement and most of the rest undecided. Only a handful

favoured British intervention on the side of France, though thes
few included Grey, the Foreign Secretary, Churchill, the Firs
Lord of the Admiralty, and Haldane. The Liberal press and al
the radical side of the parliamentary party were neutralists an
the City and the Bank of England were appalled at the prospec
of war. As the ultimata expired and the declarations of wa
followed, Germany on Russia (August 1st), and on Franc
(August 3rd), the debate continued. It was aggravated by th
agonized representations of the French who had left thei
northern sea coasts to be defended by the Royal Navy under th
Staff Agreements of 1912. A vain attempt was made to secur
German agreement to French neutrality but the German genera
staff proved unable to alter its plans despite the Kaiser's inter
vention. On August 2nd, the British officially promised th
French that their northern sea coasts would be protected agains
German attack, and the Royal Navy was officially mobilized.

The position was changed by the German ultimatum t
Belgium which was officially presented on the afternoon o
August 2nd. The Belgian rejection was followed by a Germa
refusal to accept it, and at 7 AM on August 4th, German troop
crossed the Belgian frontier en masse. The news of the Germa
ultimatum to Belgium was crucial. On August 4th, the Britis
ultimatum was despatched to Berlin. No answer being received
Britain entered the war at midnight. The Army was mobilize
at 4 PM that afternoon. Only two members of the Cabine
resigned. Britain's ally, Japan, followed with a declaration o
war on Germany at the end of August.

There remained the strange anomaly of Austria-Hungary
The German intervention against Russia had, in fact, prevente
any use by Russia of her mobilization against Austria-Hungary
And for five days after the German declaration of war on Russia
both the original protagonists, Austria and Russia, remaine
strangely reluctant to go to war with one another. This did no
suit Germany's strategic plans at all. If the main weight of th
German army was to be brought against France, Austria's rol
was to help the weak German forces opposing Russia to war
off the expected Russian offensive. The Austrians, however, ha
been looking to Germany to protect them against Russian diplo
matic pressure. And, as the bulk of their armed forces were t
be deployed against Serbia, they expected Germany to continu
to protect them against Russia militarily. It took the German

until August 6th to overcome the resistance of the Austrian general staff and secure a declaration of war against Russia from Vienna. The Russians on their side were so little concerned with the Austro-Serb dispute which had provoked their original intervention that they were content to wait. As for France and Britain, it was August 12th before either brought themselves to declare war on the Austrian empire, and then it was false information of Austrian troop movements towards the Franco-German frontier which turned the trick.

This delay in 'regularizing the situation', more than anything else, underlines the hiatus between the Austro-Serbian war and those between Germany, France, Russia and Great Britain. The foregoing account shows that there were three main factors in bringing about the German declarations of war on France and Russia. First was the Russian conviction that she could not afford an Austrian take-over in Serbia, and that not only Austria but Germany was determined on securing this, whether this involved war with Russia or not being a matter of indifference to them. Russian moves to head off Austrian pressure on Serbia were first made before the Austrian ultimatum. Though they can be explained in part by the rumours which began around July 14th or so of impending Austrian action against Serbia, there was never any disposition in Russia to share in the almost universal European condemnation of Serbian support for the assassination. With this attitude Russia demonstrated her detachment at all but the *élite* level from the main currents and values of European civilization. Once the Austrian ultimatum to Serbia was delivered the Russians reached the substantially correct conclusion that this had been concerted with Berlin. Thereafter the Tsar's advisers were unanimous in seeing Germany as the enemy, and rejecting any mediation except on terms which preserved Serbia's freedom to continue to threaten the cohesion and interests of the Austrian state.

The second factor was Germany's inability to exercise any restraining influence in Vienna. This inability was the result of the previous assurances given to Vienna, the conviction of the German military that war with Russia was inevitable, and their consequent contradiction of the diplomatic pressure brought to bear on Vienna by the Chancellor, and the determination of the Austrian Cabinet not to allow anything to prevent their planned chastisement of Serbia. In giving their original assurances to

Vienna, the German Kaiser and Chancellor misjudged both th
degree to which Vienna would take advantage of them and th
strength of the subsequent Russian reaction.

The third factor was simply the failure of the German Kaise
and of his Chancellor properly to control their military, an
their willingness to countenance military planning which le
Germany no alternative but pre-emptive war not only again:
Russia, not only against France, but also involving an invasio
of Belgian neutrality and a breach of Germany's own guarante
to Belgium. This was the more disastrous in that, while i
Russia and Austria the only obstacles to war were the reluctanc
of Tsar and Emperor to send their peoples to destruction, i
Germany the Kaiser and his Chancellor belatedly realized whei
their ally was leading them and did their best to find a way ou

On this showing, the main responsibility for the outbreak
war between Germany, France and Russia must lie between th
Tsar's advisers in Russia, who never hesitated in their drive fc
war, and the German military's fears, in that they could conside
no alternative but a pre-emptive strike against France throug
Belgium. The main responsibility for war between Britain an
Germany must lie squarely with the same military men, an
with the Kaiser and Chancellor who failed to restrain them. /
dominant school of historians have long argued that had Britai
made it clear that she would enter the war on the side of France
Berlin would have been given pause; but these arguments ru
counter to the evidence. The German authorities did what the
could to secure British neutrality, but they had already accepte
the possibility of British entry on the side of their enemies an
discounted it. British hesitations did the British very little credit
but their main effect should have been felt in Paris and S
Petersburg. There is no evidence that this was the case.

There remains the responsibility for the original outbreak
And here we return to the actions of the Serbian extremists
whether in the *Black Hand* or the Serbian government. The
planned the assassination. They willed the destruction of Austria
They were prepared to hazard a European war and the destruc
tion of Europe to secure a union with the South Slav people
under the Habsburg crown, who, it is fair to say, were a long wa
from sharing their desires. They relied on Russian backin;
which was freely given them. Never can the essentially destruc
tive anarchic element in nationalism have been so well demon

strated as in the barbarian determination of this handful of ambitious politicians, unscrupulous military and sick-minded and -bodied adolescents to pull down a civilization which seemed to overshadow them.

Second only to them in the responsibility for the outbreak of war, is the despair of the advisers, civilian and military, to the Austrian Emperor. Their inability to control Serbia or to resolve the internal conflict between Slav and German had driven them to a state bordering on paranoia. The two Balkan wars had seen a considerable deterioration in Austria's position in the Balkans; but this deterioration was not so serious that a determined diplomatic offensive based on Serbia's enemies might not have countered it. The assassination of Franz Ferdinand, unpopular as he was with them all, struck them with a shock that is rarely given its proper weight in a world where nationalism has always been taken to be in the right. It led them to an unshakable determination to excise the Serbian cancer. They knew the operation would be perilous to the patient. But their main efforts were directed to thwarting those who might stop them, efforts which involved misleading not only their German ally but their Emperor. If they had been content to secure guarantees of good behaviour, more effective in prosecuting their examination of the assassins, and swifter to act they might well have succeeded in neutralizing Serbia for a decade. But their over-estimation of their freedom of action was only matched by their incompetence in playing their hand; and they were to prove almost as criminally indifferent to the continuance of that European civilization of which Vienna was one of the principal props as the barbarians outside.

Studying the decade before 1914 in Europe, one is struck by the growth of violence, of anarchism that demanded victory-or-death, of recklessness and dissatisfaction with the existing atmosphere of civilization and society not merely among those who had little or no place in it, but among those who ruled or dominated it. These phenomena were essentially nationalistic and have to be set against a corresponding growth in inter-nationalism, in Europeanism, in the centripetal forces of Euro-pean civilization. The tragedy was that for a crucial month these destructive centrifugal forces gained control, aided by the pressures and challenges of that great power which had only in part been absorbed into Europe, Tsarist Russia. The autocrats played an equivocal part in this disaster, it is true, all three contributing in some degree to the sense of urgency which accompanied the weeks immediately after the assassination of Franz Ferdinand and then attempting to rein back when they realized how near to the abyss they had come. All three then had to be cajoled or cheated by their advisers into signing the fatal mobilization orders.

A major part in the initial processes which led to the unleashing of the armed forces was played by a kind of desperate and irrational conservatism seizing what it felt to be its only chance of avoiding social or political revolution. This anarcho-conservatism, for that was what in essence it was, was to continue into the war years, to render any chance of a compromise peace impossible, to ensure that revolution, when it came, would be violent, bloody and republican. When peace came, it was not to be a peace of the dynasties. The age of the emperors, kaisers and tsars, of imperial courts and chancellors, of aristocratic advisers and noble generals, was over.

Chapter 12

The Great War: the Disappearance of Victory, 1914–16

THE outbreak of the war was greeted with wild scenes of popular enthusiasm throughout Europe. In Vienna, Berlin, Paris, St Petersburg and London the scenes were the same: with the sides of their railway carriages plastered with slogans, trainloads of garlanded reservists left to join their units amidst hysterically cheering crowds drunk with hurrah-patriotism. Volunteers swarmed to the colours both in Germany and in Britain, from those who had escaped conscription in the one country, and those to whom Continental ideas of universal military service had always seemed mere militarism, in the other. Young women made drunk with patriotic fervour paraded the streets of London, handing out white feathers, the badge of cowardice, to all young men not in uniform. 'Now God be thanked, who has matched us with this hour', wrote the English poet, Rupert Brooke; he voiced the sentiments of his generation.

In this welter of patriotic emotion, the old sentiments of class solidarity and loyalty disappeared overnight. Of the member parties of the Second International, those of Italy, the Netherlands and Scandinavia remained neutral. The French party, deprived of leadership by the assassination of Jean Jaurés in the week before war broke out, did nothing collectively. The German party, for years the largest and most dominant socialist party in Europe, voted to a man for the credits necessary to finance Germany's war effort. All the long denunciations of war as a capitalist-imperialist plot, which the workers of the world could defeat in its opening stages by a concerted General Strike, were forgotten. Individual pacifists disappeared behind bars or were metamorphosed into ultra-patriots of the most violent kind. Socialist international solidarity gave way to what the Russian revolutionary, Lenin, watching sourly from his exile in Switzerland, dubbed 'social patriotism'.

In those heady days the idea that party strife was unpatriotic dominated the political leadership of the belligerents. In Germany the Kaiser proclaimed a 'court peace' (*Burgfrieden*). In France, the parties joined together in the *Union Sacrée*. In Britain the parties declared a truce. The civil war which threatened over Ulster was suspended as the Liberals agreed not to implement the Home Rule Bill until the war was over. In Austria, the pressure on the Czechs was relaxed a little. Even in Russia the parties of the Duma rallied behind the Tsar.

This voluntary cessation of activity on the part of the political parties in Central and Western Europe foreshadowed the primacy of the military which was to hamstring the political direction of the war in Britain, lead to violent political strife in France, and produce a virtual military dictatorship in Germany. With the concentration of public attention on the battlefields the leading military men, particularly those whose names were associated with military success, were to come to enjoy a degree of popular support that in many cases amounted to idolization, making it virtually impossible for the civilian governments to remove them from office. Their power was increased in France and among the Central Powers by legal precedents of some antiquity which placed part or all of the country under military jurisdiction in time of war. In France, one third of the Chamber of Deputies were of military age and in fact rejoined their regiments on the outbreak of war. From August to December 1914, the French parliament did not meet. Patriotism was leading to the abdication of civilian rule. All of this was based on the hypothesis that the war would be a short one, and that there would be 'victory by Christmas'. Only the British, advised by Field Marshal Lord Kitchener, the victor of the Boer War, whom the Cabinet made Minister for War, began to prepare for a long conflict. Yet final victory eluded the Generals in 1914. Not a single one of the prewar military plans succeeded.

The opening months of the war were dominated by four great battles of collision between the opposing forces. The army staffs of Europe had spent the years before the war elaborating and perfecting plans for victory through attack. Germany pinned her hopes to the modified Schlieffen Plan of 1912 which swung the main weight of the German armies in a great turning movement through neutral Belgium and western France with the aim of encircling and driving the bulk of the French armies against their own frontier. The French, imbued with an irrationalist belief in the primacy of morale above material things, prepared to fling themselves into the offensive to regain the lost provinces of Alsace and Lorraine. In the East, the Russian armies planned to drive into East Prussia and into Austrian Galicia, to break out of the great Polish salient and to prepare for an invasion of Silesia. The Austrians planned two offensives, one, on their northern front into the centre of the Polish salient, aimed at Brest-Litovsk, and another on the southern front, to pinch off the northern end of Serbia. The Germans preferred to stay on the defensive in the East, stationing the bulk of their forces in East Prussia on the northern flank of the great Polish salient. Of the four armies the French were really the only equals to Germany in military science. But they lost any chance of making this equality tell by their senseless devotion to the offensive *à l'outrance*.

The western front, accordingly, was dominated by the great German offensive movement. The German armies swept through Belgium, using enormously heavy artillery to demolish the great Belgian fortresses of Liege and Namur. The Belgian army withdrew to the flanking position of Antwerp, and the French Fifth Army and the small British Expeditionary Force moving into Belgium to their aid were forced back deep into France. The French frontier offensives into Alsace-Lorraine and in the Ardennes were repulsed with enormous losses (over 300,000 killed and wounded), and the whole French line pushed back on a great arc between Verdun and Paris. The French Supreme Commander, General Joffre, however, kept his nerve, and purging the less successful army commanders, waited for the right moment to go over to the attack.

In their pursuit of the retreating French armies, the individual German armies over-reached themselves, not only exposing their flank to the fortified camp that was Paris, from which the French government had prudently removed itself to the safety of Bordeaux, but allowing a gap to open between the two armies in their centre. Into this gap, in the engagement known as the Battle of the Marne, moved the revivified British Expeditionary Force and part of the French Fifth Army. At this moment, the nerve of General von Moltke, the German Supreme

Commander, proved less strong than that of General Joffre, and he ordered a general retreat to the line Noyon–Verdun along the river Aisne, which he ordered to be entrenched and fortified. Thereafter, each of the two opposing armies tried desperately to envelop the other's western flank, in what has come to be known as the 'race to the sea'. The fighting was bitter, bloody, and inconclusive. Both sides dug themselves in and, by the end of November 1914, an unbroken line of trenches, dugouts and barbed wire stretched between the two sides from the Swiss frontier to the North Sea. In these battles, the French lost 380,000 killed and 600,000 wounded, including 80 per cent of their infantry officers. The German casualties were a little less, but on much the same scale.

On the eastern front, the Russians did not wait for their full mobilization to become effective. After initial successes on the borders of East Prussia, their armies were lured into a rash attempt to break through to the sea and isolate the Germans into a pocket around Königsberg. But by brilliant manoeuvres the Germans evaded the trap, turning the tables on the Russians. In the successive battles of Tannenberg and the Masurian Lakes, one Russian army was destroyed and a second badly mauled. The remnants of the Russian forces then withdrew from East Prussia. Russian casualties in dead and wounded were enormous and the Germans took over 150,000 prisoners.

On the Galician front, the Austrian and Russian offensives met head on. There followed nearly a month of confused fighting, in the course of which the Austrians' deficiency in leadership was demonstrated. At its end, the Austrians retreated precipitately over more than 200 miles to the river Dunajec in front of Cracow. In the south, the Austrians fared even worse. Their invasion of Serbia was rolled back by the Serbian Army. By December 15th, 1914, their forces had been completely expelled from Serbian territory. The Austrian collapse forced the Germans to form two new armies to attack towards Warsaw in the hope of relieving Galicia of some of the Russian pressure. But a new Russian offensive caused their withdrawal; and only Russia's extraordinary weakness in arms, munitions and means of transport, saved the German and Austrian armies from disaster. At the end of 1914, Russian troops had regained all but the most westerly section of Russian Poland, and lay along the foothills of the Carpathians. And a joint offensive in the snow in January 1915 by German and Austrian troops failed to dislodge them.

The end of 1914 then saw virtual stalemate on both the major fronts. In the west, all chance of a war of movement had ended, and for three years siege conditions existed all along the line. The ability to overcome fortifications requires a heavy weight of artillery, trained assault troops capable of taking heavy casualties, meticulous planning and long preparation before an assault is made. But the generals were for long deceived by the absence of recognizable fortresses. And it was only gradually that they learned that siege warfare on a front stretching several hundred miles against trenches, barbed wire and machine guns required a weight of war material in shells, artillery, bombs and motor transport which only a major industrial mobilization of a nation's entire economic resources could provide.

Throughout 1915, the British armies, which were prepared only for field warfare, unlike their German and French counterparts, were desperately short of these essentials. Manpower was the one thing as yet they had in abundance, owing to the enthusiasm with which the pick of the nation's youth responded to the call for recruits launched by Lord Kitchener, whose photographed figure, grimly moustached, finger pointing at his audience with the slogan 'Your Country Needs You', adorned every public wall. But manpower meant human lives, which were spent in the years 1915-17 with a prodigality whose cost to Europe can never be properly calculated.

Every Allied offensive in the west took the same form. First, came a bombardment which, it was hoped, would silence the enemy's artillery and machine guns, cut a way through his barbed wire defences and take a heavy toll of the garrisons of his trench systems. Then the guns moved on to bombard the rear positions while the infantry attacked through the barbed wire, and the enemy's machine guns. Ideally, the infantry should first break into the enemy's trench-line and then break through. But they never did. And the cavalry, which had been brought up in anticipation of a break-through and a pursuit, would retire disconsolate but comparatively undamaged to their camps, while the infantry counted their losses. The Germans tried poison gas to secure an easy break-through in April 1915, and the British employed tanks for the same purpose in 1916. But in each case the new weapon was used in penny packets and on an inadequate scale. And the generals on all sides remained obstinately devoted to the frontal assault. And in every case where initial successes were scored the defenders' reserves arrived more quickly to plug the line than the attackers could regroup to break through.

This stalemate in the west was used by both sides during 1915 to divert forces to other fronts. The Germans decided to turn their main efforts against Russia in the hope of saving the disintegrating Habsburg Empire. At the end of April 1915 a joint German-Austrian offensive broke through the Russian lines near Gorlice in Galicia. There followed a steady German advance and an equally steady Russian withdrawal. By December 1915, the Central Powers had advanced nearly to Riga in the north and their front ran due southwards from the River Dvina through the Pripet Marshes in Central Poland to the eastern Galician frontier. The Russian armies managed to evade the successive German attempts to envelop them, but all the same they lost an unknown number of dead and wounded and over three hundred thousand Russian prisoners were taken.

The disappointment of the hopes placed by each of the belligerents in an early victory and the stalemate which was established in the west after November 1914, with the German army so firmly entrenched in Northern France that only a long and protracted war seemed likely to expel them, naturally led the *Entente* Powers to search for allies, especially from those powers which could most effectively bring pressure to bear on the Central Powers. Such allies, it was very quickly realized, could be found not only among the nations already in being but also among the suppressed nationalities of the German, Austrian and Turkish Empires. The Central Powers, on their side, tried naturally to thwart the approaches of the *Entente* Powers to the neutrals. But they also realized the extreme vulnerability of the Tsarist Empire to encouragement of the subject nationalities; and they toyed too with the support of the Irish, and attempted to enlist the support of Islam, to subvert Persia, Afghanistan and India, and to raise Abyssinia against the rear of the British position in Egypt.

The first of the neutrals to enter was the Turkish Empire. The 'Young Turks', the military junta which had full command of Turkish affairs in August 1914, were already thoroughly committed to Germany, with the Liman von Sanders mission reorganizing their army, German capital heavily engaged in developing the Turkish railway system and Krupps acting as their main supply of armaments. But they had little to lose and much to gain from staying neutral. They were tipped towards war partly by their hatred of Russia and partly by their confidence in a German victory. But the action of the British Navy in commandeering two modern battleships they had under construction in British shipyards, and the successful evasion of the British Mediterranean squadron by the German battle cruiser *Goeben* with its attendant cruiser the *Breslau*, which sought refuge in the Sea of Marmora and were promptly transferred by Germany, together with their crews, into Turkish service, finally decided them to declare war on Russia in November 1914.

By this time Japan and Portugal, as Britain's allies, had formally entered the war on the side of the *Entente* Powers and interest shifted to Italy. Nominally, a member of the Triple Alliance with Germany and Austria-Hungary, Italy had in fact virtually abandoned the Alliance around the turn of the century; and at the outbreak of war Italy proclaimed her neutrality. Italian entry into the war was determined by a kind of auction of Austrian territories in upper Italy in which inevitably the Germans, inhibited by the fact that they were dealing with the territory of their allies, came off second best. In April 1915, by the Treaty of London, Britain and France promised the Italians the Trentino, the South Tyrol, Trieste, Gorizia, Istria and Dalmatia and the Turkish province of Adalia if Italy would enter the war on the Allied side. Italy declared war on Austria on May 23rd, 1915.

The Italian entry into the war was preceded in Italy by a debate between the advocates of the doctrine of *sacro egoismo* (holy egotism) and those of *parecchio* (much) who argued that Italy could obtain most by staying neutral. This spirit of unashamed and admitted desire for national aggrandizement was not rewarded by any immediate gain. The Austrian position was very strong naturally and had been systematically prepared. By the end of 1915 the Italians had lost over 250,000 men in successive battles on the river Isonzo and had advanced only as far as the Austrian main defences.

More success attended the next entrant into the war, Bulgaria. The *Entente* Powers made desperate attempts to keep her neutral. But Bulgaria's ambitions lay all in the territories Serbia and Greece had taken from her in 1913 in the second Balkan war. Under German pressure, Turkey ceded her land west of the Maritsa river. On September 6th, a secret German-Austrian-Bulgarian treaty committed Bulgaria to join in operations against Serbia. On October 14th, Bulgaria entered the war. The German and Austrian offensive against Serbia had already begun, and the Bulgarian forces succeeded in cutting off the Serbian escape route to Salonika in Greece, where two *Entente* divisions had landed. The Serb army was driven into a desperate retreat across the mountains to Durazzo on the Adriatic where the survivors were evacuated to the Greek island of Corfu. A quarter of a million Serbian casualties, killed, wounded and prisoners, were lost in this campaign.

The course of events in Greece was less smooth, the country being deeply divided between the pro-German King Constantine and his followers, whose main strength lay in those sections of Greece which had gained their independence in the early part of the nineteenth century, and the Liberal leader, M. Venizelos, whose main support came from the Greek islands. In January 1915, the *Entente* Powers offered Greece the Turkish city of Smyrna and its hinterland in return for Greek concessions to Bulgaria and Greek support of Serbia. Venizelos wished to accept but the King would not agree and dismissed him. Elections in June 1915 returned Venizelos to power again but the Allied failure to carry Gallipoli made him less enthusiastic to intervene in the war unless the presence of a large *Entente* force at Salonika could be guaranteed. The obvious move of Bulgaria towards the Central Powers also made him more cautious. Greece refused to come to Serbia's aid against Bulgaria but connived at the landing of two Allied divisions at Salonika. The *Entente* troops, in fact, came too late to save Serbia; and uncertainty as to the intentions of the Greek armed forces made them abandon their first offensive. They did, however, stay in Salonika. Venizelos resigned yet again and the Greeks moved back towards an occupied neutrality.

The Turkish armies, meantime, were engaged on their only front with Russia in the Caucasus. Here, megalomania on the part of Enver Pasha drove the Turks into a winter offensive towards Kars in which the Turks lost 77,000 men out of an army of 95,000. The Turkish defeat was quickly repaired by German direction and the Russians, in their turn, were caught early in 1915 and only brilliant Russian generalship defeated the subsequent Turkish offensive.

In the meantime, the Turks and Germans between them had been attempting to preach a *Jehad*, a holy war of Islam, against the British and French. The position of the Ottoman Sultan as Caliph gave them a springboard and his proclamation of a *Jehad* was duly endorsed by the *Ulemas* of Istanbul. But the *Jehad* floundered without the support of Hussein, the Sharif of Mecca. And Hussein saw in British support the chance of forming an Arab kingdom which would comprehend the whole of the Arab east. In October 1914, the British, desperately anxious for the security of the Islamic population of their empire, and remembering Abdullah's approach to Kitchener in February 1914, opened contact with Hussein and promised him aid and support in the event of an Arab rising against the Turks. The Indian government at the same time began similar approaches to ibn Saud. As the Turkish forces in the Yemen were preparing an offensive against Aden which was to take them as far as Lahej before it petered out, the matter was urgent.

There followed, however, a year or more of negotiations in which the British authorities in Egypt offered Hussein an outright alliance and the recognition of a single Arab state in the Arabian peninsula. But Hussein's ambitions stretched to Damascus and Baghdad; in return for British support of these ambitions, he offered the British a defensive alliance and economic hegemony within the new Arab state. The British, however, were in no position to accept such proposals, in view of the interest and ambitions of their French ally in the Lebanon and Syria. And the final British note sent to Hussein in October 1915 reserved the Syrian areas west of Damascus, Homs, Hama and Aleppo, and provided for a 'special form of administration' with British participation in the provinces of Basra and Baghdad. Even that did not settle matters and the negotiations dragged on into 1916. In the meantime, the only Arab forces to take the *Jehad* seriously were the Senussi of Cyrenaica, especially after their self-styled overlords, the Italians, joined the *Entente* Powers. A joint Turkish-Senussi force caused considerable trouble with its irruptions into Egypt, until the capture of its able Turkish commander in February 1916 brought its effective activities to an end.

In the war at sea, the balance of power lay overwhelmingly in favour of the *Entente* Powers. The British battle fleet, the Grand Fleet as it was called, consisted of 35 Dreadnoughts, 27 pre-Dreadnoughts and 10 battle cruisers, 72 ships in all, which from their bases at Rosyth and Scapa Flow effectively bottled the German fleet into the North Sea. The German fleet with its 22 Dreadnoughts, 16 pre-Dreadnoughts and 8 battle cruisers was thus completely unable to exert any strength against Britain's supply lines, all of which terminated in ports on Britain's south and west coasts. And the naval folly of Admiral Tirpitz's construction policy, with its concentration on gun-power and heavy armour at the sacrifice of range of operation, was revealed. For so long as the Grand Fleet survived, Britain's commerce was largely invulnerable to attack by surface warships, once the few German warships outside the North Sea in August 1914 had been hunted down. It was for the German battle fleet, numerically the weaker of the two, to lure the Grand Fleet into action, in the knowledge that unless it was exceptionally well-handled and fortunate in the lottery of war, it faced inevitable defeat by superior numbers. Not surprisingly, sorties by the German battle fleet tended to be few and far between.

The hunting down of the German warships outside the North Sea was only a matter of time. The German Mediterranean squadron, as related above, evaded British capture and took refuge in the Sea of Marmora. The German Pacific squadron under Admiral Graf von Spee caught its weaker British equivalent at Coronel off the coast of Chile in November 1914 and destroyed it. But, thereafter, except for the cruiser *Emden*, which managed for a time to terrorize British and Allied shipping in the Pacific, Graf von Spee's squadron was lured by faked German signals sent out by British Intelligence to the Falkland Islands, to be destroyed in December 1914 by a superior British force. The *Emden* was caught and sunk by an Australian cruiser, the *Sydney*, in the Indian Ocean in November 1914, and the *Dresden*, sole survivor of Graf von Spee's squadron, was sunk in March 1915 in the Pacific. The last German cruiser, the *Königsberg*, was caught in African waters in July 1915. Thereafter, only German U-boats and the occasional German merchant cruiser appeared outside the North Sea to harass British commerce.

The German battle fleet was handled with extreme caution in these first two years of war; though isolated German cruiser and battle cruiser raids were made into the North Sea, their fate precluded more large-scale operations. In August 1914, and again in January 1915, at the battle of the Dogger Bank, British battle cruisers caught German cruiser squadrons engaged on such raids and damaged them severely. A German battle cruiser attack on the British coast in December 1914 managed to evade interception; but their fate in general convinced the German Naval High Command that the only hope of victory at sea lay in U-boat raids on all shipping engaged in supplying Britain. In February 1915, therefore, the German Naval High Command issued a formal warning that all shipping found in the waters around the British Isles would be liable to be sunk without warning, neutral shipping included. But the Germans lacked the numbers of U-boats as yet to make their threat real, and its only effect was greatly to exacerbate German relations with the United States, especially after the sinking of the passenger liners *Lusitania* and *Arabic* in May and August 1915 with considerable loss of life to the passengers, who included American citizens. American protests were so strong that in September 1915 the German government greatly modified its orders to U-boat crews and U-boat attacks in the waters around Britain notably diminished.

This was the first sign of the issue which was eventually to bring the United States into the war. On its outbreak in August 1914, the United States had proclaimed its formal neutrality. In practice, most American opinions, save among the members of the German, Irish, and Jewish minorities, were either indifferent or profoundly pro-Ally. And their pro-Allied sentiments were reinforced once Britain began placing large orders with arms and steel manufacturers, raising loans on the New York money market to finance these orders and making pre-emptive bids for the whole American cotton crop in order to prevent it from falling into German hands. The combined effect of all the Allied orders for war material and supplies in America was to introduce a general upswing in the American economy which up to the summer of 1914 had been in the throes of a depression. British and Allied orders which were largely financed by the mobilization of Britain's immense overseas investments were to keep American industry operating at full capacity for the next three years.

The British blockade of Germany, however, also had its repercussions on Anglo-American relations. As Britain had failed to ratify the pre-war conventions on contraband, the British Navy was free to issue its own lists of goods whose export to Germany was forbidden, and, as always, it arrogated to itself the right to stop and search any neutral ship suspected of carrying contraband to its enemies, the Central Powers. This right was extended to include shipment to the ports of neutrals such as the Netherlands or Scandinavia, where trans-shipment to Germany, because of the territorial contiguity of the neutral to Germany, could not be checked. Shippers found it safer to clear their cargoes with British blockade authorities in advance and arm themselves with certificates, 'navicerts' they were called, against boarding and search by British warships. And such boarding and searching with its constant reminder that the sea could only be used with British permission grated deeply on the nerves of the one world power that was not yet involved in the war.

In addition to making possible the blockade of Germany, Britain's dominance of the sea made the conquest of the German colonies merely a matter of time. Those in the Pacific fell to Australian and New Zealand action. The naval station at Kiou Chou on the Shantung peninsula of North China was reduced by Britain's Japanese ally. German South-West Africa fell easily to South African forces once a rebellion by Boer extremists in South Africa itself had been put down. Togoland was caught between British forces moving from the Gold Coast and the French advancing from Dahomey. The Cameroons fell after eighteen months' fighting to British, French and Belgian forces moving in from three sides. Only in German East Africa, where disease took a frightful toll of the Allied troops, did the German garrison, led by a genius, General von Lettow-Vorbeck, succeed in holding out until the end of the war. The very considerable body of African troops, twenty-two battalions in all, raised by the British to conduct this campaign, had a considerable impact on the development of African nationalism in East Africa in later years.

In the war at sea, British naval supremacy, as was pointed out in an earlier chapter, rested not only on her superiority in the actual strength of her fleet but also in her control of most of the major 'narrows', outlets for European seapower to the open oceans, bottlenecks through which maritime commerce virtually had to pass. Of all these narrows, only one, and that perhaps the

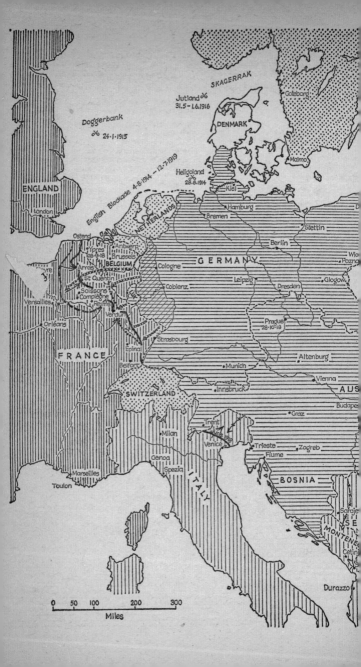

SKAGERRAK

Jutland ⚔
31.5 – 1.6.1916

Goteborg

Doggerbank
⚔ 24·1·1915

DENMARK

Malmö

ENGLAND

London

Heligoland
⚔
28·8·1914

Kiel

English Blockade 4·8·1914 – 12·7·1919

Hamburg

Stettin

NETHERLANDS

Bremen

Berlin

Wlo

Ostend

Antwerp

Cologne

G E R M A N Y

Poznan

Ypres
28·9·18

Brussels

BELGIUM

Leipzig

Dresden

Glogow

Arras

St Quentin

Coblenz

vre

Soissons

Compiègne

Reims

Verdun

Prague
28·10·18

Altenburg

Versailles

Strasbourg

Orléans

Epinal

Munich

Vienna

A U S

F R A N C E

Belfort

SWITZERLAND

Innsbruck

Budape

Graz

Trent

Milan

Venice

Trieste

Zagreb

Flume

Genoa

Spezia

Marseilles

BOSNIA

Toulon

I T A L Y

Saraje

SE

MONTENE

Cetin

Durazzo

0   50   100   200   300
Miles

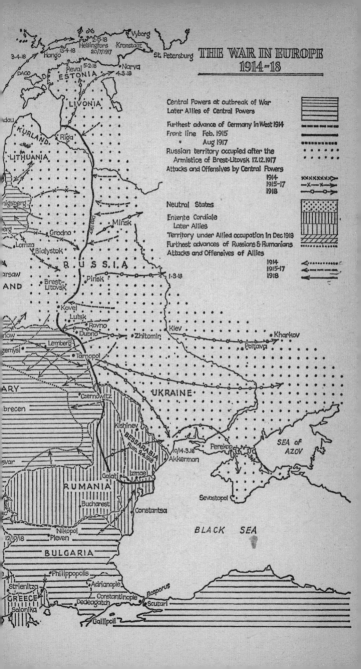

THE WAR IN EUROPE
1914-18

Central Powers at outbreak of War
Later Allies of Central Powers

Furthest advance of Germany in West 1914
Front line Feb. 1915
    "   Aug 1917
Russian territory occupied after the
    Armistice of Brest-Litovsk 17.12.1917
Attacks and Offensives by Central Powers
                                1914
                                1915-17
                                1918

Neutral States

Entente Cordiale
    Later Allies
Territory under Allied occupation in Dec 1918
Furthest advances of Russians & Rumanians
Attacks and Offensives of Allies
                                1914
                                1915-17
                                1918

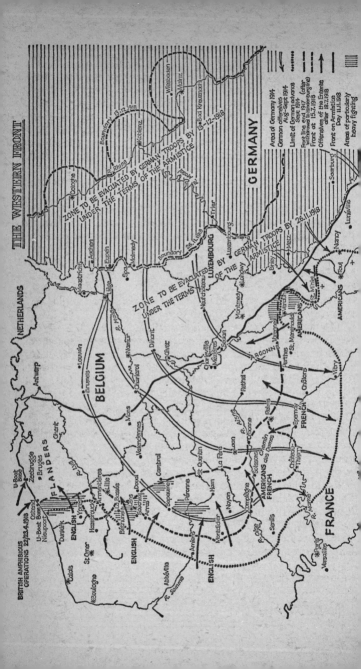

THE WESTERN FRONT

NETHERLANDS

Antwerp

BELGIUM

Brussels
Louvain
Namur

GERMANY

Maastricht
Aachen
Eupen
Spa
Malmédy

Cologne
R. Rhine
Koblenz
13.12.1918
Bad Kreuznach
Mainz
Wiesbaden

ZONE TO BE EVACUATED BY GERMAN TROOPS BY 13·12·1918
UNDER THE TERMS OF THE ARMISTICE

Trier

LUXEMBOURG
Luxembourg

ZONE TO BE EVACUATED BY THE GERMAN TROOPS BY 26.11.1918
UNDER THE TERMS OF THE ARMISTICE

Boundary 26.11.1918

Liège
Dinant
Givet
Charleroi
Mons
Valenciennes
Charleville
Mézières
Neufchâteau
Longwy
Longuyon
Montmédy
Briey
Metz
Saarburg
Saarbrücken
Lunéville
Nancy
Toul
AMERICANS
St. Mihiel
Verdun
Montfaucon
ARGONNE
Varennes
AMERICANS
St. Menehould
Perthes
Vitry
Châlons
FRENCH
Épernay
Reims
FRENCH
AMERICANS
FRENCH
Rethel
R. Aisne
Laon
Soissons
La Fère
Chemin des Dames
Château-Thierry
St. Quentin
Ham
Péronne
Noyon
Compiègne
Montdidier
R. Oise
Senlis
ENGLISH
Amiens
R. Avre
R. Marne
Versailles
Paris
FRANCE
R. Somme
Abbeville
Calais
Boulogne
St. Omer
Dunkirk
U-Boat Bases
Nieuport
Ostend
Zeebrugge
Bruges
Ghent
FLANDERS
Ypres
Hazebrouck
Armentières
Béthune
Lille
Douai
Bois Bossu
Cambrai
Arras
Bapaume
ENGLISH
BRITISH AMPHIBIOUS
OPERATIONS 22/23·4·1918
U-Boat
Bases

most vital to Britain, the Suez Canal, was really vulnerable to attack by land. Once the Turks had entered into the war, Suez was an obvious target for the Ottoman forces in Palestine. Expecting such an attack the British authorities moved two Indian divisions to Egypt in November 1914 and used Egypt as the assembly point for the first two divisions from Australia and New Zealand. They were thus easily able to repel a Turkish attack across the waterless Sinai desert in February 1915.

Before the Turkish entry into the war the British government moved troops to the frontiers of Mesopotamia at the head of the Persian Gulf to protect the oil installations at Abadan, which was commanded by a Turkish fortress on the island of Fao on the opposite side of the Shatt-al-Arab. On the Turkish entry into the war, the Turkish fortress was captured. From this there developed a full-scale advance up the Euphrates river towards Baghdad. But at the end of 1915 the British forces, rebuffed before Ctesiphon some twenty-five miles south of Baghdad retired on the town of Kut-al-Amara where they rashly allowed themselves to be besieged by the Turkish forces and were eventually, in April 1916, forced to capitulate.

The main use made of Britain's command of the sea in 1915, however, was in the amphibious assault on the Dardanelles which became the Gallipoli campaign. The scheme represented a deliberate attempt to get away from the 'continental' strategy to which Britain had committed herself before 1914 in order to return to the traditional 'maritime' strategy of the past; in this traditional strategy British seapower was used to land British armies wherever on an enemy-dominated European coastline they would create the maximum disruptive effect and could secure the most important immediate success. It had as its immediate aim the opening of a direct supply route to Russian warm-water ports so that the manifold and paralysing deficiencies of the Russian war industry could be made up from the Allies. The British Admiralty before the war had wanted to launch the Army in an amphibious assault on the German North Sea coast. In late 1914, it toyed briefly with the idea of using Britain's great store of pre-Dreadnoughts to force a way into the Baltic. But in January 1915, the decision was taken to attempt to force the Dardanelles. A purely naval attempt in February 1915 failed with the loss of three British and French capital ships; its only success was to draw Turkish divisions away from the Caucasus front, and to give warning of Allied interest in the Dardanelles area.

Thus, when, in April 1915, amphibious landings were made on the Gallipoli peninsula at the mouth of the Dardanelles they ran into heavy Turkish resistance organized by the future president of the Turkish Republic, Kemal Ataturk. And a second landing in August came to grief when the British troops failed to exploit the initial surprise achieved by the landing. In December 1915, the Allied forces were secretly and safely evacuated. British losses totalled 213,980 killed, wounded, hospitalized and missing, of which two out of three were casualties from disease rather than enemy action. As an exercise in 'maritime strategy' the Dardanelles campaign was a costly failure.

The effects of the first days of war in enhancing all the nationalist centrifugal forces in European society and opening fissures between nation and nation were greatly intensified by the hardships, privations and strains of war, above all by the impact of the ever-lengthening casualty lists upon the morale of the middle classes from whom the bulk of the volunteer and reservist officer corps of the new mass armies in Europe were recruited. These feelings of internecine hatred of English and French for German and *vice versa* were only exacerbated by the growth of considerable propaganda machines on either side designed to convince both domestic and neutral opinion of the justice of the nation's cause and the barbarism of the enemy. To this effort all but a very few of Europe's intellectuals lent their aid; and their efforts aborted for most of the following generations the development of any common European intellectual culture except among a small and *avant-garde* minority. The British were particularly effective, so all agreed, at this novel form of European intellectual *hari-kari*; so much so that, from a country where German intellectual influences had once been overwhelming, knowledge of contemporary German intellectual developments became almost as esoteric an accomplishment as expertise in Indian ceramics or the writings of Lao-Tse.

This was, however, only of significance in that it accentuated the long-term development of fissiparous as against unifying forces in Western and Central Europe. Of more immediate importance was the accentuation of internal divisions, the revival of party strife in Britain, France and Germany under the increasing strains of 1915's succession of sanguinary and unsuccessful attempts to break the strategic deadlock.

In Britain, the main lines of the struggle became clear from January 1915 onwards. On the one hand, was a small group in the Liberal party, led by David Lloyd George, which was becoming appalled by the rate at which Britain was dissipating her financial resources and the calm with which the military commanders, backed by Lord Kitchener the Field Marshal whom Asquith had made War Minister, were prepared to take extremely severe casualties and yet have nothing to show for it. For this group the main urgency was to re-establish civilian control of the military. The Conservatives were increasingly dissatisfied with their exclusion from power and had lost confidence in the abilities of all but a handful of Liberal ministers. Both groups were highly critical of Asquith's powers of leadership. In May 1915, the Conservatives forced a coalition on the Liberals. The casualties, however, continued and by the end of 1915 it was clear that Britain would have to introduce conscription.

In France, Parliament did not meet at all during the months of crisis in the autumn of 1914, and the French High Command flourished without criticism. When Parliament did re-convene it was obvious that General Joffre, with the help of the Minister of War, Millerand, was determined to tolerate no parliamentary interference with the conduct of the war. In June 1915, General Joffre precipitated a crisis in internal politics by summarily dismissing the commander of the Third Army, General Sarrail, who had a strong parliamentary following that wished to see him Commander-in-Chief. The failure to restrain Bulgaria and the need to make some gesture towards Serbia led to Sarrail's appointment as commander of an Allied expedition to Salonika. In the resultant crisis, Briand replaced Viviani as Premier, and General Galliéni became War Minister. The *Union Sacrée* between left and right had been disturbed: but the real crisis was to follow in 1916-17.

In Germany, it was the unequal social effects of the British blockade that were mainly to blame for the gradual ebbing away of the feeling of social unity which sprang up so spontaneously in August 1914. Although there was an official rationing scheme for food, it was easily circumvented, and rationing tended to operate according to the size of one's purse rather than on the basis of one's need. The Chancellor, Bethman-Hollweg, did his best to satisfy the Social Democrats, who were, after all, the largest party in the *Reichstag*. But his only reward was to induce in the conservative right the conviction that victory was essential as a means of restraining the further advance of parliamentarianism, so that social discontent could be sublimated in the exultation of an annexationist peace. The revival in social tension within Germany was not reflected in the *Reichstag*, however, until December 1915, when the left wing of the Social Democrats began to break away and opposed the vote for war credits.

In the Far East, the absorption of the Great Powers in the war in Europe left Japanese expansionists virtually a free hand. Japanese troops expelled the Germans from Kiou Chou and Japan fell heir to the German sphere of influence in the Shantung peninsula. In January 1915, Japan secretly presented to China a list of 'Twenty-one Demands' in five groups, Chinese agreement to the last of which would have given Japan an economic protectorate over Northern China and effective control of the Chinese armed forces. China managed to mobilize a certain amount of diplomatic support, which enabled her to evade discussion of the last group of demands, but she was forced to make very considerable concessions in the economic sphere.

The effect was to exacerbate internal tensions in China. Yuan Shih-kai was encouraged by the overwhelming support he received from all branches of Chinese opinion to proceed with his ambitions to found a new dynasty in China, despite international opposition from the *Entente* Powers. With Japanese support, however, the republicans rallied and anti-Yuan forces raised revolt throughout the south of China. The controversy ended in part at least with Yuan's death in June 1916.

At the end of 1915, the war was beginning to move into a new and more extreme phase. Up to that date, a negotiated peace might have been possible, and the losses which Europe had so far suffered in men and material, though extremely serious, could possibly have been overcome. But in each of the major countries the tides of parliamentarianism and anti-militarism which had flowed so strongly in the years immediately before the war were in retreat, and the military leaders, with their instinctive preference for social conservatism and political authoritarianism and their almost universal contempt for civilian parliamentarianism enjoyed the strongest popular support. For their part they had reached in all countries virtually the identical conclusion, that victory could only come when the forces of their enemies had been numerically worn down and their morale broken in the process, in short, a strategy of attrition. For Europe as a whole, however, attrition meant self-attrition; and as the process continued, the world balance shifted inevitably, irretrievably, away from Europe.

Chapter 13

Total War and the Self-Mutilation of Europe, 1916–17

1916, THE YEAR OF ATTRITION

As 1915 ended the supreme commanders in France and Germany were both convinced that ultimate victory could only be reached on the Western Front. Joffre planned a great Anglo-French offensive in the summer to be supported by simultaneous attacks on the Russian and Italian fronts. He secured the reluctant agreement of the British commander in France, General Haig, to that offensive taking place along the river Somme, an area selected not for any strategic importance but because, being in the area in which the French and British forces touched one another, it would make the problems of command easier. The aim of the offensive was principally that of attrition. The German commander, von Falkenhayn, who had replaced von Moltke after his failure at the Marne, had a similar aim, to bleed the French army white in the hope of knocking France out of the war. With this aim he proposed to concentrate his attacks on the fortress of Verdun, which lay in a salient with poor communications easily commanded by the German artillery, and which, he correctly estimated, French sentiment would make it impossible to abandon. He was unable to carry his Austro-Hungarian allies with him; they preferred to concentrate on knocking Italy out of the war by an Alpine offensive.

The German attack on Verdun began on February 21st. Its strategic aim succeeded magnificently. French troops were poured into the defence of the great fortress system which General Joffre had previously dismissed as outmoded, and many of the reserves he had earmarked for the great summer offensive were killed or wounded. The Germans, however, became equally committed to Verdun, as the final casualty total, 362,000 for France and 336, 831 for Germany, reveals. Neither side made any significant gains in territory.

As a result the planned Anglo-French offensive on the Somme became virtually an all-British affair. Launched with insufficient artillery preparation, the Somme offensive was based on a system of attack better fitted to the battlefield of Waterloo than to one dominated by the machine gun. The first day's casualties amounted to nearly 60,000 British killed and wounded. But the battle continued until mid-November when the advance of winter made further fighting impossible, with heavy reserves being committed on both sides, the Germans using 161 divisions to 20 for the French and 55 for the British. The German casualties outnumbered those suffered by Britain and France, and the German professional army was said by historians on both sides to have been virtually destroyed in the battle.

The failure by either the French or Germans to achieve victory led to the dismissal of Joffre and his deputy, General Foch, and Germany's General von Falkenhayn. Nivelle, the hero of Verdun, succeeded Foch, and Hindenburg, the victor of Tannenberg, succeeded von Falkenhayn. The British Commander, General Haig, was promoted to the rank of Field Marshal. All three promotions reflected more on the effectiveness with which their beneficiaries had built up their military reputations at home than their actual military capabilities, and Nivelle's ill-judged optimism was soon to lead France to the edge of collapse.

If the British forces had secured a partial victory in France, the rest of the Allied fronts in 1916 showed nothing but disaster. On the Italian front, it is true, the Austrian offensive in the Trentino was repelled with heavy losses on both sides. But four further Italian offensives on the Isonzo advanced the Italian lines only a few miles around Gorizia at the cost of very heavy casualties.

On the Russian front, the great offensive planned to coincide with Joffre's originally planned assault in the Somme was advanced in date to ease Austrian pressure on Italy in the Trentino. Under General Brusilov's leadership, it was at first amazingly successful and over 400,000 Austrians were taken prisoner. But the Russian casualties were extremely severe and they lacked the reserves of men, material and mobility to exploit the victory. Germany's command of the interior lines enabled her to move troops from the Western front; although the German counter-offensive was unsuccessful, these fresh German

troops were able to control the new Russian offensives launche
in July, August and October 1916. Ultimate victory continue
to elude the Russian armies; and in the meantime the Russia
will to victory was being steadily eroded by the lack of material
Tsarist bureaucratic mismanagement and the appalling casual
ties. About one million men were killed, wounded and missin
on the Russian side in 1916.

The worst *Entente* disasters occurred in Rumania and Irac
In Iraq, the British forces at Kut were forced to surrender t
their Turkish besiegers. In Rumania, the apparent success c
the Russian summer offensive brought the Rumanian govern
ment to a hasty abandonment of their neutrality in return fc
promises of post-war gains at Austria-Hungary's expense i
Transylvania and the Bukovina. But by the time Rumania'
claims had been finally conceded by the *Entente* Powers, by th
Treaty of Bucharest of August 27th, 1916, the Russian offensive
had lost their momentum and a force of German, Austriar
Bulgarian and Turkish forces was being rapidly assembled t
deal with her. The Rumanians chose to ignore *Entente* pleas fo
a southern offensive to link up with the *Entente* forces a
Salonika so as to cut the Central Powers' link with Turkey
Instead they concentrated their forces against Transylvania
Here, they caught the Austrians off balance and advanced ir
some places over forty miles; but the effect was only to exhaus
and scatter their forces and leave them less able to stand up t
the German counter-offensive when it came. The German attac
duly began in October 1916. By December, the Rumanians ha
been pinned into the north-eastern corner of their own countr
at a cost of over 300,000 casualties. And Rumania's oilfields, gran
aries and her great wealth of wheat-lands fell into German hands

In the meantime, the Greek government continued to giv
trouble to the Allied forces in Salonika. In June 1916, Anglo
French forces blockaded Athens and demanded and secured th
demobilization of the Greek army and the dismissal of the pro
German government. In August, reinforced by the survivors c
the Serbian army from Corfu, the *Entente* forces launched ar
offensive against the Bulgarians. But it was repelled and th
British flank was weakened when a German-Bulgarian counter
offensive was accompanied by the voluntary surrender of
Greek army corps to the Germans on the Graeco-Bulgariar
border.

With *Entente* encouragement, Venizelos, the Greek Liberal leader, then raised a revolt in Salonika and the islands, established a provisional government and declared war on the Central Powers. The *Entente* Powers sent an ultimatum demanding the dismissal of the representatives of the Central Powers and landed troops near Athens in support. They withdrew only after the Greeks had agreed to withdraw all Greek forces from Thessaly. In December, the British decided to recognize the Venizelos government, and a second offensive re-established Serb forces on Serbian territory in the town of Monastir. Troubles with the Greek Royalist government in Athens continued until, in June 1917, after fresh French landings on the Isthmus of Corinth, King Constantine abdicated in favour of his second son, Alexander, and a Venizelist government was established. In July 1917, the new *régime* declared war on the Central Powers and the Greek army joined the *Entente* forces on the Salonika front.

The Caucasus saw major Russian victories in 1916. Under the Grand Duke Nicholas, transferred to this theatre in disgrace after the Russian defeats in Poland in 1915, the Russian winter offensive caught the Turks completely off balance. By mid-July, the Turkish fortresses of Erzerum, Trebizond and Eringhian had fallen and the Russian armies had advanced into the heart of Anatolia. But the primitiveness of the communications and the general weakness of the Russian supply system brought them to a halt. The Turkish forces in the Caucasus were in a complete state of demoralization and a new army was sent to replace them.

The Suez and Palestine fronts saw a further Turkish defeat in August 1916 when a Turkish offensive against Suez was stopped by superior British forces on the Mediterranean coast of the Sinai peninsula. The British forces were, in the meantime, engaged in solving the engineering problems of launching a campaign through the Sinai desert. In December 1916, they advanced up to the borders of Palestine. And the same month a new British offensive was launched in Mesopotamia and by February 1917 Kut had been recaptured.

At sea, the year 1916 began with a new man in command of the German High Seas fleet, Admiral Scheer. He began by intensifying cruiser and submarine warfare against British shipping. But the sinking of the Folkestone-Dieppe packet, the *Sussex*, in

March 1916 with the loss of several American lives led
Kaiser to one of his rare, and as it proved his last, interventi
in the conduct of the war and the temporary rescinding of
order for unrestricted submarine warfare under the threat of
American break in diplomatic relations.

Scheer then attempted to lure the British Grand Fleet i
battle. There followed two German sorties in March and A
1916 with the bombardment of seaports on the British No
Sea coast. A third sortie at the end of May, made with
deliberate intention of luring the Grand Fleet into action off
coast of Norway, resulted in collision between British and G
man battle cruisers. A rather confused engagement between
main battle fleets, known to British historians as the Battle
Jutland, to Germans as the battle of the Skaggerak, follow
from which the Germans managed to escape under cover
night. Both sides claimed a victory. Tactically, perhaps,
Germans had the edge, having sunk three British battle cruis
for the loss of one battleship and one battle cruiser, and th
cruisers for the loss of four light cruisers. One further Gern
sortie in July passed without an engagement between the t
fleets. But the strategic success scored by the British at Jutl
was underlined by the fact that this was the last move by
German High Seas fleet for the rest of the war. Its existe
continued to dominate the Baltic entrances and to tie up a la
mass of British light craft in the North Sea. But effective
Jutland marked the end of the German High Seas fleet as
offensive weapon of war. Its crews were to become the m
objects of the decline in morale and the growth of revolution
feelings in Germany. For Britain, Jutland was hailed as a succ
by her propagandists; but it was difficult for public opinion
accept it as something to place alongside the classic na
victories of British tradition.

The impact of the campaigns of 1916 and the progress
destruction by death, disease, capture or nervous breakdo
('shell-shock' in contemporary parlance) of the whole eighte
to thirty-five-year-old age group in the principal belliger
countries resulted in a marked intensification of the strains t
had already begun to show themselves. As previously noted,
war losses were particularly felt among the educated middle a
professional classes from whom the junior officers in the n
mass armies were largely drawn, an infantry lieutenant's

pectation of life on arrival at the front being reckoned at about a month. In Germany, the effect was mainly to drive these classes towards the right, war-service giving their members admission to the class and status of a member of the pre-war Prussian ruling class, and to accentuate the divisions between these classes and the German industrial and agricultural workers.

In Britain, the main effect was to drive enmity for Germany deep into the national sub-conscious. On the conscious level, the main strains worked themselves out in the battle for the un-orthodox but inspired leadership of Lloyd George as against the uninspired committee chairmanship provided by the Liberal leader, Herbert Asquith. The Conservatives found themselves increasingly dissatisfied with his personality; pressure built up within political circles for the creation of a small streamlined War Cabinet, without the large and lengthy debates of which no real record was kept, which were the main feature of Asquith's cabinets. Asquith himself proved unable to understand the real nature of the criticism directed against him; and when in December 1916 a gathering together of the most dynamic members of his own and the Conservative party broke up the coalition, he virtually defied his opponents to form an alternative government. David Lloyd George, his War Minister, succeeded in bringing together the Conservatives, Labour and a large section of the Liberals under his leadership. The split in the Liberal party was never quite healed again, and Lloyd George, losing control of the party political machinery, lacked the organizing genius to create his own. For the moment, however, he was supreme, except in his relations with his generals.

In Italy, similar discontents were beginning to break out. Salandra, the Italian premier, had by no means had a majority of the Italian people behind him when he took Italy into the war. The hope of immediate victory had, however, silenced opposition and as late as February 1916 he had secured an overwhelming vote of confidence from the Italian parliament. The Austrian offensive in the Trentino in May 1916 was, however, too much for Italian opinion, and the King turned to a seventy-eight-year-old nonentity, Signor Boselli, in the hope that he would prove a successful leader of a national coalition which embraced all but the consistently pacifist Italian Socialist party.

In Japan, a similar crisis broke out in May 1916. Count Okuma's cabinet had failed to push through the most far-reaching

of the Twenty-One Demands, while at the same time its in
creased reliance on parliamentary support rather than that c
the elder statesmen of the court deprived it of the patronag
necessary to enable it to withstand the nationalist extremists i
the armed services. Okuma was replaced by a non-party govern
ment under Count Terauchi which, despite its use of officia
influence, was unable to secure a general majority in th
parliamentary elections which followed.

Japan, however, remained free to pursue a more active polic
in the Far East by securing the political support of its allies fc
its continental ambitions. The accession to power of th
Terauchi government was followed by a prolonged pres
campaign against the Anglo-Japanese alliance which included
discussion of an alternative German connexion. At the sam
time Russo-Japanese negotiations led in the summer of 1916 t
a secret agreement by which Russia recognized Japan's gains i
China. A similar agreement was reached in February 1917 wit
the British government recognizing Japan's general rights to th
succession of the German position not only in the Shantur
peninsula but also in the Central Pacific.

These internecine strains in the domestic politics of th
Entente Powers were accompanied by far greater activity on eac
side in subverting the minority national groups within the riv
political groupings. The Easter 1916 rising in Ireland provide
the most effective example, though the arms sent by German
were captured together with the renegade Anglo-Irish diploma
ist, Sir Roger Casement, as he attempted a clandestine landing
Southern Ireland. The would-be revolutionaries in Irela
represented a much younger generation than the Irish leaders
England's parliament, a generation which had lost all confiden
in the chance of obtaining anything for Ireland by parliamenta
methods; nor would they have been satisfied by Home Ru
alone had they got it, being out-and-out advocates of Iri
independence. The Easter rising was put down with th
peculiarly drastic brutality which was so often the hallmark
British policy in Ireland; but its occurrence made it impossit
for post-war Ireland to be content with Home Rule.

The Arab revolt broke out formally two months later, in Ju
1916. In all but form, it was a revolt of the Arabs of the Hedj
alone. The Sharif of Mecca, Hussein, and his three sons, Feis
Abdullah and Zaid, had been in contact with the Arab national

ecret societies in Syria, where the Turks had been exercising
heir own peculiarly drastic methods of dealing with local
discontent. The need not to be challenged by these, much less
Anglophil, Syrians, played its part in making Hussein both all-
embracing and unwilling to compromise in the territorial side
of his negotiations with the British. But the revolt itself provoked
ittle response in Syria and the only Arab officers to join Hussein
were volunteers from those captured by the British in Meso-
ootamia. They included the future Nuri es-Said, for twenty
vears the dominant figure in Iraqi politics.

The revolt came in time to thwart a new Turco-German
nilitary mission aimed at the capture of Aden, the subversion
of Ethiopia and the setting-up of a tenuous link with German
East Africa. But after the initial capture of Mecca and Jeddah
he revolt came to a dead halt and for a year or so was only kept
going by frequent injections of British money and advisers, and
he constitutional inability of the Turks to fight desert campaigns.

The divided country of Poland saw an equally dramatic change
of fortune. At the beginning of the war the Polish nationalist
novement was divided into three main strands, the Russian
Polish, the Austrian Polish and the German Polish parties. The
first was the most revolutionary, the second the most sophisticated and the last was the weakest. Of the four Polish leaders
who set up the Polish state in 1918, Joszef Pilsudski, who had
ed the Polish socialists in the 1905 rising, and Roman Dmowski,
eader of the Polish National Democrat party in the Russian
Duma, came from Russian Poland; Professor Jaworski, the
eader of the Polish Conservatives and Ignacy Daszyński, the
veteran Socialist, came from Austrian Poland.

The main motive forces in the Polish movement in the first
years of the war were first Pilsudki's National Socialists, and the
Polish legions he raised to fight at first on the side of the Central
Powers, and, second, the Polish *emigré* movement in London,
Paris and, ultimately, in the United States. The main division
of opinion in the movement was whether to back Russia or
Austria-Hungary. Pilsudski's supporters were thoroughly anti-
Russian; Dmowski and the majority of Russian Poles saw
Germany as their worst enemy. Polish military units fought on
ooth sides at different times.

The Polish movement offered obvious chances of exploitation

to all three of the Eastern autocracies, though none of the three
wished to see a situation in which Polish aspirations could get
out of hand. And with their decisions to exploit the Polish
question against their opponents, there was raised at once
the question of frontiers. A Russian-backed Poland could
advance its frontiers deep into Germany and Austria-Hungary.
But it would have to abandon all its claims in Lithuania, White
Russia, the Ukraine or Austrian Ruthenia (Eastern Galicia). A
German-backed Poland could push its frontiers deep into the
Ukraine and Byelo-Russia: but only at the price of abandoning
its claims on Prussian Poland, on Danzig and on Lithuania.

The Russians were, in fact, first in the field with their proclamation made by the Grand Duke Nicholas, commander-in-
chief in the west, on August 16th, 1914, promising religious,
linguistic and administrative autonomy to the Poles, within the
general framework of the Tsarist empire. But the great Russian
retreat from Poland in 1915 made those promises seem remarkably unconvincing. The Germans on their side began by
inclining to an 'Austro-Polish' solution, one which envisaged
the inclusion of most of Russian Poland into a Polish state
within the Habsburg empire. The Convention of Teschen of
September 15th, 1915, which established boundaries between
the German and Austrian zones of occupation in Russian Poland,
represented a part of this policy. But the Austrian military, who
were progressively increasing their power *vis-à-vis* the civilians
in Vienna, disliked even the dualism of the *Ausgleich* with
Hungary and thus were unlikely to look with favour on the
addition of a third Polish element to make the dual monarchy
into a trinity. The Austrians preferred outright annexation.

The Germans, therefore, turned increasingly towards the idea
of a satellite Polish kingdom under German protection, an
idea they were encouraged in by those who hoped to recruit
Polish manpower to swell German armies. The Polish legionaries
fought excellently against the Brusilov offensive in July 1916,
and converted to their support the increasingly powerful and
otherwise very Pan-German and annexationist High Command
in the East, Hindenburg and Ludendorff. The main obstacles
the Germans had to face were the continuing anxieties of their
Austrian allies and the resistance of those who still hoped for a
compromise peace with Tsarist Russia. The collapse of secret
negotiations with Tsarist representatives in the autumn of 1916

emoved the objections of this latter group. Austrian resistance, however, restricted German action essentially to their zone of occupation. The German proclamation of November 5th, 1916, promising the erection of an independent Polish kingdom with its own constitution and army was thus effectively confined to the provinces of Warsaw and Lublin. This was followed on January 14th, 1917, by the setting-up of a Polish Council of State in Warsaw. But the German hopes of a large Polish army were disappointed. And soon the revolution in Russia made it seem less urgent to them than it had appeared in 1916.

Inter-allied relations also underwent severe strains in this period, particularly in the near East. The pre-eminence of British forces in military matters in this theatre, in the Gallipoli campaign, in Sinai, the Arabian peninsula, Persia and Mesopotamia was far from universally welcomed in St Petersburg or Paris; especially as the Turkish choice of the Central Powers as her allies seemed to have removed all reason for any British or Russian acquiescence in the perpetuation of the Turkish Empire. As early as January 1915, when the Dardanelles operation was still under consideration, the Russians had asked their allies to agree in principle to the post-war Russian control of the Turkish Straits. The British and French concurred by secret agreements, signed on March 12th and April 12th, 1915, subject to the satisfaction of their own aspirations in the region. And the Treaty of London with Italy promised her the province of Adalia, if the Ottoman Empire were to be partitioned.

Egypt had already been formally proclaimed a protectorate in December 1914, and Britain concluded agreements in 1915 not only with the Sharif of Mecca, but also on December 15th, 1915, with ibn Saud, recognizing him as ruler of Nejd with a British subsidy. By all the accepted laws governing Great Power relations, these advances of British interest demanded the granting of compensation to France. On May 16th, 1916, the so-called Sykes-Picot agreement recognized Russian claims to Turkish Armenia and Northern Kurdistan, and French claims to Turkish Cilicia. French pre-eminence in Western Syria and the Lebanon was recognized up to the Damascus, Homs, Hama and Aleppo line. Britain, in return, was to be granted primacy in the Palestinian coast, and the provinces of Basra and Baghdad. The area between was to be divided into a French zone covering northern Syria and Mesopotamia and a British zone covering the

rest of Arabia and what is now Jordan. These terms were difficul
if not impossible to reconcile with the promises made to th
Sharif of Mecca – and the British negotiations in Cairo, seekin
a new British empire over the whole Arab world, may well hav
been deliberately out of step with the Foreign Office in Londor
Nor could the assurances given to ibn Saud by negotiator
responsible to the government of India be altogether reconcile
with those promises made to the Sharif.

The Sykes-Picot agreement contained one very odd provisior
that Palestine, or rather the old Turkish province of Jerusalen
should be under an international administration. This claus
represented a combination of three rather different lines c
thought in London. The first was the theory that it would b
desirable to have a buffer between the French zone of influenc
in Syria and the Suez canal. The second was a genuine wish t
internationalize this land which was holy to every brand c
Christianity as well as to Islam and Judaism. The third was th
influence of British sympathies with Zionism.

The international Zionist movement had been split by th
outbreak of war into separate German and western section:
supposedly coordinated by a bureau in neutral Copenhager
The German wing had devoted itself systematically to pressur
on the German government to secure concessions from i
Turkish ally; but its efforts had been largely in vain. Mor
successful was the British wing, led by a brilliant industri
chemist, Chaim Weizmann, whose war work brought him int
contact with Lloyd George during his days as Minister c
Munitions. Playing on the sympathies of those British leader
whose Anglican or non-conformist religion had made then
familiar with the Old Testament, and arguing for somethin
to combat the hostility aroused among the large Jewis
minority in the United States by the anti-Semitic measure
of England's ally, Tsarist Russia, Weizmann gradually converte
one member after another of the British government to th
Zionist cause.

In October 1916, Weizmann opened formal negotiations wit
the British Foreign Office, while a colleague, Nahum Sokolov
won the support of France and Italy. In March 1917, matter
had gone far enough for Weizmann to speak openly of Britis
support for the establishment of a 'Jewish Commonwealth'. H
announcement, however, stirred up the opposition of all tho

Jewish citizens of Britain who had been working so long for equal rights in Britain, who felt that the creation of a Jewish state with a 'secular Jewish nationality' would again make them aliens within a strange country. For them their Judaism was a messianic religion, and their Jewishness of the same significance within Britain as if they were Scots, Welsh or Cornish. Much of their support lay, it should be added, among the older Sephardic Jewish communities of Britain; while Zionism was much more the creed of the refugees from Russian Poland. With the support of Edwin Montagu, the Jewish Secretary of State for War, they succeeded in modifying the text of the British declaration designed to satisfy Zionist aspirations so that instead of a reference to Palestine 'as the National Home of the Jewish People', the British government pledged itself to 'the establishment *in* Palestine of a national home for the Jewish people'. Palestine's Arab inhabitants appeared only in the text among the 'existing non-Jewish communities in Palestine', whose 'civil and religious rights' were reserved. This pledge was duly issued on November 2nd, 1917, in the form of a letter from Arthur Balfour, the British Foreign Secretary, to the Jewish financier, Lord Rothschild, and is known as the Balfour Declaration.

Neither side had much doubt at this time that what was foreshadowed was a Jewish state. The British either dismissed the Arabs as natives on a par with the Bantu of Africa or expected that the Jews, themselves Semites, would lead to a regeneration of the Arab world in a Judean-Arab union. Weizmann himself believed that agreement could be reached with the Arabs. And he was able to present the Zionist movement, despite the strong radical populist anti-imperialist sentiments of both its Russo-Polish and American wings, as a possible vehicle for British liberal imperialist policy. It was to be twenty years before the vision of Israel as a self-governing dominion within the British Empire was finally to expire, ten before Weizmann's hopes of Arab-Jewish cooperation were revealed to be hopeless. Zionism was not strong enough as a movement, and the Arabs were far too advanced in their disunity, for the ideals behind the Balfour Declaration to be realized. And the state of Israel had to be established against the opposition of Britain and the Arabs alike.

Prospects of a successful mediation by the United States were greatly reduced during 1915–16. Outraged by the contempt with which both the German and British Admiralties treated American neutral rights at sea, President Wilson had called in November 1915 for a great rearmament effort by the United States under the slogan 'preparedness'. The National Defence Act of June 1916 enlarged the American regular army; the Naval Appropriation Act of August 29th satisfied the long-term aspirations of American navalists in setting out a major battleship construction programme designed to secure 'a Navy Second to None' (i.e. equal in strength to that of Britain) by the year 1925; the US Shipping Board Act of September 7th satisfied the aspirations of those navalists who maintained that greatness at sea could only rest on a large nationally-owned merchant marine.

The approach of the Presidential elections on the other hand demanded a rather different kind of policy. In February 1916, Wilson dispatched his intimate adviser, Colonel House, on a tour of exploration of the prospects of a mediated peace in Europe. House visited Britain; but his main efforts were devoted to obtaining a statement of Allied peace aims sufficiently moderate for Wilson to be able to use them to bring the Central Powers to negotiation. The British agreed, in the hope of securing American entry into the war on their side after the refusal, which they took for granted, of the Central Powers to accept such terms as a basis for peace talks. But their hopes were disappointed. Lacking a slogan of mediation to campaign on, Wilson chose to campaign in October 1916 on the slogan 'He kept us out of war', a slogan which he used narrowly to upset what promised to be an inevitable Republican victory.

Wilson's re-election encouraged the German Chancellor, who was under very strong pressure from the General Staff to reverse the Kaiser's decision of May 1916 and authorize the renewal on a far larger scale of unrestricted submarine warfare, to appeal to Wilson on December 12th, 1916, to mediate between the Central Powers and those of the *Entente*. Wilson, the balance of whose suspicions of the belligerents were still weighted against Germany, chose to appeal to both sides to state their terms for peace.

In their reply of December 26th, the Central Powers chose to ignore this request to define their war aims in detail. The *Entente* Powers replied on January 10th, 1917, in terms which made it clear that they had irrevocably chosen to destroy the

tructure of pre-war Europe. Belgium, Serbia and Montenegro were to be evacuated as was the German-occupied
territory of France, Rumania and Russia. Alsace-Lorraine was
to be returned to France: and, more significantly for Europe's
future, they demanded that Europe be re-organized 'on the
basis of nationalities'. Italians, Slavs, Rumanians and Czecho-
slovaks were to be freed from foreign (Habsburg) rule. All the
subject nationalities of the Turkish Empire were to be liberated,
and Turkey was to be expelled from Europe. The terms did more
credit to the *Entente* Powers' ideals than to their military realism,
considering the strategic circumstances of January 1917. They
must be seen, therefore, as making explicit a definite ideological
choice, already largely made in domestic discussions of war aims,
against any continuation of the system of balance between the
Great Powers in Europe such as had made the limited stability
of the Concert of Europe possible in the previous century. They
made the war in Europe essentially a revolutionary struggle; and,
as such, they also represented a renewed bid for the ideological
sympathy of the United States.

In this, they went a good deal further than Wilson, who was
essentially a realist save where he was himself making ideology
his own weapon. His preference was still for 'peace without
victory'. The German terms given to him confidentially on
January 29th, 1917, were much more his idea of reality save in
their colonial chapters where Germany demanded the granting
of colonial territories to accord with her population and needs.
The territorial clauses on eastern Europe, which envisaged the
creation of a large Polish satellite for Germany, represented no
more than Germany controlled politically already. But the whole
discussion was made almost academic by the German decision
taken on January 8th, 1917, three weeks earlier, to risk everything, including American entry into the war, on six months'
unrestricted submarine warfare against Britain, and to attempt
to distract the United States by formenting Mexico against
her.

In Mexico, the Germans had discovered an easy target. By the
end of August 1914, the Huerta *régime* had collapsed and General
Huerta himself abdicated. Carranza, Huerta's successor, was, if
anything, even less amenable to American views than Huerta had
been. The American government began therefore to support his
general and would-be rival, Pancho Villa. But Carranza was

more than a match for Villa and drove his forces steadily into the wild country of Northern Mexico, and the United States found herself forced, on October 19th, 1915, to recognize the Carranza *régime*. Villa, thereafter, turned violently anti-American and began to kill all the American citizens who fell into his hands. Still worse he raided American territory in March 1916.

Public opinion in the United States was now violently anti-Mexican. President Wilson, under strong pressure to intervene in force, pursued Villa by sending a large-scale punitive expedition into Mexico under General Pershing. Alarmed by its size, Carranza called in April and May 1916 for its withdrawal. A second raid into New Mexico on Villa's part made this impossible and there followed in June 1916 the inevitable incident between a unit of Pershing's so-called 'Punitive Expedition' and Carranza's forces. Wilson managed, however, to restrain his hotheads, and new negotiations with Carranza opened. In October 1916, a general election gave Carranza a Constitutional Assembly, and in March 1917 Carranza was elected President of Mexico. The Punitive Expedition was finally withdrawn at the end of January 1917 and Carranza's government recognized *de jure*. But the whole incident had placed Mexican relations with the United States under a strain from which they were only to begin to recover in the late 1920s, and in January 1917 the Germans might be forgiven for feeling that Mexico could be incited against the United States.

Their feelings were, however, mistaken; disastrously so. The Instructions to the German Minister in Mexico City, known to history as the Zimmermann Telegram, fell into the hands of British Intelligence. The announcement of the German decision to wage unrestricted submarine warfare had already led President Wilson to break off relations with Germany and propose the arming of American merchantmen. The publication of the Zimmermann Telegram and the sinking of American ships led inevitably to the declaration of war by the United States on April 6th, 1917. It was, however, to be more than a year before the real weight of American power was to be felt by Germany.

In the meantime, the German submarine blockade of Britain raged at full force. British losses rose monthly, until in April 1917 over 169 British merchant ships totalling 849,000 tons, one out of every four ships that left the British Isles, were sunk by German submarine attack. The tide turned slowly with the introduction of the system of convoying merchant ships with escorts of warships in May. But, at first, this system was only confined to ships coming into British waters and was not extended to outward-bound vessels until August 1917. The losses of ships by torpedo fell slowly to a mere 90 a month in December 1917; and the coupling of the convoy system with the introduction of a really effective control of shipping, and the concentration of British and American naval resources on anti-submarine warfare gradually gave the naval powers the upper hand. But it proved a necessary part of the battle that those senior naval officers in the British Navy to whom traditional objectives and conventional methods were all-important should be removed from office. And for most of 1917 the battle was touch-and-go.

1917, THE YEAR OF DISASTER

In 1917, the process of European self-immolation continued and intensified. America entered the war, dragged in by German miscalculations. In Russia, the Tsarist *régime* dissolved into revolution, and the parliamentary *régime* that followed dis-integrated, falling into the hands of the Bolsheviks. American influence was asserted in the Pacific. China entered the war. The French armies mutinied and the British took a mauling in Flanders that added the word 'Passchendaele' to the English language. German submarine warfare brought Britain to the edge of defeat. Yet the advocates of a war to the bitter end were strengthened in France and Germany. The Pope's attempt to mediate was much less successful than even Wilson's effort had been.

On the Western front, General Nivelle had succeeded Joffre with a great fanfare of optimism as to the chances of a major break-through in France. Tactically, he pinned his faith as a gunner to a colossal bombardment preceding the attack. But when the plans for the attack had all been settled the Germans destroyed their main base by executing a strategic withdrawal to a carefully prepared system of fortifications known as the Hindenburg Line. The line was much shorter and enabled the Germans to release many divisions to the reserves. Nivelle insisted, however, on continuing his offensive, which took place in April. The French losses were high and the territorial gains negligible. German losses were even higher. But the defeat of the hopes pinned on Nivelle and the apparent failure of the French command to evolve any variation in their offensive tactics led to a total breakdown of French army morale and widespread mutinies in no less than fifty-four of the French divisions. The secret of the mutinies was well kept, not even a whisper of them reaching the Germans.

Their effect, however, was to throw the main burden of fighting on the Western front on to the British. In April, British forces had attacked near Arras in an offensive intended to act as a diversion for that of General Nivelle, and had scored some success at the cost of 160,000 casualties. But the French mutinies called for a much greater effort. The British admiralty, unable to cope with the great German submarine offensive, urged that the coast of Flanders be cleared of the German submarine bases. On June 7th, the Messines ridge, the principal geographical obstacle to an offensive into the plain of Flanders, was successfully captured. But the main British offensive, six weeks later, ran into heavy rain; and the prolonged bombardment which generals now thought essential to any offensive merely resulted in the complete destruction of the natural drainage system of the Flanders plain, not to mention all sign of metalled roads. The offensives now known as the battle of Passchendaele made some significant advances around the town of Ypres. But the cost to each side was approximately one quarter of a million casualties. In November, the British launched a frontal offensive at Cambrai with no preliminary barrage and behind massed tanks, the first heavy use of the new British arm. The initial success was overwhelming but Passchendaele had denuded the British army of adequate reserves and the Germans were able to recover most of the ground the tanks had taken.

In Italy, even greater disaster was to strike the *Entente* Powers. Two further offensives on the Isonzo had secured little or no gain when on October 24th a joint German-Austrian force attacked in heavy fog. They scored an immediate break-through, in what became known as the Battle of Caporetto, and the Italian army collapsed. A new front line was not established until the Italian forces had withdrawn to the river Piave, over one hundred miles to the rear. The Italians lost over 300,000 casualties, and eleven British and French divisions had to be rushed from France to Italy to stiffen the new Italian line. The Italians were, however, able to hold the line of the Piave and the crucial pivot of Monte Grappa against very heavy Austrian and German attack. As a result, Italian morale recovered as quickly as it had broken.

In Rumania, greater disaster struck in August 1917 when German and Austrian troops began to clear the remainder of the country. In December 1917, a truce was signed to be followed in May 1918 by a definite treaty of peace between Rumania and the Central Powers. The treaty of Bucharest of May 7th, 1918, ceded Dobruja to Bulgaria and the Carpathian passes to Austria-Hungary. Germany took a ninety-year lease on the Rumanian oilfields. Rumania was allowed, however, to annex Bessarabia which had broken away from Russia in the Russian revolution.

Iraq and Palestine saw the only real victories on the *Entente* side. In October 1917, General Allenby, appointed to Palestine after the part he had played in the Arras battles in April 1917, finally pierced the Turkish positions at Gaza. The break-through was well-exploited and on December 11th the British forces entered Jerusalem and held it easily against Turkish counter-attack. Earlier in 1917, British troops had cleared Lower Mesopotamia and on March 11th, 1917, entered Baghdad. New advances began in December 1917. At the same time, Colonel T. E. Lawrence succeeded in revitalizing the Arab revolt and in raising its guerilla activities to the dignity of minor military operations.

The increased strains of war, which had already shown themselves in the overthrow of the Asquith government in Britain in December 1916, expressed themselves among the other belligerents in 1917. In France, the end of 1916 had seen the removal from office of the French commander-in-chief, General Joffre. In March 1917, the cabinet of Briand was overturned by a parliament suspicious of its subordination to the French military. Its successor, headed by Alexandre Ribot, an aged nobody, Finance Minister in the outgoing government, was dominated by the Minister of War, Paul Painlevé. Painlevé had the greatest doubts as to the success of the Nivelle offensive. With its failure, he replaced Nivelle with Pétain and Foch, under whom French strategy turned into a waiting game predicated on the arrival of American troops in force on the battlefield, an

event which was not expected to occur until the summer of 1918
The Ribot cabinet proved vulnerable, however, in its failure t
act decisively against defeatism and German fifth colum
activity. Painlevé succeeded Ribot as Premier in Septembe
1917. But the scandals continued and the gradual uncovering
of the full truth of the Nivelle failure and the subsequen
mutinies led to Painlevé's succession in November 1917 by
Georges Clemenceau, the ruthless, patriotic, embodiment o
victory, whose one policy was, 'I wage war'.

In Germany, the decision to wage unrestricted submarin
warfare was made despite the opposition of the Imperial Chan
cellor, Bethman-Hollweg, and marked the victory of the military
Germany became virtually a military dictatorship. Field Marsha
von Hindenburg had succeeded to the supreme command i
August 1916. His deputy, the Chief Quartermaster-General
General Ludendorff, was able to use Hindenburg's prestig
thereafter as an infallible weapon of political power. Those whom
he distrusted or disliked, those who opposed Army policy as h
formulated it, those who advocated a policy with which h
disagreed, were denounced to the Kaiser as persons for whom, o
for whose policy, Ludendorff 'could not assume the responsibil
ity'. And the implied threat of resignation left the Kaiser n
option but to get rid of the offenders. It was with this weapo
that he secured the resignation of the German Chancellor
Bethman-Hollweg, in the summer of 1917 and his replacemen
by an obscure Prussian bureaucrat, Dr Michaelis.

In the German parliament and country, the continuance o
the war was now linked to the increasing social dissatisfactio
with the existing system of power. The parliamentarians of th
Reichstag, National Liberals, Centre Party and majority Socia
Democrats, began to agitate for the establishment of parliament
ary control over the government and army. On the left revolu
tionary factions broke away from the Social Democrats, first th
extremists who were to organize themselves into the *Spartacu*
League, and then the so-called Independent Social Democrats
the USPD. The parliamentarians succeeded in obtaining i
April 1917 an undertaking that the Prussian electoral system, o
which the power of the German right was based, would b
reformed after the war. Their attempt to establish civilia
control, even in principle, over the Army was ignominiousl
rebuffed. In July 1917, therefore, the Centre's leader, Matthia

Erzberger, chose to challenge the Army head on, with the introduction into the *Reichstag* of a motion demanding a compromise peace without annexations or indemnities. It passed the *Reichstag* on July 19th, 1917 by 212 votes to 196.

The resolution was rendered pointless by the new Chancellor's acceptance of it with the rider, 'as I understand it'. The *Reichstag* thus remained powerless even when, in October 1917, the new German Chancellor, Michaelis, over-reached himself in attempting to secure its approval for the suppression of the USPD. Michaelis' defeat led to his replacement by what appeared to be a parliamentary *régime* under Count Hertling, a member of the Centre Party, and von Payer, of the Progressives. But as real power remained with Ludendorff the significance of 1917's events lay in the creation of a united middle class and Social Democrat opposition to his military dictatorship, which would be able to take over power when the defeat of Germany broke the power of the military.

That year saw two other significant events in German politics. With Ludendorff's encouragement the right-wing Conservatives and National Liberals began to gather together in a new party, the Fatherland party, determined to prevent a compromise peace. Only a peace with major annexations could, in their view, save Germany from a social and political revolution. On the left the USPD came into contact with discontent in the German navy. There were disturbances and political demonstrations in which the sailors' suspicion that their officers did not share their own poor food rations played a part. They signified the growing social discontent in Germany, discontent which went so deep as to give revolutionary Communism deep and almost permanent roots in Germany between the wars.

In Austria-Hungary, the war had aggravated the bad relations between Hungary and the non-Magyar parts of the Empire. It had also driven the Czechs into passive resistance to the central government, elevated the military authorities, dominated by Pan-German sentiments, and had brought upon the Empire a series of defeats which discredited the monarchy both in the eyes of its German allies and of the peoples of the Empire. At the opening of the war the military authorities took over, the *Reichsrath* was prorogued, and there began a long struggle for political power between the military and the civil powers in the Czech, Ruthene and Slovene provinces of the Monarchy. The military, however, were unable to impose their will in Hungary, and the Hungarian government, in control of the major part of the Empire's food supplies, gave so little food to Austria that privation was already raging in Vienna by the middle of 1916.

In October 1916, the Austrian premier was assassinated. A month later the aged emperor, Franz Josef, died of pneumonia. The Archduke Charles, who succeeded him, did not feel strong enough to challenge the Hungarians head on. Moreover, he felt bound by his coronation oath as King of Hungary. On the non-Magyar side, however, he took severe steps to reduce the power of the military. General Conrad von Hötzendorff was dismissed and Charles set himself the task of winning back the loyalty of the non-German nationalities. An essential part of this plan was the convocation of the *Reichsrath*, which met in May 1917. Its meeting showed that the military authorities had already succeeded in completely alienating the main Slav groups. The Czech spokesman demanded that the Empire be changed into a federation of free and equal states. The Yugoslavs demanded the union of Serbs, Croats and Slovenes into an autonomous democratic state under the Habsburg crown. The Emperor did his best to conciliate them. And it is just possible that he might have succeeded had it been possible for Austria to make peace at that time, though he would have faced stiff resistance from the German population of Austria proper.

It was the desperate condition of the Monarchy in fact which drove the Emperor to open secret peace negotiations with France through his brother-in-law, Prince Sixte of Bourbon. France and Britain were very interested. But their promises to Italy stood in the way; and it proved difficult to persuade Charles to make sufficiently far-reaching concessions to satisfy the Italians. Individual negotiations continued through the summer culminating in a meeting in Switzerland in December 1917 between Count Mensdorff, the former Austrian ambassador in London, and General Smuts, the South African premier and member of the British War Cabinet. But an actual Austrian break with Germany would have been impossible at this time unless Austria was prepared to fight Germany. The *Entente* Powers on their side were unable to win over Italy. The main effect of the secret negotiations was to postpone for nearly a year effective British, French and American support for the Czech and Yugoslav *emigrés*.

On their side the *emigré* leaders of the Czechs and Yugoslavs had an uphill task trying to win support for their aims. The vast mass of the Czechs were passive rather than active. They resented having to fight against the Russians and deserted or surrendered to them in large numbers. But their principal leaders preferred to persist with their policy of inactivity in the hope of a Russian victory rather than to take an active part in winning support for their cause in the West. It was left to the leader of the small Czech Realist party, Professor Thomas Masaryk, to go into exile to win support for Czech independence in France and Britain.

The southern Slavs in the Empire were in greater difficulty, since the principal enemy in the south was Italy, whose far-reaching claims on the Dalmatian Coast involved Slav territory. Moreover, they were still very much divided between advocates of a Greater Serbia and Croat advocates of a Federal Yugoslav state. Not until Italy's defeat at Caporetto did the future begin to appear more cheerful. The year 1917 was a grim period for every section of opinion in Austria-Hungary.

However, these signs of strain and incipient revolution in France, Germany and Austria-Hungary were very minor incidents compared with the events of 1917 in Russia. During 1916, dissatisfaction with the Tsar and his entourage had been rising in all sections of Russian society, even among the aristocracy who had been disgusted with the Tsar's reliance on the drunken and lecherous self-styled holy man, Rasputin. The capitalists, merchants and industrialists of Moscow had been outraged by the total breakdown of the Tsarist bureaucracy under the demands of total war. The old Tsarist army, officers and men alike, had been virtually destroyed by the casualties of three years of war. And in March 1917 strikes and bread riots in St Petersburg led to a complete collapse of the dynasty and a take-over of power by the politicians of the Duma.

The new Provisional Government consisted of a coalition of the Constitutional Democrats, the Cadets, and the Social Democrats. But its claim to power was disputed throughout Russia by the spontaneous formation of councils, *Soviets* in their Russian name, dominated by left wing Socialists, Social Revolutionaries and Bolsheviks. And the Social Democrats felt obliged to express the mood of the soldiers, workers and peasants who had elected them to the Soviets. For these the revolution involved much more than the mere transfer of power from the Tsar to the Duma. It involved the destruction of the whole police apparatus of the Tsarist state, from the oppressive military discipline of the army to the land ownership and taxation system in the villages. And under their demands Russia slid steadily downhill into chaos, disturbance and civil war.

The effect of this steady disintegration was to drive the middle class parties and the Social Democrats steadily apart from one another, and to alienate them from that section of the army that wished to continue the war and maintain order at home as an essential part of this. The Provisional Government might have been able to save itself if it had immediately concluded peace with the Germans, no matter what sacrifice was demanded. But the Provisional Government were both patriots and realists. To modernize and rebuild Russia after three years of war would necessitate large amounts of foreign capital, and Russia was already heavily in debt to the *Entente* Powers. Moreover, both Miliukov, the leading spirit in the first Provisional Cabinet, and Kerensky, who became premier in July 1917, hoped that a victorious offensive might recreate the sense of national unity which the revolution seemed to have destroyed. The Russian offensive of July 1st, 1917, was at first successful. But German counter-attacks soon reduced it to the status of a major disaster; and the Germans followed their victory by a major offensive into the Baltic coastlands which took Riga in September and overran most of Latvia.

In March 1917, the Bolshevik party had very little influence in Russia, and all its leading figures were in exile in Siberia or Switzerland. In April 1917, the German authorities, hoping deliberately to accelerate the breakdown of order in Russia, offered Lenin and the other Russian revolutionaries in Switzerland passage through Germany to Russia. On Lenin's arrival at St Petersburg, he immediately took control of the Bolshevik party, and began building up Bolshevik military units, or Red Guards, in the factories. In June and July, his supporters got out of hand, and Lenin was forced to seek refuge in Finland for safety. Allegations that Lenin was largely financed by German money and the revelation of the Bolshevists' desire to seize power temporarily discredited him.

But peasant disturbances and desertions from the army continued to spread, and the collapse and defeat of the July offensive only accelerated the process. In September 1917, alarmed at the deterioration on the home front, General Kornilov, commanding the remaining Russian armies in the west, attempted to seize power. To resist him, Kerensky was forced to turn to the Red Guards and release those Bolshevik leaders he had arrested. The way was now clear for the Bolsheviks to take over control of the congress of Soviets in St Petersburg, to arrest the members of the Provisional Government, and to establish a nominal coalition government dominated by the Bolshevik leadership. With this Russia passed under the control of a *régime* that thought of itself as the spearhead of revolution in Europe, but was in fact to isolate itself from, and be isolated by Europe, so as to become something quite different and apart from the main stream of European culture and civilization.

In the Far East, the Chinese government was lured into abandoning its neutrality and declaring war on Germany in the hope of extracting a diminution of foreign influence in her territories. Chinese labourers were, in fact, widely used behind the front in France. But the main effect of China's entry into the war was to increase Japanese domination, since only Japan was prepared to supply China with loans to cover her additional financial expenses. Only the United States remained as a check on Japanese ambitions in China. By an exchange of notes in November 1917 between Lansing, the US Secretary of State and M. Ishii, Japan's Special Ambassador to the United States, America recognized Japan's special interests in China in return for Japanese assurances that the Open Door policy and China's integrity would be maintained. The Lansing-Ishii agreements were to prove a very inadequate check, however, on Japan's ambitions in the Far East.

The Russian revolution gave new impetus to a series of movements which had been stimulated by the earlier strains of war: the casualty lists, the constant flood of abusive propaganda, the reckless dissipation of Europe's reserves of manpower, money, materials and morale, and the destruction of her cities and countryside in the war zones. These movements represented a new series of efforts on the part of the three most important supranational movements of the pre-war era, firstly, that which had produced the Hague conferences and the World Court, secondly, the second, socialist, international, and thirdly, the Papacy, to re-establish themselves against the forces of nationalism and to secure a negotiated peace.

The first movement was the strongest in the English-speaking countries and in France where it was infused with utopian aspirations. It centred on the settlement to be obtained when peace negotiations should eventually be entered upon; and it looked to a world so re-organized as to make it impossible for any war, on the scale of the one on which they were engaged, ever to break out again. The desire most favoured in discussions in the Anglo-Saxon countries was a 'League of Nations', as it was called in Britain, a 'League to enforce peace', as it was called in the United States. The sponsors of the movement in these two countries came from two rather different and previously opposed groups. One group represented a continuation of the radicalism which had begun to express itself prior to 1914 in international organizations and in a persistent critique of conventional diplomacy and power politics. The second embodied an aroused conservatism, particularly strong among international lawyers, but well represented elsewhere which had come to regard modern war as essentially subversive of the established order. Lord Robert Cecil, who was to make himself the driving force behind the idea in the British government, typified this approach. In 1917, the Lloyd George government was induced to set up a committee under Lord Phillimore to consider and report on a possible draft constitution for a League of Nations. And the theme of such a league was to play a large part in Allied propaganda thereafter.

The movement was to see its agitation crowned by success; although it had little support among the Central Powers. Here the moderates chose to press for a compromise peace, without annexations or indemnities, as in the *Reichstag* Peace Resolution of July 1917. Their slogan was originally taken from the Bolsheviks. But the movement for a compromise peace enjoyed only limited support in Britain. The most spectacular support came from the former Conservative Foreign Secretary, the aged Lord Lansdowne, who appealed, in a letter published by *The Daily Telegraph* on November 29th, 1917, for a negotiated peace as the only alternative to a war of attrition which was eliminating an entire generation in Britain and Europe and preparing the way for chaos and revolution. The letter caused no little stir in Britain. But its main effect again was to play a part in forcing the British Government once more to define its peace aims. The terms, as defined, could only have been acceptable to Germany as an alternative to outright defeat; and few in Germany outside the innermost circles of government contemplated this possibility.

The only support any movement for a compromise peace secured in Britain was that sponsored by the Social Democrat parties of the Netherlands and Scandinavia, which reached its culmination in the so-called Stockholm peace conference in September 1917. This conference was the last of a series at which the remnants of the old Second International had sought to restore their movement's shattered internationalism. Earlier conferences had met in Switzerland, at Zimmerwald in September 1915 and at Kienthal in 1916, where Lenin's influence had secured the publication of a *communiqué* saying that there could be no real solution of the conflict without the conquest of political power and the ownership of capital by the peoples of Europe themselves. Such a resolution, even if valid, was unlikely to lead to a negotiated peace, and in July 1916, at a second conference confined to delegates from the European neutrals (thus excluding Lenin and the Russian Social Democrats) the Dutch Socialists attempted to persuade their colleagues in the belligerent powers to agree to attend a conference to discuss the terms of a possible peace.

In this effort the Dutch were abandoning their own earlier inclination, in which the influence of the Belgian Socialist, Vandervelde, the chairman of the Second International, can be seen, to feel that there could be no peace without a total German withdrawal from Belgium. The influence of the belief that the German invasion of Belgium made the war a just war and not an imperialist manifestation could be seen still at work in the preference, expressed by the Labour movement in Britain and the Socialists of France, for working for an agreed statement of Allied war aims.

The Russian revolution of March 1917 provided a new spur to the Dutch efforts, more effective in that, since January 1917, there had been a Labour member of the British War Cabinet, Arthur Henderson. But divisions within the British Labour party, which refused to have anything to do with the breakaway Independent Labour Party, prevented the assembly of a British delegation, and the whole project was most bitterly opposed by Lloyd George and the Tories in the War Cabinet. Henderson resigned from the War Cabinet in August 1917 as a result to be replaced by another Labour leader, George Barnes. But no British delegation, and no French delegation, came to Stockholm; and the conference as such never met. Instead the Dutch-Scandinavian committee held a series of discussions with delegations from the German, Austrian and Russian parties, and a good many individuals. But these meetings had little or no effect.

A rather similar fate befell the Papal Peace Message of August 1st, 1917. The Pope had been waiting for some time for the right moment to intervene, and the stalemate of the summer seemed to offer the best opportunity. But the moment was, in fact, ill chosen. The *Reichstag* peace resolution, as has been seen, was virtually ignored by the German Government, and the conjunction of the Papal intervention with it merely laid the Pope open to accusations of allowing himself to be used as a German catspaw. The real stumbling block at this stage was the determination of the Lloyd George government and the Americans to overthrow the German Empire and secure Alsace-Lorraine for France, and the equal determination on the German side not to abandon their gains on the Belgian coast and frontier, let alone give up Alsace-Lorraine.

The fact of the matter was that in Britain, France and Germany, the governments were now dominated by those who were determined to fight *à l'outrance*. Alone among the leaders of these three countries, Lloyd George was capable of thinking internationally. But being the nominee of a coalition of Conservatives and Liberals determined on victory he could only express his international leanings in terms of redevelopment of the world after victory. In the United States, President Wilson was grimly determined now on the punishment of aggression and the overthrow of autocracy and militarism as necessary pre-conditions to a just peace. American opinion was indulging in an orgy of nationalism and chauvinism to which, among others, the IWW, pacifists to a man, were to fall victim. Their leaders disappeared behind bars, all save one, who was lynched. Everything was set for the collapse of Europe.

Chapter 14

1918—Victory and the Collapse of Europe

THE WINTER of 1917–18 was a long and hard one in Central Europe; and its privations made themselves felt in a wave of strikes of a semi-political nature in Austria-Hungary and in Germany. By January 1918, the flour ration in Vienna was reduced to 165 grams a day. The spontaneous demonstrations that followed developed into a major strike movement which spread into Lower Austria and to Budapest. The strikers usually combined political demands with their demands for more food. Echoes of the November revolution in Russia could be heard in Austria where extreme criticism met the severe peace terms being demanded of Russia by the Austrian and German governments. In February, sailors of the Austrian fleet mutinied, demanding peace. In March, Austrian ex-prisoners of war began returning from Russia bringing with them a ferment of ideas and stories of the Russian revolution. From May onwards, there was a succession of mutinies among Austrian army units especially among the Czechs and Slovenes.

The strike movement in Germany broke out almost at the same time as the demonstrations in Vienna, though the fact that these events occurred almost simultaneously seems to have been a coincidence. As in Austria, the strikes were on a very large scale and dominated the large cities such as Berlin, Hamburg, Essen and Leipzig. The strikers, as in Austria, published a series of protests against the unfairness of the food rationing and the excesses of military government which were combined with demands for the reform of the Prussian electoral system and the conclusion of an immediate peace 'with no annexations and no indemnities'. The strikes were more easily suppressed in Germany than in Austria-Hungary. But in both countries they revealed that the determination of the autocracies to secure an

310 A HISTORY OF THE WORLD IN TWENTIETH CENTURY

annexationist peace as the only alternative to social revolution had become self-defeating; it had created instead a large group of citizens for whom nationalism and loyalty to their rulers were no longer relevant. The German ruling *élite* in the military and ultra-patriotic circles had produced what was to be a permanently revolutionary element in their country; they had alienated a section of the working-class tradition permanently from its national roots.

At the time, the military authorities in both of the Central Powers were inclined to see behind this wave of strikes the influence of the 'new diplomacy' introduced into European affairs by the two non-European powers represented in the Bolshevik leadership in Russia and the Democratic President of the United States. On November 8th, 1917, the new *régime* in Russia had adopted a 'Decree on Peace' proposing the immediate opening of negotiations for a 'just and democratic peace without annexations and without indemnities'. On November 21st, they had called for an armistice on the Eastern front, and on December 15th an armistice was signed. On December 22nd, peace negotiations were opened at Brest-Litovsk. The Bolshevik negotiators chose deliberately to conduct the negotiations in open session and to accompany them with a barrage of appeals to the peoples of Europe and the colonial territories under European rule. In their view revolution was imminent in Europe; and they did their best to subvert the German units with which they came into contact. They found themselves confronted instead with demands for the attachment to Germany of Poland, Lithuania, Kurland (Latvia) and the Ukraine. There followed a prolonged and agonizing debate within the Soviet government. On February 18th the Germans denounced the armistice and resumed their advance towards St Petersburg. On March 3rd, 1918, the Bolshevik government gave way and signed the peace of Brest-Litovsk.

The treaty of Brest-Litovsk accelerated the process, which had already begun, of the separation from Russia of the subject nationalities. In March 1917, the Provisional Government had abolished the restrictive legislation passed by the old Tsarist *régime* against the so-called national minorities, and had announced the beginning of national self-rule. The administration of the border-lands had been placed in the hands of prominent local figures. But the same factors which in Russia proper were to make the triumph of Lenin possible, popular restlessness, the demand for land and peace, the inability of the Provisional Government to provide firm authority, led to an immense growth in separatist national movements in the non-Russian areas. In the Baltic, White Russia and the Ukraine the landlords were Russian. In the eastern border-lands beyond the Caspian Sea, nationalist feeling expressed itself against the Russian colonists brought in by the Tsars. Under such circumstances, the Bolshevik party inevitably became the party of the Russian colonists and the arm of Russian colonialism. The collapse of the Tsarist empire and the failure of the Provisional Government left pockets of Russian troops, sailors and settlers scattered throughout the non-Russian territories. Civil war between them and the nationalities was virtually inevitable. Until the fall of the Provisional Government, Lenin's followers collaborated with the 'nationalities'. Thereafter, they were to become their bitterest enemies. The fate of the nationalist movements thereafter depended on the degree to which they could call on German and then Allied support against first the Bolshevik Red Army and then the White counter-revolutionaries. Finland and the Baltic states, Lithuania, Latvia and Estonia, were to establish and maintain their independence. The Ukraine, Byelo-Russia, the Crimea, Transcaspia, Turkestan, cis-Caucasian Daghestan and the three Transcaspian states of Georgia, Armenia and Azerbaijan, at various times proclaimed their independence, but none proved able to maintain it; though isolated resistance to Soviet rule was to continue in the Turkic areas of Transcaspia until the middle of the 1920s.

Among the non-Russian members of the Tsarist empire, Finland was the most successful in winning independence. The Finnish achievement of independence began after a vicious civil war which lasted from January to May 1918, in which the anti-Communist forces, the Whites, were greatly aided by the German Baltic division under General von der Goltz. Thereafter, the Finnish 'Whites' became involved with the Allied intervention in Northern Russia, and suffered a serious defeat in the course of an attempt to annex East Karelia from Russia. On the German signature of an armistice with the *Entente* Powers in November 1918, they found themselves abandoned by Germany; but they managed to re-establish friendly relations with the *Entente* Powers by intervening to help the Estonians beat back a Soviet invasion while wisely refusing to intervene in the Civil War in Russia. Estonia, Latvia and Lithuania, being much weaker than Finland, survived through 1918 only under the occupation of German forces intent on annexing the whole area to the German crown. The German collapse in November 1918, left them still under German occupation, which the *Entente* Powers tolerated as a means of protecting them against the Red Army. A British naval squadron was eventually to play a large part in aiding native forces to beat off the combined attacks of German, Soviet and 'White' Russian counter-revolutionary armies. Polish troops also participated in the last stages of the fight with the Soviet Red Army.

The Ukraine and Byelo-Russia were not so fortunate. Both operated in areas claimed by other minorities, the Lithuanians and Poles having designs on Byelo-Russia, the Cossacks of the Don and the Poles operating at various times across the territory of the Ukraine. Both had large Russian elements hostile to native nationalism. Both built up national councils, *Radas*, in 1917, both claimed their independence after the November Revolution, both found themselves under attack from Bolshevik forces, and both turned to the Germans who forced the Soviets to recognize their independence at Brest-Litovsk. However after Brest-Litovsk, the Ukraine and Byelo-Russia found themselves forced to accept German-sponsored puppet governments and to be exploited for German supply purposes. German withdrawal in November 1918 left the Ukraine the main theatre of civil war between the White Russian armies of General Denikin, native Ukrainian forces, Poles and the Soviet Red Army. Byelo-Russia's fate was similar, save only that the very weak nationalist movement collapsed completely during the German occupation. In both territories, the sole-lasting monument to local nationalism was their establishment as separate Soviet republics in a Soviet Federation with nominally separate Communist parties under central Russian control.

The Moslem element in the Tsarist empire was divided between those liberal reformists who hoped to unite the sixteen million Moslems of the Tsarist empire either on a basis of national cultural autonomy or within a federal state, and the advocates of independent nationhood for the separate parts on a more orthodox Moslem basis. By December 1917, the Pan-Moslem element had succeeded in setting up an Executive

Council, the *Shura*, in St Petersburg, and an Assembly, the *Medzhilis*, at Kazan on the Volga. The seizure of power by the Bolsheviks in November 1917 was followed by the capture of this machinery by Moslem Communists, who, against the wishes of the Bolshevik leaders, evolved a grandiose plan for an autonomous Moslem republic to cover all Russian Central Asia. The Moslem Communist movement collapsed, however, in June 1918 when the Czech legionaries originally recruited by the Provisional Government to fight on the Eastern front, clashed with the Bolsheviks in the course of their immense withdrawal across Russia and Siberia to Vladivostok. The Kazan *Medzhilis* collapsed and the Moslem Communist movement with it. The survivors were ruthlessly absorbed into the Russian Communist party in November 1918.

Only the Turkic separatists, the Crimean Tatars, the Kazakh and Kirghiz who, in 1916, had staged a major rebellion against the loss of their lands to Russian colonists, the Turkestanis, the Circassians, Chechens and Ingush of the Caucasian mountains were left to fight the battle for independence on their own. Some fell victim, especially in Turkestan, to the panic-stricken violence of the Russian soldier and settler population. Some fought for a time for the White Russian armies of General Kolchak. However, they were eventually driven to the Bolshevik side by the ultra-nationalism of the White Russian officers. Some rallied, especially in Turkestan, into the *Basmachi* movement of mounted partisans, defying Soviet forces until well into the 1920s. In the Kazakh-Kirghiz areas, famine was to kill over a million natives in 1921–22. The Crimean Tatars, occupied first by Germans, then by Soviet forces, then by the White armies of General Denikin, suffered a fate similar to that of the nationalists of the Ukraine. Throughout these areas, Soviet victory meant a resumption in a new and more oppressive form of the colonization of the Tsarist days; and the network of Autonomous Regions, Autonomous Soviet Socialist Republics and People's Soviet Republics, set up by the victorious Bolsheviks, were to be autonomous in name only.

The Transcaucasian states of Georgia, Armenia and Azerbaijan were divided from one another by language, race and religion, and caught between the Russians and the Turks. The Armenians were virulently anti-Turk, the more so as in 1915 the Ottoman government had set itself deliberately to exterminate the Armenian minority in Eastern Turkey, over one million Armenians perishing between 1915–17. Georgia with its own language and alphabet was thoroughly Social Democrat. Azerbaijan was Moslem. All three were in the front line of the war with Turkey; and the Russian armies on the Caucasus front did not begin to disintegrate until after the Bolshevik revolution in November 1917. By the Treaty of Brest-Litovsk, the territories of the Transcaucasus found themselves handed over to the rule of the Ottoman Empire. To proclaim their independence was the only alternative.

To maintain their independence proved more difficult. For a time the Azerbaijanis looked to their Turkish co-religionists and the Georgians to the Germans. The armistice of November 1918 brought British and White Russian forces in their stead. British withdrawal in the autumn of 1919 left them open to division between the Red Armies from the north and the revived military power of the new Turkish republic. Here again separate Federal Socialist Soviet Republics were continued after the Russian reconquest. But the return of Bolshevik rule meant the return of the old centralism practised by Tsarist Russian nationalists. Nationalism now only expressed itself within the Communist movement.

The Russian revolution had thus run full circle from the enlightenment towards the subject nationalities shown in the early days of March 1917 to the repression of their independence from 1919 onwards. The Bolshevik party similarly had begun as the extreme Russian wing of the European socialist movement. In capturing Russia it became more and more separated from that movement and less and less European in its socialism. Soviet Russia was to retire into and be isolated in the non-European traditions of Russia.

Before this process of withdrawal was well under way, the Soviet leadership was to bequeath to Europe a new style in diplomacy, one concerned not with relations between governments nor with influencing governments, but with influencing peoples behind and against their governments. The 'new diplomacy' was essentially subversive, not to say revolutionary; and it was to play a very considerable part in the destruction of pre-war Europe brought about in the year 1918, in ensuring that defeat brought not reform but revolution. This 'new diplomacy' was not, however, directly the creation of the Soviet leadership. Rather it was adapted by them from the European radical left, especially from the intellectual radicals of Great Britain, particularly from that group which had drawn away from the Liberal party and had not yet joined Labour, the radicals of the Union of Democratic Control.

In the circumstances of 1917, the 'new diplomacy' was essentially concerned with peace. For the Soviet leadership it took two forms, publication of the secret treaties concluded by the western *Entente* Powers with the Tsarist Empire during the war, and the public demand for a peace 'without annexations or indemnities'. The Soviet leadership also announced its intention of abolishing secret diplomacy and conducting all negotiations 'absolutely openly before the entire people'. The peace decree was directed not to governments but to their peoples. It was to be coupled with a series of appeals to the peoples of Europe's colonial empires in the sacred name of 'self-determination'.

These Soviet moves found an immediate reaction in Britain and the United States. In Britain, the impact of the Soviet peace decree was observable well beyond the radical and Labour circles to whom it might be expected to appeal. It certainly influenced Lord Lansdowne to publish his peace letter which was to find a considerable echo in other conservative circles. Further it drove the British premier and those who felt that war *à l'outrance* was essential to define British war aims in such a way as both to make them accord with the radical-populist ideals of the British Labour movement and to make it inconceivable that there could be any peace with Imperial Germany without there first being a major revolution. In a speech of January 5th, 1918, made significantly not to Parliament but to the British Trades Union Congress, Lloyd George called for a territorial settlement based on 'government with the consent of the governed', 'national self-determination', and the creation of an international organization 'to limit the burden of armaments and diminish the probability of war'.

Lloyd George's appeal was almost immediately taken up by President Wilson for the United States. In the election campaign of 1916, Wilson had moved much closer to the American Progressives; he had indeed only defeated his Republican opponent with the support they gave him in 1916 and refused him in 1912. Once engulfed in war, his aim, like those of the

Union of Democratic Control (UDC) in Britain, was to us
the war to bring about reform in the international system
Wilson himself drew a great many of his ideas and much of h
programme from the UDC either directly through emissarie
in Britain or indirectly through UDC influence on his Progressiv
supporters. He was determined to use the position of militar
and financial pre-eminence in which he knew the United State
would end the war to secure acceptance of his ideas. Ironically
however, he did not represent more than a minority of th
American electorate in this plan. Majority opinion in Americ
at this time was thoroughly martial and chauvinist, dominate
by the kind of war psychosis which had swept Europe in Augus
1914. Like his Soviet opposites, Wilson was acting as an immens
amplifier for the ideas and notions of Europe's progressives.

Wilson's vehicle was the famous 'Fourteen Points', set out i
an address to the American Congress on January 8th, 191:
These were to be followed by the 'Four Principles' of Februar
11th, the 'Four Aims' of July 4th, 1918, and the 'Five Partic
ulars' of September 27th, 1918. They represented much th
same ideas of national self-determination, justice and ope
diplomacy through a League of Nations as Lloyd George ha
voiced; though Wilson was precise where Lloyd George prefe
red to be vague. Wilson added two favourite ideas of America
progressivism, the Freedom of the Seas, so that maritime traff
might pass in peace and in war without interference by be
ligerents, and the removal of all economic barriers to trade. Bu
the first was defeated by British obstructionism (to Britis
opinion it could only seem an attempt to deprive them of th
blockade weapon, the major weapon in their armoury as
Great Power). For the second it was impossible to obtain publi
acceptance in the United States itself.

The British and American replies to the Soviet appeal to ope
diplomacy both represented an implicit determination, whateve
the qualifications introduced into the speeches, to destroy th
German, Austro-Hungarian and Ottoman Empires; though s
long as there still seemed a chance of a separate peace with th
Habsburgs, reference to Czech and Yugoslav nationalis
aspirations was muted. It was apparently assumed that thes
could still be accommodated within the framework of a Habs
burg state reconstituted on federal lines. Only the Poles, workin
through representatives in London and America, had secure

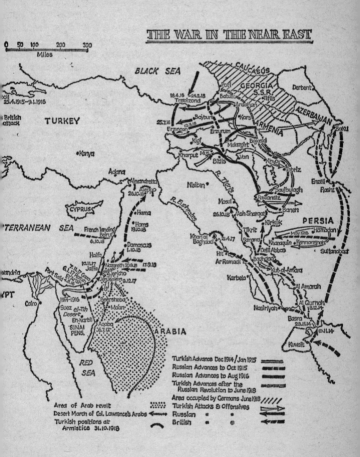

THE WAR IN THE NEAR EAST

0 50 100   200   300
Miles

BLACK SEA

CAUCASUS

GEORGIA
S.S.R.

Derbent

AZERBAIJAN

18.4.16 24.2.18
Trebizond

Batum

Tiflis

Ardahan

TURKEY

25.7.16

Bayburt

Kars

ARMENIA

Baku

British
attack
23.4.1915–9.1.1916

Konya

Erzincan

12.2.16

Erzerum

Malazgirt

Bagdad

Adana

Kharput

M.2.5

Bitlis

Van

Khoi

Tabriz

Enzeli

Rasht

Alexandretta
26.10.18

Aleppo

Nisibin

R. Tigris

Sauibulagh

Sardandiz

CYPRUS

French landing
Beirut
6.10.18

Hama

Homs
19.10.18

R. Euphrates

Mosul

26.10.18

Ash Sharqat

PERSIA

TERRANEAN SEA

Khan al
Baghdadi

21.4.17

Tikrit

Kirkuk

May 1916

Hamadan

Kermanshah

Haifa

Damascus
1.10.18

Samarra

Khanaqin

Sultanabad

Jaffa

6.11.17 Gaza
31.10.17
7.11.17
Nazareth 20.9.18 17.9.18
Jericho

Hit

Ar Ramadi

Deli Abbas

Baghdad
11.3.17

Kut-al-Amara

XPT

Cairo

1914–1916

Suez

el-'Arish

Beersheba

Jerusalem 9.12.17

Karbela

Al Amarah

Port Said
Alexandria

En-Nakhl

Maʻan

SINAI
PENS.

Aqaba
6.7.17

ARABIA

Nasiriyah

Al Qurnah
3.12.14

Basra
23.11.14

Kuwait

10.11.14

RED
SEA

Area of Arab revolt

Desert March of Col. Lawrence's Arabs

Turkish positions at
Armistice 31.10.1918

Turkish Advance Dec 1914 / Jan 1915
Russian Advances to Oct 1915
Russian Advances to Aug 1916
Turkish Advances after the
Russian Revolution to June 1918

Area occupied by Germans June 1918
Turkish Attacks & Offensives
Russian ,, ,,
British ,, ,,

EUROPE, NORTH AFRICA, THE
NEAR AND MIDDLE EAST circa 1923.

0 100 200 300 400 500 Miles

NORWAY
Oslo

ATLANTIC
OCEAN

Edinburgh
Belfast
IRISH FREE STATE
Dublin

DENMARK

NORTH SEA

London
The Hague

R. Elbe

Berlin
R. Oder
SILESIA

GERMANY
Brussels
RUHR
Cologne

Paris
Metz
SAAR
Strasbourg

Prague
CZECHOS

FRANCE
Munich
Vienna

Geneva
SWITZERLAND
TYROL
AUSTRIA
HU

Locarno
Trieste
Fiume

Marseille
Venice
YUGOSL

Lisbon
Madrid
CORSICA
Rome

PORTUGAL
SPAIN
ITALY
ADRIATIC SEA

Gibraltar
BALEARIC IS.
Naples

Tangier
SARDINIA

Algiers
SICILY

FRENCH MOROCCO
Tunis
Malta

ALGERIA
MEDITERRAN

Tripoli

LIBYA

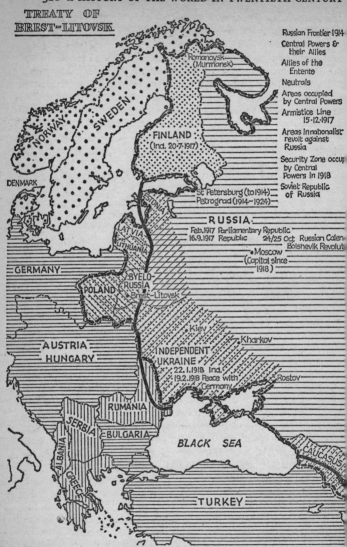

TREATY OF BREST-LITOVSK

Russian Frontier 1914
Central Powers & their Allies
Allies of the Entente
Neutrals
Areas occupied by Central Powers
Armistice Line 15·12·1917
Areas in nationalist revolt against Russia
Security Zone occup by Central Powers in 1918
Soviet Republic of Russia

NORWAY
SWEDEN
DENMARK
FINLAND (Ind. 20·7·1917)
Romanovsk (Murmansk)

St Petersburg (to 1914)
Petrograd (1914–1924)

ESTONIA
LATVIA
LITHUANIA

RUSSIA
Feb.1917 Parliamentary Republic
16.9.1917 Republic   24/25 Oct Russian Calen Bolshevik Revolut
Moscow (Capital since 1918)

GERMANY
POLAND
BYELO-RUSSIA
Brest-Litovsk

Kiev
Kharkov
INDEPENDENT UKRAINE
22.1.1918 Ind.
19.2.1918 Peace with Germany
Rostov

AUSTRIA HUNGARY

RUMANIA
SERBIA
ALBANIA
GREECE
BULGARIA

BLACK SEA
CAUCASUS

TURKEY

Allied support for the creation of a Polish state, and such support figured prominently in both Lloyd George's and President Wilson's pronouncements. Hopes of detaching Austria-Hungary from Germany were, however, revealed as baseless on April 2nd, 1918, when Count Czernin, the Austrian Foreign Minister, in an unhappy attempt to turn the techniques of the new diplomacy against the Western powers, revealed the peace talks with them, and sought to ascribe their failure to France's insistence on the recovery of Alsace-Lorraine. He also denounced the Czech political leaders within the Monarchy as no better or, by implication, no less treasonable than the exiles in France, Britain and Russia.

The Czech answer came very quickly. On April 9th, Czech, Croat, Serb, Rumanian and Polish exile leaders met in Rome. Italian ambitions in Dalmatia and along the coast of the Adriatic, as expressed in the Treaty of London in 1915, had long stood as a barrier to Allied recognition of Serb and Croat national aspirations. But the defeat of Caporetto in 1917 had caused the Italian government to change its attitude, and had ended the Serbs' attempt to put Serbian aggrandizement before union with their Croat and Slovene brethren. The Pact of Corfu in July 1917 had already bound its signatories to form an independent 'Yugoslav' national state. Now the Italians were prepared to back this movement for its disruptive effect on the Habsburg empire. In February 1918, a meeting of Allied experts on propaganda in London decided deliberately to encourage all the anti-German minorities in Austria-Hungary as a means of breaking her power as the weakest link in the German alliances. The meeting at Rome now styled itself the 'Congress of Oppressed Nationalities' and demanded the abolition of Austria. On April 13th, the Czech leaders within the Empire convened a meeting of Czech and Slovene notables in Prague and adopted a National Oath and, on May 16th, a second meeting in Prague brought together representatives of the Czechs, Poles, Yugoslavs, Slovaks, Italian and Rumanian minorities in a pledge to work together for independence and democratic government. At the same time Czech and Polish national units were forming with Allied encouragement in France and Italy. In addition, the terms of the Treaty of Brest-Litovsk had alienated the Polish units that had hitherto been fighting on the German side. In February 1918 the Polish Council in Warsaw broke off relations with Austria-Hungary and a brigade of the Polish legion deserted to the Russians. Almost simultaneously the Czech legion in Russia obtained Soviet agreement for its withdrawal from Russia via Vladivostok. In June 1918 the French recognized the Czech exile National Council as 'the basis for a future Czechoslovak government'. And in America, Masaryk concluded at Pittsburgh an agreement with representatives of the Slovak *emigrés*, looking to the establishment of a Czechoslovak state. Recognition by Britain and the United States followed soon thereafter.

These developments took place against the background of the German spring offensives on the Western front. It was on these attacks that the German military leadership pinned their final hopes of victory. The aim was to force the British to sue for peace. New infantry tactics had been developed, involving infiltration by independent battle groups, using smoke to hide their movements. Known strongpoints were to be encircled rather than assaulted from the front. Thirty-five divisions from the Eastern front were to be committed to the first offensive. The initial assault fell on the British Third and Fifth Armies in the Somme area. It did not succeed in separating the British and French forces but scored an advance of forty miles and inflicted a quarter of a million casualties on the Allies. A second offensive in Flanders in April scored a complete breakthrough and the Germans were only contained by the greatest effort, and a further three hundred thousand casualties. In May, a third German offensive struck the French on the Aisne river, broke through and advanced to within thirty-seven miles of Paris before being halted. Two more major attacks in June and early July scored minor successes but were soon contained. The German army had shot its bolt at a cost of eight hundred thousand casualties to itself. However, Germany had inflicted over one million casualties on the Allies, captured great quantities of guns and war material and carved three immense salients in the Allied line. But Allied morale had held, the armies though badly mauled had not collapsed, and American divisions, fresh, strong and vigorous, were now pouring into France. Two such American divisions had in fact held the third German offensive in front of Paris. The initiative now passed inexorably to the Allies.

This was the more welcome in that the German offensives had at last forced the Allied generals to agree to a system of unified command. The Caporetto disaster in October 1917 had led to the formation of a Supreme War Council the following month. But the British and French generals had refused to give it powers of command over themselves or to furnish it with a central strategic reserve, and the British and French prime ministers had felt themselves unable to override their refusal. The British defeat in March 1918 was compounded by Pétain's refusal to send more than a few divisions to the aid of the British, and an announcement that French troops in the event of a retreat would withdraw to the south-west to cover Paris. Such an action would have given the German general staff the separation of British and French armies for which they were working. It led the Supreme War Council to give General Foch supreme command over all Allied forces in France.

Under Foch's direction, the Allies now prepared for the counter-offensive. In the second half of July, four French armies, into which considerable American and British contingents were incorporated, drove the Germans back from their great salient pointing towards Paris. On August 8th, the 'black day' of the German army in the view of General Ludendorff, the British Fourth Army, with large Canadian and Australian contingents, over 600 tanks and very heavy air support, broke clean through the German front at Amiens and drove the Germans back to the starting line of their first spring offensive. For the first time, the morale of the German army was seen to crack. And on September 12th, the first all-American offensive (though it had heavy air and artillery support from the Allies) obliterated a salient at St Mihiel which had persisted since the fighting in 1914.

The turn of the tide on the Western front came, however, too late to forestall the opening of Allied intervention in Russia. Small elements of British and Allied troops had been landed in Murmansk as early as March 1918 at the appeal of the local revolutionary forces, to protect the large quantity of Allied stores landed there against possible German attack through Finland. They received military reinforcements in May 1918. And the Japanese military authorities had long been nursing plans to intervene in Siberia and take over the Russian Maritime Provinces, with the aim of making the whole North China Sea into an 'inland sea' surrounded by Japanese-controlled territories. There were half a million tons of Allied war stores in Vladivostok too. Since November 1917, there had been discussions in Allied circles centred on the idea of using Japanese troops to recreate the Eastern front which Russia's collapse had destroyed. But the Japanese refused to move without American agreement, although naval units were sent by Britain and Japan to Vladivostok in January 1918.

The desperate state of the Western front under the impact of the German spring offensives stirred the British and French authorities into renewed pressure for Japanese intervention in Siberia. Their proposals which envisaged a mass movement of Japanese troops along five thousand miles of Trans-Siberian railway to the Urals and beyond were so unreal as to indicate more the depths of despair to which Britain's military planners had been brought in the early summer of 1918. In April, small Japanese and British units were landed at Vladivostok to prevent local Bolshevik forces from shipping the war stores in the city out of Allied reach. And in May the Czech Legion, retreating across Russia under an agreement made by the Czech exile leadership with the Bolsheviks, clashed with Red Army units, and seized control of the whole Central Russian railway network from the Volga to Irkutsk. A section of the Legion had already reached Vladivostok. The rest determined to fight their way across Siberia to join them. At the end of June 1918, the Czechs already in Vladivostok seized the city.

The need to come to the aid of the Czechs overruled American objections to intervention in Siberia. Japanese troops began landing at Vladivostok at the beginning of August 1918 and within three months there were over 70,000 Japanese troops in Siberia. They were to be joined by much smaller contingents of American, British and Canadian troops. By this date, the Czechs had established complete control from the Pacific to the Urals. The Japanese, however, made no move to come to their aid but simply entrenched themselves in Manchuria and the Siberian Maritime Provinces. West of them were the Czechs now gradually retreating in the face of Bolshevik attack; authority was exercised by various anti-Bolshevik governments. In November 1918, these were to be united under the leadership of Admiral Kolchak. The stage was set for civil war in Russia.

The intervention in Siberia was important principally because of its scale. There had been other British landings in Northern Russia, where at the beginning of July 1918 the Murmansk

Soviet had broken with the Bolshevik leaders in Moscow, and a Social Revolutionary government had been set up in Archangel. American troops were added to those of Britain in August 1918, and the combined forces advanced deep into North Russia. Their original aim had been simply to protect Northern Russia against German and Finnish invasion; and they had been dispatched *before* the break between Murmansk and Moscow. Thereafter, they were, willy-nilly, embroiled in the civil war. Other small British forces were sent into the Caucasus and into Transcaspia to aid in the protection of the oilfields against Turkey and to forestall a possible German-Turkish drive into Persia and Afghanistan. Their presence did not outlast the year 1918. It was to be more difficult to extricate the British troops in Northern Russia.

The Allied interventions in Russia were conceived in panic and borne of too much study of small-scale maps. Their effect was to embroil the West with the new Soviet government and to accentuate the division between Russia's new rulers and Europe; to plant the Japanese military firmly in Eastern Asia and to exacerbate relations between Britain and America; and all to no avail. As has been shown previously, by the time the Japanese troops had begun to invade Siberia, the German forces were already in retreat on the Western front. In September 1918, three great offensives, in Palestine, on the Salonika front and on the Western front, were to bring total defeat to Germany and her Eastern allies, and dissolution to the Habsburg monarchy.

In Palestine, the British forces had been considerably weakened during the spring of 1918 by the withdrawal of British troops to bolster the armies in France and repair the losses they suffered during the German spring offensives. They were replaced by Indian troops, who needed a good deal of training before Allenby felt it safe to go over to the offensive again. The British offensive opened on the plains of Megiddo (the biblical Armageddon) on September 19th. A complete breakthrough was scored and Allenby unleashed his three cavalry divisions and the Hejazi Bedouin forces in a pursuit which was only to end with the conclusion of an armistice by Turkey on October 30th. Damascus was 'liberated' by Arab forces on October 1st, a day after Australian cavalry had passed through in pursuit of the fleeing Turks. The Turkish Cabinet then resigned, Enver Pasha retiring in favour of a non-partisan Cabinet appointed by the

Sultan. By the terms of the armistice, for which the Turks sued on October 14th, and which was signed on October 30th on the isle of Lemnos, the Turkish authorities agreed to open the Dardanelles, surrender all garrisons in Cyrenaica, Tripolitania, Arabia, Syria and Mesopotamia, and withdraw all forces from Northern Persia and Transcaucasia. The bulk of the Turkish army was to be demobilized and the Turkish fleet surrendered. British troops entered Mosul in late November, and British forces moved through to the Caspian Sea, reoccupying Baku. The Ottoman Empire was destroyed.

The Arab nationalists believed themselves now to have British support for setting up an Arab government in Damascus. Among the secret treaties published by the Bolsheviks in November 1917 was the Sykes-Picot agreement of 1916 providing for the division of the Arab provinces of the Ottoman world into spheres of influence between Britain and France. The Ottoman Governor of Syria lost no time in turning this disclosure to the propaganda advantage of the Turks and against the forces of the Arab revolt and their supporters in Syria. The pro-Arabs in the British administration in Cairo and Palestine and in the Arab Bureau responsible for relations with the Arab forces were encouraged by the effect of these revelations to resume their campaign for a unified Arab monarchy under British protection. Various statements were made by these pro-Arab elements (most notably the so-called 'Declaration to the Seven' of July 1918 made to the leaders of the Party of Syrian Unity formed among the Syrian exiles in Cairo), promising that the government of the territories liberated from the Turks would be based on the principle of the consent of the governed. Where the Arab forces had themselves (ie, without British military participation) 'emancipated' former Ottoman territories, the Declaration promised that their 'complete and sovereign independence' would be recognized. It was presumably to fit in with this provision that Arab forces were allowed to 'liberate' Damascus, British troops being deliberately held back to make this possible. This chicanery, for there is no other word for it, encouraged the Arabs to believe that Britain would protect them against French claims. They were to be rudely disillusioned the following year.

The offensive on the Salonika front began on September 14th, 1918. The front was defended primarily by Bulgarian troops, the

German and Austro-Hungarian contingents having been with-drawn to bolster the French and Italian fronts. By September 17th, the Allied forces had advanced over twenty miles; by September 26th, the Bulgarian army was in a state of total collapse and the road to Sofia, the Bulgarian capital, lay open. That day, the Bulgarian government requested an armistice, which was signed on September 29th. The Bulgarian army was to be demobilized and all Allied territory evacuated. Free passage through Bulgarian territory and the control of Bulgaria's transport facilities were surrendered to the Allies. The way was open to attack Germany and Austria-Hungary from the rear.

On the Italian front, the armies of Austria-Hungary had staged their last offensive across the river Piave in June 1918. The offensive involved crossing the river on pontoons within range of the Italian artillery; and although the Austrians fought with vigour and determination their margin of strength was too small to bring victory. The Italian counter-offensive was not launched until October 24th, twenty days after the Austrian government had inquired of the American government about an armistice. The Austrian forces bravely held out for five days, inflicting heavy losses on the attacking forces. But, on October 30th, they began to crumble and the Italian cavalry started a pursuit which carried them right up to and across the old Italo-Austrian frontier and which ended on November 4th, the day the Austrian armistice was finally signed. On November 3rd, Italian sea-borne forces occupied Trieste. Half a million Austrian prisoners were taken on this final offensive, known to historians as the battle of Vittorio Veneto.

The collapse and disintegration of the Habsburg Empire was already in full progress. On September 14th, the Emperor had published a last appeal for peace which had simply been ignored. On October 1st, the *Reichsrath* convened for the last time, all the national delegations taking advantage of the occasion to issue declarations in favour of independence. On October 4th, the Austrian government dispatched a note to the United States requesting an armistice and offering to make peace on the basis of the Fourteen Points. On October 16th, in a last attempt to save the Habsburg state, the Emperor issued an Imperial Manifesto proclaiming the re-organization of the non-Magyar part of the monarchy as a federal state with complete self-government for the subject nationalities. Even at this late date the government in Budapest was able to prevent its application to the territories under Hungarian rule.

But the move came much too late. On October 14th, Beneš had already announced the formation of a provisional Czech government in Paris. On October 21st, in America, Masaryk proclaimed Czech independence and on October 28th in Prague the local Czech leaders had no difficulty in formally taking over the administration of Bohemia with tacit Austrian acquiescence. The following day, Serb and Croat leaders meeting in Zagreb proclaimed the establishment of a Yugoslav state. On October 30th, a German National Council was set up for the German provinces of Austria. The next day, after the assassination of Count Tisza, strong man of the old *régime*, a Radical-Social Democratic government under Count Karolyi proclaimed Hungary's independence. Polish independence had been proclaimed in Warsaw on October 7th; and the administration of Polish Galicia was taken over from the Austrians together with that of eastern Silesia and the Austro-Hungarian zone of occupation in eastern Poland by the end of October. It was to be some time, however, before the Polish exiles and the Warsaw Poles were to be reconciled and a single Polish government recognized by the Allies. On November 12th, the last of the Habsburg emperors abdicated his throne. Balkanization, the division of Eastern and Central Europe into a congeries of small, weak, mutually suspicious and inimical states, a natural prey to Great Power pressures and ambitions, was completed.

Of all the belligerents there remained only Germany. During the spring and summer of 1918 the hold of the military over German affairs had become virtually absolute. In June 1918, at the height of Germany's victories in the West, Ludendorff had forced the Kaiser to dismiss the State Secretary in the Foreign Ministry, von Kuhlmann, for daring to suggest that the Supreme Command should conduct peace negotiations. He followed this *coup* by forcing the Kaiser to dismiss the head of his own Civil Secretariat. The Kaiser was reduced to bitter complaints, scribbled on the margin of Foreign Ministry dispatches, that he could not obtain a hearing for his views from the Chief of the General Staff. But the events of August 1918 shook Ludendorff's nerve badly; and his encouragement of the Prussian conservatives and German nationalists through the Fatherland party and the whole movement for an annexationist peace meant that any resignation of power on his part would mean at least a parliamentary, if not a socialist, revolution in Germany.

The final Allied offensives in the West opened on September 26th with a massive attack by the new American armies on the Argonne forest area. On September 27th–28th a British offensive on the Cambrai sector broke into the Hindenburg Line, and on October 5th they had forced a total German withdrawal to new positions along the Selle river. In Flanders, Anglo-Belgian forces were on the advance from Ypres. Throughout October successive offensives threw the German forces back along the line. Ostend, Zeebrugge, Roubaix, Lille, Valenciennes, all fell before the advancing armies. By the end of October, Allied troops were approaching Sedan. The events of September 27th–28th, when taken with the collapse of Bulgaria, were enough for Germany.

On September 29th, Hindenburg and Ludendorff informed the Emperor and the Chancellor that the military situation demanded the immediate institution of negotiations for an armistice. It was decided to address an appeal to President Wilson to bring about an armistice on the basis of the Fourteen Points. The generals believed that if the Allied terms should prove too onerous then Germany would fight on. At the same time, they realized that there would have to be a change of government in order to provide one that would be both acceptable to the Allies and able to maintain order in Germany. Since the only alternative source of authority was the *Reichstag*, a German staff officer was sent to tell the party leaders that the army had lost the war and that the *Reichstag* would have to make the peace. A new Chancellor was found in Prince Max of Baden, the one German state where the ruling house had established a compromise with the middle classes. This action by General Ludendorff, for he was the prime mover, represented the complete abdication of power by the army leadership. When Ludendorff came thereafter into conflict with the new Chancellor he was easily forced to resign. The real German revolution occurred between September 29th and October 3rd, 1918.

On October 4th, the new Chancellor sent a note through neutral channels to President Wilson asking for an armistice to be concluded on the basis of the Fourteen Points. The German government was to find President Wilson a stern and unbending task-master, insistent on proof that the new government was speaking not merely for the old imperial authorities but for the German people. There followed further exchanges of notes, Wilson demanding that submarine operations cease immediately and that the armistice should confirm the 'present military supremacy' of the Allied armies. He remained so obstinately unconvinced that any real transfer in power had been effected in Germany that pressure began to build up in favour of the Kaiser's abdication. On October 26th, the *Reichstag* adopted a series of resolutions which made the Chancellor and his Cabinet responsible to the *Reichstag*, established civilian authority over the armed forces and swept away the three-class system of voting in Prussia.

In the meantime, the plans made by the German naval command for a large-scale raid on the British coast led on November 3rd to mutiny in the German fleet and the setting up of workers and sailors councils on the Russian model. Mutiny spread to the army and on November 7th in Munich the Independent Socialist leader, Kurt Eisner, proclaimed a Bavarian republic and the overthrow of the ruling house of Wittelsbach. On November 9th, the revolution spread to Berlin and the Kaiser abdicated. The Social Democrats overthrew Prince Max of Baden's Cabinet and a new Cabinet under a Social Democrat Chancellor, Friedrich Ebert, took office. On November 10th the Republic was proclaimed in Berlin. The Kaiser took refuge in Holland. The Supreme Command of the Army pledged its support to the new *régime*. The German revolution was over; though attempts both from left and right to overthrow it were to be a constant feature of its first five years of life.

Throughout this period the Allied Supreme War Council was in session at Versailles, debating the terms of the Armistice. None of the Allies had ever formally accepted the Fourteen Points; and President Wilson's assumption of the leadership in negotiating unilaterally with the Germans was much resented. The British and French leaders turned therefore to writing armistice terms which would make it impossible for Germany to resume the fight again. All but a handful of Germany's modern warships and all her submarines were to be surrendered. Allied armies were to occupy all the land between the existing front and the river Rhine, including Belgium, Alsace-Lorraine, Northern France and Luxemburg; they were in addition to

ccupy the bridgeheads over the Rhine. Germany was to dis-
orge her gains in Eastern Europe. The blockade would con-
nue in force. The American authorities made no complaint
ver the terms and the German delegation accepted them over
rmy protest. On November 11th, the armistice was signed in a
ailway carriage at Compiégne. At 11 AM that day the Great
War was at an end.

The war losses were immense. In all, sixty million men were
mobilized by the belligerents excluding the United States and
apan. Of these 57·6% became casualties, with over 8 million
illed, 21 million wounded, and 7¾ million taken prisoner and
ncarcerated behind walls and barbed-wire fences until the
rmistices released them. The highest casualty rates were
uffered by Austria-Hungary (7 million casualties, 1·2 million
ead, 3·6 million wounded, 2·2 million prisoners, 90% of all
mobilized), Russia (9 million casualties, 1·7 million dead, 4·9
million wounded, 25 million prisoners, 76·3% of all men
mobilized), France (6 million casualties, 1·3 million dead, 4·3
million wounded, 0·5 million prisoners, 73·3% of all mobilized),
Rumania (535 thousand casualties, 335 thousand killed, 120
housand wounded, 80 thousand prisoners, 71·4% of all mobiliz-
d), Germany (7 million casualties, 1·8 million dead, 4·2 million
wounded, 1·2 million prisoners, 64·9% of all mobilized), Serbia
45 thousand killed, 133 thousand wounded, 152 thousand
risoners, 46% of all mobilized), Italy (650 thousand killed,
47 thousand wounded 600 thousand prisoners, 39·1% of all
mobilized), the British Empire (908 thousand killed, 2 million
wounded, 191 thousand prisoners, 35·8% of all mobilized),
Belgium (13 thousand killed, 44 thousand wounded, 34 thousand
risoners, 34·9% of all mobilized) and Turkey (325 thousand
illed, 400 thousand wounded, 250 thousand prisoners, 34·2%
f all mobilized). The direct costs of the war have been estimated
t over 180 billion dollars, or 45 thousand million pounds
terling, the indirect costs at 151 billion dollars, or just under
8 thousand million pounds sterling. But these figures are purely
otional. The casualties, to be put in their clearest light, must be
een as falling entirely on the age groups entering into the
ighteen to thirty-five years range between the years 1914–18,
n terms of an average expectancy of life in the front line of one
month for an infantry officer, six to eight weeks for an ordinary
oldier. A significant proportion of a whole generation in Europe,

especially of those with courage, dedication, and initiative w
killed or scarred physically and mentally. And attempts ma
today to belittle these figures go contrary to all the contempora
evidence.

The war produced many new means of battle. It was, in fac
the first industrialized war in history. Poison-gas, the tank, th
submarine have all been mentioned. Another major develo
men was that of war in the air. In 1914–18, aircraft we
primitive, unarmed, slow and used merely to extend the scoutir
range of the armies' cavalry. In 1918, the Allies were preparir
for a major bombing assault on Germany's cities; ground attac
techniques had been developed and proved especially effectiv
in France and Palestine. The Allies had some eight thousan
aircraft to the Central Powers three and a half thousand. Aeri
combat techniques had become advanced, air aces with tens
'kills' to their credit were national heroes. German dirigib
lighter-than-air balloons, the *Zeppelins*, and German aircra
had bombed London, causing a certain amount of panic amor
its citizens. The more imaginative had already leaped forwar
to visualizing the scenes that were to mark World War I
Warsaw, Rotterdam, Coventry, London, Belgrade, Lübeck
Hamburg, Berlin, Cologne, Dresden – even to Hiroshima.

In the world of art and literature, the war accentuated th
division of the creative and artistic intellectual groupings fro
the remainder of society referred to in Chapter XI above. Fo
many artists, of course, the war period was too short to introdu
any really startling changes in doctrine or technique. But th
development of 'metaphysical painting' (*pittura metafisica*) i
Italy, a curious combination of cubist method and surreali
themes, pointed forward to the developments of the ne
decade. Marc Chagall continued his surrealist exploration
dream-life fantasy in Russia to which he returned on th
outbreak of war. In Britain, Italian Futurism had a bri
influence in 1914–15 on the so-called Vorticist school, one whic
united painters and sculptors such as Wyndham Lewis, Jaco
Epstein, Henry Gaudier-Brzeska, and E. Wadsworth, wit
Anglo-American writers such as Ezra Pound, Ford Mad
Hueffer, Rebecca West and Osbert and Edith Sitwell, a scho
which, if it can be said to have had any theme, preached
revolutionary *élitist* assault on the received values of their ow
society.

The most significant development, however, began in neutral Switzerland in 1916. This was the so-called 'Dadaist' movement, an anarchist and nihilist assault on any notion of order, restraint or aesthetic in art and culture. For a time, 'Dada', which spread rapidly to Berlin, Paris, Barcelona, New York and Cologne, embraced artists and writers as variegated as Picasso, the Italian Futurist, Marinetti, the Russian philosopher of the Central European *Blaue Reiter* group, Kandinsky, Paul Klee, Max Ernst, André Breton and Louis Aragon. It cleared the way for the post-war development of the extreme forms of cubism and surrealism, especially the work of Paul Klee, the Swiss surrealist. For others, especially in Germany and France, it opened the way to a personal re-involvement in political activity on the side of the extreme revolutionaries, an involvement itself so anti-political as to hinder rather than help the re-integration of the artist with society. In general, it marked the revulsion and disgust of the artists and writers in Europe with the society in which they lived but with which they felt little or no identification, a society which seemed to have decided to immolate itself in an orgy of hatred and self-destruction.

The war of 1914–18 marked for Europe the end of an era of peace, stability and cooperation between the established ruling social groups of the continent's leading powers. The forces which expressed themselves in these years were divisive and destructive, both between the powers and within them, and in each case they reflected the discontent of the social groupings which, under the existing systems of socio-political power, were denied any participation in, or identification with, the processes which governed their destinies. For those social groups which thought along individualist rather than collectivist lines, peasants, professional men, small traders and business men, white-collar workers, the main enemy seemed to be the forces of cosmopolitan Europe and the foreign powers whose activity, they thought, hampered and stunted their own national development. For those who thought on collectivist lines, the alienated intelligentsias and the organized industrial workers, the main enemies became, under the privations of war, the ruling groups who seemed to want to prolong the war to satisfy their own annexationist demands. Between these two forces, political Europe as it was organized in 1914 fell to pieces to be replaced by the spurious internationalism of the League of Nations, all things to all men, in theory world-wide, in fact European in composition, which sought to outlaw war by the threat of making it universal, and ensured only that any future employment of force for national ends would be deliberate, conspiratorial, and less hindered by the check and balances of the Concert of Europe system which had broken down in 1914. The League was to last only twenty years, until a second world war destroyed what the first had left undamaged of Europe's supremacy and introduced a new balance of terror, rather than power, between the super-powers on Europe's periphery, the Soviet Union and the United States, with Europe divided between them.

SELECT BIBLIOGRAPHY

Albertini, Luigi, *The Origins of the War of 1914*, 3 vols, translated and edited by Isabella M. Massey, Oxford University Press, London, 1952–1957.

Anderson, M. S., *The Eastern Question, 1774–1923*, Longmans, Green and Co Ltd, London, 1966.

Avery, Peter, *Modern Iran*, Ernest Benn Ltd, London, 1965.

Ayearst, Morley, *The British West Indies*, Allen and Unwin Ltd, London, 1960.

Barbour, Neville, *A Survey of North West Africa (the Maghreb)*, Oxford University Press, London, 1959.

Barraclough, Geoffrey, *An Introduction to Contemporary History*, C. A. Watts and Co Ltd, London, 1964.

Black, C. E., and Helmreich, E. C., *Twentieth Century Europe: A History*, (2nd edition), Alfred A. Knopf Inc, New York, 1963.

Brogan, D. W., *The Development of Modern France*, Hamish Hamilton Ltd, London, 1959.

Bullard, Sir Reader, *The Middle East: A Political and Economic Survey* (3rd edition), Oxford University Press, London, 1958.

Cady, John F., *South-East Asia: Its Historical Development*, McGraw-Hill Book Co, New York, 1964.

Cargill, Oscar, *Intellectual America: Ideas on the March*, Macmillan and Co Ltd, London, 1941.

Carr, Raymond, *Spain 1808–1939*, Oxford University Press, London, 1965.

Chambers, Frank P., *The War Behind the War*, Faber and Faber Ltd, London, 1939.

Clubb, Oliver E., *Twentieth Century China*, Columbia University Press, New York, 1964.

Cole, G. D. H., *A History of Socialist Thought*, Vol III, *The Second International, 1889–1914*, Macmillan and Co Ltd, London, 1956.

Craig, Gordon A., *The Politics of the Prussian Army, 1640–1945* (revised edition), Oxford University Press, New York, 1964.

Dozer, D. M., *Latin America, An Interpretative History*,

McGraw-Hill Book Co, New York, 1962.

Edmonds, Sir James E., *A Short History of World War I*, Oxford University Press, London, 1951.

Edwardes, Michael, *Asia in the European Age, 1498–1955*, Thames and Hudson Ltd, London, 1961.

Esposito, Brigadier-General Vincent J. (ed.), *A Concise History of World War I*, Frederick A. Praeger Inc, New York, 1964.

Feis, H., *Europe, The World's Banker, 1870–1914*, Kelley, New York, 1961.

Gooch, G. P., *Before the War: Studies in Diplomacy*, 2 vols, Longmans, Green and Co Ltd, London, 1936–1938.

Grattan, C. H., *The South West Pacific Since 1900: A Modern History*, University of Michigan Press, Ann Arbor, Michigan, 1963.

Griswold, A. W., *The Far Eastern Policy of the United States*, Yale University Press, New Haven, Connecticut, 1962.

Hodgkin, T. L., *Nationalism in Colonial Africa*, Frederick Muller and Co Ltd, London, 1962.

Hofstaedter, R., *The Age of Reform, From Bryan to F.D.R.*, Alfred A. Knopf Inc, New York, 1955.

Hourani, Albert, *Arabic Thought in the Liberal Age, 1798–1939*, Oxford University Press, London, 1962.

Hughes, H. Stuart, *Consciousness and Society, The Reorientation of European Thought, 1890–1930*, MacGibbon and Kee Ltd, London, 1959.

Hurewitz, J. C., *Diplomacy in the Near and Middle East, A Documentary Record*, Van Nostrand Company Inc, Princeton, New Jersey, 1956.

Jones, A. H. M., and Monroe, E., *A History of Ethiopia*, Oxford University Press, London, 1955.

Kann, R. E., *The Multinational Empire: Nationalism and National Reform in the Habsburg Monarchy, 1848–1918*, Columbia University Press, New York, 1950.

Kedourie, Eli, *England and the Middle East: The Destruction of the Ottoman Empire, 1914–1921*, Bowes and Bowes Publishers Ltd, London, 1956.

Kelly, J. B., *Eastern Arabian Frontiers*, Faber and Faber Ltd, London, 1964.

King, J. Clemens, *Generals and Politicians*, University of California Press, Berkeley, California, 1951.

Komarnicki, Tytus, *Rebirth of the Polish Republic: A Study in*

the Diplomatic History of Europe, 1914–1920, William
Heinemann Ltd, London, 1957.

Langer, W. L., *The Diplomacy of Imperialism, 1890–1902* (2nd
edition), Alfred A. Knopf Inc, New York, 1956.

Lewis, Bernard, *The Emergence of Modern Turkey*, Oxford
University Press, London, 1961.

Lewis, Cleona, and Schottebeck, Karl T., *America's Stake in
International Investments*, The Brookings Institution, Washington DC, 1938.

Lindberg, Folke, *Scandinavia in Great Power Politics, 1905–
1908*, Almkvist och Wiskell, Stockholm, 1958.

Link, Arthur S., *Woodrow Wilson and the Progressive Era, 1910–
1917*, Hamish Hamilton Ltd, London, 1954.

Little, Tom, *Egypt*, Ernest Benn Ltd, London, 1958.

Mack Smith, Denis, *Italy: A Modern History*, University of
Michigan Press, Ann Arbor, Michigan, 1959.

Marder, Arthur J., *British Naval Policy, 1880–1905: The Anat-
omy of British Sea Power*, Putnam and Co Ltd, London, 1940.

Marder, Arthur J., *From the Dreadnought to Scapa Flow*, 3 vols,
Oxford University Press, London, 1961.

Marlowe, John, *The Persian Gulf in the Twentieth Century*, The
Cresset Press, London, 1962.

May, Arthur J., *The Habsburg Monarchy, 1867–1914*, Harvard
University Press, Cambridge, Massachusetts, 1961.

Mayer, Arno J., *The Political Origins of the New Diplomacy*,
Yale University Press, New Haven, Connecticut, 1959.

Mazour, Anatol G., *Finland Between East and West*, Van Nostrand Company Ltd and Macmillan and Co Ltd, London, 1956.

Morison, S. E., and Commager, H. S., *The Growth of the
American Republic* (5th edition), Oxford University Press,
London, 1962.

Morton, W. L., *The Kingdom of Canada*, McClelland and Stew-
art Ltd, Toronto, 1963.

Mowat, R. B., *The Concert of Europe*, Macmillan and Co Ltd,
London, 1930.

Mowry, G. E., *The Era of Theodore Roosevelt, 1900–1912*,
Hamish Hamilton Ltd, London, 1959.

Mumford, Lewis, *Technics and Civilization*, Routledge and
Kegan Paul Ltd, London, 1934.

National Bureau of Economic Research, *International Migration*,
The Bureau, New York, 1931.

Nelson, Harold I., *Land and Power: British and Allied Policy on Germany's Frontiers 1916–1919*, Routledge and Kegan Paul Ltd, London, 1963.

Nowell, C. E., *A History of Portugal*, Van Nostrand Co Inc, Princeton, New Jersey, 1962.

Page, Stanley W., *The Formation of the Baltic States*, Harvard University Press, Cambridge, Massachusetts, 1959.

Pevsner, Nicolaus, *Pioneers of Modern Design, From William Morris to Walter Gropius* (2nd edition), Simon and Schuster Inc, New York, 1949.

Pipes, Richard, *The Formation of the Soviet Union: Communism and Nationalism 1917–1923*, Harvard University Press, Cambridge, Massachusetts.

Reshetar, John S., *The Ukrainian Revolution, 1917–1920*, Princeton University Press, Princeton, New Jersey, 1952.

Rippy, J. Fred., *Latin America: A Modern History*, University of Michigan Press, Ann Arbor, Michigan, 1958.

Rosenberg, Arthur, *The Birth of the German Republic, 1871–1918*, Oxford University Press, London, 1931.

Sacher, Howard M., *The Course of Modern Jewish History*, Weidenfeld and Nicolson Ltd, London, 1958.

Schapiro, L., *The Origin of the Communist Autocracy*, G. Bell and Sons Ltd, London, 1955.

Schmitt, Bernadotte E., *The Coming of the War, 1914*, Charles Scribner's Sons, New York, 1930.

Seton-Watson, G. H. N., *The Decline of Imperial Russia, 1855–1914*, Methuen and Co Ltd, London, 1952.

Seton-Watson, R. W., *A History of the Czechs and Slovaks*, Hutchinson and Co, London, 1943.

Shwadran, Benjamin, *The Middle East, Oil and the Great Powers* (2nd edition), Council for Middle Eastern Affairs Press, New York, 1959.

Singer, Charles, Holmyard, E. T., Hall, A. R., and Williams, Trevor I., *A History of Technology*, Vol IV, Oxford University Press, London, 1955.

Smith, C. Jay, Jnr, *Finland and The Russian Revolution 1917–1922*, University of Georgia Press, Athens, Georgia, 1958.

Spear, J. G. P., *India: A Modern History*, University of Michigan Press, Ann Arbor, Michigan, 1961.

Spender, J. A., *Great Britain, Empire and Commonwealth, 1866–1935*, Allen and Unwin Ltd, London, 1936.

Taylor, A. J. P., *The Habsburg Monarchy, 1809–1918*, Hamish Hamilton Ltd, London, 1961.

Taylor, A. J. P., *English History, 1914–1945*, Oxford University Press, London, 1965.

Ullman, Richard H., *Anglo-Soviet Relations 1917–1921, Vol I: Intervention and the War*, Princeton University Press, Princeton, New Jersey, 1961.

Vinacke, Harold, *A History of the Far East in Modern Times* (6th edition), Appleton-Century-Crofts, New York, 1961.

Walker, Eric A., *A History of Southern Africa* (3rd edition), Longmans, Green and Co Ltd, London, 1957.

Wiedner, Donald L., *A History of Africa: South of the Sahara*, G. Bell and Sons Ltd, London, 1964.

Wilenski, R. S., *Modern French Painting* (2nd edition), Faber and Faber Ltd, London, 1944.

Winkler, Henry R., *The League of Nations Movement in Great Britain, 1914–1919*, Rutgers University Press, New Brunswick, New Jersey, 1952.

Wolfe, Bertram, *Three Who Made a Revolution*, The Dial Press Inc, New York, 1948.

Yanaga, C., *Japan Since Perry*, McGraw-Hill Book Co, New York, 1949.

Zeine, Zeine M., *Arab-Turkish Relations and the Emergence of Arab Nationalism*, Khayat, Beirut, 1958.

Zeman, Z. A. B., *The Break-Up of the Habsburg Empire, 1914–1918*, Oxford University Press, London, 1961.

STATISTICAL TABLES

The statistics that are reproduced on the following pages appeared in the complete one volume hardback edition, and also appear in all three volumes in this Pan series. There will be some statistics, therefore, that do not directly apply to this particular volume, but have been kept in so that an overall picture of the history of the twentieth century can be received.

Note: The following statistical tables have been compiled, unless otherwise noted, from the figures given in the League of Nations *International Statistical Yearbooks* (Economic and Financial Section, Geneva, 1927 to 1945) and the United Nations *Statistical Yearbooks* (Statistical Office of United Nations, Department of Economic and Social Affairs, New York, 1949 to 1964).

Some of the individual figures are estimates made on the basis of the best available information and therefore must be used with caution. Taken together, however, they present a reasonably accurate and reliable picture of trends of production, consumption and income.

The sign '. . .' indicates that the figure for that year is either unavailable or negligible.

POPULATION

In thousands, 1900–62

	1900	1913	1920	1925	1929
Egypt	...	12,144	...	14,055	14,500
Congo	...	15,000 (est.)	...	15,000 (est.)	10,000
Rhodesia	...	1,620	1,883	2,015	2,400
S. Africa	...	6,323	...	7,525	8,000
Canada	5,250	7,500	...	9,400	10,000
USA	89,000	96,512	...	116,257	123,000
Mexico	...	15,550	14,235	15,000	16,000
Argentina	4,090	7,875	...	10,087	11,000
Brazil	...	25,000	30,636	32,500	41,000
China / Taiwan	303,000 (est.)	441,900	...	448,231	452,791
India / Pakistan	287,000 (1891)	320,000	318,000	325,000	352,370
Indonesia	...	48,000	49,351	53,230	61,000
Iran	7,000 (est.)	9,000	...	9,000	9,000
Japan	43,200	53,363	...	59,737	64,700
Turkey	...	19,574	...	13,139	14,000
France	38,900	37,790	39,000	40,610	41,230
W. Germany / E. Germany	56,000	66,978	60,894	63,166	64,739
Italy	32,347	35,598	37,766	39,113	40,459
Poland	(7,960)	(10,145)	26,746	29,847	31,084
Spain	18,566	20,299	21,286	22,170	23,075
Sweden	5,136	5,639	5,875	6,044	6,112
UK	41,155	45,789	43,552	45,202	45,875
Australia	4,500	4,872	...	5,992	6,200
N. Zealand	...	1,147	...	1,415	1,450
USSR	129,000 (1897)	161,200	...	141,000	161,000

1933	1937	1946	1948	1952	1958	1962
15,210	16,008	18,835	19,528	21,421	24,666	27,285
10,000	10,154	10,622	10,885	11,763	14,254	15,617
2,602	2,781	3,456	3,554	6,676	6,450	7,265
8,430	9,805	11,420	11,890	11,912	15,035	16,640
10,760	11,339	12,307	13,227	14,430	17,120	18,600
126,000	128,961	141,235	146,571	156,981	174,882	186,591
17,600	18,737	22,779	23,876	26,922	32,895	37,233
12,030	13,490	15,912	16,420	18,056	20,060	21,418
44,900	38,687	46,650	48,350	54,477	65,740	75,271
450,000	452,460	455,592	463,493	...	646,530	...
				8,000	9,851	11,327
363,100	379,778	329,828	342,120	367,000	410,686	449,381
		72,587	73,321	...	88,762	96,558
63,500	67,938	72,290	72,000	78,163	89,441	97,765
—	16,200	17,000	17,000	19,559	19,677	21,277
67,500	70,040	75,300	80,171	85,500	91,540	94,930
15,200	16,725	19,040	19,500	21,983	26,247	29,059
41,900	41,200	40,600	41,100	42,600	44,789	46,998
65,350	57,600	47,657	48,850	50,642	54,283	56,947
		18,657	18,500	18,779	17,355	17,102
42,217	42,650	44,994	45,706	46,865	49,041	50,170
33,024	34,359	23,930	23,970	...	28,770	30,324
24,242	25,043	27,246	27,761	28,306	29,798	30,817
6,212	6,276	6,719	6,883	7,125	7,409	7,562
46,610	47,289	49,185	50,065	50,429	51,842	53,441
6,657	6,836	7,466	7,710	8,649	9,842	10,705
1,546	1,587	1,761	1,840	1,995	2,282	2,485
168,000	170,000	193,000	...	...	206,850	221,465

IRON ORE (CONTENTS)

In thousand

	1913	1920	1929	1933
Egypt	...	78	...	...
Congo	20	80	50	...
Rhodesia	...	...	7	...
S. Africa	...	2	38	25
Canada	279	117	...	170
USA	62,975[1]	68,889[1]	37,226	8,918
Mexico	...	...	123	50
Argentina	...	...	...	...
Brazil	...	...	30	9[2]
China	440[1]	1,489[1]	971	540
India ⎫ Pakistan ⎭	...	...	1,545	779
Iran	...	...	...	...
Japan	153[1]	315[1]	88	170
Turkey	...	...	...	...
France	43,054[1]	13,921[1]	16,231	9,678
W. Germany ⎫ E. Germany ⎭	7,309[1]	6,299[1]	2,089	828
Italy	603[1]	390[1]	360	264
Poland	...	184[1]	217	54
Spain	10,789[1]	5,480[1]	3,070	853
Sweden	7,476[1]	4,519[1]	6,874	1,685
UK	16,254[1]	12,881[1]	4,028	2,274
USSR	10,300[1]	160[1]	7,849[1]	7,200
Australia	176[1]	615[1]	572	490
N. Zealand	...	...	4	3·3

NOTE: The figures generally refer to the iron content of marketable
by applying a fixed percentage to the figures for production of crude

[1] Ore production, not iron content.
[2] 1961 production.
[3] Exports only.

metric tons, 1913–62

1937	1939	1946	1948	1954	1958	1962
...	...	...	...	...	89	230
7	4	...	...	...	...	...
...	...	...	15	35	84	384
295	312	656	699	1,186	1,416	2,772
850	874	773	1,456	3,673	7,847	13,920
36,991	26,423	36,154	50,891	39,952	36,572	39,672
90	111	171	227	314	581	1,091
...	...	...	17	30	29	60[2]
126[3]	363[3]	396	1,069	2,088	3,526	6,652[2]
240	297	12	...	...	...	...
1,870	1,930	1,565 {	1,483	2,675	3,739	8,137
			...	...	3	...
...	...	...	...	...	149	30
293	429	282	297	900	1,146	2,023
...	155	73	121	301	609	457
11,520	10,161	5,021	7,555	14,240	19,320	21,553
2,759	3,928 {	1,024	1,793	3,140	4,132	3,900
		...	...	419	395	493
502	468	73	280	559	650	565
268	600	143	224	536	581	682
596	1,148	750	767	1,370	2,466	2,889
9,136	8,360	4,308	8,205	9,285	11,027	13,333
4,333	4,417	3,574	3,990	4,369	4,008	4,191
14,600	14,000	...	16,231	37,321	51,513	74,298
1,255	1,727	1,229	1,356	2,300	2,580	3,175
0·3	0·6	3·4	2	1	1	1

ores mined. The data are sometimes only rough estimates obtained
ores.

	1900	1913	1920	1929	1933
Congo	...	...	...	114	...
Rhodesia	...	221	525	1,037	484
S. Africa	...	8,205	10,942	13,018	10,714
Canada	...	13,426	12,021	12,273	9,954
USA	244,000	517,060	597,169	552,309	347,608
Mexico	...	890	715	1,054	647
Argentina	...	...	...	...	...
Brazil	...	26	302	348	646
China ⎫ Taiwan ⎭	...	13,779	20,670	18,030	...
India ⎫ Pakistan ⎭	...	16,468	18,250	22,721	20,107
Indonesia	...	568	1,096	1,832	1,035
Iran	...	...	...	...	...
Japan	...	21,316	29,245	34,258	32,524
Turkey	...	843	700	1,421	1,860
France	33,400	40,016	24,303	53,780	46,887
W. Germany ⎫ E. Germany ⎭	149,000	190,109	107,525	163,441	109,905
Saar	...	...	...	13,579	10,561
Italy	0·5	1	152	223	324
Poland	...	...	30,702	46,236	27,356
Spain	...	4,016	5,421	7,108	5,999
Sweden	...	364	440	395	349
UK	228,000	292,043	233,216	262,045	210,430
Australia	...	12,614	13,011	10,532	9,238
N. Zealand	...	1,182	939	1,389	857
USSR	16,200	36,011	7,775	41,668	76,205

NOTE: The figures relate to anthracite and bituminous coal but

1937	1939	1946	1948	1954	1958	1962
36	27	102	117	379	294	76
1,029	1,118	1,613	1,696	2,748	3,535	2,826
15,491	16,890	23,602	24,017	29,315	37,085	41,275
13,411	13,364	14,776	15,296	11,609	8,558	7,283
448,303	402,156	536,837	592,911	379,154	389,355	395,552
1,242	877	893	613	1,314	1,476	1,107
...	0·5	3·1	17·5	33	136	211
763	1,047	1,897	2,025	2,055	2,240	2,448
36,469	37,527	13,890	32,430	83,660	270,200	...
		1,000	1,650	2,118	3,181	4,554
25,438	28,215	30,187	30,607	37,471	46,056	61,370
			245	563	607	990
1,373	1,781	157	540	900	603	471
...	75	150	150	252	194	158
45,258	52,409	20,368	33,726	42,718	49,674	54,399
2,307	2,696	3,831	4,023	3,690	4,075	3,893
44,346	49,147	47,155	43,291	54,405	57,721	52,359
171,124	174,698	53,940	99,814	145,758	150,005	141,999
			2,848	2,648	2,903	2,575
13,365	13,258	12,566	...	...	...	...
1,272	2,024	1,167	972	1,074	724	692
36,218	46,000	47,288	70,262	91,619	94,981	109,604
2,084	6,606	10,759	10,423	12,398	14,445	13,880
460	444	488	374	267	319	139
244,251	235,050	193,132	212,806	227,686	219,285	200,604
12,268	13,752	12,977	15,020	20,080	20,770	24,874
986	1,061	974	968	827	850	711
127,968	145,000	...	150,012	243,681	353,030	386,432

clude lignite and brown coal.

In millions of barrels, 1913-2

	1913	1920	1929	1933
Egypt	0·1	0·1	272	238
Congo (Brazzaville)	...	...	...	...
S. Africa	...	...	...	...
Canada	0·2	0·2	137	142
USA	248·4	442·9	138,104	122,536
Mexico	25·7	157·1	6,700	4,870
Argentina	0·1	1·7	1,365	1,951
Brazil	...	...	...	...
China } Taiwan	...	...	...	10·6
India } Pakistan	7·9	8·4	219	224
Indonesia	11·2	17·5	5,239	5,535
Iran	1·9	12·2	5,549	7,200
Japan	1·9	3·2	...	202
Turkey	...	...	...	...
France	0·4	0·4	75	79·2
W. Germany } E. Germany	0·5	0·2	103	238
Italy	...	...	6	26·9
Poland	(7·8)	5·6	675	551
Spain	...	...	...	...
Sweden	...	...	...	...
UK	...	...	...	...
USSR	62·8	25·4	14,477	21,48

NOTE: The figures refer to crude petroleum including shale oil thousand metric tons, 1920-62

1937	1939	1946	1948	1954	1958	1962
171	666	1,282	2,092	2,278	3,184	4,671
...	...	...	...	...	...	123
...	...	..	40	34	24	...
308	974	929	1,660	12,984	22,365	32,975
177,661	170,941	237,526	273,007	312,846	330,955	361,658
6,733	6,100	7,038	8,372	11,967	13,380	16,000
2,238	2,655	2,965	3,323	4,231	5,102	14,404
...	...	...	19	130	2,473	4,365
8·5	0·4	66·6 {	122	789	2,264	...
			3	5	2	2
297	320	301 {	249	269	203	1,025
			65	260	302	446
7,662	7,949	302	4,376	10,775	16,274	22,784
10,330	9,737	19,497	25,270	3,000	40,903	65,320
351	332	191	159	300	367	760
...	...	...	3	58	329	595
70·5	70·5	51·7	70	526	1,387	2,370
451	741 {	649	635	2,666	4,432	6,776
		...	...	...	...	...
14·4	12	10·8	9	72	1,546	1,808
501	500	117	140	184	175	202
...	...	...	1	...	72	...
...	...	...	36	84	94	...
...	3·7	56·4	156	161	146	128
30,500	29,530	...	29,249	59,281	113,216	186,242

cluding natural gasoline.

Wheat unless otherwise stated

	1910–13	1920–24	192
Egypt	93	977	1,2:
Congo[1]	272	186	3!
Rhodesia[1]	52	100	1!
S. Africa	171	185	2!
Canada	5,365	9,253	8,2!
USA	18,782	16,107	22,1!
Mexico[1]	300	2,232	1,4!
Argentina	4,002	5,345	4,4!
Brazil[1]	...	...	4,4!
China	...	...	}21,3!
Taiwan	41	23	
India	}9,575	9,427	8,7!
Pakistan			
Indonesia[1]	1,547	1,450	2,0!
Iran			
Japan	643	726	8!
Turkey	3,822	...	2,7!
France	8,862	7,405	9,1!
W. Germany	}3,765	2,493	3,3!
E. Germany			
Italy	4,989	4,849	7,0!
Poland[3]	(509)	4,996	7,0!
Spain	3,550	3,745	4,!
Sweden	220	273	5!
UK	1,587	1,952	1,3!
USSR	20,660	9,200	18,8!
Australia	2,463	3,667	3,!
N. Zealand	188	192	1!

[1] Maize.   [2] 1948–52 average.
[3] Rye.   [4] 1935–6.

1933	1937	1948	1954	1958	1962
1,087	1,235	1,089²	1,729	1,412	1,605
318	...	324²	322	320	...
104	148	212²	306	449	516
272	276	535	578	616	698
7,672	4,905	10,515	9,035	10,834	15,392
15,029	23,784	35,749	26,777	39,665	29,735
1,907	1,635	...	4,488	5,277	6,015
7,787	5,650	5,200	7,690	6,720	5,020
5,292	5,560	5,449	6,690	7,787	...
21,000	17,320	{ 21,695²	23,350	28,950	...
		13²	15	40	42
9,604	9,971	{ ...	8,014	7,997	11,807
		...	3,669	3,587	4,129
1,930	1,984	...	2,721	2,634	3,202
		...	2,100	2,700	2,700
1,051	1,372	...	1,516	1,281	1,630
2,617	3,694	4,867	5,010	8,671	8,581
9,861	7,017	7,634	10,566	9,601	14,054
5,604	4,467	{ 1,953	2,914	3,720	4,591
		941	1,081	1,363	1,315
7,923	8,064	6,155	7,283	9,815	9,521
7,073	7,253	6,304	5,844	7,329	6,703
3,762	...	2,432	4,798	4,550	4,820
795	700	...	1,021	598	890
1,700	1,533	...	2,828	2,755	3,689
27,727	30,830⁴	32,750²	42,399	76,568	70,600
4,826	5,096	5,190	4,589	5,854	8,353
231	156	...	112	164	251

In thousand me

	1900	1913	1920	1929	1933
Rhodesia	...	...	...	...	...
S. Africa	...	...	...	39	?
Canada	...	1,060	1,118	1,400	41?
USA	10,000	31,803	42,809	57,339	23,60?
Mexico	...	...	...	124	...
Argentina	...	...	...	...	...
Brazil	...	...	...	27	54
China Taiwan	...	43	52	20	3?
India Pakistan	...	63	158	584	70?
Japan	...	240	811	2,294	3,198
Turkey	...	...	...	...	
France	1,565	6,973	3,050	9,717	6,57?
Saar	...	...	...	...	1,67?
W. Germany E. Germany	6,461	12,236	7,798	16,245	7,617
Italy	135	934	774	2,122	1,771
Poland		972	1,377	833	
Spain	122	242	250	1,003	506
Sweden	300	750	498	694	630
UK	5,500	7,787	9,213	9,791	7,137
Australia	...	14	219	440	399
USSR	1,600	4,212	163	5,003	6,889

SOURCE: As stated in the introduction; also Ingvar Svennils
Commission for Europe, Geneva, 1954, p 260 for 1900 figures.
NOTE: The figures refer, as far as possible, to the total production

ns, 1900-62

1937	1939	1946	1948	1954	1958	1962
...	...	7	9	33	60	...
284	368	516	596	1,431	1,832	2,634
1,425	1,407	2,111	2,903	2,898	3,955	6,508
51,380	47,898	60,421	80,413	80,115	77,342	89,202
16	77	239	270	454	988	1,851
...	...	...	122	186	244	644
76	114	343	483	1,148	1,360	2,200
427	485 {	...	...	2,225	11,080	12,000
		...	4	25	107	182
930	1,066	1,314 {	1,277	1,712	1,842	5,112
			2	10	10	7
5,801	6,696	564	1,715	7,750	12,118	27,546
...	...	80	102	169	160	242
7,920	7,944	4,408	7,236	10,627	14,616	17,240
2,350	2,030	291	1,228			
19,849	23,633 {	2,555	6,790	20,628	26,265	32,563
		...	305	2,330	3,043	3,622
2,099	2,283	1,153	2,125	4,207	6,271	7,490
1,441	1,000	1,219	1,955	3,949	5,663	7,684
166	584	641	624	1,102	1,560	2,196
1,106	1,152	1,203	1,276	1,861	2,431	3,595
13,192	13,434	12,899	15,116	18,817	19,879	20,820
1,108	1,213	1,107	1,245	2,246	3,183	4,234
17,730	18,796	...	18,639	41,434	54,920	76,300

owth and Stagnation in the European Economy, UN Economic

de steel, both ingot and steel for castings.

Apparent consumption expressed in ter

	1900	1913	1922	1929
Egypt	...	...	...	...
Congo[2]	...	...	...	...
Rhodesia	...	...	...	...
S. Africa	...	...	...	...
Canada	...	...	...	...
USA	...	...	...	...
Mexico	...	...	...	...
Argentina	...	...	...	...
Brazil	...	...	...	...
China Taiwan	...	...	...	...
India Pakistan	...	...	...	...
Indonesia	...	...	...	...
Iran	...	...	...	...
Japan	...	...	...	...
Turkey	...	...	...	...
France	2,520[1]	4,750[1]	3,995	7,290
W. Germany E. Germany	6,650[1]	11,900[1]	9,853	11,846
Italy	...	1,150[1]	1,118	2,505
Poland	...	...	984	1,248
Spain		500[1]	585	1,285
Sweden	350[1]	560[1]	420	936
UK	4,580[1]	6,270[1]	3,023	7,450
USSR	...	...	...	...
Australia	...	...	...	...
N. Zealand	...	...	...	...

SOURCE: As stated in the introduction; also Svennilson, *op.*
pp 276–9 for European figures to 1933.

crude steel in thousand metric tons, 1900-62

1933	1937	1952	1954	1958	1962
...	191	159	275	231	474
...	41	253	196	188	66
...	52	182	190	236	211
...	941	1,736	1,751	2,154	2,376
...	1,702	5,125	4,778	6,165	6,419
...	40,999	81,337	93,260	91,206	91,058
...	326	978	820	1,332	1,890
...	846	859	1,448	1,629	1,546
...	430	1,241	1,522	1,781	2,852
...	1,504	1,049	2,823	6,290	15,240
			118	136	330
...	1,360	1,849	2,276	3,616	6,437
		...	245	329	637
...	224	218	256	268	246
...	126	43	162	336	353
...	5,590	5,308	6,808	10,954	23,011
...	164	381	456	319	560
4,692	5,451	10,616	9,478	13,458	14,923
5,931	14,851	14,640	17,507	20,918	27,804
					6,611
1,891	2,280	3,994	4,865	6,259	11,938
492	1,110	...	3,906	5,009	7,197
555	170	...	1,214	1,644	2,809
824	1,367	2,513	2,591	2,937	4,005
5,531	10,921	16,006	17,139	18,637	17,731
...	17,523	35,100	...	49,908	73,981
...	1,221	2,201	2,616	2,855	3,572
...	212	413	352	390	476

Apparent consumption, not corrected for indirect trade.
Leopoldville.

In thousand met

	1913	1920	1929	1933	1937
Egypt	...	...	180	288	323
Congo (Leopoldville)	...	...	60	11	25·5
Rhodesia	...	...	...	21·5	52·9
S. Africa	...	...	...	310	840
Canada	...	...	1,945	477	979
USA	15,707	17,059	29,481	10,912	20,138
Mexico	...	...	225	...	345
Argentina	...	...	350	514	1,060
Brazil	...	...	96	226	571
China	...	...	...	...	...
Taiwan	...	...	185	143	146
India Pakistan }	377	567	570	653	1,142
Indonesia	...	...	...	74	...
Iran				...	...
Japan	...	...	4,274	4,318	6,104
Turkey	...	...	65	143	226
France	1,930	1,500	5,787	5,221	4,285
W. Germany E. Germany }	6,833	2,550	7,039	3,820	12,605
Italy	1,365	1,050	3,497	3,554	4,258
Poland	(660)	231	1,008	411	1,289
Spain	511	480	1,820	1,407	380
Sweden	390	281	570	403	876
UK	2,923	2,333	4,776	4,471	7,361
USSR	...	...	2,367	2,710	...
Australia	...	...	720	326	732
N. Zealand	...	...	...	98	176

SOURCE: As stated in the introduction; also Svennilson, *op cit*, pp 282–3 for 1900–13 figures.
* See page 362 for Cement Consumption figures.

1939	1946	1948	1952	1954	1958	1962
368	588	768	947	1,237	1,511	2,232
35·1	81·5	127	240	346	393	162
58·5	66·4	71	...	397	796	400
949	1,180	1,308	2,021	2,162	2,722	2,658
910	1,835	2,221	2,913	3,592	5,730	6,207
21,212	28,102	35,210	42,350	46,433	54,830	58,937
410	738	833	1,757	1,783	2,539	3,352
1,130	1,154	1,265	1,545	1,683	2,471	2,945
698	826	1,265	1,616	1,683	3,790	5,039
...	...	660	...	4,600	1,300	9,000
225	97	236	447	536	1,015	1,841
1,748	2,068	1,578	3,594	4,468	6,186	8,587
		329	539	682	1,089	1,395
170	...	38	...	147	299	511
...	...	53	...	65	410	745
6,199	929	1,859	7,118	10,675	14,985	28,787
284	325	336	459	703	1,517	2,323
3,600	3,859	5,830	8,830	9,557	13,629	16,852
14,540	2,328	5,580	12,886	15,984	19,737	28,593
		...	...	2,635	3,558	5,432
6,112	2,019	3,211	6,652	8,776	12,838	20,157
1,500	1,399	1,824	...	3,403	5,058	7,544
1,194	1,835	1,803	2,457	3,323	4,817	6,788
1,185	1,462	1,486	2,116	2,465	2,510	3,054
8,344	6,679	8,657	11,316	12,152	11,854	14,253
...	...	6,455	...	18,992	33,308	57,328
882	735	1,029	1,257	1,727	2,456	2,935
233	230	238	263	323	561	631

NOTE: The figures cover, as far as possible, all hydraulic cements used for construction.

Fleets in thousands gro

	1913	1921	1929	1933
Egypt	...	...	...	46·6
S. Africa	...	...	...	523[1]
Canada	...	1,134	1,335	1,331
USA	5,429	17,026	14,376	12,563
Mexico	40	...	54	40
Argentina	215	167	297	318
Brazil	329	499	561	489
China Taiwan	} 87	163	319	400
India Pakistan Indonesia	... }	197	199	187
Japan	1,500	3,355	4,186	4,258
Turkey	157	...	172	188
France	2,201	3,652	3,378	3,470
W. Germany E. Germany	} 5,082	717	4,093	3,888
Italy	1,522	2,651	...	3,285
Poland	...	...	50	67·1
Spain	841	1,116	1,161	1,218
Sweden	1,047	...	1,510	1,658
UK	18,696	19,572	20,166	18,592
USSR	974	413	440	843
Australia	...	694	678 }	642
N. Zealand	...	...	... }	

NOTE: The figures relate to merchant shipping registered in ea
100 cubic feet or 2·83 cubic metres. Only vessels of 100 gross tons a

[1] All British colonies in South Africa.

gistered tons, 1913–62

	1937	1939	1948	1952	1958	1962
	68·5	...	82	92·8	129	237
	537[1]	629[1]	456[1]	414[1]	194	233
	1,257	1,223	2,007	1,692	1,516	1,704
	11,788	11,362	29,165	27,245	25,590	23,273
	33·5	30·4	114	160	162	201
	293	291	683	1,034	1,029	1,262
	473	485	706	794	911	1,204
	600	258	809 {	614	540	522
				...	...	486
	221	238 {	315	477	674	1,013
			...	142	128	313
					119	335
	4,475	5,630	1,024	2,787	5,465	8,870
	195	224	241	444	596	729
	2,844	2,934	2,786	3,638	4,338	5,162
	3,928	4,483	428 {	1,398	4,056	4,924
				...	21	315
	3,174	3,425	2,100	3,289	4,900	5,412
	93·2	121·6	180	278·6	458	867
	1,044	902	1,147	1,216	1,607	1,995
	1,494	1,577	1,973	2,332	3,303	4,167
	17,436	17,891	18,025	18,624	20,286	21,658
	1,258	1,316	2,097	...	2,966	4,684
	657 }	495	524	559	631	574
		175	184	232	256	241

untry on July 30th of the year stated. Gross registered tons equal
ore are included.

SUMMARY OF BALANC

From 1929 to 1938 in millions of old US gold dolla

	1929	1933	1938
Egypt (E £)	...	...	...
N. and S. Rhodesia (R £)	...	...	...
S. Africa (SA £)	−73·6	62·8	−26·2[4]
Congo (Belgian Congo F)	...	...	...
USA (US $)	95	−31	−300
Canada (C $)	−27·7	−7·7	14·5
Mexico (US $)	...	...	...
Argentina (US $)	3·3	−2·8	−72·8
Brazil (US $)	...	...	...
China ⎱	−22·8	−58·8	74·9[5]
Taiwan (US $) ⎰			
India (Rupee) ⎱	−62·6	16·6	−54
Pakistan (Rupee) ⎰			
Indonesia (US $)	−34·6[2]	3·6[2]	−39·7[2]
Iran (US $)	...	...	...
Japan (US $)	−17·7	−36·1	−23·8[5]
Turkey (US $)	−39·7	9·1	...
France (US $)	...	...	...
W. Germany (DM) ⎱	0	0	...
E. Germany ⎰			
Italy (US $)	...	...	...
Poland (US $)	−1·0	−5·5	−4·5[4]
Spain (US $)	...	−38·9[6]	...
Sweden (Kronor)	−45·3	−4·3	−12·5
UK (£)	...	...	...
Australia (A £)	−57·7	−40	−30·9
N. Zealand (NZ £)	33·1	−47·4	7·7

NOTE: No sign indicates a credit and a minus sign indicates a deb
[1]Excluding military end-items and service donated which amount
to in millions of US $:

	Canada	USA
1961	35	1,539
1958	148	2,281
1954	284	3,161
1948	...	300

1946	1948	1954	1958	1962
11·2	3·9	−0·2	−6·2	−4·0
...	...	−1·6	5·8	4·7
23·6	92	76	12	24
...	...	−147	...	...
156	1,152[1]	167[1]	488[1]	−1,025[1]
4	0[1]	0[1]	0[1]	0[1]
82	6·8	−98·6	−70	−267
−22	186·6	−98·5	1·1	−6·6
...	14	15	−161	−68
39	...	...	...	...
	...	−0·4	6·1	−1·7
45	−604	−45	−215	−89
	6·3	22·8	−25·8	−49·8
−49[2]	−9	...	−9	−41
−469[7]	10·2	−59	13·9	9
−20	26·9	17·7	71·6	5·7
−134·8	17·6	10·3	−30·8	−4·5
(M £T)				
−5	−6·9	39·5	−16·4	53·8[8]
...	...	−416	−400	400
	...	...	...	...
−101	−3·2	−35·7	37·0	−792·4
−15	...	...	...	...
...	...	11·6	−15·2	79·3
19	374	−69	464	339
68	...	−27	43	115
12	48·9	−19·3	34·5	197
...	...	−8·3	−4·7	4·95

Million Indonesian guldens.
In 1961.
In 1937.
In 1936.
In 1932.
In million rials.

CEMENT CONSUMPTION

Apparent consumption in thousand metric tons, 1913–50

	1913	1920	1929	1933	1939	1946	1950
UK	2,273	1,745	3,935	4,354	7,837	5,526	8,160
Germany[1]	5,924	2,200	6,257	3,714	14,215	2,673	9,770
France	1,652	1,885	5,720	4,764	3,228	3,894	6,589
Italy	1,332	1,053	3,482	3,463	4,605	2,078	4,850
Sweden	265	218	469	367	1,182	1,579	1,689
Poland	(590)	191	925	409	1,500	1,025	2,262
Spain	581	458	1,991	1,405	1,158	1,773	2,047

SOURCE: Svennilson, *op cit*, pp 284–5.

[1] From 1946, West Germany and Saar only.

In million US dollars, 1929-48

	1929	1933	1937	1939	1946	1948
Congo	...	19·4	41·4	33·5	77·9	190·8
	...	31·2	74·1	46·8	126·4	237·5
Egypt	454	150	193	155	330	663
	431	161	200	152	285	591
N. Rhodesia[1]	29·9	11·1	20·0	20·6	32·7	64·8
	7·6	21·0	59·3	45·6	53·1	114·7
S. Rhodesia	72·3	25·6	41·9	40·0	83·2	176·4
	50·7	15·5	31·2	25·8	68·3	106·3
S. Africa	676	272	506	404	859	1,420
	422	141	208	151	385	540
Canada	2,200	488	811	723	1,838	2,630
	1,995	645	1,012	901	2,241	3,103
USA	7,557	1,996	3,176	2,403	4,966	7,197
	9,015	2,228	3,361	3,192	9,776	12,663
Mexico	306	89	170	121	542	581
	482	121	219	150	316	465
Argentina	1,388	378	482	353	588	...
	1,537	470	758	466	1,168	...
Brazil	714	232	331	262	674	1,134
	781	291	350	305	942	1,173
China	1,254	495	280	158	561	...
	761	245	363	122	148	...

VALUE OF IMPORTS AND EXPORTS—continued

In million US Dollars, 1929–48

	1929	1933	1937	1939	1946	1948
India	1,626	488	677	560	1,077	1,561
	2,001	654	717	701	960	1,274
Iran²	130·2	55·5	85·4	58·6	119·1	...
	225·4	124·0	159·3	140·6	303·0	248
Dutch E. Indies	784	226	280	258	106	392
	1,009	333	550	418	58	683
Japan	2,142	837	1,363	1,073	305	259
	2,030	794	1,200	1,317	103	275
Turkey	210·6	59·7	90·5	92·8	113·5	196·8
	126·3	76·9	109·5	99·5	209·0	
France	3,867	1,891	1,703	1,119	1,965	3,347
	3,337	1,229	960	807	854	2,012
W. Germany	5,441	1,712	2,205	2,440	712	1,581
	5,448	1,979	2,384	2,266	227	706
E. Germany	}			}	...	...
Italy	1,898	656	735	542	...	1,499
	1,316	528	550	569	...	1,068
Poland	593	157	239	145³	144	510
	535	183	227	148	127	528

	C1	C2	C3	C4	C5	C6
(imports)	894	273	…	112[3]	302	470
(exports)	691	220	…	78	266	361
Sweden (imports)	810	320	542	602	879	1,130
Sweden (exports)	823	313	511	454	708	1,107
UK (imports)	10,128	3,838	5,185	3,783	5,267	8,381
UK (exports)	6,989	2,366	2,999	2,198	3,894	6,841
USSR[1] (imports)	767	303	256	…	…	…
USSR[1] (exports)	805	431	329	…	…	…
Australia (imports)	1,062	298	408	426	568	1,082
Australia (exports)	1,130	450	583	461	637	1,316
N. Zealand (imports)	399	117	224	179	231	448
N. Zealand (exports)	446	180	258	203	321	505

SOURCE: *UN Statistical Yearbook*, 1948.

NOTE: The top figure gives the value of imports; the bottom figure the value of exports. All figures are expressed in US dollars of the gold content fixed on January 31st, 1934.

[1] Excluding silver.
[2] Including petroleum.
[3] 7 months.

	1929	1933	1937
Egypt, million E £	...	...	...
Congo (Leopoldville), mill. fr.	...	...	...
Rhodesia, million £	14	11·1	19·2
S. Africa[2], million rand	257	278	375
Canada, million C $	4,789	2,452	4,062
USA, 1000 million $	87·3	39·6	73·6
Mexico, 1000 million pesos	2·8	2·7	4·9
Argentina, 1000 million pesos	...	...	9·3
Brazil, 1000 million cruzeiros	...	...	...
China, 1000 million yuan	...	...	...
Taiwan, million NT $	...	...	...
India, 1000 million rupees	...	...	...
Pakistan, million rupees	...	...	...
Indonesia[3], 1000 mil. rupiahs	4,971	2,070	2,768
Japan, 1000 million yen	...	11·8	16·8
Turkey, million Liras	...	...	1,606[4]
France, 1000 million NF	0·25	0·2	0·28
W. Germany, 1000 million DM	} 72·3	44	71·5
E. Germany, million DM			
Italy, 1000 million Lire	...	...	131[4]
Poland, 1000 million zlotys	...	...	...
Spain, 1000 million pesetas	...	...	...
Sweden, million kronor	8,220	6,840	10,274
UK, million £	4,178	3,728	4,616
USSR[5], 1000 mil. new roubles	28,900	48,500	96,300
Australia, million A £	726	622	832
N. Zealand, mil. NZ £	...	101·3	173·3

NOTE: National income is the sum of the incomes accruing within
country, before deduction of direct taxes, and equals the sum c
rent, interest and dividends accruing to households, savings c
income from property and entrepreneurship.

[1] In 1961. [3] Until 1939 in million guilder
[2] Until 1946 in million SA £. [4] In 1938.

1939	1946	1954	1958	1962
...	...	869·4	1,187·8	...
...	...	44,560	48,050	...
28·2	47·7	310·2	409	491·4
434	690	3,039	3,175	4,601[1]
4,373	9,821	19,002	24,986	30,509
72·5	180·38	300·3	364·7	450·3
5·7	24·1	64·4	114·7	160·5
29·3	120·3	106·3	271·2	905·6
...	...	451·2	1,046·2	...
...	...	74	125	...
...	...	18,807	32·827	58,731
...	87·3	96·1	126	140·3[1]
...	...	20,116	21,379	24,069[1]
2,933	...	91·8	174·2	...
...	2,123·6	5,984	8,359	15,421
...	...	14,785	33,873	52,603
...	26	122·3	188·6	270·6
87·2	...	{ 121·1	180·1	273·2
		{ 48,328	64,899	79,547
...	...	9,931	13,468	19,393
...	...	...	321·3	426·1
...	...	292·8	498·6	670·6
...	21,790	38,891	50,466	66,669
5,482	8,662	14,447	18,427	22,631
28,300[6]	...	84	126	166
861	1,388	3,997	4,924	6,251
210·1	365·9	802	962	1,240

ear to the factors of production supplied by the normal residents of a
ompensation of employees, income from unincorporated enterprises,
orporations, direct taxes on corporations and general government

Until 1940 in million roubles.
In 1940.

FOREIGN INVESTMENTS
IN THE UNITED STATES

In millions US dollars, according to various estimates, 1897–1919

	1897	1908[1]	1914	1919
Great Britain	2,500	3,500	4,250	1,59
Germany	200	1,000	950	55
The Netherlands	240	750	635	41
France	50	500	410	13
Canada	...	...	275	31
Belgium	20	...	...	..
Austria-Hungary	...	...	150	11.
Switzerland	75	...	...	...
Others	...	250	420	25
Floating Loans	...	400	110	32
Total	3,085	6,400	7,200	3,68
Gross American Investment Abroad	685	2,525	3,514	6,95
Net Foreign Investment	+2,710	+3,875	+3,576	−2,97.
New American Investment Abroad	−2,710	−3,875	−3,576	+2,97
American Government Loans				9,59
Total American Overseas Investment				12,56.

SOURCE: Cleona Lewis and Karl T. Schlottebeck, *America's Stake in International Investments* (Washington, D.C., 1938).

[1] This estimate, by Sir George Paish, probably exaggerates the level of investment of Germany, France and the Netherlands by contrast with the more careful calculations of 1914 which are based on the statistics of dollar investments prepared by Allied governments and the American Custodian of Enemy Property in 1919.

Index

SET EUROPE ABLAZE
E. H. Cookridge

Special Operations Executive in
Western Europe 1940-45

The truth about S.O.E. agents, their
real names, backgrounds and code
names, recruitment and training
secret laboratories
codes and cyphers
audacious feats of sabotage
treacheries and betrayals
interrogations, tortures and executions

The breathtakingly true story of the
men, and women, whose daring
exploits
SET EUROPE ABLAZE

'Packed with astounding incidents,
vivid sketches of Resistance life, and a
whole series of excellent and often
tragic adventure stories.'
Sunday Telegraph

'A vivid account of the agents' way of
life'—
The Glasgow Herald

Illustrated   **10/-**

This is the American edition of the
book published by Arthur Barker Ltd.,
under the title of INSIDE S.O.E.